FORTRESS BRITAIN

Dartmouth Castle, with the square gunports for heavy guns at basement level. (Author)

FORTRESS BRITAIN

ARTILLERY FORTIFICATION IN THE BRITISH ISLES
AND IRELAND

BY

ANDREW SAUNDERS

BEAUFORT

British Library Cataloguing in Publication Data

Saunders, Andrew, 1931–
    Fortress Britain: artillery fortification in the
    British Isles and Ireland.
    1. Great Britain. Fortifications & fortified
    buildings
    I. Title
    623′.1′0941

    ISBN 1–85512–000–3

First published in Great Britain 1989 by
Beaufort Publishing Ltd,
PO Box 22, Liphook, Hants
GU30 7PJ

Designed by Tony Garrett
Typeset by Inforum Typesetting, Portsmouth
Printed and bound in Great Britain by
The Bath Press, Avon

CONTENTS

PHOTOGRAPHIC CREDITS

The full acknowledgements for the abbreviations used in the captions are as follows:

BL	By permission of the British Library
DOE	Department of the Environment. These are Crown Copyright reproduced with permission of the Controller of Her Majesty's Stationery Office
Hatfield House	By courtesy of the Marquess of Salisbury
HBM	Historic Buildings and Monuments Scotland
IWM	The Trustees of the Imperial War Museum
NMM	The National Maritime Museum, London
Oxoniensia	By permission of the Oxfordshire Architectural and Historical Society
RCHM	Royal Commission on Historical Monuments of England

Introduction

The first crack of cannon fire on a European battlefield at an unknown date early in the fourteenth century heralded a revolution in warfare comparable to the mushroom cloud of nuclear fission seen over Hiroshima in 1945. While the consequences for mankind were nothing as horrific as the nuclear bomb, the introduction of gunpowder changed the whole dimension of war. In immediate practical terms, the use of guns on the battlefield had little more effect than very loud fireworks, frightening horses rather than inflicting casualties among the protagonists. Yet, the power of gunpowder to hurl solid missiles at the walls of castles and towns was appreciated very quickly, together with the need of the defenders of those walls to use guns themselves to repel the attackers. The physical adaptation of walls during the 1350s and 1360s to accommodate the new weapons came only a generation after the first appearance of guns. Twenty or thirty years on, came works of fortification in England designed both to resist the effects of gunfire and to deploy guns against attackers.

Whilst almost everyone would abhor violence and the practice of war, and while many would consider the concept of permanent fortification and indeed the theory of 'the deterrent' as distasteful, defence, nevertheless, has always figured prominently in man's consciousness, and has been responsible for some of the more significant changes he has wrought on the landscape. Mankind's need to protect itself and its possessions has been a fact of life since the establishment of settled communities in neolithic times.

Permanent defences commonly imply physical obstacles of deeply cut ditches and mounded-up earth and rock ramparts, and when other resources become available, these basic defensive forms may be improved with structures of brick, stone, concrete or steel. The design of these protective enclosures has inevitably evolved to meet the development of new weapons and tactics used against them.

The defences of the remoter periods of history – hillforts, Roman military works, castles, and the rest – are familiar, and much studied by academics and visited by tourists. The fortifications of more recent times are less considered. Yet they are frequently more substantial and complex. Perhaps they lack a romantic flavour. To some people the fact that a particular fort 'never fired a shot in anger' is a matter of derision, even contempt. It was another matter for those people the fort was built to protect. We forget that the absence of angry shots was what it was all about. It is also a matter of ridicule that forts were often obsolete in technological terms by the time they were completed, or only functional after the threat which inspired them had long gone. Nevertheless, people at the time felt safer because there was some visible means of protection, and undoubtedly would have suffered had it been absent. The deterrent factor of permanent fortification is a crucial one. An anecdote from the period immediately before the Crimean War bears this out. A Captain Washington of the Hydrographer's Department of the Royal Navy was sent on a spying mission in 1853 under the cover of discussing an improved form of lifeboat but really to assess the strength of the Russian Baltic fleet and the condition of the defences of its base at Kronstadt. The Russians were not unaware of his real objective and, in fact, went to some pains to demonstrate the strength of the fortifications and their up-to-date French shell-firing guns, even putting on a demonstration to show how little affected by bombardment from the sea one of the forts was. The significance of Captain Washington's subsequent report was not lost on the Admiralty, and the British fleet in its Baltic campaign, once war had started, did not attempt to challenge the Kronstadt defences.

No fortification system is infallible, all will succumb to a well equipped besieger in time, but the fact that the defences are there makes an enemy think carefully about aggression. Once an attack is initiated, the defended stronghold is a delaying factor which will allow the defender's other forces to retaliate and regroup in order to counter-attack. The existence of a defended strongpoint may be by-passed by an attacker but not ignored. If not taken it will remain at best an irritant, at worst, a threat to his lines of communication.

Artillery fortification in its various guises is a form of defence which originated and then developed in Europe, and wherever Europeans established their colonies in the wider world over the course of six hundred years. Its end came with nuclear warfare and the rocked-propelled missile. In the seventeenth and eighteenth centuries, every continental city or sizeable town was surrounded by continuous lines of defences.

Great Britain and Ireland, indicating the main concentrations of coastal defences. (Author)

In the nineteenth century, with the revolutionary improvements in artillery and more powerful explosives leading to longer range, greater accuracy, and more devastating firepower, the continuous lines gave way to rings of detached forts. These in turn were modified to accommodate the armoured cupola and disappearing guns in hardened concrete shells, later extended by infantry trenches and sunken machine-gun positions.

Examples of fortification of all dates survive throughout Europe, and in some places there are outstanding concentrations of defences, such as the lines of Valletta in Malta, the defences of Gibraltar, and the fortifications of Ulm on the Danube. Because it is part of a wider story, the history of artillery fortification in Britain cannot be studied in isolation from the ideas and practice elsewhere in Europe and later in America. Because British armies and military engineers were actively engaged on foreign soil for much of their time, and because of its island situation, Britain itself has been on the fringe of military engineering. The work of British engineers has largely been derivative, except during the latter half of the nineteenth century. Most of their efforts were carried out in North America, the West Indies and the Mediterranean and less in Britain itself.

The principal and traditional defence of the British Isles for much of our period was the Royal Navy. Many of its finest achievements relate to the defeats of enemy fleets which were preparing the way to invasion. The navy provided an early warning system and maintained a watch, and sometimes blockade, of continental ports of assembly and naval bases, as well as being a protective force. There had always to be a home fleet of some kind, besides the navy's increasingly more far-flung responsibilities that came with an expansion of colonies and empire. There was nothing an enemy could achieve by way of invasion without control of the English Channel. Since defeating the British fleet usually seemed unlikely, the only hope was to lure the Royal Navy out of position for sufficient time to effect a landing unopposed at sea.

Much of Britain's fortifications are understandably coastal. They were intended to defend naval ports and dockyards, to protect the commercial harbours and strategic islands, and to oppose the threat of invasion. Inland fortifications are less numerous. Some belong to the long period of feuding between aristocratic factions during the later Middle Ages in England and Scotland, and to the lawless area of the Scottish borders. The English settlements in Northern Ireland at the end of the sixteenth century needed defending from the native Irish. The English Civil War of the seventeenth century, and its subsequent effects on Ireland and Scotland, saw a proliferation of temporary, earthwork defences, either isolated forts or defences of towns and country houses. Finally, there are the fortifications which arose from those spasmodic occasions of in-surgency in eighteenth century Scotland and Ireland.

The periods of threat from overseas were fitful. The effect of the Hundred Years War with France was a pattern of cross-channel raiding and burning of sea-coast towns. The first coastal defence scheme on a truly national scale arose out of the danger of invasion in 1538–9 from the combined forces of the Catholic monarchs, Francis I of France and Charles V of Spain, at the behest of the Pope against Henry VIII's assumption of supremacy over the church in England and his divorce from Catherine of Aragon. The next major crisis was that with the Spain of Phillip II which had its climax in the Armada of 1588 and a continuing danger of invasion during the latter years of the sixteenth century. Nearly sixty or so years later were the wars with the Dutch, which, in English eyes, had their nadir in the raid on the Medway in 1667. The wars with France during the eighteenth century brought their tensions, and even the exploits of the American privateer, Paul Jones, led the northern ports to look to their defence. But the most serious danger of invasion came during the wars with revolutionary France and Napoleon Bonaparte. There were indeed landings of French troops in Ireland, in Jersey, and even at Fishguard in Wales. It might, however, have been thought that, after 1815, Britain's rapidly growing industrial base together with the creation of the world's most powerful navy, would have been sufficient protection, but the continuing fear of France would erupt from time to time with all the phantasy and ephemeral puff of smoke of a genie from a bottle. Such was the panic of 1859 that Parliament ordered the building of the most extensive programme of defence works ever seen in the British Isles. The debate between the 'Blue-water' school of home defence which placed reliance for national security on the navy, and those who wanted the 'belt and braces' support of coastal fortifications as well, continued into the present century. After all, it was said, the home fleet might be lured away from the Channel and, what with the rapid mobilisation and transport of troops to the coast by railway, and fast steamships to carry them across, an invasion of Britain might be effected in a matter of days – even hours. By the turn of the twentieth century, Germany had taken the place of France as the main threat, and defensively there was a clear switch of emphasis from the south coasts to those of the north-east. While coastal raiding was more of a danger than actual invasion during the First World War, the possibility of invasion in 1940 is still too close to reality in many people's memories. With the advent of nuclear weapons and missile technology, coastal defence officially came to an end in 1956.

Why then pay much attention to fortifications in the British Isles? Unlike the continent of Europe, we in Britain (Ireland apart) have not seen the counter-marching of foreign armies, the horrors of

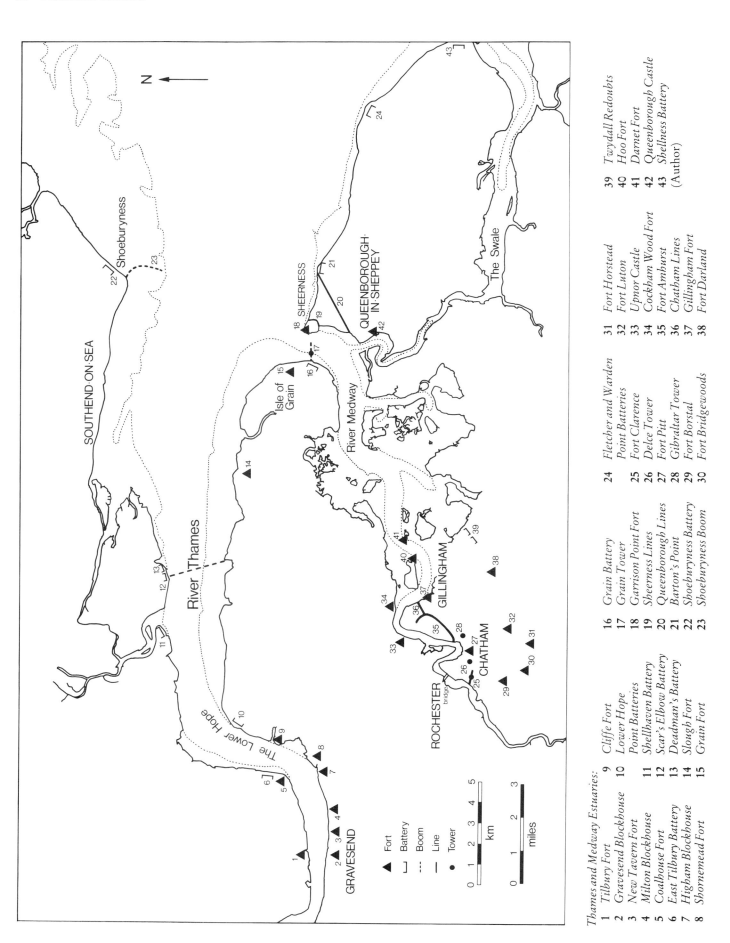

Plymouth:
 1 *Screaesden Fort*
 2 *Tregantle Fort*
 3 *Tregantle Down Battery*
 4 *Whitesand Bay Battery*
 5 *Polhawn Battery*
 6 *Rame Church Battery*
 7 *Pier Cellars Battery*
 8 *Cawsand Battery*
 9 *Maker Heights Redoubts*
10 *Grenville Battery*
11 *Hawkin's Battery*
12 *Picklecombe Fort*
13 *Garden Battery*
14 *Barnpool or Mount Edgecumbe Tower*
15 *Devonport Lines*
16 *Mount Wise Redoubt*
17 *Ernesettle Fort*
18 *Agaton Fort*
19 *Knowles Battery*
20 *Woodlands Fort*
21 *Crownhill Fort*
22 *Bowden Fort*
23 *Egg Buckland Keep*
24 *Forder Battery*
25 *Austin Fort*
26 *Fort Efford*
27 *Laira Battery*
28 *Devil's Point Tower*
29 *Western King Tower*
30 *Western King Battery*
31 *Firestone Bay Tower*
32 *Plymouth Citadel*
33 *Fisher's Nose Tower*
34 *Mount Batten Tower*
35 *Drake's (St Nicholas) Island*
36 *Breakwater Fort,*
37 *Fort Stamford*
38 *Twelve Acre Brake Battery*
39 *Brownhill Battery*
40 *Fort Staddon*
41 *Fort Bovisand and Watch-house Brake Redoubt*
42 *Renney Battery*
43 *Penlee Point Battery*
(Author)

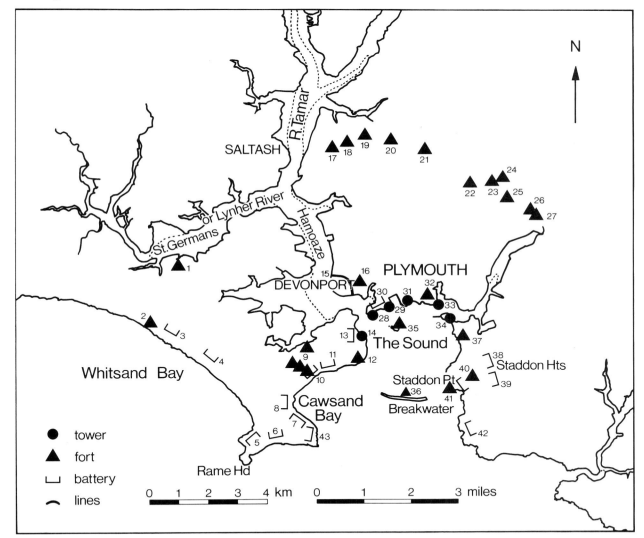

siege and the sack of towns. It is, however, precisely for these reasons that the defences of the last six hundred years which survive in Britain are so surprisingly intact. Unlike European defences, which required frequent revision and rebuilding to keep up with ever changing fashions, British fortifications were constructed at moments of crisis and then abandoned, especially since they were often outmoded by the time they were completed. As the crises came infrequently the relics of previous defences were either re-used with little change, or entirely new forts were built on new sites. They cover a very wide date range, and individually are often remarkably complete.

The intention of this book is not to list or describe all the examples of artillery fortification in the British Isles remaining to us. This is an introductory, general survey illustrated by those defence works which typify the main engineering fashions over the space of the last six hundred years. Those which are described in some detail are usually those that are accessible to the public. Nor is it a study of the development of fortification in international terms although reference is made to the main influences upon British military engineers from abroad. It concentrates attention on the fortifications themselves, placing them broadly in their historical context but avoiding detailed discussion of the history of foreign relations or domestic political history. Although it would be ridiculous to describe artillery fortifications in isolation from the weapons which were used in them and against them, this is not a history of the development of guns. Discussion of the garrisoning of forts, and of the internal arrangements and structures within them, is also limited.

The study of fortification suffers from all the limitations affecting the understanding of any structures of the historical period which survive in part or in other uses, and is no different in this respect from churches, houses, or industrial buildings. Documentary history of fortifications, even in recent times, is deficient in many details. For the earlier periods it can be positively confusing. The many plans and drawings of fortifications which can be seen in the Public Record Office, British Library and local archives, are often only proposals or depict partial adaptations which may or may not have been carried out. There are very few building accounts, and until the modern period, little description of defensive plans and lines of fire where two or more forts can be assumed to have acted together. There are accounts of sieges but few descriptions of forts by those who lived in them during peacetime. All the familiar strengths and weaknesses of archaeological methods apply: buried remains of elements long destroyed, evidence for construction and re-use in standing remains which may have been adapted and added to many times. It has to be emphasised that, recent as many of these structures are, their surviving remains cannot be taken at face value. Our knowledge is always partial, and often feats of imagination are needed to achieve a mental reconstruction.

Interest in artillery fortification is now a well established branch of the archaeology of the modern period. Fortification has always had its devotees from as early as the sixteenth century, and in the eighteenth century, no educated gentleman's library lacked volumes on military engineering. The bastioned system of fortification with its theoretical and mathematical basis fitted into the renaissance concept of natural science, as well as to the everyday experience of Sterne's Tristram Shandy. It must be remembered that Leonardo da Vinci was first a military engineer and later an artist. Allusions to fortifications and their design constantly occur in the literature of the period, and their

Portsmouth, the Solent and Isle of Wight defences:

1 *Needles Battery and New Needles Battery*
2 *Hatherwood Point Battery*
3 *Hurst Castle*
4 *Warden Point Battery*
5 *Fort Albert and Cliff End Battery*
6 *Yarmouth Castle*
7 *Fort Victoria*
8 *Golden Hill Fort*
9 *Freshwater Bay Redoubt*
10 *Bouldner Battery*
11 *Netley Castle*
12 *St Andrew's Point*
13 *Calshot Castle*
14 *West Cowes Castle*
15 *East Cowes Castle*
16 *Carisbrooke Castle*
17 *Fort Fareham*
18 *Fort Gomer*
19 *Fort Grange*
20 *Fort Rowner*
21 *Fort Brockhurst*
22 *Fort Elson*
23 *Fort Wallington*
24 *Fort Nelson*
25 *Portchester Castle*
26 *Fort Southwick*
27 *Fort Widley*
28 *Fort Purbrook*
29 *Farlington Redoubt*
30 *Brown Down Battery*
31 *Gilkicker Fort*
32 *Fort Monckton*
33 *Gosport Lines*
34 *Fort Blockhouse*
35 *Portsea Lines*
36 *Round Tower and Point Battery*
37 *Portsmouth Lines*
38 *Hilsea Lines*
39 *Southsea Castle*
40 *Spitbank Fort*
41 *No Man's Land Fort*
42 *St Helen's Fort*
43 *Horse Sand Fort*
44 *Lumps Fort*
45 *Eastney Batteries*
46 *Fort Cumberland*
47 *Puckpool Mortar Battery*
48 *Barrack Battery*
49 *Sandown Fort*
50 *Yaverland Battery*
51 *Redcliffe Battery*
52 *Bembridge Fort*
(Author)

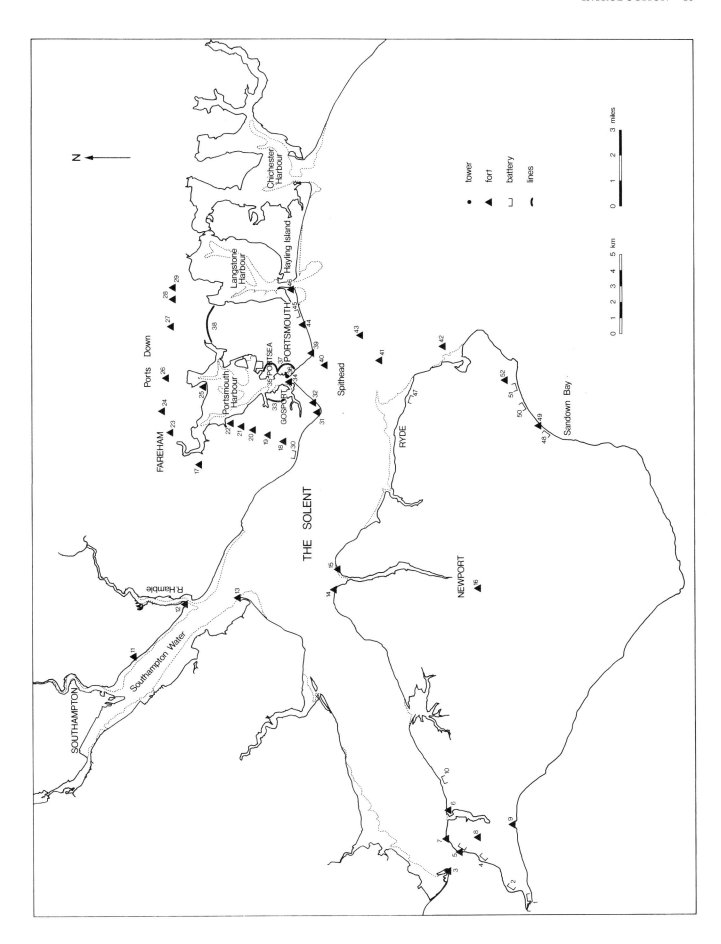

geometrical shapes could also influence such things as garden design. The first comparative study of fortification as a whole on an historical basis comes in the nineteenth century from a Frenchman, Viollet-le-Duc, followed by George Sydenham Clark, one of the first English writers on the subject, though it must be said that the writers of treatises on military engineering, whether from a theoretical or practical standpoint, have always adopted the historical method. More recently for Britain, Bryan O'Neil, a former Chief Inspector of Ancient Monuments, was the first to undertake an archaeological study of fortification. His posthumous book, *Castles and Cannon* (1960) was for a generation the only general study of British fortification up to and including the Civil War. Stewart Cruden in *The Scottish Castle* (1960) carried the story into the eighteenth century for Scotland. However, during the past twenty-five years, a growing number of articles and studies of individual fortifications as well as some notable English general works on European military engineering have appeared. In 1971, the Fortress Study Group was formed in Britain to foster the subject and has published *Fort* annually with an international readership. At a more local level, across the country, there are groups who have established themselves to study the defences of their own areas. More and more forts are being preserved and displayed to the public, and again, local initiative has matched that of English Heritage and the National Trust. For this reason this book contains a gazetteer of those fortifications which are available to the visiting public.

This is intended as a general review of the surviving elements of defensive constructions built since the employment of gunpowder which exist in Britain and Ireland, and attempting to place them in their wider context. The restrictions of book length mean that with so great a range of material the result is inevitably superficial, but it is hoped that it will serve as a framework from which the growing band of scholars and enthusiasts for the structures that impose themselves so solidly on our landscape and in our history may develop our knowledge of these past defences to greater effect.

My sincere thanks are due to many friends and colleagues who have helped me over the years by discussion, advice and criticism, especially those who are members of the Fortress Study Group, in particular Jock Hamilton Baillie, Quentin Hughes and Victor Smith. The late Bryan O'Neil introduced me to the subject, and the late Roy Gilyard-Beer provided the opportunity to develop my interest. Work in the Ancient Monuments and Historic Buildings Inspectorate facilitated a wide acquaintance with defensive structures of many periods. Much photographic and graphic material prepared by colleagues past and present is included and is mostly within the copyright of the Department of the Environment. Crown Copyright photographs of material in the Public Record Office are reproduced with the permission of the Controller of Her Majesty's Stationery Office. I am grateful for the contribution of Margaret Etherington who drew the maps and other line drawings, and to my publisher, Robert Gardiner. Over many years my family has endured many visits to overgrown earthworks and concrete batteries often in inaccessible though eventually attractive situations. My wife, Gillian Hutchinson, has put up with much of the fieldwork, and the crises of manuscript preparation. Her contributions to the research and analysis are considerable and the book owes much to her. Its faults are my own.

CHAPTER ONE

Early Artillery Fortification and Coastal Defence

EARLY GUNS

The first illustrations of guns appear in two English manuscripts written in 1326–7 by Walter de Milemete, chaplain to Edward III. They show curious, flask-shaped objects laid horizontally on trestles with an armoured soldier putting fire to the touchholes. That the projectile appears to be an arrow rather than solid shot is a further curiosity; yet the cannon's strange shape as shown in the illustrations is confirmed by an actual bronze 'gunpowder bottle' found at Loshult in Sweden, and believed to belong to the fourteenth century. It is the earliest gun to survive and its flask-like shape is due to the thickening of the metal at the breech end to withstand the explosion of the gunpowder charge.

The discovery and application of gunpowder in Europe and the development of firearms lie outside the scope of this book but it is necessary to know that the use of cannon in warfare was established in primitive form by the early fourteenth century, and may be even earlier. Perhaps the first reference to the manufacture of guns is the instruction for the making of brass cannon and iron balls to accompany them in a Florentine manuscript of 1326. From then on, references to the use of guns in battles and sieges become increasingly common. Whether the 'crakes of war' employed by Edward III against the Scots in 1327 were indeed cannon is uncertain but there seems little doubt that guns were used by the English in the Crecy campaign. After this victory, Edward immediately wrote to England asking for all available guns in the Tower of London to be sent to him for the siege of Calais. The Tower was the royal arsenal and early guns were also made there, although others were obtained from elsewhere. Towards the end of the century, the Tower took on a more significant role as the centre of arms production and the main storehouse of cannon for English kings.

In order to understand the effectiveness of such early cannon against contemporary defences, and in turn how guns were deployed by the defenders, we must appreciate the kinds of weapons involved. The earliest flask-shaped guns were anti-personnel weapons with little muzzle velocity or accuracy. They were portable and can be described as the first hand-guns. Small calibre iron hand-guns, with reinforcing rings shrunk over a tube, were also made during the fourteenth century and became widespread. As gun-makers developed their skills, barrels became longer and the gunpowder charges stronger. As a check to increasing recoil many pieces were equipped with a projecting lug or hook which could be fixed on or against the sills of embrasures or on forked rests. In England, as later developed, they were known as hackbuts or hagbuts. By about 1370, mentions of larger pieces of wrought iron and bronze became still more common, and heavy guns began to appear; some of them were very large indeed, capable of firing 150- to 200-pound stone shot, as their battering power in siege work came to be recognised. Larger guns were later made in cast iron and were distinguished by the size of their powder chambers. The increase in calibres and the lengthening of barrels required new manufacturing techniques. Instead of tubes, iron bars, arranged like barrel staves, were forged together to form a hollow cylinder and strengthened by shrinking iron hoops over the bars in order to contain the pressure of the fired gunpowder. The heavier pieces were generally muzzle-loaders but smaller cannon were sometimes made in two parts with the chamber detachable so that it could be charged with powder before being wedged or screwed into the barrel ready for firing. Separate screwed breeches were frequent in later fifteenth century cast bronze guns, such as the Dardanelles gun in the Tower of London. Small calibre iron breech-loaders whose detachable chamber was wedged into the breech became common. The advantages of comparatively rapid fire they gave were offset by lack of efficiency due to escaping gases round the less than perfectly sealed breech. English examples of late fourteenth century guns were recovered from Castle Rising Castle in Norfolk. The two survivors were wrought iron and tubular. Contemporary guns found elsewhere

Fifteenth century illustration of a siege. The besiegers are employing a shielded bombard as well as using hand-guns behind gabions. The defenders are also using hand-guns from the battlements and have erected a timber-fronted barbican or bulwark in front of the gateway to the town. (From Die Schweizer Bilderchronfen)

in Europe were sometimes still mounted on their original flat timber beds. Some guns of larger size retain elements of axle and solid wheels forming a rudimentary carriage.

By the fifteenth century there were three main types of gun in use. The hand-gun or fire stick, which might be fired by an individual unaided, or used on a rest, or on the sill of an embrasure. Light artillery pieces, often breech-loaders and often known as serpentines, were frequently mounted on flat wooden beds or pivoted on sill beams in embrasures inside towers and on battlements. There was also a wide variety of heavier pieces, or bombards, for siege work, which were often mounted on wheeled carriages. Illustrations of this range and variety of weapons can be seen in many late medieval illuminated manuscripts.

Many technical developments took place during the fifteenth century. The Hussite wars in central Europe saw the introduction of mobile field artillery with medium cannon mounted on wheeled carriages and light cannon fixed on stands which were set up in wagons drawn up as defensive barricades. As well as light breech-loading guns equipped with two or three chambers providing a fast rate of fire over a flat trajectory, there were high-angled mortars and howitzers also in use. At the time of the Hussite wars, Conrad Kieser of Eichstatt wrote a manual for gunners called *Bellifortis*. It summarised all that was then known about artillery and was continually re-published throughout the fifteenth century. Although longbows and crossbows continued to be the long range weapons of the infantry until well into the sixteenth century, guns of all shapes and sizes had become an essential part of warfare. Whatever the limit to their effectiveness in terms of range, accuracy and rate of fire, they clearly were the coming weapon. The change that had taken place in warfare, and which ended some of the old attributes of chivalry, is nowhere more graphically described than in the account of Sir John Talbot futilely and fatally charging the massed and dug-in French artillery at Castillon in 1453, an action which effectively ended English possession of Gascony and ensured final French victory in the Hundred Years War.[1]

Guns were expensive and prestigious – 'the last argument of kings'. Siege trains were beyond the means of almost everyone other than the king himself. They could be works of art as well as of war. Gunfounders in bronze were capable of producing highly decorative pieces which served not only as presentation pieces but could serve on the gun decks of the *Mary Rose*. But guns were not only familiar objects to kings and their armies. Little more than a hundred years after their first employment in England they were such an every day fact of life that Dean Gunthorpe of Wells Cathedral (1472–98) could punningly use as his rebus a chambered serpentine. In the alterations to his deanery his masons carved projecting gun barrels from the outer face of the oriel window to his hall, while inside, accurately carved breech-loaders on their beds were cut into the spandrels of fireplaces and door arches. Even Gunthorpe's coat of arms was quartered by three gun chambers.

From 1450 bronze was increasingly used for the heavier cannon, although the most famous example of a great bombard in this country is the wrought iron *Mons Meg* at Edinburgh Castle, having a bore of 20 inches (508mm) and imported into Scotland from Flanders in 1437. Cast bronze made it possible to provide a constant thickness of metal which was a great improvement over wrought iron. Shot fitted the bore better and therefore the propellant gasses were more effective. Nevertheless bronze was expensive. Chamber cannon, serpentines, continued to be produced in

Dean Gunthorpe's rebus in the spandrel of a fire surround, Wells Cathedral Deanery. (Author)

numbers. As the number of guns increased the differing sizes and calibres acquired distinctive names. Heavier pieces became known as cannon and culverins and very much smaller pieces, almost hand-guns, were called fowlers and drakes. Multi-barrelled guns were developed quite early and were known as *ribauldequins*. There was in fact great variety and virtually no uniformity or consistency in bore among the hand-forged pieces.

The French brothers Bureau are credited with significant improvements both in artillery and projectiles, and the manner of their deployment by the mid-fifteenth century. Important innovations of fundamental significance came to emerge after 1450, most notably the addition of trunnions to cannon barrels, which did much to reduce the destructive force of recoil on carriages and allowed better elevation and depression of the piece. By 1530 artillery had become so essential to any army that manufacturers began to effect much greater standardisation. This enabled mass production of cast iron cannon balls which were at the same time of the correct calibre. Smooth-bore cannon were soon to attain their basic elements which were to continue with very little change until the mid-nineteenth century.

The Dardanelles bombard, Tower of London. (Author)

Berry Pomeroy Castle, Devon: gunport in the Margaret Tower. (Author)

Interior view of a keyhole gunport, Cooling Castle, Kent. (Author)

THE FIRST ARTILLERY DEFENCES

The castles and town walls into which the first guns were inserted had changed little in essentials from the defensive systems developed in the classical world of Greece and Rome. Medieval fortifications were a combination of high towers and enclosing curtain walls often with projecting mural towers, which allowed flanking fire across the front of the defences as well as fire to the field. Where possible the walls were surrounded by a wet moat or dry ditch. Vertical defence came from projecting timber hoards or masonry machicolations at the wall tops. Entrances were protected by additional towers, often brought together to form gatehouses of varying elaboration, sometimes given additional forward defences or barbicans. Sieges were usually a matter of investment and blockade but, where it was active, the besiegers might employ missile-throwing engines – springalds, trebuchets and the like – as well as mining to bring down a length of wall. More commonly, they might attempt to force an entry by escalade or try overtopping the defended battlements by siege engines known as belfries. 'Greek fire' might be used by attacker or defender alike but the principal anti-personnel missile weapon was the longbow or crossbow. The provision of long slits through wall faces for the despatch of arrows and the battlemented walltop are familiar features of medieval fortification.

The first firearms were a noisy and smoky variant of the bow and arrow, and were employed in the same manner within defensive positions. Differences arose from the need for a circular hole in the wall face to allow for the muzzle of a gun. So the first gunports took this simple form. The earliest example of a gunport in England, supported by documentary evidence, is to be seen in the precinct wall of Quarr Abbey in the Isle of Wight.[2] The sequence of simple, circular gunports possibly belong to *c*1365, when a licence to crenellate (or fortify) was granted to the abbey. Small circular holes cut through the gatehouse towers of Carisbrooke Castle, also in the Isle of Wight, may be primitive gunports as well. The most common type of early gunport, however, can be described as an inverted keyhole; in other words, a circular hole combined with a vertical sighting slit. In Southampton there are keyhole gunports, probably of the mid-1370s, and therefore among the earliest in the country.[3] They have exceptionally long sighting slits, which might also have served as arrow loops, in the blocking walls built across the fronts of twelfth century houses behind the Arcade on the Western Esplanade. The Arcade itself was a battlemented wall-walk carried on arches built outside the blocking walls and continued the town defences along the waterfront. These loops or gunports occur at intervals of 30 to 40 feet (*c*10 metres), the exact interval being determined by the position of a convenient blocked opening. Behind the wall, a hand-gun could have a traverse of 30 degrees within the embrasures, and it has been demonstrated diagrammatically that, assuming all the embrasures in the Arcade were similar in size, every point more than 20 yards (*c*18 metres) from the wall was covered from two embrasures. This type of gunport was used in the walls of towers and curtain walls alike from the late fourteenth to the mid-sixteenth centuries, and later still in some Scottish tower-houses.[4] There are many, often elaborate, variations of this form of gunport but there is no clear typological sequence which can securely aid the dating of a defence work. Some of the variants do cater for different types of weapon in the same embrasure. At Berry Pomeroy Castle, Devon, the combination of cross-loop and round hole appears to provide separately for crossbows and cannon. Elsewhere, some variants seem to be mainly decorative. The keyhole gunport in its simplest form was universal, and is frequently represented in contemporary illustrations of late medieval castles and town walls. This type of gunport is the clearest sign that a medieval defensive work acknowledged the role of gunpowder artillery as a major weapon.

Early gunports were intended for close defence, and often were intended to fire on fixed lines. Their size and that of the embrasures within the wall thickness could only accommodate hand-guns or small artillery pieces usually strapped to flat wooden beds. Any heavier weapons, and certainly any piece capable of conducting an artillery duel with a siege battery, required greater space and manoeuvrability. If such heavy guns were part of the garrison's armament they might be mounted on the tops of towers, on raised platforms behind the curtain wall, or in earthwork batteries forward of the walls. Unfortunately, the physical evidence for the deployment of heavy cannon does not normally survive. Earthworks and timber platforms are soon removed or eroded, and the parapets of walls are the most vulnerable to decay, ruination or replacement in another style. An indication that towers may have been intended for the mounting of heavy guns is the evidence of vaulting to carry a gun platform on the roof of a tower; likewise the apparent over-provision of heavy or additional timber joists. There are also parapets on late medieval towers which have unusually wide embrasures quite unlike the normal pattern of crenellation. Such embrasures would enable the traversing of guns mounted on wheeled carriages, perhaps protected by wooden shields.

The introduction of artillery into British fortifications, on surviving evidence, belongs to the latter part of the fourteenth century, and relates directly to the insecurity of the Channel coast following the death of Edward III, and with the decline in English military fortunes during that stage of the Hundred Years War. Cross-channel raiding was a frequent and destructive event. Many towns along the south coast suffered at the

Cooling Castle, inner gateway. (Author)

hands of the French and Bretons: Southampton in 1338; the Isle of Wight, 1369; Rye, 1377 and Winchelsea, 1380 are just some of the places plundered and burnt. Richard II's government attempted to meet the danger by strengthening the royal castles and encouraging both individual lords to defend their coastal estates, and merchant communities to provide themselves and their towns with better walls. Archaeological evidence for the strengthening of royal castles with guns in the 1380s can be seen at Portchester and Carisbrooke. Licences to crenellate manor houses, with coastal defence as the principal reason, applied to Cooling Castle in Kent near the mouth of the Thames, at Hever, Scotney and Saltwood Castles also in Kent, and at Bodiam Castle in East Sussex, where Sir Edward Dalyngrigge obtained a licence in 1385, 'to strengthen with a wall of stone and lime and crenellate and construct and make into a castle his manor house at Bodyham, near the sea in the county of Sussex for defence of the adjacent country and resistance of our enemies'.[5] Towns which have major artillery fortifications remaining from the late fourteenth century are Canterbury, Southampton and Norwich.

The two castles which were built anew with guns in mind, Cooling Castle (1381) and Bodiam (1385), are still essentially medieval castles with gun-

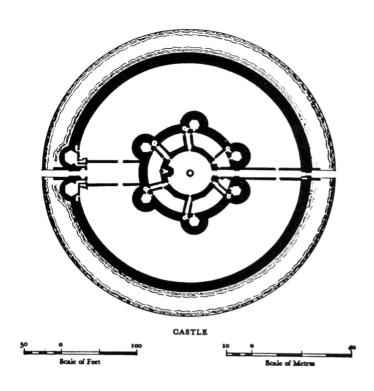

CASTLE

50   0   100   10   0   40

Scale of Feet   Scale of Metres

Queenborough Castle, Kent (from an Elizabethan plan at Hatfield House). (DOE)

Canterbury West Gate. (DOE)

ports instead of arrow loops. Both are quadrangular enclosures with round towers at the angles and at the entrances. The towers at Cooling contain circular openings with vertical sighting slits for hand-guns; the outer gatehouse has four simple round openings, perhaps for small cannon. Cooling also has the distinction of having the earliest description of gunports in this country. The building accounts specify the provision of, '*x arket holes de iij peez longour en tout et saunz croys . . .*'.[6] The dimensions in the text fit the existing keyhole gunports, which indeed are without cross slits. At Bodiam, the castle's gunports are concentrated in the main gatehouse, with two keyhole gunports in the ground floor of each tower and others covering the causeway leading to the entrance.

The fortification which might have demonstrated the latest in military thinking at this formative period was Queenborough Castle, Kent, built by Edward III for coastal defence in the 1360s, but totally destroyed after the Civil War. Queenborough's plan is novel for its date, anticipating the centrally planned castles of Henry VIII nearly two hundred years later. It is unlikely that a castle of such advanced design would have failed to be equipped for defence by gunpowder artillery. Guns were provided, but the castle also contained the traditional stone-throwing engines and trebuchets. It was these which were fired off when the king carried out an inspection. Queenborough is the missing link in England between defences designed for missile throwing by the principles of tension and torsion and the new weapon employing the propellant force of gunpowder.

The earliest surviving purpose-built artillery defences where guns were the main weapon are to be found in the towns of Canterbury, Southampton and Norwich. The existence of guns and gunners in Norwich is documented as early as 1365. The West Gate of Canterbury is superficially like many another twin towered gatehouse but distinguishing it are three tiers of keyhole gunports skilfully arranged to give overlapping fire in front of the gate. The building is firmly dated to 1380, and marginally the earliest fortification in Britain designed specifically for defence with guns. The Cow Tower at Norwich also has tiers of gunports providing overlapping fields of fire covering the most vulnerable areas. The distinction here is that the Cow Tower is an isolated, self-contained circular gun-tower on the river bank. A detailed account for its building in 1398–9 includes reference to payment 'to Robert Snape, mason for 12 shotholes at the Dungeon, price 9d. a piece, 9s'. Without this description there might be some doubt that the curious, small cross-loops that survive in the twelve openings were intended even for hand-guns. Internally, the embrasures would have given room for those working guns mounted on flat wooden beds laid upon the sill, and the low level of the loops would inhibit their use for crossbows. Unlike the

God's House Tower, Southampton. (Author)

Canterbury West Gate, a further tier of heavier weapons might have been accommodated on the roof to fire between the massively thick and lofty merlons in the parapet.[7]

The slightly later God's House Tower at Southampton projects from the earlier God's House Gate at the south east angle of the town walls. It controlled the sluices filling the defensive ditches, and also flanked the most vulnerable quarter of the town. The addition consists of a rectangular, two-storey block, with a square tower of three storeys at the end. As an addition to the town walls it dates from 1417. The tower doubled both as an artillery defence provided with large keyhole gunports for small cannon on the first floor, and as residential quarters for the town gunner. On the roof of the tower was the main gun platform with wide embrasures in the parapets for large guns. The platform was slightly over 21 feet (6.4 metres) square. Each side contained a single embrasure in the parapet averaging 15 feet (4.5 metres) in width leaving a single merlon at the angles, quite unlike normal medieval battlements. The wide embrasures seem intended for heavy artillery pieces perhaps on wheeled carriages capable of traversing widely, and are a feature which can be paralleled in northern France, at Dieppe Castle, and on one of the mural towers of St Malo.

The Cow Tower, Norwich, the earliest English gun-tower. (Author)

Most of the later mural towers of Canterbury possess keyhole gunports. At Norwich, there are many short, straight slits along the circuit of the wall, which look too small even for crossbows and may be gunports, as well as two eroded loops which appear to be of keyhole type. One of the mural towers at Southampton could also have supported a gun platform. This is the Catchcold Tower which is significantly larger and more prominent than earlier towers. It has considerably greater projection from the curtain wall (about 15 feet, 4.5 metres) which suggests an increasing stress on flank defence. There is a high level chamber containing three keyhole gunports and a wall recess, perhaps for munitions. The existence of the heavy stone vault to this chamber, or casemate, strongly suggests that large guns were meant to be used on the platform above.

FIFTEENTH CENTURY CASTLES AND COAST DEFENCES

The military success of Henry V in France led to a relaxation of defensive postures along the English south coast and lessened the requirement for domestic fortification. Normandy was under English control and therefore no threat until the collapse and expulsion of English forces from France in the 1450s. After that, only Calais remained in English hands. The new English defences equipped for the use of guns during the last years of the fourteenth century had little strength to resist siege cannon. They were intended simply for close defence. None of the walls, whether towers or curtains, were particularly thick or bombard-proof. Few, if any, had been backed with earthwork.

Polruan blockhouse with the town of Fowey beyond. (By courtesy of B T Batsford Ltd)

Perceptions were different on the Continent after the turn of the century where the passage of large armies and siege trains could be expected. Towers became larger and were given greatly thicker walls. Specially designed earthworks reinforcing medieval town walls are recorded in the accounts of the campaigns in France during the latter half of the Hundred Years War. These defences were often thrown up outside the gates of towns, sometimes of a temporary nature but occasionally intended to be permanent. The description by an Englishman of one of the barbicans or bulwarks in front of the gates of Harfleur in 1415 illustrates their function in contemporary warfare. In front of every gate

> the enemy had already cunningly constructed a strong defensive work which we call a barbican but the common people 'bulwerkis'. The largest of them was circular, reinforced by thick vertical tree trunks close set all the way round almost as high as the towns walls. Reinforced inside by timbers, earths and beams hollowed out into cavities and recesses from which to receive an enemy and his attacks and with apertures, embrasures and small casemates through which their canelle (which in our language we call gunnys) and with missiles, crossbows and other weapons of offense they would harrass us. And it was circular in construction with a diameter greater than the putting distances of the 'shot' which our common people in England are used to playing with in the butts.[8]

On a hill outside Dieppe during the abortive siege of 1442–3 there was a bastille or detached fort. During the siege of Orleans, 1428, the lines of circumvallation included a line of detached bastilles. The English armies were soon to copy these fortifications. The preparations to defend Calais in 1436 against the Duke of Burgundy were described by an English chronicler:

> A fair broad dike [was cast up] on the south side of the town and made three strong *bullwerkes* of earth and clay, one at the corner of the castle without the town, another at Boulogne Gate and another at the postern by the Prince's Inn. And at the Milk Gate there was a fair bulwerk made of brick.[9]

Features like these, and the use of trenches and earthworks, were changing the traditional form of medieval fortification.

The threat of violence and destruction to coastal towns was posed once more with the end of English control in France. The defences of these towns needed to be repaired and improved. Sandwich, Kent and Fowey, Cornwall were both plundered in 1457. Fortifications took on a different pattern. There was no major construction or rebuilding of town walls, except for places like Tenby, Dyfed, in 1457. Instead, additional outworks, which were often of a temporary earthwork nature, were thrown up, and more specific protection given to harbours to resist hostile shipping.

In 1420–2 a masonry blockhouse was built at the mouth of Portsmouth harbour to protect the King's ships and the launching point for many royal expeditions to France. The Round Tower at Portsmouth Point is still there, though now refaced with no fifteenth century features visible. The tower protected the end of a chain boom defence across the harbour mouth linked to a timber tower on the Gosport side. Another chain boom was belatedly fixed between Fowey and Polruan after 1457, protected at either end by small, square masonry blockhouses, one of which survives almost intact on the Polruan side. It still has a keyhole gunport on the upper level and also evidence of a timber baulk set in the embrasure on which a small gun might be fixed.

Away from the areas at risk from invading armies or the briefer but equally destructive raids from sea-borne enemies, what was happening to castles and country houses following the appearance of cannon? It is a complicated and highly individualistic picture in England and Wales, and only slightly less so in Scotland where a military stance was more necessary. It is complicated because England and Wales were generally untroubled by war for much of the later Middle Ages. The English nobility had fought their wars in France. At home there were family feuds, banditry and thuggery, it is true, but by comparison with the continent of Europe at the time, there were no prolonged military campaigns which could leave large areas devastated and where defensive provisions were an inevitable fact of life for lord or community alike. In Britain the nobility and even some of the lesser gentry had their armed retainers, sometimes on a very large scale, but the only soldiers who in any way represented a standing army were either the professionals of the Calais garrison or the King's personal bodyguard of 200 archers. Even the Wars of the Roses were only spasmodic eruptions of violence which did not involve great hardship on the non-combatant population. The Wars of the Roses were unusual in not following the accepted pattern of continental warfare. There were few sieges of any duration, and instead a series of pitched battles, short and sharp affairs which led to a heavy toll among the nobility.

On only one occasion during the Wars of the Roses was the royal siege train put to its ultimate use. In 1464 it accompanied the Earl of Warwick mopping up Lancastrian strongholds in the north of England. It included such great bombards as the *Newcastle*, the *London* and the *Dijon*. Alnwick and Dunstanborough Castles capitulated without a fight but the last surviving Lancastrian castle, Bamburgh, held out. It was hoped that a full siege could be avoided for eminently sensible reasons.

The King our most dread Sovereign Lord, specially desires to have this jewel (Bamburgh) whole and unbroke by artillery, particularly because it stands so close to his ancient enemies the Scots and if you

Threave Castle: gun-tower on the outer curtain wall. (Author)

are the cause that great guns have to be fired against its walls then it will cost you your head and for every shot that has to be fired another head down to the humblest person within the place.[10]

Sir Ralph Grey refused the offer. The bombards produced the inevitable destruction, and Sir Ralph paid the penalty.

Kings of Scotland had fewer scruples about using their siege trains against troublesome nobles or against occupying English garrisons. James I bought a great bombard of brass, called the *Lion*, from Flanders as early as 1340. The Stuart kings were fascinated by artillery, and this for James II had fatal consequences. While supervising a salute for his queen, Marie of Guelders, during the siege of Roxburgh in 1460, a gun exploded and fatally wounded him.

Some of the nobility and gentry, nevertheless, felt it necessary to show their neighbours that guns were part of the defensive provisions of their residences whether or not the gunports were an illusion or truly purposeful. No clear pattern emerges. There were obviously areas – notably in Scotland, the Borders or close to the sea coasts – where defence needed to be a reality. Elsewhere, a few castles of advanced design were built where gunpowder artillery had its place. By contrast there were a good number of great houses built during the fifteenth century by some of the most significant men in the land and leading figures in the faction fights known as the Wars of the Roses which are grand houses without any defensive pretensions whatsoever. Examples of the latter include Tattershall Castle, Lincolnshire, and South Wingfield Manor,

Ravenscraig Castle: gunports in the landward front. (Author)

Derbyshire (both built on the instructions of Ralph, Lord Cromwell, formerly Lord Treasurer), and Haddon Hall, Derbyshire, and Dartington Hall, Devonshire.

Between the two extremes of undefended and highly defensible houses and castles, there are many manorial houses, old and new, which appear to pay lip service to the new weapon. Across the country there can still be seen today the occasional keyhole gunport, often high up in a tower, and as far as can be judged, apparently of little practical use, as at Minster Lovell Hall, Oxfordshire or at Gainsborough Old Hall, Lincolnshire. Elsewhere, we can have more confidence in the serious intentions of the gunports which cover an entrance. Caister Castle in Norfolk has its thin brick walls punctured with gunports, some so high up the lofty tower as to be useless, and others opening from confined newel stairs which must have been unworkable. Nevertheless, an inventory of c1470 describes twenty guns of various kinds about the castle and perhaps present at the time of the well known siege. Across the country there is much variety and we have frequently to stand back and ask whether the defensive trappings, the machicolations, the battlements as well as the gunports are not part of an empty military show.

Away from the obvious danger zones, the castles which now seem to demonstrate advances in military engineering are few, but significant. In Scotland, this does not become architecturally apparent until about 1450. An example is Threave Castle in Galloway where the artillery defences are in a similar mode to the English artillery works at Canterbury, Southampton and Norwich but are disposed with greater sophistication. Recent archaeological excavations have demonstrated that the artillery wall and towers wrapped round the rectangular tower-house of Archibald 'The Grim', third Earl of Douglas, of c1370, were erected by either the eighth or ninth earl in about 1450. Dendro-chronological evidence suggests that the construction may perhaps be narrowed to 1447. The castle stands on an island in the river Dee. The enclosing curtain walls were 4 feet 6 inches thick (1.5 metres) at ground level, with a distinct batter, and are pierced with slits at close and regular intervals for either handguns or bows. The angle towers are the most interesting element, three storeys in height and provided with gunports in the lower two storeys, three at each level. The gunports take two forms. On the ground floor they are of the dumb-bell variety (two circular holes one above the other linked by a slit) with internal splayed embrasures. On the floor above, the gunports were the more familiar keyhole type. The topmost level had a tall parapet pierced by three wide crenells somewhat similar to those at the Cow Tower, Norwich, and suggesting the existence of a gun platform.[11]

Elsewhere in Scotland, Ravenscraig Castle, Kirkaldy, was first and foremost an artillery fort before it was a residential castle. It was built between 1460 and 1463, its defence concentrated across a narrow promontory. Massive round towers of considerable thickness, at either end of a long frontal range, project well into the ditch, and contain well-positioned keyhole gunports to enfilade the front. These gunports were operated from their own vaulted gunrooms in what amount to fully-fledged casemates, and the earliest example of such in a British fortification. Slightly later in date are round-ended horizontal loops of French type in the heightening of the curtain wall above the entrance.

Another castle of innovatory design, this time in Wales, is Raglan Castle. Raglan combines the richness of architectural detail of a palatial residence of the 1460s with the ground level austerity of an artillery fortress. The main circuit of the castle was completely covered by small circular gunports, and the towers, especially the main entrance, were multangular in order to enhance flanking capabilities. The most remarkable feature is the detached Great Tower, sometimes known as the Yellow Tower of Gwent, sited in advance of the more traditionally designed castle and covering its entrances. It is therefore not a keep of last resort. This tower is unlike anything else in the British Isles and perhaps has something of a French or Italian flavour to its design. Anthony Emery has recently demonstrated that it was built by William Herbert, Earl of Pembroke, probably between 1461 and 1466 as a focal point for Yorkist activity in South Wales and the border.[12] The

detached tower is hexagonal, of five storeys, with a pronounced batter to each side which continued up to a heavily machicolated parapet. The tower provided a self-contained residence with its own kitchen but the lower two floors have walls pierced by cross-loops and plain, circular gun-loops. Outside the tower was a low, enclosing apron wall of hexagonal plan, with low half-round turrets at the angles and separated from the tower by a narrow passage. Outside the apron wall was a wet moat. The half-round towers also contained cross-loops. The Great Tower at Raglan is remarkable on several counts. Its concentric hexagonal plan anticipates to some extent the basic characteristic of Henry VIII's coastal defences. Its situation as an advanced work before the castle proper makes it akin to French bastilles.

Kirby Muxloe in Leicestershire was intended to be defended at ground level from keyhole gunports in conventional square towers but was left unfinished with the execution of its owner. The building accounts describe the gunports as 'murtherholes'.[13] Warwick

Raglan Castle: The Great Tower with the main gatehouse behind. (DOE)

Kirby Muxloe Castle: entrance front at the time of the excavation of the moat in 1914. (DOE)

Castle was also intended to have a substantial gun-tower which was begun by Richard III in 1484 and left unfinished. The present Bear and Clarence Towers, with their circular gunports similar to those at Raglan, were but the outward facing angle turrets of a proposed self-contained keep-like great tower. According to Leland, 'King Richard III pullyd downe a pece of the waulle and began and halfe finished a mighty tower of strengthe, for to shoute out gunns.' The two seven-sided turrets flank the ditch and cover the ground to the front.[14]

It is in Scotland that we see the long continuation of providing gunports in tower-houses, both of the keyhole type and the horizontal 'wide-mouthed' sort. Noltland on Westray, Orkney, of the mid-sixteenth century, presents up to four tiers of both types, and all-round cover of its Z-plan. Cruden has said that 'notwithstanding the advances in artillery and firearms, the wide-mouthed port introduced into use at the royal works at Holyrood House and Falkland about 1500 were unchanged at the time of the building revival in

the last quarter of the sixteenth century.'[15] As in England, the placing of such features in structures, which were becoming increasingly domestic in character, was highly individualistic. At many there was determination to provide all-round cover. At others the siting was arbitrary and apparently of little real significance. Many towers have no gunports at all, particularly the more substantial houses of Aberdeenshire: Glamis, Craigievar and Crathes. Elsewhere, ornamental gunports are not uncommon, for example at Edzell and the Earl's Palace at Kirkwall. Some gunports are even rebated for glass! By the sixteenth, and certainly the seventeenth century, gunports were fashionable rather than essential items of defensive equipment.

LATE MEDIEVAL TECHNICAL IMPROVEMENTS

The close of the fifteenth century saw the beginnings of an advance in English fortification which has been recognised in the major harbours of the South West. At Dartmouth, Devon, the townsmen began to build a stone tower near the water's edge in 1481 replacing an earlier castle that lay further back from the tideline. The importance of this local initiative was not lost on central authority and Edward IV granted £30 towards its building, with a further £30 for five years on condition that the 'strong Tower and Bulwark' was to be finished as soon as possible and to be kept 'garnished with guns and artillery . . .' Dartmouth Castle is of considerable significance in the development of English artillery fortification. The original intention had been to construct a small round tower but the design was soon altered and the fort was enlarged by the addition of a rectangular tower. The addition contained the main armament, located in the basement close to sea level: seven embrasures for large guns on flat beds firing through large rectangular gunports 2½ feet (76cm) high and 2 feet (68cm) wide, rebated on the outside for wooden shutters to keep out the sea spray. These large gunports with slight internal splay of the embrasures enabled larger guns to be mounted than had been customary, and allowed a greater field of fire. This was a significant step forward in the deployment of guns. The defence of Dartmouth was further improved in 1491 when the Kingswear blockhouse was begun on the opposite side of the estuary. This was square in plan with similar, large rectangular gunports. At the southern end of the town, further within the haven, is an irregular shaped blockhouse, added in about 1509–10, and known as Bayard's Cove. This has eleven large, squarish gunports at water level.[16]

Similar gunports are to be found elsewhere in south western coastal defences erected during the next generation. St Catherine's Castle at the entrance to Fowey harbour in Cornwall, was built c1520, again as a piece of local initiative. Similar works were carried out at Plymouth. There are references in the Old Audit Book of Plymouth to guns and bulwarks as early as 1504–5.[17] Blockhouses were built on the eastern side of the Hoe, below the seventeenth century Royal Citadel, and further west, defending the approaches to the river Tamar. Among the latter is the blockhouse at Devil's Point which is seven-sided, three of which have rectangular gunports with internally splayed embrasures and hand-gunports in the parapet merlons. As at Dartmouth Castle and St Catherine's Castle, Fowey, this blockhouse provided accommodation for a small garrison with fireplace and privy as well as a defended entrance. Other blockhouses existed at Brixham and Salcombe in Devon and St Ives in west Cornwall; all indicative of the threat posed from the direction of Brittany and the western harbours of France.

These south western blockhouses, improved as they were in firepower, were still deeply in the medieval tradition. Elsewhere along the south coast existing defences were strengthened by additional bulwarks of timber and earthworks of the sort familiar to those who had campaigned during the latter part of the Hundred Years War. None of these temporary struc-

Devil's Point Blockhouse, Plymouth, with its rectangular gunports. (Author)

tures survive in England other than the roughly D-shaped earthwork, 'the bulwark in the Snook' at Berwick-upon-Tweed. Their existence is usually only attested in documentary reference. Thus at Rye in East Sussex in 1456–7, Thomas Hoget was paid 6d 'for makyng of a pytte to laye in a gunne besyde the North Gate'.[18] More substantial was the bulwark built at Sandwich, Kent, in 1451, which was two storeys high within a water-filled moat. It was the key to the town's defence and was described as '*ung bollewerk rempare nouvellement*' in the account of the French raid of 1457.[19] It was repaired after the raid and another bulwark, built of brick, was erected at Fishergate. There were earthen bulwarks at Southampton in 1456–7, and there is an illustration of this sort of thing on a map of Kingston-upon-Hull of c1538–9. This bulwark was built of earth revetted with timber and, as was frequently the case, acted as a barbican to the Water Gate. Three embrasures are depicted and four cannon mounted on timber beds outside it. Thykpeny's bulwark at Plymouth is mentioned in 1486 when William Bovey was paid 7s 6d for keeping it for a year,[20] while at Portsmouth, by 1522–4, the town itself was enclosed by a 'mud wall' flanked by five rounded bastions.

The advantages of earthwork were obvious at a time when guns were becoming more numerous and effective. Earth absorbed the shock of impact while masonry shattered. It was quick and cheap to throw up. With the use of timber supports and revetments the defenders could contrive protected gun chambers and casemates within the earth mass. The disadvantage lay in the fact that earthworks required constant maintenance and were essentially temporary. Where defences needed to be kept on a regular footing, as at the border

Berwick-upon-Tweed: the Great Bulwark in the Snook.
(Author)

strongholds of Calais and Berwick-upon-Tweed, earthworks acquired some elaboration. At Berwick five earth bulwarks were constructed in 1522–3. One was at the north western corner, near the junction between the town wall and the castle, one stood before the north eastern angle and was entered by a postern in the walls, another stood in front of Cow Gate, and a masonry work, 'the Stoone Bulwarke of the Sandes', projected from the south eastern corner of the walls. The Great Bulwark in the Snook still survives in a much eroded condition opposite Windmill Bastion. The largest of these was 'the gret bullwerk by the belle tower'. It measured 21 yards (19 metres) across its base towards the walls and projected for 70 yards (64 metres) outward from the Bell Tower and was 9 yards (8.2 metres) across its furthest extremity. Timber was used in its construction but it had besides masonry 'Gown holes' and 'loupes of stone'. Berwick also demonstrated other developments and amendments which affected medieval defences elsewhere. Towers were reduced in height

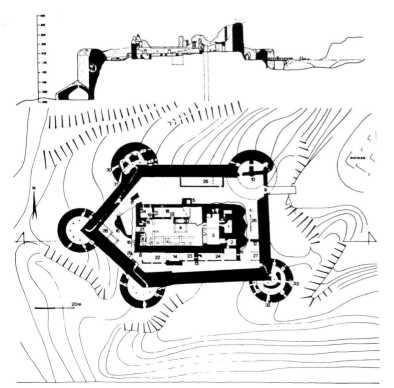

Franchimont, Belgium: as seen from the section, the round angle 'towers' are low-level ditch defences. (From Patrick Hoffsummer, *Étude Archéologique et Historique du Château de Franchimont à Theux*)

and were infilled with earth to create solid gun plat-forms, and curtain walls were reinforced with an earth backing or countermure. This was not a new military device but it necessarily came into prominence in order to resist bombardment. A further refinement of mason-ry united with earthwork by means of internal buttres-ses or counterforts became the normal manner of ram-part construction until the mid-nineteenth century. The resulting rampart behind the wall provided plat-forms for guns, and their easy movement around the defences. At Berwick, the countermure varied between 18 and 28 feet (5.5–8.5 metres) in thickness. Tunnels with masonry side walls and timber roofs gave access through it.[21]

By the turn of the sixteenth century the tradi-tional medieval defensive forms were undergoing con-siderable changes in the face of improved artillery which had now given the attack superiority over de-fence. The changes, however, only went so far. The brothers John and Gaspar Bureau had so reformed the French artillery of Charles VII that successful sieges now took days rather than months. One of the features of the invasion of Italy in 1494 was the way in which the French guns were deployed in support of the infantry in the initial stages of the assault. The great effectiveness of siege trains produced an inevitable response from defenders. Medieval curtain walls and mural towers were demonstrably inadequate. New and stronger towers with thicker walls, shot deflecting surfaces, greater attention to ditch defence and the introduction of elaborate outer works began to appear across north-ern Europe. In Italy, as we shall see, the defensive innovations were revolutionary.

Such changes taking place in England were a pale reflection of what was happening on the continent where many new gun-towers were intended to resist siege guns by the very strength and thickness of their walls. These were equipped with tiers of enclosed gun casemates as well as gun platforms on top, which together could provide substantial firepower. It was recognised that these enclosed casemates could only function if the resulting smoke from the exploding black powder could escape by means of vents within the wall thickness. These massive new gun-towers were lower in height, unless their function was to command high ground beyond the fortress. The use of casemated guns was frequently applied at the base of walls so that the ditch could be scoured by fire from strongly pro-tected positions. A combination of these features can be seen in many places on the continent but the fortress of Franchimont near Liege, belonging to the first decade of the sixteenth century, provides a good example. Here, an earlier rectangular castle was enveloped by massively thick walls on three sides culminating in an angled front on the fourth. On the most vulnerable side, overlooked by high ground, the earlier donjon was thickened with a beaked front and solid half-round

Salses Castle, France. (Author)

towers for guns. At one angle of the new work was a massive gun-tower which also commanded the high ground and covered the entrance. At the foot of the other four angles of the enclosure were circular, single-storey, conical-roofed, casemated batteries or capo-niers controlling the ditch bottom. Pairs of gunports in the caponiers covered the foot of the curtain wall entirely. Access to the caponiers was by long wall passages from the internal courtyard, but they also had sallyports at ditch level enabling the defenders to make offensive sorties. The casemates themselves were venti-lated. Similar ditch defences can be seen elsewhere, as at Langres in France but those at Franchimont are fine and accessible examples.

Another example of the sort of changes over-taking castle design is Salses Castle in southern France in the foothills of the Pyrenees. Salses was built by the Spanish engineer Ramiero Lopez to defend the approaches to Roussillon. In plan terms it is traditional, square with round angle towers and a high powerful keep in the centre of one side. As was then customary in Italy, the walls of the towers and curtain were steeply scarped to deflect shot. The curtain walls were about 50 feet (18 metres) thick. But the significant features of

Tantallon Castle, showing outer earthworks. (HBM)

Salses, which foreshadowed later developments, were the low-lying profiles of the fort set within a deep ditch, the curved and thick parapets to deflect shot, close attention to ditch defence and the provision of detached towers acting as ravelins in the ditches. Substantial outworks of this sort were also appearing in Italy at this time; the ravelin at Sarzanello is thought to be the earliest example of this feature still surviving.[22]

Evidence for similar novel ideas in early sixteenth century British fortification are best seen not on the English south coast but in Scotland and in the Borders: at Dunbar, Craignethan and Tantallon Castles; at Berwick, Norham and Wark. After the defeat of the Scots at the hands of the English at Flodden in 1513, the influence of French military personnel assisting the Scots made its mark. For example, Dunbar Castle had five French gunners under James IV's gunner, Master Wolf, in 1517, which suggests that the 'great outer blockhouse' may have been built at this time as a counterweight to the English fortress town of Berwick. The castle had already been reconstructed for James IV in 1496–1501, but the 'great outer blockhouse' stands detached on a neighbouring, island-like promontory joined now to the castle only by a traverse

wall built across a tidal cleft in the rock, and containing a covered passage. The plan of the blockhouse is polygonal, somewhat in the shape of an angle bastion. The walls are massively thick (21 feet or 6.5 metres) and contain four large, ground-level casemates with segmental vaults equipped with smoke vents. Two of the casemates have two gunports each, divided from one another by a pier of masonry. Other casemates have single gunports, and there is another gun position in the salient angle. The gunports are horizontal, round-ended openings with external splay from a circular gun hole at the inner face. This type of gunport became characteristic of sixteenth century Scottish military works.[23]

At Tantallon Castle, on the east coast, the most conspicuous defence is the medieval towered curtain wall across the neck of the promontory above the sea. In front of the castle are several earthworks, the easternmost being a massive bank and ditch shielding the lower part of the high curtain wall, and likely to be contemporary with the siege of 1528. Its gateway, and the ditch before it, were defended by a traverse wall and a small round flanking tower furnished with gunports, similar to those at the Dunbar blockhouse.

The other notable innovative Scottish artillery fortification is at Craignethan Castle in Lanark-

Tower and capannati *after Francesco di Giorgio Martini.*
A Ciglo
B Covered-way
C Capannati
D Ditch
E Lower ditch
F Mid-ditch wall
G Gun platform
H Flank batteries
(From Simon Pepper and
Quentin Hughes, 1978)

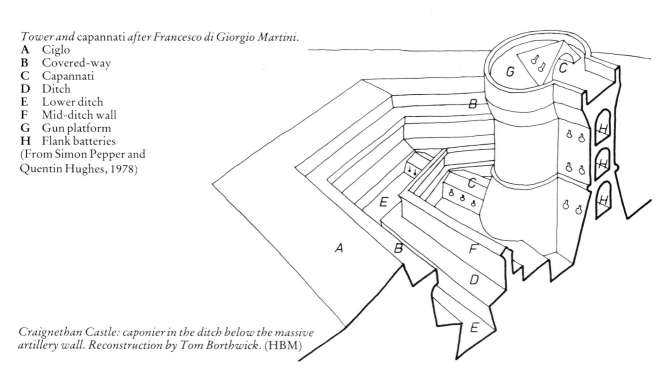

Craignethan Castle: caponier in the ditch below the massive artillery wall. Reconstruction by Tom Borthwick. (HBM)

shire, a private stronghold of the Hamiltons, built
c1530. The site of the castle is overlooked from high
ground to the west. The domestic buildings, however,
are masked by a massive, high scarp wall clearly intended to counter the threat of besieging guns on the
high ground. This wall was not protected by an outer
earthwork as at Tantallon. Instead, the promontory in
front of the scarp wall was cut by a deep, straight-sided
ditch revetted in stone and defended by a fully developed, true caponier – a vaulted and loopholed
covered gallery – extending right across the ditch. This
caponier is a remarkably sophisticated feature unknown elsewhere in Britain then and for many years to
come.[24] It is a form of defence to be found in Francesco
di Giorgio Martini's treatise on fortification, written
towards the very end of the fifteenth century. Such a
device can only have appeared in a baronial castle in
Scotland as a result of experience in Italian warfare on
the part of the designer or the presence on the Hamilton
payroll of a foreign adviser.

Norham Castle, a few miles west of Berwick
and further up the Tweed on the English side, had been
severely damaged as a result of a Scottish attack in 1513.
It was subsequently repaired by the Bishop of Durham,
whose castle it was. The inner ward was strengthened
by Clapham's Tower, designed for artillery, with a
casemated gun position covering the approach to the
ward. The tower also had an unusual angular front.
This angular plan was more distinctly applied to the
four towers added to the outer ward. Each had obtuse
angle fronts, and were described in Thomas, Lord
Dacre's report of 1521, as 'bulwerks'. They may be an
ill-conceived attempt to follow the then little known
Italian concept of the angle bastion. It has been suggested that these 'bulwerks' are almost identical with
Martini's *capannate* or prototype caponiers.[25] The
Norham structures, however, were not sited in the
ditch as Martini would have expected. Nor were they
vaulted and low-lying, but raised to the height of the
curtain and therefore mainly self-defeating in practice.

At Wark, the other major castle covering a
ford over the Tweed, the new works of 1519 were in a
more traditional mould. This castle too had been easily
captured in 1513, and in 1517, Lord Dacre, guardian of
the East and Middle March requested that the master
mason at Berwick be sent to Wark to 'devise the
fortifications'. Two years later Dacre wrote to Wolsey
describing the new works. The most important structure was the polygonal keep or donjon four storeys
high and on each floor were 'fyve grete murdour holes,
shot with grete voultes of stone, except one stage wich
is with Tymbre, so that grete bumbardes may be shot
out at icheon them'. Each floor had a central trap door
to enable the guns to be lifted and mounted in position.
Little remains of the castle today, and the form of the
gunports is unknown. Dacre's emphatic description
suggests that they were major features, perhaps double

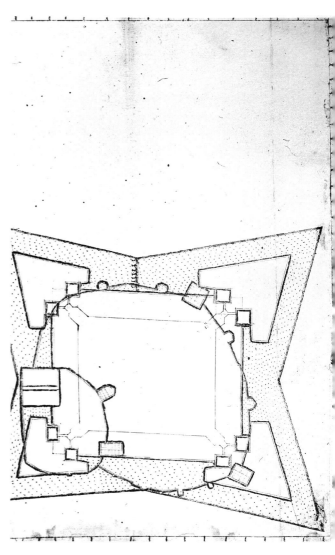

*Norham Castle: sixteenth century plan of the castle with the
'bulwarks' on the outer curtain and Rowland Johnson's
scheme for converting the castle into a bastioned fortress.*
(Hatfield House)

splayed loops on a par with Dunbar. The Earl of Surrey
visited Wark in 1523 and described the keep as 'the
strongest thing I have seen', and wished that 'the keep
at Guisnes [in the Calais Pale] were like it'.[26] It did
indeed survive a Scottish attack the same year, but it is
hard to see such a lofty gun-tower being anything more
than an anachronism, easily susceptible to an army with
a substantial siege train.

Gun-towers were more suitable for the protection of harbours where the target was primarily
shipping, and a landing party unlikely to be equipped
with heavy guns, unless it was an outright invading
force. It is therefore unsurprising that the fort to protect the harbour at Camber near Rye, East Sussex,
completed in 1514, was circular with ten double-
splayed gunports on the ground floor allowing greater
traverse for the guns. This for England was an important advance in fortification technique.[27] In spite of

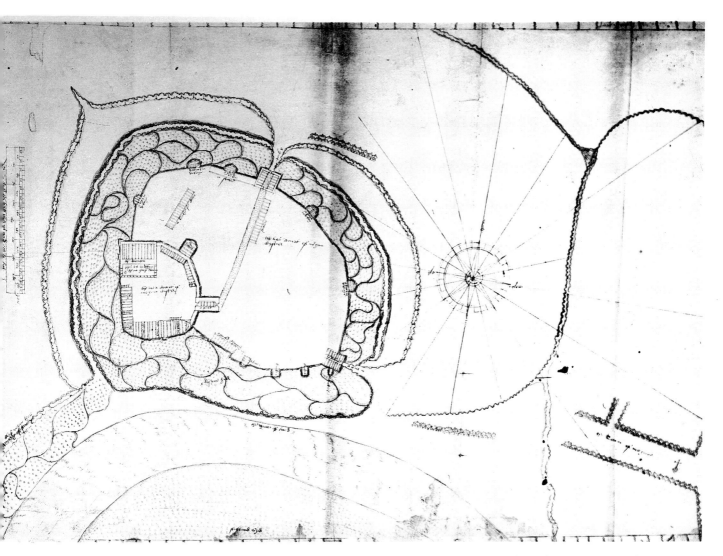

this, as Kenyon has pointed out, the gunports still had a restricted field of fire which did not even meet, let alone overlap.

The fortifications designed or adapted for the use of guns in the British Isles during the hundred and fifty years since their first influence on military architecture became apparent were built piecemeal as reaction to an assortment of threats. They were conceived, built and paid for by a variety of people from the king, the powerful and often independent lords, down to minor lords, religious houses and merchants. There was little appreciation of a national policy and at this date we should not expect to see defence primarily as a central responsibility. There were many who had seen active service on the battlefield and at the siege of strongholds who knew what they wanted. There were gunners technically qualified at their craft and master masons who understood the practical considerations required for the building of fortresses. But there was no one who can be identified as possessing the qualifications required of a military engineer. While there were a few

books on the practice of warfare there was scarcely anything which approached the science of fortification. Such treatises as there were were still out of reach of those on the western fringes of Europe. Changes there certainly were, but as England was not involved in any Continental wars after 1450, there were limited examples and experience to work from. The Burgundian chronicler Commynes commented on some English troops who were serving in the Burgundian army in 1477, that 'because the English had not fought outside their Kingdom for so long they did not understand siege warfare very well'.[29] The only body of soldiers approaching a standing army was the Calais garrison. It is not surprising therefore to see innovations arriving in Scotland through the agency of French specialists rather than into England. This sequence of *ad hoc* solutions to spasmodic threats was not to change until there was a very real threat of invasion and danger of conquest for the country as a whole, combined with the presence of an English king who had the political authority and the resources to deal with defence on a national scale.

CHAPTER TWO

Henry VIII and the Emergence of a National Defence Policy

Under the first two Tudor kings England acquired a degree of internal political stability which had been lacking for much of the previous half century. Not only were the Wars of the Roses over, the aristocracy depleted and exhausted, but the concepts of the nation state and the New Monarchy were strengthening in both England and Scotland. The revolution in ideas, technology and art, which we term the Renaissance, was spreading across Europe from its Italian and Mediterranean source. It was not a sudden revolution, nor were the changes necessarily noticeable at the time, but in many important respects the attitudes of the Middle Ages altered during the sixteenth century. The lands of the New World were discovered across the seas because men rejected the traditional belief that the earth was flat. The 'Universal Church' was divided by the individual conscience of Protestantism, and residual feudal society diminished with the rise of capitalism on the one hand, and absolute monarchy on the other. Kings now possessed standing armies and, fitfully, had the resources to pay for large bodies of mercenaries, and they had more and better gunpowder and guns. The revolution in technology applied equally to warfare and weapons. Kings were thus better able to impose their will on over-mighty subjects and to embark on aggressive adventures against their neighbours.

Henry VII was plagued by pretenders to the throne playing the Yorkist card but he was not seriously threatened from abroad or from Scotland. Little attention needed to be paid to coastal defence although some improvements were made to the fortifications of Calais. Apart from encouraging the independence of Brittany, Henry was little concerned with France, though he briefly led an expedition there, and, inconsequentially, besieged Boulogne. The real world of power politics involved the Holy Roman Emperor and the French king, and was a world in which Henry VII had no part. The military campaigns which mattered for the development of fortification were in Italy where Charles VIII of France swept all the city states before him with the power of his siege train, a display which

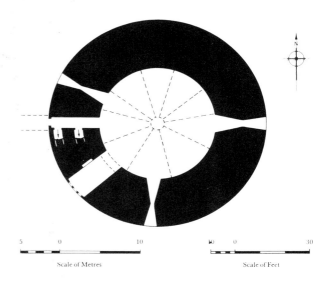

Tournai, Tour Henri VIII. (DOE)

caused universal alarm throughout western Europe. England was peripheral to these events in Italy but Henry took the opportunity to negotiate a Spanish bride for his eldest son, Arthur, so that there would be an ally in case of serious threat from France.

Henry possessed some military power. The Yeomen of the Guard were formed as a small personal bodyguard for the king in 1485. Of more practical importance were the guns housed in the Tower of London. Henry also maintained the nucleus of a small permanent navy as well as adopting the traditional practice of hiring merchant ships for war service when occasion arose. Henry added six new warships to the existing fleet, and in order to maintain them, he built the first drydock for the royal navy at Portsmouth between 1495 and 1497. This choice of site, together with the shipbuilding capacity of the river Hamble, emphasized the importance of the Solent and Southampton Water in future defensive considerations.

By contrast, the youthful Henry VIII, due to his father's prudence, had the means and the ambition to strike an attitude on the continent of Europe and attempt to join the political big league. This was in fact

Dover Harbour Bulwarks: the gun-towers are of different dates and stages of development. (Author)

the 'Holy League', whose purpose was to defend the papacy from its enemies, and in practical terms involved a treaty with Spain binding England to attack France before the end of April 1512. This involved a brief but successful campaign in France in 1513 and the capture of Tournai. Henry at the same time successfully dealt with a 'second front' on his northern border stimulated by the 'auld alliance' of France and Scotland, which led to the crushing English victory of Flodden on the very border itself. For Scotland, defence was a serious matter and the influence there of French engineers has already been noted. There was no necessity for additional defences in England until 1519, and again in 1533, after Charles V's indignant reaction to the annulment of his aunt's (Catherine of Aragon) marriage to Henry and her supplanting by Anne Boleyn.

The capture of Tournai in 1513 was a pointer to the way English fortification was moving. The old castle of the counts of Flanders and the extensive circuit of medieval town wall were not susceptible for conversion into up-to-date artillery fortifications except at prodigious cost. It was therefore decided to build a citadel within the city which would combine both a strongpoint and accommodation for the English garrison. It was the first new defensive work to be erected by the Crown since the construction of Queenborough a century and a half earlier, if we leave aside improvements to existing defences at Calais, Berwick and Southampton. The new defences were not complete when Tournai was eventually given up in 1519, but one tower remains as evidence of their considerable scale.

The surviving Tour Henri VIII, the north east tower, is 90 feet (27 metres) in diameter with walls 22 feet (7 metres) thick. There are two superimposed vaulted chambers each containing three gunports. Those in the upper chamber are long, narrow, double-splayed loops with rectangular openings but with such lack of manoevrability for the guns they must always have been intended to fire on fixed lines. The main armament was clearly intended for the platform, whose present parapet is rounded. The tower does not represent any major advance in design but it is novel in English terms by anticipating the greater destructive force of heavy siege artillery.

By contrast, Edward Guldeford's gun-tower at Camber, Sussex, begun a few years previously in 1512, and which still survives, was a flimsier construction altogether with walls less than half as thick. Similar gun-towers were built by the townspeople on the end of the first pier at Dover harbour, and are represented on the Cowdray painting of the embarkation of Henry VIII for the Field of the Cloth of Gold in 1520. The two towers appear to be of different dates (c1500 and c1518). The older of the two has two tiers of rectangular gunports and a battlemented parapet, mounting guns on field carriages. The other tower has only one tier of rectangular gunports in much thicker looking walls. It is much more sophisticated in appearance, particularly with its thick curved parapet. Both towers and pier had a short life. At Berwick, small, round gun-towers were added in c1530 to the north west curtain of the castle and to the north side of the long wall which extends down the cliff from the castle to the Tweed.

The eventual divorce of Catherine of Aragon, the breach with Rome, the assumption by Henry of the title, Supreme Head of the Church in England, and a parliament sympathetic to the economic outcome of the Protestant Reformation, left England, and more particularly the king, isolated. For the first time in three hundred years there was a serious threat of invasion and the overturning of political power by external enemies. In 1538, Francis I, king of England's traditional enemy, France, and the Emperor, Charles V of Spain, with the double motive of personal affront and dedication to defending Catholicism, signed a peace treaty. At the same time Pope Paul III threatened a Bull excommunicating Henry, releasing his subjects from their allegiance, and also tried to stimulate Francis and Charles into leading a crusading army against him. Warnings of a coming invasion came from various parts of Europe, including a report that Charles had made a truce with the Turks giving him freedom for the enterprise of England.

The crisis was short lived. The would-be allies had more pressing internal problems of their own, and by the middle of 1539 the threat had evaporated. Nevertheless, the fright was deeply felt and led to a national defence programme on a scale never attempted since the creation and fortification of many West Saxon

Map of the English and French fortifications of Boulogne. (DOE)

towns by Alfred and, after his death, in Mercia, as resistance centres to the Danish armies in the late ninth and tenth centuries. There was too much at stake. Henry's throne was of course at risk, but so were the proceeds of the dissolution of the monasteries and the dispersal of their enormous landed wealth among the aristocracy and gentry. Too many people had a vested interest in maintaining the Reformation in England.

The recurring threat, which included the French landing on the Isle of Wight, and more serious invasion intentions in 1545, the dangers to the land frontiers with Scotland and at Calais, led to defensive preparations becoming one of Henry's preoccupations for the rest of his reign. This and the English siege and capture of Boulogne, produced rapid developments in the mid-1540s in English military engineering with which Henry became personally involved. He was very much a renaissance man. Beyond the more obvious attributes of kingship, his interests and accomplishments were wide: as an athlete, scholar, musician, even linguist. It is therefore not surprising that military matters interested him, particularly those pertaining to guns and fortifications. His personal involvement with fortification extended beyond strategic considerations and designs were clearly approved and amended by the King himself.

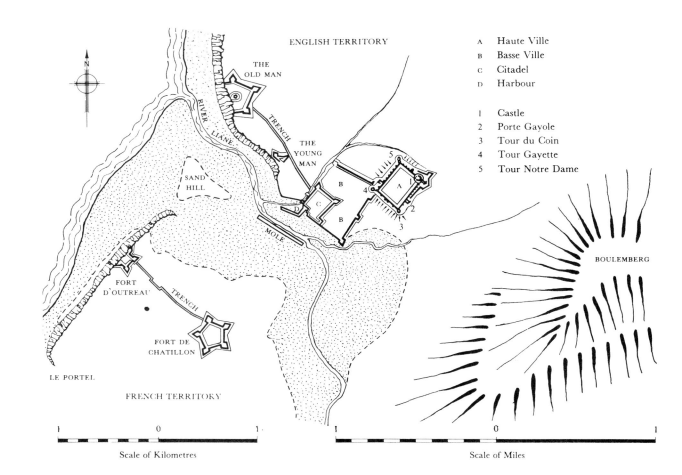

THE INVASION CRISIS AND THE 'DEVICE' FORTS, 1539–43

Henry's response to the invasion crisis of 1538 was prompt and coherent. It was summed up by the contemporary chronicler, Edward Hall. The king reviewed the condition of the navy in 1539 and ordered musters of men fit to serve in the army in March.

> Also he sent dyvers of his nobles and counsaylours to view and searche all the Portes and daungiers on the coastes where any meete or convenient landing place might be supposed . . . And in all suche doubtful places his hyghnes caused dyvers and many Bulwarks and fortifications to be made.[1]

The initial document the 'Device by the King' was drawn up in February naming commissioners to advise on improvements for Calais and Guisnes and to search and defend portions of the English coast and South Wales, shire by shire.[2]

As a result, new fortifications sprang up along the south coast: the entrance to Falmouth harbour, Weymouth Bay, the Solent, Rye harbour, Folkestone, the Downs, up the east coast to the Thames estuary, the mouths of the Blackwater and Orwell, and on to Hull. To the west, the entrance to Milford Haven was protected. Nor were the coastal forts and batteries all that was done. The French ambassador, Marillac, wrote to Francis I that

> the English continue to fortify the frontiers in all haste and take musters everywhere . . . 5 or 6 ships do nothing but circle round the Kingdom in order to explore and correspond, if need be by fires, with those who watch by night upon certain gardes of wood lately erected; so that no foreign vessel could show itself without the whole country being warned.[3]

The strategy behind the siting of fortifications was not primarily to repel an actual landing, but rather to deny the enemy a harbour or anchorage which he could use as a base for sustaining an invasion. It is axiomatic that having established an initial bridgehead an invader would need somewhere through which reinforcements and supplies could safely land and pass through to the field army advancing towards its principal objectives. Individual forts protected harbour entrances, and, where distances were too great for effective artillery range, castles or blockhouses were sited to support each other. The major castles were of a design which was self-contained, self-defensible and carefully sited. Early in 1539, the Earl of Southampton and Lord St John took a boat into the Solent to note how the circumstances of wind and tide would influence shipping at the junction of Southampton Water with the Solent.[4] This determined the siting of Calshot and East and West Cowes Castles. Although the first defences early in 1539 were temporary affairs, earthworks thrown up in the panic of imminent danger, they were

The 'Device' castles of Henry VIII: comparative plans to a common scale.
1 Walmer
2 Portland
3 Camber (final phase)
4 Sandgate
5 Pendennis
6 Hurst
7 Deal
8 St Mawes
9 Calshot

soon replaced by permanent fortifications sometimes showing changes of mind in design while building was in progress. The threat was real, and if it receded for the time being, it could occur again.

There were some thirty separate fortifications built as a result of the 'Device'. By the end of December, 1540, the names of twenty-four new works were listed as already garrisoned. They were large and small, forts and blockhouses. The major works, the ten great 'castles' – Deal, Walmer, Sandown, Camber, Sandgate, Calshot, Hurst, Portland, Pendennis and St Mawes – share striking similarities of plan and detail. All, save Sandown, still survive, some little altered from their original form. There is a sophistication and an overall design concept which could be applied individually to suit the needs of the location, and withstand the

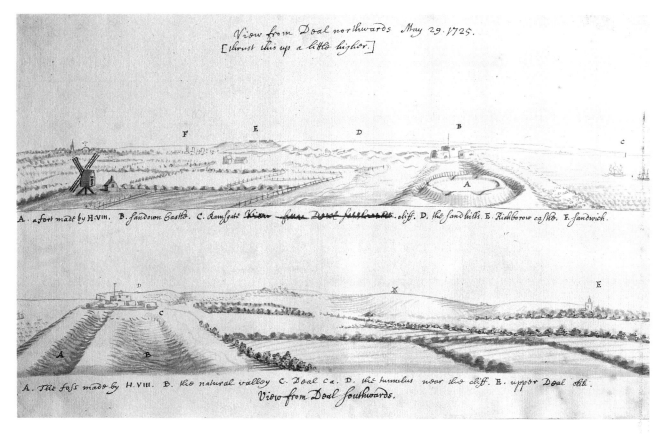

View from Doal northwards May 29. 1725.
[thrust this up a little higher.]

A. a fort made by H.VIII. B. Sandown Castle. C. Ramsgate ...... cliff. D. the sand hills. E. Richborow castle. F. Sandwich.

A. The foss made by H.VIII. B. the natural valley C. Deal Ca. D. the tumulus near the cliff. E. upper Deal cliff.

View from Deal southwards.

idiosyncracies of the master mason concerned. They were all centrally planned, sometimes starting as a single round tower with additional concentric elements applied either from the start or soon afterwards. Unlike the traditional medieval castle, they were much more squat and less of a target as well as more shock absorbing. There were at least three tiers of offensive armament in each castle; that is, provision for long range guns firing out beyond the limits of the work. At the same time, separate provision was made for the weapons providing close defence, sometimes in two tiers, covering entrances, moats and inner courtyards. The offensive and the defensive firepower were not interchangeable and had their own fields of fire. The traditional defensive elements relating to entrances continued: drawbridges, portcullisses, and murder-holes in the vaulting of entrance passages. Besides possessing thick walls, (14–15 feet or 5 metres in the castles in the Downs, generally 11 feet or 3 metres elsewhere), other shot deflecting features were employed. Curved walls and parapets were used. Round bastions were usually open at the gorge, and floored across in order to mount two tiers of heavy guns. The open gorge prevented them being used as strongpoints against the defenders should the attackers break in during a siege. In some of the castles hollow bastions have subsequently been filled to provide more solid gun platforms. The gunports and casemates generally show a marked development from earlier English artillery fortifications. Emphasis on wide external splays

gave better opportunities for traversing guns, with internal splayed openings in the thickness of the walls wide enough to allow for the working of the pieces. Where there were casemates, vents were provided and taken through the wall thickness to allow smoke and fumes to escape. This applied to hand-gun ports as much as to the large casemates. Garrison accommodation naturally centred on the inner tower or keep, though in the larger castles, accommodation was also provided in the bastions.

Such were the common design characteristics. The principal grouping of fortresses was 'the three castles which keep the Downs': Deal, Walmer and Sandown. Sandown no longer exists, except for a fragment eroded by the sea. The loss is not too serious since it was virtually identical with Walmer Castle. The Downs castles were deservedly the most formidable, individually and collectively, linked as they were by entrenchments and with circular earthen bulwarks in the intervals. The 'Downs', which they protected, were four miles of semi-sheltered water within the Goodwin Sands and of very great strategic importance as an anchorage. The three 'castles' were among the first works to be built in the new scheme of permanent coastal defence.

Deal Castle, or 'the Great Castle', was the most powerful of all the 'Device' fortifications. The core is a large, central, circular tower with six small, rounded bastions, or lunettes, attached to it at basement, ground and first-floor levels. The central tower

◀ *Two views of the Downs earthwork bulwarks as sketched by* ▶
William Stukeley in 1725. (Society of Antiquaries of London)

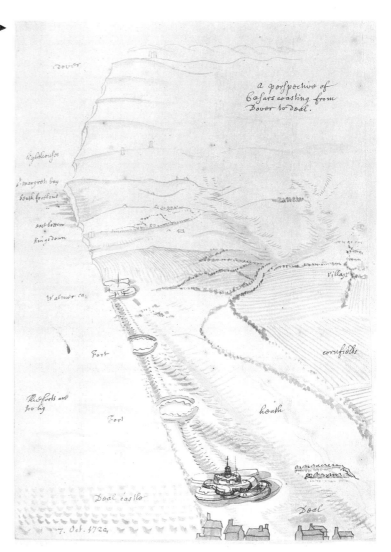

rose above them. Separated from this core by a narrow, passage-like courtyard is an outer ring of six larger rounded bastions with a wide, deep and stone-revetted moat outside it. The main armament was mounted on the central tower and on the inner and outer bastions. The defensive armament of hand-guns was provided for by small ports in the inner lunettes to cover the narrow courtyard. Similarly, fifty-three gunports in the outer bastions, connected by a continuous passage known as 'the rounds', covered every part of the moat. Walmer and Sandown Castles were similar except that they were based on a four bastion plan rather than six and lacked the inner lunettes.

Hurst Castle and St Mawes have plans based on three outer bastions and a central tower. Hurst guarded the western entry to the Solent through the Needles Passage. This passage had been protected by Worsley's Tower belonging to the 1520s, on the Isle of Wight below the cliff at 'Round Tower Point'. During the Earl of Southampton's reconnaissance early in 1539 this squat and octagonal structure was described as 'one of the worst devised things' he had seen.[5] Hurst was built on the mainland at the end of a shingle spit, which enabled it to defend both the Needles Passage and the shallow anchorage at the mouth of the Avon Water. The distinguishing feature is its angularity. The central tower is twelve-sided, and so is the outer ring of defence, at least internally. Externally, the three half-round bastions project beyond the salient angles of the curtain wall. St Mawes, on the other hand, while it has a

Deal Castle: as envisaged c1545 by Alan Sorrell. (DOE)

conventionally circular tower, has it eccentrically placed. There is no surrounding curtain, just a clover-leaf plan with the central tower rising above three rounded bastions set to the front. St Mawes was one of two forts commanding the entrance to Falmouth harbour. The other was Pendennis Castle. At each fort are remains of two small blockhouses at the waters-edge, which may have been built slightly earlier, in 1537 or 1538. Sandgate Castle, near Folkestone, was another variant of the three-bastion type. It was the only coastal fort that did not defend a harbour or anchorage. In-

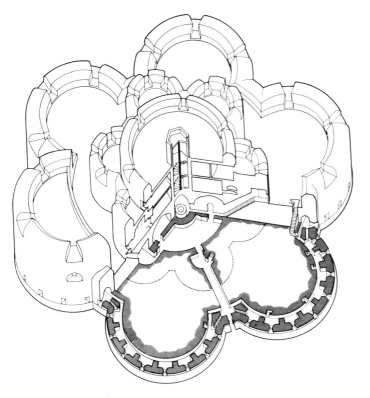

Deal Castle: an axonometric view. (DOE)

St Mawes, Cornwall: remains of earlier blockhouse at the waters-edge. (Author)

stead, it protected Dover from an attack from the rear as it commanded the coast road to the south.

Calshot and Pendennis Castles are at first glance alike with their simple circular, central towers, surrounded by multangular curtain walls set some distance away to give a wide courtyard. Calshot commanded the entrance to Southampton Water at the end of a shingle spit on the western side, covering the deep water channel. The curtain is circular externally, rising from a moulded plinth at the top of a sixteen-sided sloped apron which ran down into the moat. Pendennis Castle began as a simple round gun-tower. The sixteen-sided curtain was clearly an after-thought since its parapet masks the lower tier of primitive circular gun-ports in the ground floor of the tower. Portland Castle is a variant of the previous examples. The two-storey tower is only a segment of a circle set at the centre point of a segmental gun battery. It was one of a pair of forts designed to cross their fire over Portland Roads and was in commission by 1541 or 1542. Its partner is of the nature of a blockhouse in plan and will be described later.

Camber Castle is the most complicated of all; perhaps due to the fact that it did not begin on a virgin site but was an adaptation of Sir Edward Guleford's tower begun in 1512. It had three main building periods which produced major changes in the plan. In its final form, four new massive, circular bastions linked by an eight-sided curtain and a heightened central tower replaced a precocious, if muddled, intermediate predecessor for the protection of the harbour of the Camber beside Rye.[6]

These then were the great 'castles': low, bulbous, self-contained and self-defensible. There were besides sixteen other works of a smaller and simpler kind which were described as bulwarks or blockhouses, and were also part of the 'Device' programme. Their functions were broadly similar to the larger castles, but they were conceived more as 'ship-stopping' batteries, rather than all-round defensive works capable of resisting attack from landward. They range from substantial masonry structures like Sandsfoot and West Cowes Castles to earthwork batteries such as those along the Essex coasts. Few have survived and our knowledge of them has only recently been advanced by archaeological excavation.

The most substantial survivor is Sandsfoot Castle, the partner of Portland Castle. Even so the octagonal battery has almost entirely gone over the cliff leaving just the substantial rectangular residential block to the rear. The latter does not appear to have been strongly defensible, and the landward approaches were only later protected by earthworks. Of the two forts which guarded the entrance to the Isle of Wight's principal harbour, the river Medina, only West Cowes Castle remains to any degree. It is now a substantial part of the clubhouse of the Royal Yacht Squadron. Its

Calshot Castle, Hampshire. (Author)

partner, East Cowes, was abandoned only seven years after its construction. West Cowes was another centrally planned structure having a round tower with short, single-storey rectangular wings to east and west, a D-shaped battery to the front and a rectangular walled ditch to landward.

  Continuing eastwards, the next blockhouses were at Dover for the protection of the harbour. In March 1539, Marillac, the French ambassador, saw 'new ramparts and bulwarks in the rock where the sea beats . . . and well furnished with great and small artillery.'[7] Three bulwarks were built. They were all earthworks revetted with timber. One was at Archcliffe, also described as the bulwark of earth upon the hill above the south pier. The second was the bulwark in the cliff, and after 1542 known as the Black Bulwark in the cliff, covering the harbour itself. Lastly, to the north, was the turf bulwark under Dover Castle, subsequently known as Moats Bulwark after its second captain, Stephen Mote. A fourth bulwark, the Black Bulwark at or near the pier of Dover was probably in occupation in late 1544.

  Somewhat surprisingly the entrance to the river Medway did not form part of the 1539 pro-

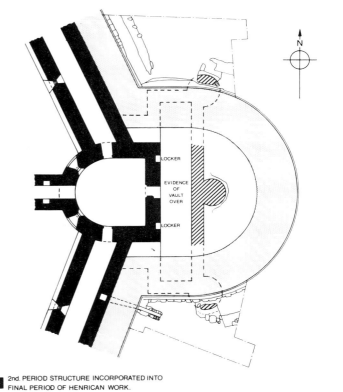

2nd. PERIOD STRUCTURE INCORPORATED INTO FINAL PERIOD OF HENRICAN WORK.

2nd. PERIOD STRUCTURE DEMOLISHED.

FINAL PERIOD WORK. (GUN PORTS OMITTED)

LOCKER

EVIDENCE OF VAULT OVER

LOCKER

Camber Castle, Sussex: plan of the east bastion after excavation showing Haschenperg's idiosyncratic attempt to provide flanking cover in the second period structure and later suppressed in the final period by a conventional rounded bastion. (DOE)

Remains of the Gravesend blockhouse following excavation.
(Author)

Castle Rushen, Isle of Man: circular gun-tower on the glacis.
(Author)

gramme. The Thames however was, partly to stop warships advancing on London, partly to protect the dockyards at Deptford and Woolwich, and also to protect the main ferry crossing of the Thames between Tilbury and Gravesend. Here were five small bulwarks or blockhouses, two on the Essex bank at West and East Tilbury, and three in Kent at Gravesend, Milton and Higham. Again, none has survived but they are known from later plans and drawings. Something of the plan of Gravesend bulwark has been revealed by excavation, and the site of the Milton blockhouse located. Both West Tilbury and Gravesend were essentially elongated D-shaped brick towers. The semi-circular front formed the battery with a rectangular block to the rear for accommodation. Additional earthwork batteries were provided on either side.

Although the 'Device' intended the defence of the Essex coast, nothing was done until 1543, except for the strengthening of the medieval walls of Harwich with trenches and earthen bulwarks in 1539. The additional bulwarks were added at Harwich (three), Landguard Point, at 'Langar Rode', St Osyth's, and one at East Mersea opposite Brightlingsea.

On the opposite side of the country, the entrance to Milford Haven was protected by two blockhouses which were in existence by 1546. That at Angle was described by George Owen, the Elizabethan historian of Pembrokeshire, as 'a rounde turrett never yet finished'. That in Dale parish was also a round tower, 20 feet (6 metres) in diameter with eight 'portes or loopes for great ordnance'.[8] The south western coasts of England were also surveyed and a map of *c*1540 shows where forts were proposed and 'not made' as well as those existing, such as Dartmouth, Plymouth, Stonehouse, Fowey and St Ives, together with the castles of Powderham and St Michael's Mount.[9]

Not part of the royal programme of defences, but likely to be contemporary with it, are some unusual works on the Isle of Man. Edward, third Earl of Derby added a sloping glacis beyond the moat of Castle Rushen to mask the curtain walls from gunfire. This is probably the earliest appearance of a feature which was to become commonplace in bastioned fortification. There were three low, round gun-towers with conical roofs sited on the glacis, one of which still remains. A detached round gun-tower was built in advance of Peel Castle and the isolated, circular Derby Fort has gunports reminiscent of Bayard's Cove, Dartmouth.

Many coastal towns such as Fowey, Dartmouth and Harwich were reported to have added to their defences on their own initiative. At Portsmouth, which was of particular importance as a victualling base, the king himself took a hand. Apart from the existing boom defences at the harbour mouth and other works along the sea front, the first major programme of fortifications took effect in 1522–4 with ditches, walls and bulwarks around the town. Some of the outlying

Derby Fort, Isle of Man. (Author)

bulwarks were also built at about this time, such as Palshed's or Windmill Bulwark on Southsea Common. In 1539 there was greater impetus to the work, and the French ambassador reported that the fortifications were well advanced.

The crisis of 1539 did not only require attention to coastal defences: the Border strongholds of Carlisle and Berwick, Calais and Guisnes were also vulnerable. On the Scottish Border, Berwick was the most important. In January 1539, the Master of the Ordnance, Sir Christopher Morris, surveyed the artillery and the condition of all the Border fortresses and was appalled: 'withoute I had seen it with myne eyen, I wold not have believed it to be so ill.'[10] Improvements were made at Berwick Castle and elsewhere but the chief result was the commencement of a new work at the north east angle of the town defences, the Lord's Mount. This was a massive gun-tower in the same idiom as the works along the south coast. Its plan was three-quarters of a circle, clasping the north east corner of the town wall. Carlisle in comparison with Berwick was a poor relation. Platforms were contrived on the castle walls with other improvements. However, a novel feature for England was the construction of the so-called 'Half-Moon Battery', in fact a low gun-tower specifically for ditch defence. Another novelty was the citadel at the entrance to Carlisle from the south. It was intended to be a self-contained strongpoint on the site of the former Botcher Gate, consisting of two massive round towers with a connecting masonry wall and a half-round tower to the north commanding the city itself, and joined to the round towers by curtain walls. On that other frontier, the Calais Pale, a similar review was undertaken.

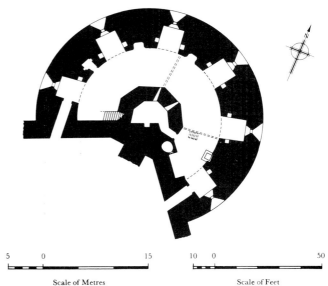

Scale of Metres   Scale of Feet

Berwick-upon-Tweed, Lord's Mount. (DOE)

DESIGN, CONSTRUCTION AND MANNING

There is thus remarkable consistency about the fortifications arising from the crisis of 1539. They were very traditional in basic conception but they were accomplished works showing confidence in their rounded, centrally planned forms. There were certainly far more advanced technically than anything else built in England previously: 'The "Device" fortresses were massively beautiful machines designed for the maximum emission of balls and bullets.'[11] There was clear recognition of the need to keep works as low as possible, to make the walls massively thick and to strive for all-round flanking cover. Over and over again the reports to, and instructions from, the king stress the need to improve splays and loops. At the same time, there was a fixation with massive firepower at several levels which was incompatible with low-lying defence that was less of a target. There were advantages in employing tiers of guns against warships but few against a land-based enemy. It is, however, interesting to see the deliberate separation of the self-defensive armament from the offensive. This practice was not to become an article of faith again until the mid-nineteenth century.

Who was responsible for this common theme? Most of the advisors and commissioners carrying out the surveys and supervising the works were 'amateurs' in the sense that they were officers at Court, great nobles and prominent landowners, not engineers. They might include the Master of the Ordnance and skilled master masons, but the element that is frequently omitted from the accounts is 'devisor'.

There was only one named engineer associated with the 'Device' forts, and that was a Moravian, Stephan von Haschenperg. It is known that he was responsible for Sandown Castle, phase II of Camber Castle, the earth bulwarks in the intervals between the Downs castles and the works at Carlisle. Haschenperg's Sandown and Camber noticeably lie outside the simple plan forms of the bulk of the 'Device' fortifica-

tions. Both were exceedingly complex and over-elaborate, particularly with regard to self-defence. Whereas the plan of Walmer was of four massive round bastions clustered around the central tower, Sandgate's three-bastion scheme becomes three small towers linked by curving curtain walls with an outer curtain wall lacking any flanking cover. Furthermore, the internal space between the central tower and the three outer towers was divided into three compartments by what amounts to two-storey caponiers. At Camber, the four outer bastions with their internal stirrup-towers or cavaliers were linked by caponiers to a narrow passage encircling the central tower, again dividing up the internal spaces into small compartments. This emphasis on self-defence seems excessive and unnecessarily complex. For what were intended to be gun-towers controlling anchorages from hostile shipping, the other 'Device' forts had the right answers. The impression gained from Haschenperg's designs is that here was an engineer whose experience lay in close siege work from land-based armies. Indeed his work at Carlisle suggests that he was more at ease there. The so-called 'Half-Moon Battery', and some of the outer works at the castle were ditch, or casemated flank defences, which were not uncommon in early sixteenth century continental fortifications but in the 1540s were still novel in England. The Citadel at Carlisle was modest and straightforward, and it is ironic that Haschenperg was sacked for incompetence while he was engaged in an

Carlisle: Half-Moon Battery in the early nineteenth century. (DOE)

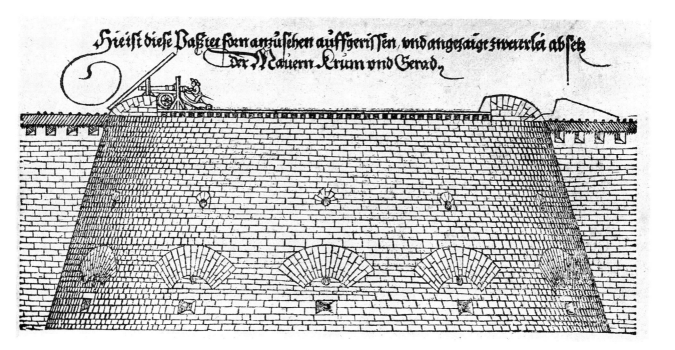

Dürer's proposal for a bastion with casemates and smoke vents and curved parapet. (Society of Antiquaries of London)

area where he seems, with hindsight, to be much more assured. While Haschenperg's experience clearly lay in northern Europe, he does however appear to have had an inkling of the new developments taking place in Italy. The strange form of his bastions at Camber, now masked by conventional 'Henrician' bastions of the Hurst Castle type, indicate an awareness of different defensive techniques and a willingness to experiment (see illustration on p41). Although his bastions were still rounded, they were low profiled and were faced with a sloping bank or glacis of shingle, backed by the cavalier-like stirrup-towers providing an upper tier of guns. More significantly, there appear to be positions for recessed flanking guns behind projecting 'ears' (*orillons*) covering the faces of the multangular curtain.[12]

We are still faced with the question: who designed the mainstream 'Device' forts? The Englishmen who were shortly to become Henry's leading military engineers, Richard Lee and John Rogers, were busy at the time at Calais and Guisnes. Sir Richard Morris, Master of the Ordnance, and James Needham, Surveyor of the King's Works, were much involved and were described as devisers of the bulwarks in the Thames. The Earl of Southampton and William, Lord St John were others closely concerned. Without clear authorship, the inspiration for the underlying design factors came from northern Europe, and, if there was a theoretical source, it is likely to have been *Etliche Underricht zu Befestigung der Stelt schloss und Flecken* by Albrecht Dürer, first published at Nuremberg in 1527. It is the earliest printed book confined to artillery fortification which, nevertheless, did 'not put forward a new system of fortification, it is rather a synthesis of ideas and practice already current in Germany and a

wide area of Europe.'[13] The book concentrates on the bastion itself and not its relationship to the line of defence as a whole, though Dürer pays attention to casemated flank and ditch defences. The bastions are D-shaped, massive in scale, with very thick walls and tiers of guns. Many of the detailed features are described: rounded parapets, battered outer walls, gunports with wide external splays, smoke-vents, low-level galleries for ditch and flank defence, frequently with projecting works in ditches similar to later caponiers. In 1535, a Latin translation, *De urbibus, arcibus castellisque cendendis* was published in England in time for the great coastal fortification programme. Machiavelli's *Libro dell'arte della guerra* (1521) may also have been known at the time. This advocated the value of earthworks with ditches flanked by casemates.

Probably the leading and unifying influence behind the fortifications of 1539–43 was the king himself. There are many references to Henry's personal concern in the building of fortresses, from the programme of works planned for Calais in 1532, to visitations while construction was in progress, and to the 'splais' which 'the King's grace hath devised'. It is also established that the skilled works teams employed on the royal palaces – Hampton Court in particular – were transferred to fortress building. This must explain the general excellence of the masonry and detailing of the castles themselves. It is likely that much of the skilled and arduous work of designing so many complex structures was done by the King's works office, but it is quite possible that Henry himself saw many of the schemes and gave them his approval.

A good deal is known about the cost and administration of building operations at Henry's castles.[14] Sandgate, Pendennis and St Mawes cost rather more than £5000 each, Portland slightly less. Camber appears to have cost nearly £16,000, and the castles and bulwarks in the Downs £27,000. By contrast, the cost of building one bulwark in the Thames was estimated at £211 13s 4d. For most of the fortifications, the names and offices of those administering the work are known. There was usually a paymaster, responsible for financial control, a comptroller in charge of the administrative, purchasing and supply organisation, an overseer watching the general conduct of the work, and a master carpenter and master mason looking after the technical side, but also sometimes acting in the capacity of a contractor, and to a certain extent responsible for the details of construction. A member of the local gentry was frequently connected with the work, such as Sir Thomas Treffry at St Mawes, who acted as paymaster. Ultimately, the defences were the responsibility of the Lord Admiral.

Details of the actual building are more hard to come by, though sometimes the progress of the work can be followed in such evidence as pleas from the paymaster for funds to meet the wages of the workmen. Fortunately the 'ledgers' of Sandgate Castle exist, and a close examination of them provides a reasonably complete picture of the progress of the building operations which must be typical of them all.[15]

In the spring of 1539 most of the workmen – masons, quarrymen, limeburners and wood fellers – were occupied preparing the building materials, while 'scapple men' and rock breakers were 'digging and casting beach from the foundation of the castle, breaking rocks, carrying them from the sea, loading earth and stone'. At this stage there was little need for carpenters, and those present made scaffolding, barrows, tubs, hods and other apparatus of a building site. In the first months, 225 men were engaged and 12 overseers. Throughout the summer the number of men rose until the daily average was 500. Bricklayers eventually became more numerous than stone masons, and there were more than 50 carpenters and sawyers. Less than half the total were identified as labourers. During the winter the labour force dropped, as might be expected, to just over 100 and temporary accommodation was provided for them. There was a three-week break over Christmas. By June 1540, the daily average on the site was 630 and the job was finished by that autumn with the provision of the drawbridge, completion of the lantern and the gilding of the great vane.

In the Downs, 1400 men were at work in May 1539. The stone came from local quarries and from the sea shore and, as in nearly every other fortress, from the now disused buildings of neighbouring religious houses. Stone from Beaulieu Abbey went into Calshot Castle, the Carmelite Friary at Sandwich into the Downs castles and much Caen stone from the Norman masonry of St Augustine's Abbey, Canterbury, went back across the Channel to the works at Guisnes. It is therefore unsurprising that the visitor to Henry's castles today sees fragments of moulded Gothic windows and vaulting ribs built into their walls. The bricks at Sandgate were likely to have been local in origin as would have been the lime; 44,000 tiles were used, most of which came from Wye in Kent. The sources of timber were similarly not far away. Lime kilns and a forge were established, fired with local brushwood and coal from the north of England. Many ready-made goods were bought in London, ranging from tents for the workmen to pre-fabricated wooden panelling. At Sandgate, however, the masons were recruited in Somerset and Gloucestershire. Skilled men received 7d or 8d per day. Labourers received 5d or 6d. The 5d rate of pay produced a strike among the labourers demanding the top rate at Deal in 1539.

Although there are various lists of ordnance at each place, it is extremely difficult to determine precisely how the castles and bulwarks were armed. The probability is that there never was a fixed number

Sandgate Castle, Kent: sixteenth century view showing the D-shaped gatehouse in advance of the ditch and the nature of the armament. Also, on the left-hand side are two beacons. (Hatfield House)

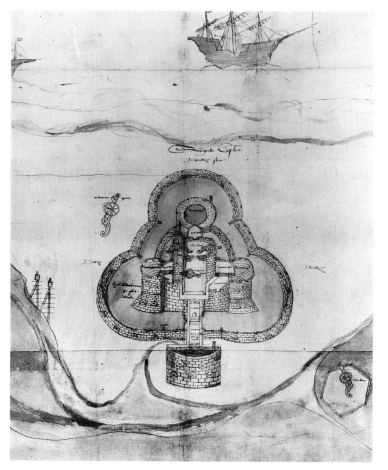

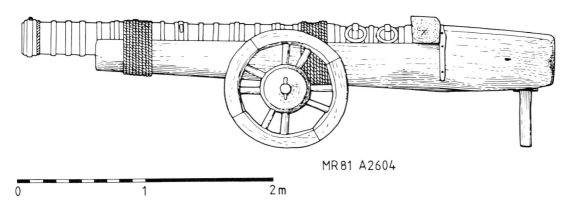

MR 81 A2604

0   1   2 m

Stave-built breech-loading gun on a wheeled carriage from the Mary Rose. (Mary Rose Trust)

of guns allocated, even theoretically, to any one fort. Captains of castles obtained what ordnance they could when they could, and according to their complaints there was never enough. Ordnance was almost entirely the property of the Crown and administered from the Tower of London. Individual guns were moved from fort to fort depending on emergencies, but some stayed in one place and were accounted for from time to time.

During the first decades of the sixteenth century there had been technical improvements in refining iron, enabling guns to be cast more easily. At the same time, cannon were conforming to a more-or-less regular range of sizes according to the weight of shot fired. Therefore, a saker came to fire a 6-pound shot, a culverin 18-pound, demi-cannon 32-pound, etc. These more uniform pieces are identifiable among the 'Device' forts' armament lists, but there were also many more primitive pieces still in use. At the Downs castles, demi-cannon, culverin, demi-culverin, saker, minion and falcon are frequently listed. The hackbut or arquebus, fired on the matchlock principle, was common as a personal weapon and for service in the gunports covering moats and courtyards, but the bow and arrow was still commonly in use. Among the primitive ordnance were stone-firing perriers, breech-loaders such as slings and bases of various kinds. There does, however, appear to have been some measure of fixed distribution at the Thames bulwarks according to the list of 1540. On the Essex bank the bulwarks had three brass guns of nearly similar calibre, and each had an iron bombard. Smaller guns varied in number from eight to eleven. On the Kent side, there were more brass pieces, six or five, though again, each had an iron bombard. The smaller guns were in relation to these figures, thirteen to twenty-four. The heavier guns were mounted on wheels, differentiated as shod or unshod.

Much more is known about garrison strengths, at least as far as the gunners are concerned, and this is the first time that such information is available. The Master of the Ordnance, Sir Christopher Morris, in 1540 compiled a book which gave not only the numbers of the garrisons but also their rates of pay.[16] Captains usually received 1s to 2s a day, the deputy 8d, the porter also got 8d and the soldiers and

gunners 6d. At Sandown there were 10 gunners, 11 at Walmer and 16 at Deal; and at the small blockhouses in the Thames, the number of gunners and soldiers varied: 2 soldiers and 6 gunners at Gravesend, 3 soldiers and 6 gunners at Milton, 2 soldiers and 4 gunners at West Tilbury and at East Tilbury, and 4 soldiers only at Higham. Altogether there were 2220 individuals listed, and their wages amounted to £2208 8s 0d a year. It must be remembered that these were simply holding garrisons. In time of crisis they would expect to be supplemented from local musters. Accommodation was provided within the forts, but the internal arrangements and woodwork do not survive to any great extent. St Mawes still has some internal doorcases with good carving on them. At Deal it is possible to see on the upper floor how the rooms were partitioned off and entered from a passage round the central stairs.

All the forts were well organised and a strict code of discipline was intended. The regulations were contained in the *Ordinances and Statutes devised by the King for the rule, establishment and surety of his Majesty's castles, bulwarks and other fortresses appointed to the survey of the Lord Admiral.*[17] All breaches of the rules had a scale of forfeiture of pay. The men had to supply their own weapons, and every gunner was expected to provide himself with a hand-gun or hagbush at his own expense. 'No gunner is to shoot off any ordnance nor hail any ship without the leave of the captain or his deputy on pain of losing his place.' Additionally, the Statutes and Ordinances for Berwick-upon-Tweed provide a great deal of information about garrison life there during the sixteenth century.[18] There was a permanent garrison of 40 soldiers including a constable, 2 porters, watchman, priest and 10 gunners. The regulations attempted to deal with the usual problems applying to garrison towns. This nucleus of trained officers and gunners, paid directly by the Exchequer, provided an important new element in coastal defence.

THE ANGLE BASTION AND EXPERIMENTS WITH THE ITALIAN SYSTEM, 1545–7

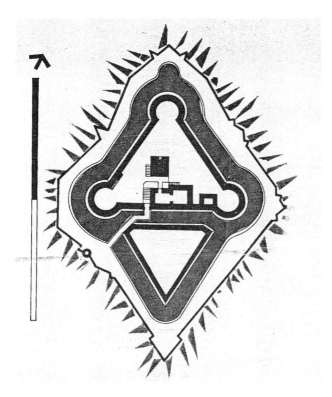

Sarzanello, Fortezza di Firmafede. (From Quentin Hughes *Military Architecture*)

Although the coastal defences of 1539 shared common elements which were developed from the well tried practical examples of north European fortification, they were completely outside what was to become the mainstream of military engineering during the next three hundred years: that is to say, the defensive system based on the angle bastion. During the Middle Ages the round tower had generally superseded the square tower because of its inherently greater strength, and because it had no angles and was less vulnerable to mining. Rounded forms, in plan and elevation, continued to be favoured in the initial phases of artillery fortification since they also provided a glancing surface for the deflection of shot. Yet round towers possessed a fundamental weakness which was to be more serious as siege work became more systematic. They presented an area of dead ground in front of the tower or bastion which could not be commanded by flanking fire from adjacent towers. By contrast, the salient of a pointed or angle bastion provided the minimum of a target and no dead ground. It became axiomatic in artillery fortification that lines of defence should be drawn so that every portion of the *enceinte* could be covered by gunfire. Enfilade fire was far more effective than direct fire for checking the rush of assaulting troops on a breach. The

flanks of the angle bastion provided greater firepower, and for this reason the angle bastion remained the dominant element in fortification design until the middle of the nineteenth century when technological improvements in artillery itself forced equally radical changes in defensive methods (see illustration on p248).

J R Hale has examined the early development of the angle bastion in central Italy, from the adaptation of round tower forms in the middle of the fifteenth century to the achievement of a true angle bastion in the fortresses built by Giuliano da Sangallo in the early years of the sixteenth century, which established the bastion as the principal and normal element of a fortress. Hale has also suggested that the origin of the recessed flank, so much favoured by Italian engineers and their disciples during the sixteenth century, may be derived from the junction of a steeply battered or scarped round tower with a similarly steeply scarped curtain wall, features especially common in Italian fortifications of the sixteenth century, which produced the opportunity for concealed gun positions – *traditori* ('traitors') as the Italians called them. The hallmark of the Italian school throughout the sixteenth century was to be the recessed or withdrawn flank protected from direct fire from the field by projecting *orillons* or ears on the faces of bastions.[19]

The first military treatise to include fortification is by Francesco di Giorgio Martini.[20] It may have been a compilation over a number of years but seems to reflect the period of the 1480s, or even the early 1490s. It antedates the period when Italy was the main European theatre of war, 1494–1539, when the pressure to develop better defensive forms was more insistent. Martini's work is all the more important because he not only documents a transitional stage in fortress design, he anticipates the coming angle bastion forms. In many ways his drawings are conventional, showing concentric defences with heavy guns in an earthwork rampart in front of masonry walls with lighter guns on the walls and towers. Yet, he introduces primitive angle basions which begin with pointed towers, and then explores the triangular trace as the smallest figure that could be completely flanked using bastions at the salients. Martini's drawings combine tall, multi-tiered gun-towers with triangular bastions, but many of his maxims were of universal application. The strongest elements of the defences, he argued, must always be placed in the most vulnerable sections of the perimeter. Circular *enceintes* he condemned because they restricted the line of fire. The strength of a fortress depended upon the quality of its plan rather than the thickness of its walls. He stressed the importance of the ditch, both as an obstacle to infantry, and for the reason that it shielded the lower parts of the scarp from artillery. The ditch was to be defended from the flanks of the towers, and with obstacles on the ditch bottom, including bombproof gun positions (*capannati*, see illustration on p31). In

Martini's treatise, the role of the covered-way on the outside of the ditch, and the sloping glacis beyond is formulated for the first time. Martini was a follower of the Vitruvian theory that a well proportioned human body was the guiding principle of all art, and provides an image of the ideal fortress in terms of the human figure. According to Hale, 'During the transitional period, not only was there no distinction between "art" and military engineering, but the mathematical interests of art theorists were particularly suited to the development of a type of fortification based on geometrical principles.'[21]

Leonardo da Vinci, Michaelangelo and Filareti are the most prominent of the artist/military engineers of the early renaissance who applied themselves to fortress design. It is, however, the Sangallo family, and in particular, Antonio da Sangallo the younger, to whom the credit should go for the evolution of the angle bastion in Tuscany, rather than to Vasari's claim on behalf of Sanmicheli at Verona. Francesco Giamberti, the eldest of the Sangalli, designed the fort at Sarzanello in 1493 as an equilateral triangle with round corner bastions. In 1497, a huge triangular, detached bastion was added to the most vulnerable side and the fort was surrounded by a covered-way complete with *places d'armes* which appears to belong to the early sixteenth century, and therefore, perhaps the earliest to survive. Giuliano da Sangallo, among a large repertoire, designed the fort at Nettuno in 1501–2, which appears in plan to have typical angle bastions with flanking guns in recessed positions behind rounded *orillons*. The bastions are, however, lofty angled versions of conventional mural towers. It is with Antonio da Sangallo's fully bastioned *enceinte* round the port of Civitavecchia in 1527 that the Italian bastion system may be said to have arrived. From the 1530s, Italian engineers had grasped the new principles, and were applying them across Italy, and to those parts of Europe whose princes could afford their services. At the same time, the new ideas were being transmitted in the growing Italian literature on fortification.

Through the 1520s and 1530s the impetus provided by the campaigns and initial successes of the French invasion of Italy caused the angle bastion to be used more and more. But it had not yet become universal: round bastions continued to be built in Italy into the 1530s and even 1540s, reinforced by the revival of interest in Vitruvius who claimed that while blows directed at angles could shatter them, 'in the case of round towers they can do no harm, being engaged, as it were, in driving wedges to their centre'.[22] The concept of the angle bastion was, however, beginning to spread northwards, largely as a result of the French military campaigns in Piedmont and Savoy during the mid-1530s. When the French captured Turin in 1535 it was surrounded by an earthwork *enceinte* of angle bastion Italian form. The French and Imperial armies began to

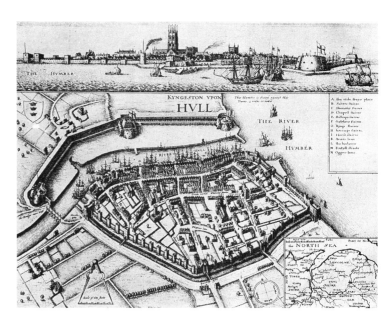

Hull castle and bulwarks by Hollar. (Author)

employ Italian engineers and as a result bastioned *enceintes* appeared at Le Havre in 1540 and at Antwerp in 1542–3.[23]

Military engineers in England during the early 1540s were, it seems, aware of revolutionary changes in fortification design taking place without understanding the rationale behind them. Haschenperg fumbled towards retired flankers behind *orillons* at Camber Castle. John Rogers was moving away from the rounded bastion at Guisnes and experimenting with elliptical, trefoiled forms or rounded bastions drawn to a sharp salient. The design of the flanks in these hybrid forms gave protection for the guns which would have a clear line of fire down the length of the curtains and past the face of adjacent bastions. The siting of the gunports in the trefoils made possible a degree of cross-fire over the field yet the lobes of the trefoils still produced significant areas of dead ground.

This transitional form of bastion first appears in mainland England among the various drawings for the defences of Kingston-upon-Hull. Hull was intended to be refortified as part of the 'Device' programme, but nothing was done to secure the town from seaborne attack until the King visited it in 1541. Work was delayed to the next year and John Rogers, was transferred from Guisnes to undertake a major scheme of defence which consisted of two large bulwarks, one opposite each end of the harbour, with a 'castle' midway between them, and all linked by a crenellated wall, nearly half a mile long, running parallel to the river. The two blockhouses were each trefoil-shaped in plan with pointed segmental bastions enclosing a square central building. The entrance to each was through the middle of a rectangular 'stalk' at the gorge. The central castle was square with a pointed segmental bastion on opposite sides. The curtain wall joined the other two sides.

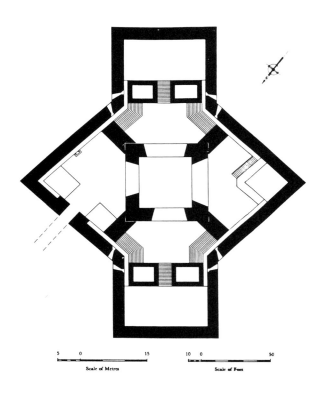

Scale of Metres   Scale of Feet

Southsea Castle, Hampshire: plan based on the existing remains and earlier surveys. (DOE)

Inside the square enclosure was a central rectangular keep. In some respects the works at Hull maintained the basic Henrician theme of central planning, but the pointed segmental bastions suggest a move towards the angle bastion and was a design peculiar to Rogers, only seen elsewhere at Guisnes. There was, however, no conception of proper flanking cover. The gunports in the bastions did not cover the side of the rectangular figure or link effectively with the adjacent bulwarks.

Another indication of change was the plan of Southsea Castle built two years later in 1544, at the southernmost point of Portsea Island, commanding the deep-water channel between Spit Sand and Portsea. Southsea was centrally planned, just as the other main castles, but with a square keep. Two rectangular gun platforms were sited on either side of the keep and separated from it by a courtyard. On the other two sides, the sea and the main landward approach, the curtain was produced into two projecting, straight-sided salients or triangular bastions. As a slightly later improvement, a pair of gunports was inserted into the obtuse angle formed by the bastions and the curtain to provide complete flanking cover along the whole of the long sides of the fort, an improvement on the works at Hull. Internally, the courtyard was divided by four caponiers springing from each angle of the square keep, a device reminiscent of Haschenperg's schemes for Sandgate and Camber.

At the same time as Southsea and Hull were

building, other smaller works were filling gaps left among the 1539–43 defences. Southampton Water and the entrance to the Hamble were strengthened by Netley Castle and St Andrew's Castle. Netley was built by Lord St John and shared some of the plan characteristics of Southsea Castle. St Andrew's Castle lay on the west side of Hamble Common, but has been completely eroded by the sea. Descriptions around the turn of the seventeenth century suggest that it consisted of a high square tower with the main armament on a lower semi-circular bulwark. Brownsea fort was built at the mouth of Poole harbour by the town of Poole, with financial aid from the King, a little later between 1545 and 1547. It was intended to consist of a square tower, which never rose above a single storey, with an hexagonal wall extending from it enclosing a gun platform at ground level. None of these minor works showed any real development of design.

Moving away from mere domestic considerations, Henry VIII was ever anxious to play a part in European politics and again joined in the Franco-Imperial conflicts. In 1543, he gave token support to Charles V in his campaign against Francis I at the siege of Landrecy, and in the next year Henry besieged Montreuil and Boulogne himself. This was to be a school of war for the English commanders. It put them alongside a cosmopolitan Imperial army, and in particular, put them into contact with Italian engineers, both in their own camp and also with those advising the French. Italians were now in English pay. It is reasonably certain that the new ideas in military engineering were beginning to filter across the Channel from this source.

That this was so can be seen in the style of some of the new defences which were built between 1545 and 1547 to meet a renewed threat of French invasion. The French fleet entered the Solent in July 1545, and not only was the flagship, *Mary Rose*, lost in this action but the French landed on the Isle of Wight. The Scots too had earlier repulsed an English raid at Ancrum Moor and were then reinforced from France. There were therefore threats to the south coasts, danger in the north, and with Henry's capture of Boulogne the year before, an overseas possession to be defended. All this gave rise to a substantial new fortress building campaign and bore with it hints that the new Italian ideas on angle bastions and more organised flanking fire for fortifications were influencing English engineers.

These new ideas seem to have been best understood and expressed in the English fortifications of Boulogne. John Rogers was chiefly responsible. The new works at Boulogne were in an accomplished Italian style and set out on clear geometrical principles without, it seems, the benefits of Italian colleagues on the spot. The defences included not only the repair of the town's medieval defences but the construction of de-

tached works outside the town and a citadel within the
Basse ville. All these works were laid out, to judge from
the drawings, with proper regard to lines of defence and
the flanking function of bastions (see illustration on
p36). Similar bastioned fortifications were designed in
1546 by Rogers for the inlet at Ambleteuse along the
coast to the north of Boulogne, and another fort a few
miles further north of Cap Griz Nez. These and much
of the new defences of Boulogne were in earthwork
with masonry reserved for gateways and flankers. Because they were earthworks they regularly fell into
ruins every winter and had to be reconstructed in the
following spring.

The translation of the Italian methods to England was not effected with the same assurance as Rogers
achieved at Boulogne. Much of the English fortification
was in the hands of Richard Lee, Roger's contemporary
at Calais, who seems to have been a slow learner. He
was, however, the builder of an angle bastion with a
recessed flanker on the Italian model at Portsmouth in
1546. Among the 'certain fortification to be made
according to the King's Majesty's device' was a 'great
bastillian to be made before the Gate'.[24] There is no
mistaking its shape on contemporary drawings, irregular though it is. It was an addition to an earlier tower.
The bastion had little forward projection but one long
face terminated in a rounded *orillon* to the west, masking a very small flanker. The opposite flank appears to
be used as an entrance thereby neutralising its true
purpose. Sketches exist to show a scheme for additional
improvement to the Portsmouth earth walls which
were based on the Italian system but not carried out
apart from another 'bastillion' between the Round
Tower and Point Gate.

Elsewhere, Italian ideas had their influence
but were imperfectly understood. Sandown Bay in the
Isle of Wight – another potential bridgehead for an
invader, and omitted in the earlier defensive programme – was given a fort in the summer of 1545. An
Italian engineer, Giovanni Portinari, was in charge of
the construction, but it was a hybrid design of a rectangular walled enclosure with a square keep to landward supported by two bastions. One of the latter was
a simple square set on an angle of the main enclosure,
the other had a semblance of an arrowhead bastion. On
the seaward side of the enclosure was the now familiar
half-round bastion providing the main gun platform.
Sharpenode Fort, also on the Isle of Wight at Sconce
Point commanding the Needles Passage was even
odder. It was described as a blockhouse and was a
square platform with two acutely angled salients projecting at either corner of the landward side as putative
bastions. The work was described in 1559 as follows:

yt is a massy platforme only walled wyth planke . . .
wythout aney dytche aboute yt. This bulwark up
about xxxvii fote square and viii fote high to the sea
wardes, and hath two flankers wyth a hier wall to the

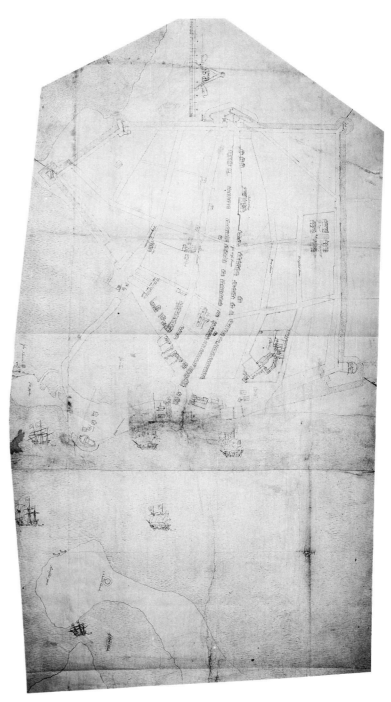

*Portsmouth in the mid-sixteenth century: the 'great bastillion'
is to the north east.* (Hatfield House)

landewardes wherby they may flanker the pece wyth
hercubusses that elles might beate them from the hill
at ther backes.[25]

Another part of the coastline hitherto neglected, except
for the then still existing Queenborough Castle, was
the Medway. In 1545 the decision was taken to build
three blockhouses. Sir Richard Lee was responsible but
without a very clear idea of the Italian form to judge by
later drawings. The blockhouse that was built was a
square tower with a square and thickly walled enclo-

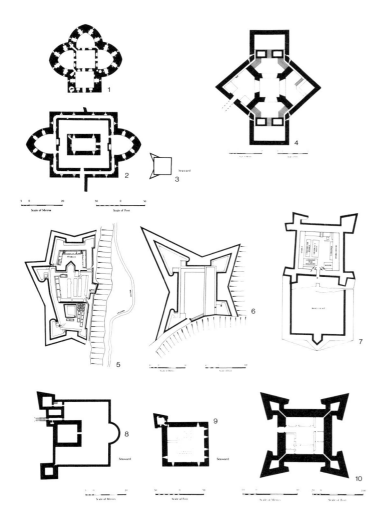

The development of the bastioned system:
1   *Hull, the northern blockhouse*
2   *Hull, the central castle begun in 1542*
3   *Sharpenode, Isle of Wight, 1545–7*
4   *Southsea Castle, 1544*
5   *Lauder, Scotland, 1548*
6   *Dunglass, Scotland, 1548*
7   *Broughty, Scotland, 1548*
8   *Sandown, Isle of Wight, 1545*
9   *Yarmouth, Isle of Wight, 1547*
10 *Harry's Walls, Isles of Scilly, 1551.*

sure well provided with embrasures. At one angle, to seaward, was a polygonal bastion with the salient angle flattened. It was a gun platform rather than a device for self-defence.

Henry VIII did employ other Italian engineers. Girolamo de Treviso arrived as early as 1538 as an expert on fortifications and he was killed in 1544 during an attack on Boulogne. Antonio de Bergamo and Gian Tomasa Scala of Venice were both sent to assist Lee with the re-fortifying of the castle at Tynemouth in January 1545. They were no doubt responsible for the somewhat crude bastioned trace across the land front, complete with recessed flankers, of which there is a plan. It is probably the earliest plan to show an

English version of an Italian *orillon* bastion. Scala's unpublished treatise on fortification contains a revealing autobiographical note: '. . . *fisi la forteza de timor* [Tynemouth] *che son sulla bocha de la fiumare de novo castel* [Newcastle] *et in quel ano fisi la traversa a barwich* [Berwick] *et fisi quel de uarch* [Wark]'.[26] He returned to Venice on the death of Henry VIII. It was Rowland Johnson who was responsible for a plan for enclosing the medieval castle of Norham within a bastion trace (see illustration on p33).

In his last years Henry maintained his personal involvement with fortifications and clearly was up to date in the new ideas and technical terms. The word bastion had come into royal vocabulary following the capture of Boulogne in 1544. Among the first defensive measures he demanded was the construction of a 'bastillion' round the Roman lighthouse. Although Italians were employed, Henry put his reliance on his two English engineers, Lee and Rogers. The ideas were drawn from foreigners but their execution was entrusted to Englishmen.

The reign of Henry VIII is of the greatest interest to the student of English military engineering. It is a period of transition, and during the final three years or so of his life, one of dramatic and rapid development. The great defence programme of 1539–43 marks the high point of the progression from mural tower to *rondelle*, from simple gun-tower to concentric fort. Although they were nevertheless at a dead end in terms of fortification design, the massive concentric works when used as coastal defence were functional, if over-provided for in terms of firepower. The circular form served well against shipping or indeed a landing, and while they were obviously obsolete in their details, Sandgate and Hurst Castles were sufficiently well sited and structurally sound to be converted into Martello towers 230 years later. The 'castles' for the most part also observed that prerequisite of a coastal battery, all-round defence, in the event of an assault from a landing party. Within two or three years from the construction of the new coastal forts there was a move from the round to the square or rectangular. Was this part of the progression towards the angle bastion whose concept was firmly grasped once Henry had broken out of his temporary insularity and mixed with foreign captains conversant with the new Italian ideas?

CHAPTER THREE

The Establishment of the Italian Bastion System in the Sixteenth Century

THE BASTION SYSTEM

The most characteristic feature of artillery fortification, its most enduring image, is the four-sided angle bastion. This feature remained a constant element in military engineering from the middle of the sixteenth century until quite late into the nineteenth, whether defences were planned on a regular geometrical figure or formed an irregular *enceinte* designed to fit the terrain. During the six hundred years in which gunpowder artillery has existed and influenced the form of defensive systems, the angle bastion was the underlying concept for half that time. The bastion system was the dominant factor in fortification world-wide; or rather throughout Europe or wherever Europeans colonised. It was thought to be equally applicable against the armies of Louis XIV as against the armies of the Mogul Empire in India or even the Red Indians of North America.

The earliest angle bastions concentrated upon effective flanking cover across the intervening curtain

Plan of Palmanova. (Author)

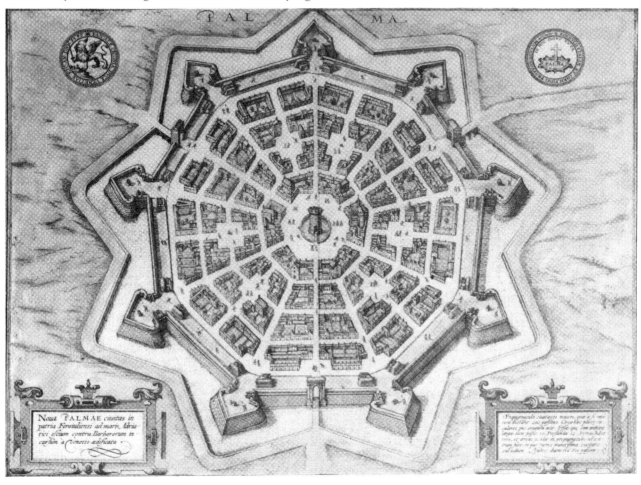

wall, but, as the bastion system developed, the emphasis moved towards defence in depth. These outer defences were themselves dependent upon the bastion principle. Outworks of whatever complexity grew out of the line of capital through the salient angle of the bastion, and were influenced by the 'line of defence' drawn from the flank of one bastion to the salient of the next. The defences moved outwards in layers: ditch, covered-way, sometimes a further ditch and glacis beyond, with the various projections providing more and more flanking cover, and reflecting the dominant factor of the bastions on the primary *enceinte*. The bastion system in fact was the reduction of the traditional elements of defence by ditch, rampart and projecting tower to a logical form emphasising the necessity for complete flanking cover of the whole. It subsequently led to the requirement for means by which the attackers were kept under fire for as long as possible, and for prolonging resistance step by step. Greater emphasis was given to making the range of different weapons govern the length of the line of defence. Fortress artillery in the sixteenth and seventeenth centuries had an effective range of about 600 yards (550 metres) and the musket not much more than 200 yards (180 metres). The attackers therefore had only a short distance to cover under opposing small arms fire, and the density of fire to which they might be subjected was not very great because the weapons used allowed only a slow rate of fire. The decisive phase of the attack was in the area about one hundred yards from the parapet. Therefore every effort was made to pin down the attackers within that zone and to concentrate upon them as heavy a fire as possible.

The bastion trace with its outworks had this principal purpose. The frontal fire from the parapets was arranged to graze the slope of the glacis. The faces of the bastions contained the offensive batteries capable of firing into the field. By contrast, the flanks of the bastions had a defensive role and were intended to bring gunshot along the ditch in front of the curtain and across the face of the opposite bastion This raking enfilade fire would be most effective at the point where the attackers were endeavouring to scale the walls or surge through a breach. Breaches, therefore, were usually sought in the faces or salient angles of bastions. But this represented the last throes of the defence. The enemy's advance needed to be delayed, if not halted, by outer obstacles. In the process of time, various types of outworks were devised. Within the ditch the *tenaille*, a long bank of earth, was intended primarily as a screen to the escarp of the curtain with the intention of reducing damage to the escarp revetment, or it might cover a sallyport. The ravelin was another advance work in the ditch, also in front of the curtain. Its function was not only to protect the curtain but also to bring flanking fire over the ground in front of the bastions on either side of it, and thus force the attacker

to capture the ravelin before he could assault the bastions. Ravelins were important, and were often employed in front of an entrance through the fortifications, thereby controlling communications. Angled counterguards covered the faces of bastions. Outworks known as hornworks, crownworks, *demi-lunes* etc, were constructed in front of the ravelins and the salients of bastions and beyond the covered-way on the counterscarp of the ditch in order to delay the attackers still further, and to push outwards the point on which they must make their first attack, or to occupy difficult pieces of terrain. Retrenchments, such as that done at Pisa in 1499, might provide an internal line of defence if the main parapet was breached. Batteries mounted on raised positions, known as *cavaliers*, gave command by height, and might be sited within specially important bastions. Underground defence, with countermines, often extending from below the salients of bastions, was a frequently used device. A citadel, or keep of last resort, was sometimes provided within a major fortress or defended town for use after the main lines had fallen. Engineers tried to meet every eventuality. The complex geometry, and the defensive systems developed from the sixteenth century through to the seventeenth and eighteenth centuries, moved towards a futile search for impregnability.

The adoption of the angle bastion could mean a great deal more than an improvement in defensive capability. It could influence town planning. Indeed, the geometrical and methodical conception of the bastion system was admirably suited to the idealised proportions and mathematical basis in renaissance theory.[1] Military theorists, by creating their ideal defensive forms on geometrical figures, could, at the same time, fill the interiors of those figures with a regularly planned town. The urban plan might be radial, the plan adopted at Palmanova near Venice, or it could be designed on a grid pattern as proposed by Pietro Cataneo, with further combinations of both grid and radial plan. The regularity, balance and proportion of the bastion system were also mirrored in the concepts of Vitruvius as applied to architecture. It is, perhaps, more than just coincidence that the bastion system began when classical architectural forms were supplanting Gothic, and declined at the time when the revival of Gothic and other architectural styles started to replace the traditional proportions and conventions of Palladianism as well as those of the neo-classical movement. The architectural parallels can be maintained when we realise that the high-point in the complexity and over-indulgence in the bastion system was contemporary with the achievements of the Baroque. The pervasive influence of fortification, theoretical or real, combined with a style of warfare dominated by sieges rather than pitched battles, gave the subject both an intellectual and vicarious appeal to the educated man. The conventions of siege warfare, and the tech-

Yarmouth Castle, Isle of Wight: two-storey orillon *bastion flanking the original entrance.* (Author)

nical terms of the military engineer entered contemporary speech and literature. They might even influence the design of gardens. Even today it is possible to discuss surviving fortifications, both in the actual mass and in their theoretical designs in terms of art.[2]

COASTAL DEFENCES AFTER HENRY VIII

The death of Henry saw no change in relations with France. In fact, revived hostilities with Scotland only increased England's vulnerability during the 1550s. The strategic pattern of coastal defences which had evolved under Henry was further strengthened on the Isle of Wight and expanded to the Isles of Scilly and the Channel Islands. The Needles Passage, the western approaches to the Solent, had been protected but the town and port of Yarmouth on the north western end of the Island was completely open. A fort was built in 1547. Originally it was a square, walled enclosure with a ditch on two sides and the sea washing the other two. At the south east angle, covering both ditches was a two-storey angle bastion of true Italian inspiration, but imperfectly applied, so that the stubby square-ended ears or *orillons* were too short to protect the flankers adequately. Inside the enclosure, ranges of buildings were set against the walls leaving a small central courtyard. There were two tiers of gunports in the walls with heavier armament at parapet level. This presented a hybrid piece of fortification which was remodelled in the 1560s when three-quarters of the interior was infilled, its height reduced by 9 feet (2.75 metres) and the fort converted into a substantial gun platform. The *orillon* bastion remains little altered and at full height, and is the earliest surviving angle bastioned fortification to be seen in the British Isles.[3]

Another transitional fort is Upnor Castle

opposite Chatham Dockyard, Kent. Although it was designed by the leading English engineer, Sir Richard Lee, as late as 1559, its use of a partial bastion plan does not suggest complete confidence in the true function and purpose of the angle bastion. Upnor was the only new fortification, apart from the monumental defences of Berwick-upon-Tweed, being built in the first years of Elizabeth's reign. Its purpose was to protect the Queen's warships while 'in ordinary' (that is, moored, out of commission) in the Medway below Rochester Bridge. Initially the fort consisted of a great, angled, water bastion just above water level at full tide with a rectangular residential block behind it, built over and against the river bank. Despite Lee's experience of bastioned fortification in France and at Berwick, he appears at Upnor to have misjudged its significance as a device for achieving flanking cover. The employment of an angle bastion for a river battery severely limited the firepower which could operate against oncoming warships. Perversely, the landward defences of Upnor, which might have benefitted from a bastion trace, were woefully deficient, and had to be made good nearly fifty years later. Upnor contains other anachronisms such as a river frontage with tall, slender angle turrets containing keyhole gunports, which might be just excusable in the earlier Henrician castles but not in a work of the latter half of the sixteenth century. Perhaps Upnor was a deliberate piece of nostalgic romanticism![4]

A surprising omission from Henry's defensive scheme is the lack of up-to-date fortification for the Isles of Scilly. The view of Sir Francis Godolphin, Governor of the islands in 1602, was that an enemy who captured the islands might 'soon make [them]

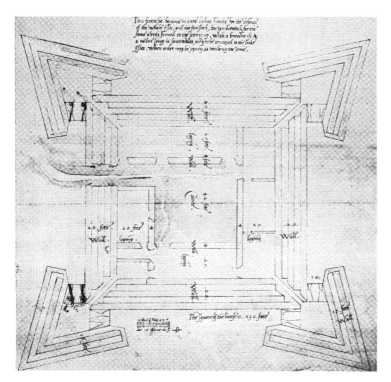

Harry's Walls, Isles of Scilly. Plan of 1552–3. (Hatfield House)

impregnable and use [them] as a rendezvous of his navy, a citadel or scourge against the realm'.[5] This was equally apposite seventy years before. There was a small medieval castle on St Mary's but the first evidence for Tudor interest in fortifying Scilly followed a visit to the islands by the Lord Admiral Seymour in 1547, who intended to prevent the islands becoming a base for pirates or something politically more sinister. At first the defensive centre of gravity lay in Tresco but, in 1551, an order came from the Privy Council 'to make the forte in our Ladies Isle of Silly upon the little hill betwixt the freshe water and St Marie Roode, where of to receave a plat at his [John Killigrew] sonnes hands'. This is the unfinished fort now known as Harry's Walls. Only one length of curtain and two *orillon* bastions of copy-book Italian plan remain. In its eroded state it is the most advanced piece of military engineering for its date to be seen in this country. A contemporary drawing gives the complete plan of the unfinished fort. The dimensions match the surviving masonry and an inscription reads 'This fortress begonne in oure ladies Ilande for the defence of the whole Isles, and not finished . . .'. The plan shows a square symmetrical fort with acutely pointed bastions and recessed flankers and square-ended *orillons*. The plan also suggests that the armament in the bastions was intended only for the flanks. It is unclear where the heavier guns, intended to command the harbour of Hugh Town, were mounted. Yet, in 1554 two sakers were in position. The failure to complete this sophisticated design must be due to lack of attention to topo-

graphical realities. The plan was clearly a drawing office production with no allowances made for the practical difficulties of the site. The hill on which it was placed was too small for a fort of this size so that the bastions were awkwardly sited on steeply sloping ground and could not have functioned properly.[6]

By contrast, on the neighbouring island of Tresco, a fort of entirely traditional design was simultaneously under construction. What is now known as King Charles's Castle was built between 1548 and 1554 at the northern end of the island to guard the entrance to the sheltered harbour of New Grimsby. The castle is basically in two parts: a semi-octagonal battery with a gunport in the centre of each of the five sides towards the sea, and a rectangular barrack block to the rear. The latter has small square projections at the north east and south west corners and a larger square projection in front of the main entrance in the centre of the back wall. These square projecting 'bastions' gave this part of the castle something of a cruciform plan and could have provided partial but inadequate flanking cover. By comparison with Harry's Walls, King Charles's Castle harks back to the plans of the Thames blockhouses of 1539–40 and, more closely, to the two-storey gun battery of Sandsfoot Castle, Weymouth and the battery on Brownsea Island. The gunports too have an archaic flavour to them. As a piece of artillery fortification it represents perhaps the last fling of traditional castle building at the moment when the angle bastion was finally established in England. It is ironic to see the two styles being expressed simultaneously in the same place; the obsolete form being completed and the modern version a functional failure.[7]

Commanding the harbour of Old Grimsby, on the western side of Tresco, is a contemporary masonry blockhouse. It is a simple rectangular battery with living quarters attached. It survives minus its roof. The sites of two others lie on the north side of St Mary's. The other significant and recently discovered work of fortification on Tresco is a defence line across the neck of the headland on which King Charles's Castle stands. This consists of an earthwork, now almost eroded, with two lengths of curtain with a bastion in the centre and a demi-bastion at the eastern end with possibly another on the west, close to the castle itself. The central bastion has recessed flankers and *orillons* and would therefore seem to be of sixteenth century date but not necessarily contemporary with the archaic castle.[8]

The other area where new defensive schemes were put in hand was the Channel Islands. Although in theory neutral, the islands were both useful and vulnerable. The French did indeed land on Sark in 1549. There were existing medieval castles: Castle Cornet, guarding the harbour of St Peter Port in Guernsey, and Mont Orgueil above Gorey harbour in Jersey. The experienced engineer, John Rogers, was sent to Guernsey in

Mont Orgeuil Castle, Jersey, from the north: Grand Rampier flanked by a demi-bastion. (Author)

1551 and a considerable sum of money was issued to the Captain of Guernsey, Sir Peter Mewtis, for repairs and fortifications at the castle the following year.

At Jersey, the Duke of Somerset, who was governor from 1537 to 1550, attempted to make Mont Orgueil less vulnerable to siege guns which could be mounted on the hill overlooking the castle from the rear. This involved the addition of a massive and irregular tower to the earlier keep, with a further enormous gun platform in front of it at a lower level. The object was to create platforms for heavy guns which could command and make the opposite hilltop untenable. This remodelling of a medieval castle employed the latest thinking. The Grand Battery or Rampier below the Somerset Tower was flanked by an irregular demi-bastion at the north east corner, with a recessed flanker sheltered behind an *orillon*. At the base of the tower itself is a mutilated casemate intended to provide flanking cover through a long embrasure cut through the masonry of the south west corner of the Somerset Tower.

Alderney had hitherto been undefended but the French threat to Sark in 1549 led to the construction of fortifications. Both John Rogers, 'late surveyor of Boulogne', and 'John [*sic*] Rydgeway', visited the island and, by May 1551, £5000 had been spent on works. These were concentrated in Longy or Longis Bay. Part of this work survives in what is now known as Essex Castle and there are other traces at 'Chateau de Longis' or 'the Nunnery'.

SCOTTISH CAMPAIGNS AND BERWICK-UPON-TWEED

Protector Somerset's attempt to link the two crowns of England and Scotland by marriage failed by diplomatic means, and led to The War of the Rough Wooing. Somerset's invasion, in September 1547, both mastered the Scottish field army at Pinkie, and then set out to create an English 'Pale' in Scotland by the construction of a network of new forts in the eastern Lowlands. Somerset established three centres under English control: Eyemouth, Hume and Roxburgh. From Leith detachments were sent to the island of Inchcolm in the Forth, and to Broughty Castle on the Tay. On the west, garrisons were established at Castle Milk and Dumfries. France quickly came to the support of the Scots, and sent an expeditionary force in 1548. English control was soon lost in the south west but substantial fortresses were constructed at Broughty, Lauder and Haddington. Further reinforcements led to the building of a fort at Dunglass. During this war, England made its most determined attempt to gain control of Scotland since the time of Edward I but, through the intervention of the French, its forces were eventually driven out during 1550.[9]

The capture of defended places was the usual way of obtaining control. Somerset introduced a policy whereby the rapid construction of new earth and timber forts for the protection of garrisons would exert the necessary military and political pressure to force the Scots to accept the marriage and political union. Plans of most of these forts are preserved and there are

Eyemouth, Berwickshire: aerial photograph of the headland with the English fort with its single central bastion and the French fort beyond it flanked by two demi-bastions at either end of the curtain. (HBM)

Inchkeith, Firth of Forth: remains of a French fort with a casemate in a bastion flank. (HBM)

considerable earthwork remains at Eyemouth, Dunglass and Roxburgh. Sir Richard Lee held the post of 'General Surveyor' and was responsible for the design of Eyemouth and Roxburgh. There was also present, Ridgeway, described in 1548 as 'Surveyor of the woorkes about Barwick', who was much involved with Roxburgh and other garrisons. Sir Thomas Palmer was closely concerned with the design of Haddington. Thomas Petit was responsible for Lauder. Accompanying these home-grown engineers were Giovanni di Rossetti also known as 'Mr John the Ingineer' or 'the Italian' or just 'the engenour', and Archangelo Arcano, another Italian adviser of long standing. Rossetti designed the works at Broughty.

The first fort to be built was at Eyemouth. The defence consisted of a single bastion in a re-entrant angle of an earthwork cutting off the headland. Although seemingly up-to-date, the recessed flanks were much too small, and in order to protect the faces of the bastion, Lee had to insert two tunnel-like casemates through the curtain. The surviving English earthworks compare unfavourably with the French fortifications at the same spot some ten years later. Broughty was needed to protect a base for seaborne supplies. Although designed by an Italian, its plan seems very unsure and irregular. Square in shape its bastions were decidedly eccentric and inconsistent but they did have the merit of providing complete all round cover. Lauder, by comparison, was much more Italian looking, though designed by Petit. Here was a mixture of straight-sided bastions, one with two tiers of guns, with large *orillon* demi-bastions protecting the most vulnerable side. In 1548, the strategically important town of Haddington was enclosed by a ditched, square fortification with angle bastions at the corners. The ramparts were very thick, and as well as concealed flankers in the bastions, there were additional earthworks protecting the hackbutters, with cavaliers giving raised platforms for artillery. It clearly impressed the enemy. A French mercenary fighting for the English, wrote '*que Adingthon aisny fortiffié est une des plus belles et fortes places après Thurin [Turin] qu'il est possible*',[10] The French commander, Andre de Montalembert, was shocked by its strength. Indeed, the defenders were well capable of resisting the siege and it was distractions in England which led to a withdrawal. Haddington was the only success among the English forts in Scotland. Dunglass suffered from a poor location and was of little real strength. Lee had provided a mixture of straight-sided and *orillon* bastions of different sizes but again with very short flanks.

'In Scotland during 1547–50, as at Boulogne in 1545–50, the new Italian technique of fortification was tested in the field as perhaps nowhere else in Europe at the time. It has to be said that it was not wholly successful, at least as practised by the English.'[11] The forts of Scotland's French allies, such as

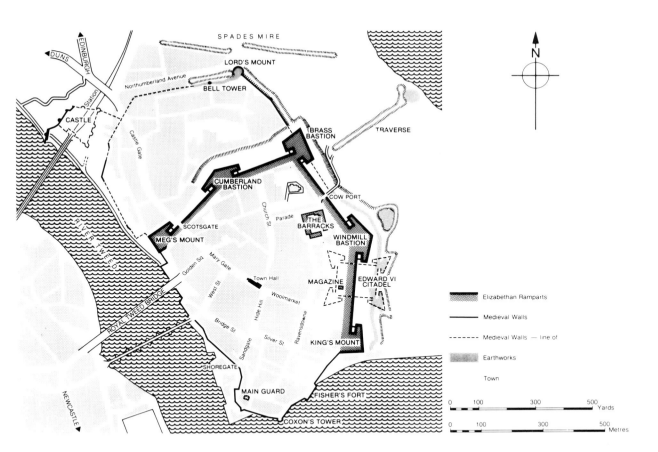

Berwick-upon-Tweed, Northumberland: plan of town including the circuit of the medieval walls, the outline of the citadel and the bastioned enceinte. (DOE)

their base at Leith, had a brighter ring of confidence about them. This is well demonstrated by their more effective solution for defending Eyemouth. The French fort has a longer curtain much further inland scoured by demi-bastions at either end. Other important French defensive works included a similar fort to Haddington at Aberlady nearby, and on Inchcolm in the Forth.

The failure of the English attempt to garrison southern Scotland and the presence of a French expeditionary force on the Border led to renewed attention to the defences of Berwick. Ever since its recapture from the Scots in 1482 the fortifications had been spasmodically improved. The Edwardian town walls enclosed a large area on the north east bank of the Tweed and, immediately outside the walls to the north west corner was the medieval castle. Improvements under Henry VIII added bulwarks and gun-towers to, and in front of, the walls but these were obsolete and now insufficient. For many years the inadequacies of the castle had been obvious owing to its low-lying position in regard to the town.

In July 1550 Sir Richard Lee and Sir Thomas Palmer were commissioned to survey the Border fortresses. Berwick was, of course, the most important,

lying as it did on the most favoured invasion route into and out of Scotland. Their recommendation was for a new fort or citadel on the high ground on the eastern side of the town, which would stand higher than the castle, and command both the town and the harbour. They proposed a rectangular fort with four angle bastions. The nature of the high ground ensured that the citadel would straddle the line of the town wall. Although designed by Lee and Palmer, the engineer in fact responsible for carrying out the work was William Ridgeway. Like other forts of this date, the bastions were very small and acutely pointed. This produced, correspondingly, restricted flanks behind their square *orillons*, closely similar to the bastions of Harry's Walls in the Isles of Scilly. Work on the citadel proceeded slowly, and in 1557, Ridgeway was instructed to increase the number of men employed but in fact the work was never completed and is no longer visible as an entity. It was overtaken by political events and a new drastic remodelling of Berwick's defences.[12]

In 1557 relations with Scotland were no better and, more worrying, the French army, estimated at 3000 men, had become a permanent force, based on strong modern fortresses at Leith and Inchkeith and, more close at hand, at Eyemouth. Again, Sir Richard Lee was brought in to take a radical review of Berwick and impose a modern defensive system on the medieval structure. The half-finished citadel was inadequate for the needs of the town as a whole. Lee's plan was the

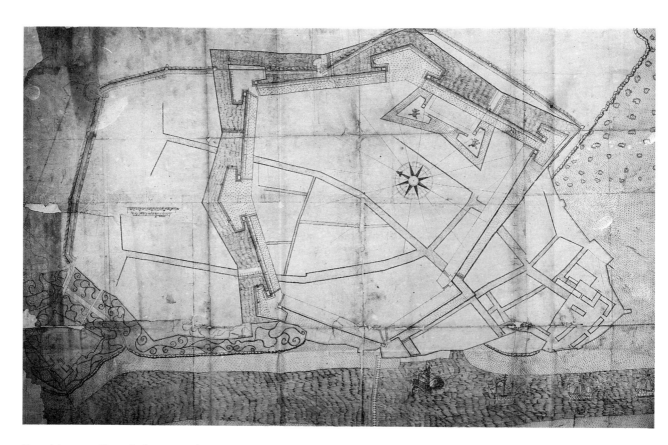

Berwick-upon-Tweed: the sixteenth century enceinte.
(Hatfield House)

abandonment of the medieval enclosure and the reduction by about a third of the defended area. The reduced *enceinte* consisted of a massive stone-faced rampart, three *orillon* bastions and two demi-bastions at the ends of the circuit where it met the river wall on the one hand and the sea wall on the other. Although never fully finished, the ramparts of Berwick are the most impressive and substantial works of sixteenth century fortification in Britain. Indeed they are of European significance. The defences were technically more advanced than anything previously attempted in Britain, and their construction is so well documented that Berwick provides a detailed example of current military engineering practice.

The shape of the bastions was very different from those of the earlier citadel. Their salient angles were much less acute. Both bastions in the middle of the north and east sides were obtuse-angled and very flat towards the field. All the bastions in the original design were small with small flankers behind short, flat, *orillons* no more than 40 feet (12 metres) broad. They were subsequently enlarged. The scarp wall, 20 feet (6 metres) high, was strengthened internally by a system of buttressing called counterforts. At cordon level at the top of the scarp was a *chemin des rondes*, and there was intended to be an earth rampart rising up behind the parapet for a further 16 feet (5 metres) in height. In

fact, this upper rampart was never completed. The ditch in front was not intended to be wide, and the counterscarp lacked a covered-way. The proposed scarp profile of masonry and earthwork divided by a *chemin des rondes* was unusual, and did not comply with contemporary Italian practice, where the scarp was carried to its full height in masonry. Lee clearly intended that his masonry revetment should be masked from direct artillery fire, and in this respect he was anticipating later practice. On the angle of batter for the masonry scarp Lee was also out of fashion. The Italian engineers, who were called in later, recommended a batter of 26° instead of Lee's near vertical scarp of 6°. The bastions were first planned to be symmetrical about their line of salient with long *orillons* to protect the two levels of guns in the recessed flankers. The lower level was a casemate covered by timber decking entered from vaulted tunnels through the ramparts. In it were two guns firing through square ports in a wall 6½ feet (2 metres) thick. The upper storey of the flanker also had provision for two guns which fired through embrasures in a 12 feet (3.6 metres) thick parapet. The flankers were later enlarged and in some instances the rear was deepened and arched over. The flankers of the later Windmill Bastion omitted the upper tier of guns leaving the flankers open.

In the first years of construction Elizabeth's government became worried about the enormous cost involved. Not only were members of the Council sent to Berwick to check on value for money but the leading resident Italian engineer, Giovanni Portinari, was called in to see if Lee's design was up to the mark. Portinari did indeed have serious criticisms but Lee, with a good deal of ruthless and petulant obstruction, deflected any change of course. In 1564, however, there was increasing anxiety in London, and Portinari was again called in, this time with another Italian engineer, Jacopo Contio, and an Englishman, William Pelham. Lee was now more ready to listen to other opinions. Portinari's original criticism that the whole peninsula between the Tweed and the sea should have been included within the fortifications was accepted by adopting a compromise solution of throwing up an earthwork traverse from Brass Bastion to the sea. The Italians did not approve Lee's scarp design but Portinari's report, in justification of Lee, referred to the town of Hesdin as a recent example of the combination of revetted and unrevetted earthworks. There was strong criticism of the size of the flankers of the bastions, and the access into them. Portinari quoted the example of Ambleteuse, part of the Henrician defences about Boulogne, whose flankers were the same size and plan as those at Berwick. He reminded Lee that in the siege of Ambleteuse in 1549 the first shots of the French put out of action the guns in one of the flankers. This example demonstrated that there was too little space to handle artillery and to replace damaged pieces, so that the English defenders were forced to abandon the fort. Large flankers, 40 feet (12 metres) by 50 feet (15 metres), with wider access tunnels were recommended, and this modification can be seen to have been carried out at Brass Bastion. To enable a more active defence Portinari suggested the provision of sallyports from the flanker through the *orillon* and into the ditch, and that the main gate should be protected by an adjacent flanker and covered from direct fire by a ravelin. He also recommended a covered-way on the counterscarp of the ditch, a conventional enough device. However, the political impetus to fortify Berwick slackened towards the end of the decade and Portinari's proposed improvements were not put into effect. The ditch was never completed and the covered-way, like the upper ramparts, had not been adopted when work petered out in 1569.

THE SPANISH THREAT

The reign of Queen Elizabeth I was rarely free from the threat of invasion or, at the very least, coastal raiding. At first it was the presence of the French in Scotland, then from 1582 until the turn of the following century, it was the menace of Spain, whether from Spain itself, from the Spanish Netherlands, or from a combination of the two. Apart from the massive commitment to Berwick and the building of one entirely new fort at Upnor to protect the Medway fleet anchorage, much of the defence expenditure in these years went towards the

Berwick-upon-Tweed: flankers and curtain. (Author)

Berwick-upon-Tweed: traverse across the headland and earthwork bulwark. (Author)

navy and spasmodically maintaining existing fortifications. Henry VIII had adopted a serious strategic conception behind his coastal defence programme, and his castles and blockhouses were still well sited and functional. Defence policy under Elizabeth was directed less towards coastal defences and more towards opposing any threat at sea. This meant greater expenditure on ships and encouraging privateering. The policy was to change after the Great Armada of 1588. The new defences of the latter part of the century mainly lay in the South West – the Isles of Scilly and the Channel Islands – to meet a continuing Spanish threat.

The most substantial piece of re-fortification undertaken shortly before the Armada, and in some ways similar to what had been done at Berwick, was that carried out at Portsmouth. Unfortunately, none of this Elizabethan work survives today. It is, however, well documented.[13] Although Henry's reconstruction of the town ramparts had continued on into the 1550s, the inadequate state of Portsmouth's defences was widely known across the Channel. A survey of 1571 presents a picture of general decay except at the waterside where some ordnance was mounted. Suggestions were made in the following year for new works but nothing of substance was done until 1584. Out of several schemes, one, by the engineer William Pers, had similarities with Berwick by proposing the reduction of the defended area of the town. Another proposal suggested a square, bastioned citadel sited near the Square

Portsmouth in c1586: orillon bastions had replaced those of Henry VIII. (Hatfield House)

Tower and Saluting Platform near the Camber. Richard Popinjay (who in the 1570s had been closely concerned with the 'New Fortification' at Castle Cornet, Guernsey), William Pers and William Spicer were the principal engineers involved at Portsmouth. Divided authority, and seemingly lack of clear directions, contributed to the construction dragging on for about ten years. There are detailed descriptions of the work. In 1586, the embryo angle bastions and the traditional round bastions of the Henrician trace were reformed into large Italianate *orillon* bastions with something approaching regularity of plan. The exception was a new, obliquely angled, almost flat bastion, Pembroke Mount, opposite the four brewhouses, and breaking the long eastern curtain midway between East Mount and Wimbledon's Mount (later King's Bastion). The flankers were in two tiers and were 40 feet (12 metres) wide and 60–70 feet (18–21 metres) long. The length of the *orillons* extended 40 feet (12 metres) beyond the flankers, and the total length of the face of the bastions was usually 240 feet (73 metres). The average height of the bastions was 24 feet (7 metres). The ditch was intended to be wet, with the water retained by two *batardeaux*, and was complete with *cunette*. At Portsmouth there was noticeable progress towards greater regularity of plan and standardisation of individual features. The idea of an internal citadel was, however, dropped. While works were in progress at Portsmouth, attention was given to Carisbrooke, the pivotal defence position of the Isle of Wight. Brian Fitzwilliam and Pers, then employed at Portsmouth, drew up plans for the old castle. It would seem that the two mural towers at the corners of the south curtain wall were rebuilt at this time in shallow angle bastion form and named 'knights', or more conventionally, *cavaliers*.

The lengthy build-up to the Armada crisis of 1588 demanded the encouragement, training and rationalisation of a home defence force in the shape of the militia, the refurbishment of existing batteries and gun platforms around the coasts, the construction of new emergency works and the mobilisation of the traditional 'early warning' beacon system. There was no standing army, and little experience of warfare on land other than among those few who had served in the Low Countries in support of the Protestant Dutch. The east coast of England was most at risk since it was anticipated that the main invasion threat would come from Parma's veterans in the Spanish Netherlands. At Great Yarmouth, for example, the townspeople, who had strengthened the medieval town walls in 1569, set about further improvements early in 1588. Some of this work is still to be seen as earthen ramparts and mounts outside the town wall. Elsewhere in Norfolk plans were drawn up for bastioned earthworks at Weybourne Hope. Plans were also prepared for Southwold, Dunwich and Aldeburgh in Suffolk as well as elsewhere along the south coast as at Pevensey. Local

▲ *Weybourne Hope, Norfolk: bastioned earthwork beach defences.* (Hatfield House)

Pevensey Castle, Sussex: remains of a small earthwork battery of the Armada period. (Author)

Pevensey Castle: demi-culverin found near the earthwork battery mounted on a replica Elizabethan field carriage. (Author)

defence was encouraged and large numbers mobilised when invasion seemed imminent but it was as well that the Armada was dispersed at sea and the piecemeal coastal defences and the amateurish militias were not tested. If the over-ambitious plan for linking Medina Sidonia's Armada with the troops of Parma in a combined operation in the region of Ramsgate in Kent had not failed, it is unlikely that there would have been much to prevent an early capture of London.

The English government could not be certain where the feared landing would take place. Its doubts emphasised the great strategic importance of the Gravesend–Tilbury crossing of the Thames. This was the scene of that most famous occasion in 1588, apart from the defeat and dispersal of the Armada itself, when the army was assembled at Tilbury and was addressed by the Queen herself. The two Henrician blockhouses of West Tilbury and Gravesend control-

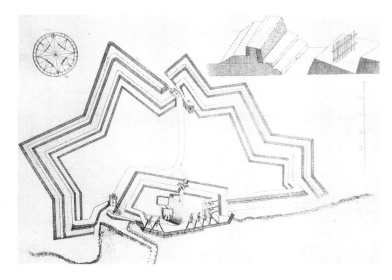

Tilbury Fort, Essex: Genebelli's outer earthwork enceinte.
Public Records Office SP 12/217 No 5. (PRO)

led the lowest crossing of the river and the ferry which would be essential to convey the field army, camped on the Essex bank, into Kent, depending upon the actual invasion point. On both sides of the river fortifications were erected at the last moment to the design of Frederigo Genebelli, an Italian military engineer, who had come into English service in 1585 following his sensational attempt to destroy Parma's bridge of boats during the Spanish siege of Antwerp. Genibelli at Tilbury was described as trenchmaster or colonel of the pioneers and gunners. A drawing exists which purports to show the new works beyond the blockhouse. They consisted of a substantial earthwork enclosure of an irregular but acute-angled *tenaille* trace without conventional bastions. The new defences were temporary and, such is the nature of earthwork in marshland, they had all but disappeared by the 1630s.

The failure of the Great Armada was by no means the end to the Spanish threat. Indeed, it has been said that the Armada experience made the English newly aware of their vulnerability and that 1588 was a psychological victory for Spain.[14] Invasion fears were just as real during the 1590s, and there was a very destructive raid on West Cornwall, as well as the discovery of a plot to sieze Falmouth for an invasion base. Between 1592 and 1601 attitudes to permanent defensive works changed and there was much fortifying, particularly in the South West and the Channel Islands. Much of this work was in progress simultaneously and was the responsibility of three engineers: the Italian, Genebelli, and two Englishmen, Robert Adams and Paul Ive or Ivey.

Robert Adams was more of an architect than engineer; he was appointed Surveyor of the Queen's Works at Whitehall shortly before his death in 1595. He had earlier been sent to the Low Countries to the fortifications at Flushing and Ostend, and superin-

tended repairs there. He supplied plans for Portsmouth's defences but his main achievements were at Plymouth and Scilly. Plymouth was especially at risk since it was virtually undefended, apart from the earlier gun-towers along the shore line. The local population understandably wanted protection around the developing town, but, strategically, it was more important to defend the Sound. In 1548–9, a tower and battery had been built on St Nicholas Island (later to be known as Drake's Island) which supplemented the earlier towers. Adams was sent to Plymouth to appraise the position, and his recommendation in 1592 was for a fort on the high ground at the Hoe to guard against sudden surprise. Work began the next year under Adams's supervision but, after his death in 1595, the fort was completed by its first captain, Sir Ferdinando Gorges, a man with considerable military experience. Genebelli visited the fort following its completion in 1598, and drew up a plan, which was not taken up, for a bastioned *enceinte* enclosing the town. The fort was in two parts, an upper enclosure on the higher ground, and a lower one extending down to the waters-edge. The upper fort was triangular with a ditch 20 feet (6 metres) wide, and two large bastions with flankers covering the approach from the land. The main armament was in the more irregular lower enclosure on the cliff, to control shipping in the Sound. Some of this fort was incorporated into the late seventeenth century Royal Citadel and influenced the southern part of its plan.

During his first visit to Plymouth, Adams was diverted to inspect the Isles of Scilly, but he was not appointed surveyor of works for a new fort on St Mary's until 1593. The fort on Hugh Hill, now the Star Castle Hotel, has an eight-pointed star trace. This was not an unusual plan and appears often in the textbooks. The fort was little more than a blockhouse for a small garrison. Its armament was economically sited in the re-entrant angles of the trace, and giving complete flanking cover. The captain of the islands, Sir Francis Godolphin, continued with other defensive measures, and the bastioned land front across the neck of the promontory above Hugh Town was built by 1600, and was the beginning of the almost complete circuit of fortification which later came to be built around the Hugh or the Garrison.

Genebelli was the leading fortification consultant but he was much blamed for exceeding his estimate for bringing Carisbrooke Castle up to date. Rather than continue tinkering with the medieval walls, Genibelli enveloped the whole castle in a new bastioned *enceinte* between the years 1597 and 1601. He saw Carisbrooke as the key to preventing the Isle of Wight being seized by the Spaniards and used as a base against the mainland. This was sound advice since capture of the Island was indeed the fall-back strategy for the 1588 Armada. This re-fortification represented the last full

▲ *Star Castle, St Mary's, Isles of Scilly: entrance to the outer enclosure, roof of the central building to right.* (Author)

▼ *Carisbrooke Castle, Isle of Wight: Genebelli's Italian bastioned* enceinte *enclosing the medieval castle.* (DOE)

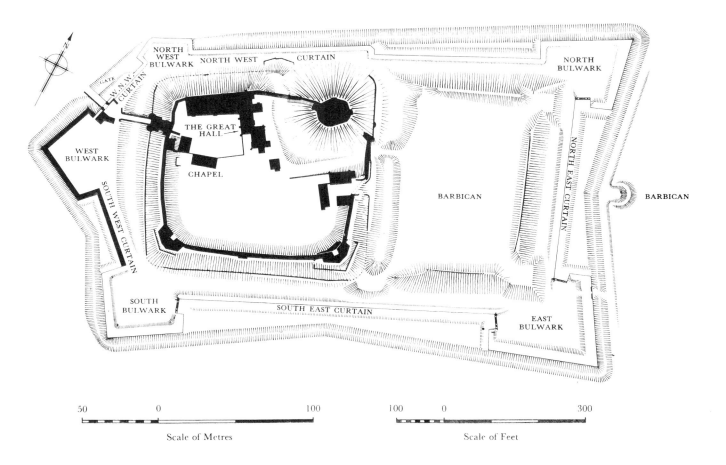

Carisbrooke Castle: aerial photograph. (DOE)

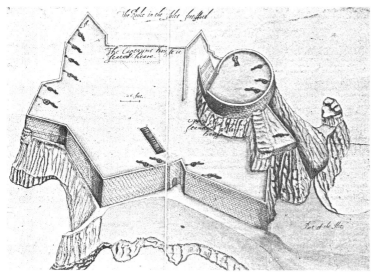

Elizabeth Castle, Jersey: Paul Ive's birds-eye view of his new fort. British Library [BL] Cotton MS, Augustus I i, 30. (BL)

scale example in Britain of the 'Italian School' of bastion design. The long-familiar form with recessed flankers and protecting *orillons* after fifty years of active life was now passé. Experience in siege work proved that flankers in this form were much too restrictive in the ground they could cover, and were a death-trap if the enemy found the means of enfilading them with gunfire. The growing fashion, particularly among those engineers who had experience in the Low Countries, was for straight flanks usually at right angles to the curtain. However, Genebelli stuck to the old ways.

The three bastions on the more vulnerable east and south sides of the castle have short, flat *orillons*. One has recently been excavated archaeologically.[15] In its original form the flanker had two embrasures commanding the ditch with a further tier of guns recessed behind the upper gun floor, carried on a vault. The one full *orillon* bastion has a salient angle of 77°. The distance between the south and the east bastions is roughly the prescribed length, 670 feet (204 metres), but the curtain between the east and north bastions is only 390 feet (119 metres). A rare device for Britain at this period is the surviving *tenaille* which Genebelli provided in the ditch before almost each curtain to mask the scarp. A further sophistication was the construction of flankers canted to provide a grazing fire across the adjacent face.

Paul Ive, however, represents a landmark in British military engineering, being the first native engineer to write and publish an original treatise on fortification as well as being a successful practitioner.[16] Ive was employed in the Channel Islands between 1593 and 1595, completing the new outer line around Castle Cornet in Guernsey and various works at Mont Orgeuil Castle, Jersey, before it became redundant and, more importantly, devising the first stage of Elizabeth Castle which replaced it. For the latter we have not only the fort itself – mercifully little mutilated by Second World War additions – but Ive's perspective drawing of the finished work. Adapting a fort to a rocky crag does not allow the display of the finer points of the bastion

Pendennis Castle, Cornwall: aerial photograph showing Ive's bastioned enceinte *enclosing Henry VIII's castle.* (DOE)

system but this is a skilful piece of work. Ive also served at Portsmouth, and was brought in to overhaul the Cinque Ports defences in 1596. His major work, which should be compared with Genebelli's at Carisbrooke, is the re-fortification of Pendennis Castle at Falmouth in 1598–9. The new fortress enclosed the Henrician castle within the restrictions of a narrow headland. The result is an irregular trace with bastions very much smaller than those used at Carisbrooke and mostly employing straight flanks. The flanks are at various angles to the curtain depending on the fields of fire required, though some do not adequately flank their adjacent bastions. As he did at Castle Cornet, Ive used a wide salient projecting towards the sea. The land front at Pendennis was given two *orillon* bastions, since reformed, but elsewhere on the *enceinte, orillons* were omitted. By the turn of the century *orillon* bastions had completely gone out of fashion in English fortification. This was demonstrated clearly in Ive's last work, Castle Park at Kinsale, Ireland (see illustration on p69).

Paul Ive's treatise, *The Practice of Fortification*, was not entirely given over to theory. As Ive himself stressed, the book was concerned with the practical application of military engineering: 'in this business the opinion of a soldier who hath had experience of the defence and offence, is to be preferred before the opinion of the Geometrician or mason, who are inexpert, of the practises that an enemie may put in execution.'[17] He had had such practical experience in the Low Countries, and drew his examples from the fortifications he had seen there. British military men were no longer as ignorant of European warfare and its technical developments as they were at the beginning of the century. While there was little internal conflict, mercenary service or volunteering into the armies of co-religionists engaged in continental campaigns was training for many. Ive's basic ideas of design in 1589 still show Italian influence. He stressed the fundamental importance of bastions which should not be acute angled, and should not be further apart than 200 paces. He described bastion flanks, with and without 'cullions' [*orillons*]. He considered that the flanks should have sufficient width for two cannons, with at least 50 feet (15 metres) allowed for their recoil. Emphasis was also placed on the ditch, though the proposed musketry casemates on the edge of the *cunette* before the salient of the bastions, look decidedly vulnerable. The covered-way, he wrote, should be 19 feet (nearly 6 metres) broad and well protected by its parapet, and when strengthening old walled towns, he advised the use of ravelins in front of the curtains.

The bulk of the expenditure on Elizabethan fortifications was met by the Exchequer but every opportunity was taken by the Crown to reduce its burden, either by shifting responsibility on to a county or town, or even on to an individual captain. In the case of very large works, like Berwick or Portsmouth, it was unavoidable that central government paid. Also the fortification of coastal towns was a matter of national importance, and if local people could not maintain them they had to be helped. Nevertheless local resources could be brought in particularly at moments of crisis. For example, the Isle of Wight volunteered to find £400 towards the work at Carisbrooke in 1597, the offer being inspired by the immediate fear of invasion.[18] The financial responsibilities of captains of forts varied considerably. In some instances they might be expected to keep the fort repaired and armed out of their own pockets.

Engineers would be expected to advise on the siting of the fort, to produce designs, and prepare the working 'plat'. They might be in practical charge of the works, or this might be delegated to others. In some instances they might be contractors for materials themselves, as, for example, was Sir Richard Lee. Portsmouth provides a schedule of duties for the surveyor of the works which gives a detailed picture of the organisation of a major building operation in 1584.[19]

The guns mounted on the late Tudor forts were still of many types, patterns, calibres and weights, and were made of both brass and iron, although much had been done to standardize and reduce the number of different types.[20] The best basis for the classification of sixteenth century guns, and which was followed by most of the theorists, was that adopted by Robert Norton in *The Gunner* of 1628. All pieces normally in use were divided under four heads: Cannons of battery, Cannon periers, Culverins and Mortars. In day to day practice there was no fixed establishment of artillery at the forts. Pieces were moved, became unserviceable and were always a scratch lot containing an assortment of types and calibres.

IRELAND

Nothing has been said so far about artillery defences in Ireland. The use of heavy guns in sieges came only late in the fifteenth century, and descriptions of specialised defences later still. The siege of Maynooth in 1535 involved artillery deployed by the defenders in earthwork positions and there was even mention of a 'bulwark'. Some coastal fortifications were constructed during the reign of Edward VI at the entrance to Cork harbour, Kinsale, Galway and elsewhere as part of the attention paid to the south west coasts. The latter half of the sixteenth century saw an increasing involvement by Spain in Irish affairs as a means of embarrassing England, and this drew an inevitable response from Elizabeth. Duncannon Fort at the mouth of the estuary at Waterford was begun in 1587, as well as further fortifications at Cork and the building of the citadel at Galway in 1584.[21]

English problems in Ireland were always internal as well as external. Here English strength lay in the towns as well as the coastal districts. The native Irish maintained intermittant resistance to the English colonists in the countryside. Much as in Scotland, there was a long standing multiplicity of castles, tower-houses and other strongholds where the increasing stock of firearms meant the introduction of loops for hand-guns. Carrickfergus Castle was provided with gun embrasures and, as the new fashions in military engineering took hold, an angle bastion replaced a corner tower at Limerick Castle in 1611. The houses of the landowning class also took on the plan and functions of military works. Rectangular, central blocks with projecting corner towers were a common form, with the towers strongly loopholed for hand-guns. Mountjoy Fort in Co Tyrone and Monkstown Castle in Co Cork show how widely separated this house type could be in the early seventeenth century. Rathfarnham Castle, Co Dublin and Raphoe Palace, Co Donegal have their corner towers pulled out into an angle bastion plan with the faces brought to an acute angle. Perhaps the finest house of this kind is Portuma Castle built in 1618 in Co Galway. This large semi-fortified house combines much classical detail with defensible corner towers.[22]

By the 1590s, the native Irish rebellion had become more cohesive under the Ulster chieftain Hugh O'Neill, second Earl of Tyrone. He had built up a more than usually disciplined Irish force armed with guns he had bought from Scotland with Spanish subsidies. In the previous rebellions of James Maurice Fitzgerald (1568–73), and of the Earl of Desmond (1579–83), the Irish had attempted a defensive course by retreating into their strongholds only to be taken by the English with their superior guns and siege work. O'Neill had contemplated converting his castle at Dungannon into an up-to-date fortress with the help of a foreign engineer but instead, it was the English Lord Deputy who found himself bottled up in a remote fort in 1598. The relieving force was wiped out at the Battle of the Yellow Ford within sight of the Blackwater Fort, whose garrison promptly surrendered to the rebels. In response to this rising, Elizabeth relied on Lord Mountjoy, who arrived in Ireland in 1600 as Lord Deputy. Very much a professional soldier, Mountjoy was able to deal with the Irish guerilla tactics but, in 1601, a Spanish expedition landed at Kinsale on the south coast. Mountjoy made his first priority the capture of the harbour castles, and cut off the town from the sea. O'Neill's Irish army had shadowed Mountjoy in his march to the south but, in a joint attack with the Spaniards on Mountjoy, they were crushingly defeated. The Spaniards later agreed to evacuate Kinsale and return home.

A plan of the siege of Kinsale shows the nature of the fortified camps and enclosed batteries of the English. The earthwork enclosures were generally rectangular and well flanked with angle bastions but also included round bastions as well. Following the siege of Kinsale, Castle Park, which had been occupied by the Spaniards, was enclosed by a new fort, which today is called James Fort. This was the final engineering work accomplished by Paul Ive who was to die at Kinsale. It is a mature pentagonal design, well fitted to the terrain. The bastions are all straight flanked, with the flanks sometimes at right angles to the curtain and sometimes at an obtuse angle. It was intended as permanent fortification with the ramparts revetted in stone. Since there was an expectation of further Spanish landings, Mountjoy advised the building of more defences at Galway, Limerick, Cork, Waterford and Carlingford. Elizabeth Fort at Cork, Haulbowline Island Fort in Cork harbour and a detached fort outside the walls of Galway were constructed at this time.

With the accession of the Stuarts and the union of the two crowns of England and Scotland, there was an accommodation with Spain and a reduction of tension in the Borders. Coastal defences were allowed to deteriorate, and unfinished work left undone. By 1620 the Portsmouth defences were said to be ruinous and the fortifications in the Channel Islands reported incomplete and defective. Some were concerned at the lack of security at home, but others saw opportunities for economies in the military establishment. In 1623 the Lieutenant-General of the Ordnance, Sir Richard Morrison, and two military colleagues were instructed to survey all the forts on the south coast of England. It was decided to demolish most of the temporary batteries and defence works which had been erected during the war with Spain, and to cease manning them. However, the Commission did recommend that some new permanent forts should be built at places where there had only been temporary works before. Amongst these was Harwich. As a result, the only significant fort to be constructed during the reigns of the first two Stuarts was Landguard Fort at the mouth of the Orwell Estuary. It was built in 1626–8, a simple square, bastioned fort which was totally replaced, almost on the same site, by another in 1716.[23]

The part of the British Isles where fortifications were still being built in some numbers during the early decades of the seventeenth century was Ireland. The fortifications were, however of another kind, and were principally in the north. These were the defences of the Protestant settlers in newly 'planted' areas in Ulster. The defences could take the form of enclosed towns, usually new creations with planned interiors laid out with regular plots for the incomers. Coleraine, Carrickfergus and Belfast were surrounded by earthen ramparts and flanking bastions. The earthworks of Derry were, however, overrun by the followers of Sir Cahir O'Doherty in 1608. Later, in 1613, the City of London became responsible for the settlement and it was then enclosed by stone-faced ramparts flanked by nine bastions. The settlements were also in small forts, such as Charlemont Fort, built by Charles Blount, Lord Mountjoy, in 1602, burned in 1920 but with its outer earthworks still remaining. And then there were

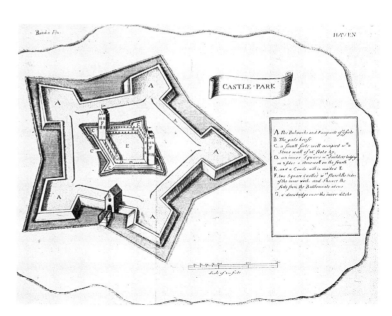

James Fort, Kinsale, Co Cork: Ive's plan, from T Stafford, Pacata Hibernia, *London 1633.* (Author)

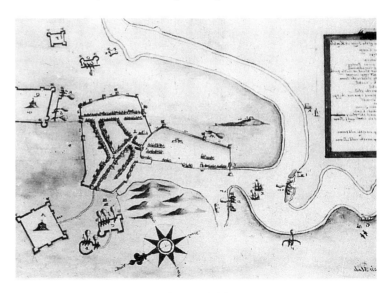

Siege of Spanish forces at Kinsale. (Hatfield House)

fortified houses in abundance, often with a defensible walled enclosure or bawm. Even these, frequently amateurish, defences against a hostile population had their walls flanked by angle bastions, so pervasive had this form of fortification become.

CHAPTER 4

Civil War

By 1640 Britain had escaped prolonged warfare for the better part of a hundred years. England and Wales had indeed experienced little more than an occasional insurrection since the Wars of the Roses. Following the

Early seventeenth century siege work taken from Les Travaux de Mars. (Author)

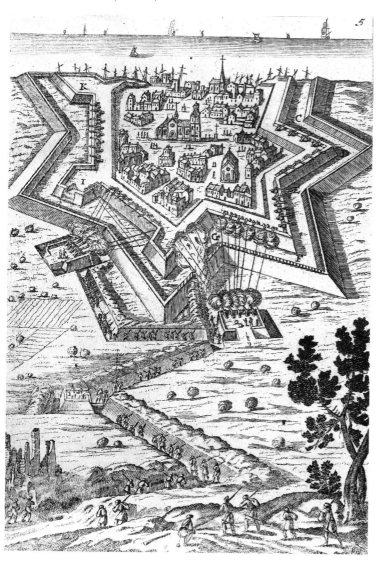

Anglo-Scottish wars of the late 1540s and early 1550s, Scotland suffered upheavals caused by religious conflict and struggles for power among the nobility during the reign of Mary, Queen of Scots, but with the eventual union of the crowns in the form of James I and VI, Mary's son, warfare with England seemed to be at an end. Only in Ireland was there a permanent state of hostilities between the native Irish and the English rulers and new settlers during the early years of the seventeenth century. By contrast, in this period the continent of Europe was enduring protracted warfare of appalling intensity and ferocity fought by large mercenary armies over an extensive area of central Europe. Nominally the causes of the Thirty Years War were religious, the conflict between the forces of the Protestant Reformation and those of the Catholic Counter-Reformation, but inevitably political and national motives were interlinked. The large professional armies were ill-provisioned and erratically paid so that the main sufferers were the peasantry whose crops and persons were constantly at the mercy of the soldiery. It was a period of total war over such a wide area and for such a long time that had no previous parallel and was perhaps unequalled for its horrors until the twentieth century.

The Thirty Years War was, understandably enough, a training ground for those soldiers who took part in it. The leading protagonists were widely known and regarded as military exemplars, so that the Parliamentary divine, Hugh Peters, could, in 1645, report to the House of Commons, 'That when I look upon the two Chiefs of our Army, (Fairfax and Cromwell) I remember Gustavus Adolphus, and Oxenstern . . .'[1] The Thirty Years War, in particular, saw the development of field tactics, of weapons and military equipment, fortifications and siegecraft. 'We see the face of war and the forms of weapons alter almost daily; every nation striving to outwit each other in excellency of weapons,' wrote Lupton in a military treatise.[2] It was a cosmopolitan affair. Men from many countries saw the war as an opportunity for adventure and enrichment. Many saw it as a means for obtaining military experience in what was still the highest secular social calling of all. Religious conscience was not a paramount factor in choice of sides: Protestants fought for the Imperialists and Wallenstein, and Catholics for the Swedish armies of Gustavus Adolphus. There were regiments of English and Scots in Holland, France, Spain, Sweden, Denmark, Austria and Russia but they served most frequently in the Dutch and Swedish armies. The contingents which were sent on the occasional national expeditions such as to Cadiz in 1625 and to the Isle de Rhé in 1627 were pressed men with no training, and were generally unfit for service. The expeditions ended in disaster. There were individual soldiers, however, who achieved very high rank in the continental armies. Fairfax, Goring and the royal brothers, Rupert and Maurice, had served under Frederick Henry of Nassau at the siege of Breda in 1637, and Alexander Leslie, Earl of Leven, had been governor of Stralsund and other Baltic fortresses between 1628 and 1631. Others returned to Britain as self-proclaimed military experts and wrote serious works on the arts of war.[3]

The Civil War in England was on a totally different scale, both in terms of the underlying causes as well as intensity of hostilities. There was a certain religious undertone. The king as defender of the established church also inclined towards Catholicism, and was certainly not averse to recruiting troops among the Catholic Irish to be employed against his subjects. Parliament inclined towards strict Protestantism and parts of its army were dominated by extreme sects which ultimately were to influence the whole pattern of domestic politics. The presbyterianism of the Scots and their desire to apply their beliefs to England had an important influence on political affairs, helping to precipitate the initial crisis, and was a constant factor in the relations between the two countries throughout the war. The deep seated cause of the conflict was the struggle for dominance between the Crown and people, as represented by the Parliament of the day. Charles I believed in the 'divine right' of kingship and found it impossible to accept that Parliament should limit his personal rule. While the monarchy in countries such as France achieved absolute power, the movement towards restricting such absolutism in England was advanced by withholding consent to taxation and thus limiting the Crown's ability to act in isolation from Parliament. Such political struggles had been common in Elizabeth's reign but, under the less politically astute early Stuarts, the friction became more intense. Both sides drifted into war. There was great reluctance to fight against the lawful king but it was Charles himself who first anticipated military action. Desperate for money to maintain an army in the North in order to oppose the Scots who had crossed into northern England and were in secret communication with the opposition in the English House of Commons, Charles attempted a *coup d'etat* by using milit-

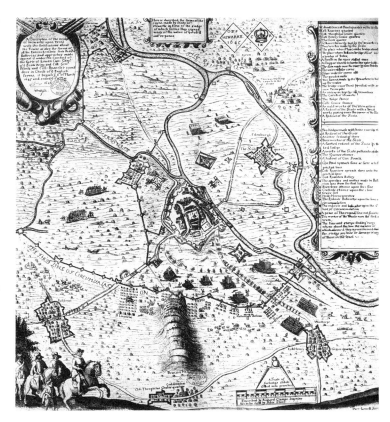

Newark, Nottinghamshire: Parliamentarian siege plan by Richard Clampe from the engraving in the British Library. (Royal Commission on Historical Monuments [RCHM])

ary force to arrest the five most prominent members of the Commons. His failure led him to leave London and seek military support from his followers in the North. On 22 August 1642 Charles set up his military standard outside Nottingham. It was the traditional signal for assembling retainers and feudatories for military service. It was a declaration of war.

This is not the place for another account of the campaigns and progress of the Civil War which has its own prolific literature. There were few major pitched battles in the four years of the first Civil War, many encounters and skirmishes, and sieges of houses and towns. Our concern here is with these latter events, often very fully described by participants at the time, which show the nature and varieties of fortifications which were pressed into re-use or were newly constructed, and the development of the engineering branches of the respective armies.

EARLY SEVENTEENTH CENTURY MILITARY ENGINEERING: THE DUTCH SYSTEM

The early seventeenth century produced a spate of books on military subjects in English. Many were translations from the French and Italian but many were derived from Dutch theorists, and from first-hand

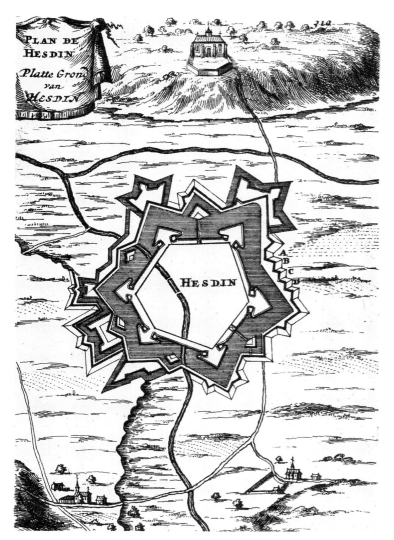

PLAN DE HESDIN

Platte Grond van HESDIN

HESDIN

A
B
C
D

Hesdin, a characteristically fortified Low Countries town, from Les Travaux de Mars. *(Author)*

experience in the wars in the Low Countries. Soldiers like Robert Barret in *The Theorike and Practike of Modern Warres*, Francis Markham in *Five Decades of Epistles of Warre* of 1622, and Robert Ward, 'Gentleman and Commander', who wrote the *Animadversions of War* in 1639, described the conventions and practices of the contemporary battlefield and the whole military art.

Immediately before, and during the Civil War, the most readily understood and practised school of military engineering in England was the Dutch. French methods were also in use and some Frenchmen served as engineers in the Royalist armies. However, in terms of the written word, Dutch methods were the most fashionable, and were to remain so until well after the wars and into the 1670s. In 1638 Henry Hexham translated Samuel Marolois's *Fortification ou architecture militaire tant offensive que deffensive* of 1615. Hexham went on to publish *The First Part of the Principles of the Art Military, Practised in the Warres of*

the United Netherlands in 1642–3. Hexham was a veteran of the Dutch wars, and served as quartermaster to Goring. Robert Ward held that the Netherlandish way of fortification was the 'most absolutest manner that can be invented'.[4] For some years after the Civil Wars, military books continued to reflect the principles and practises that operated at that time. Written as a supplement dealing with fortification to the 1659 edition of Elton's *Complete Body of the Art Military*, Thomas Rudd's contribution stemmed from personal experience. He is described as 'Captain Thomas Rudd, engineer to King Charles the First'. As late as 1672, Thomas Venn's *Military and Maritime Discipline* contained a translation of Andrew Tacquett's *Military Architecture* by John Lacy which reflected closely the Dutch School. The new French school of fortification associated with Antoine de Ville and the Compte de Pagan was less well known, but it was described in Gerbier's *Interpreter of Fortification* of 1648.

The Dutch school arose out of the eighty-year-long war with Spain which dragged on from 1566 to 1648. The wars were struggles of attrition, dominated by fortifications and sieges. From makeshift beginnings, the defences of Dutch towns became highly developed, and exploited the natural advantages of water and earthwork. Military engineering and the creation of a corps of engineers were developed by Prince Maurice of Nassau in the years around the turn of the seventeenth century. Notable among the specialists Prince Maurice gathered about him was the military and water engineer, Simon Stevin, as well as Marolois and Freitag who translated defensive practices into treatise form.[5]

The dominant characteristics of Dutch fortification were the use of the earthen rampart and the wet ditch. They suited the topography and could be thrown up at low cost. Maurice's achievement was to develop the complete earthen *enceinte*. The scarp of the thick earth rampart was unrevetted, and ideally was intended to have command above the surrounding land of 25 feet (7.6 metres). It was protected against escalade by sharpened horizontal palisades, or 'storm poles'. Below the rampart, and about 15 feet (4.5 metres) out from its foot, was a low outer rampart, or *fausse-braye* which gave the defenders command of the ditch and the covered-way beyond. The *fausse-braye* was an important characteristic of Low Countries methods. Of the major elements, the salient angle of the bastion varied from 60° in a square figure to 90° in a dodecagon. The faces met in narrow salient angles, and could supplement the cross-fire of the bastion flanks. This left the main task of frontal defence to the curtain and the outworks. The flanks were regularly perpendicular to the curtains. This enabled a spacious open gorge at the back of the bastion to be used for retrenchments as a desperate last defensive measure. The 'line of defence' – that is the line from the junction of the flank with the curtain to the salient angle of the adjacent bastion – was always devised with the range of musketry in mind. It was usually no longer than 60 Rhineland rods, or about 240 yards (220 metres). Ditches, or wet moats, were wide, 50 yards (46 metres) or so, with a *cunette* or additional ditch with vertical sides and about 20 feet (6 metres) wide, running down the centre of the moat. On the counterscarp of the ditch was a continuous protected path or 'covered-way', 15 feet (4.5 metres) broad, with a parapet and sloping glacis beyond it. Ravelins within the ditch, according to the Dutch method, should have faces of 33 yards (30 metres) in length, and to be traced so as to be flanked from the curtains of the main *enceinte*. Dutch defensive systems often employed complex outer works such as an additional ditch, together with *demi-lunes*, which were ravelin-like works set in front of the principal bastions. 'Hornworks' were large figures fronted with demibastions ('crownworks' had a small centrally placed full bastion as well) set beyond the main ditch. These large outworks often occupied a particular point of strategic importance, or provided additional flanking fire.

As well as fully enclosed fortresses and towns, there were small earthen redoubts, or *Schanzen*, sconces which were constructed to control river crossings and river lines with the least possible number of men, and to act as advance and early warning posts. The Dutch school was at its best at exploiting flat, wet terrain, and with its multiple lines of defence and elaborate outworks 'it contributed an important extension of the principle of defence in depth to European fortification as a whole'.[6]

MILITARY ENGINEERING DURING THE CIVIL WARS

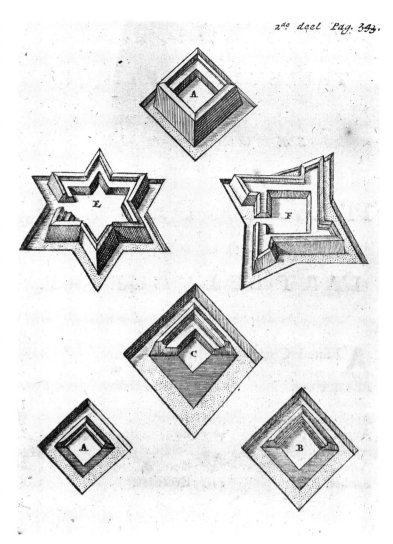

Various forms of sconces from Les Travaux de Mars. (Author)

The strategic conduct of the First Civil War for both parties was concentrated on the need to capture and retain areas of population and the resources they controlled. Both sides were preponderant in certain areas. The king's strength lay mainly in the North East, Wales and the South West, but there were important Parliamentarian strongholds at Plymouth, Taunton, Lyme, Gloucester and Hull within this area of Royal dominance. Parliament had its main support in London and the South East, East Anglia and a corridor across the Midlands and into the North West. Nevertheless the Royalists had many strongholds within this area, and Charles's main military and political base at Oxford posed a constant threat to London. While the general military situation was fluid, many superannuated castles, country houses and towns underwent often prolonged sieges. At the same time, both sides created isolated strongpoints covering lines of communication, advance warning posts, and, in some instances coastal defences. All this activity in attempting to control territory and win strategic advantage involved the re-furbishing of old fortifications and, more particularly, the construction of new ones.

Who were the designers and military engineers carrying out these defensive works? There was no standing army, no establishment of professional engineers. Both sides looked to the county 'trainedbands' for soldiers, and attempted to seize the militia's magazines. The king began raising men by issuing commissions of array empowering county notables to produce the nucleus of a field army. Many volunteers joined both armies out of political and religious motives. Both sides did possess a handful of 'professional' soldiers, men who had served foreign armies with varying distinction, and now appeared among their respective officer corps. But the English Civil War was essentially an amateurish, muddled and ill-equipped affair. Examples abound, and its character can, perhaps, be illustrated by the following anecdotes.

Amateurishness comes through all too clearly in the memoirs of Colonel Hutchinson. At the Parliamentarian siege of Newark in 1644,

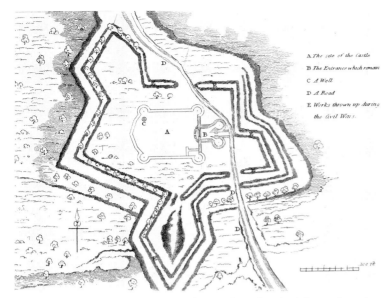

A *The site of the Castle*
B *The Entrance which remain*
C *A Well*
D *A Road*
E *Works thrown up during*
    the Civil Wars.

200 ft

Donnington Castle, Berkshire: later sketch of the earthworks of the Civil Wars surrounding the medieval castle. (DOE)

The forces that Sir John Meldrum commanded before this towne, were gather'd out of severall associated counties, and the commanders so emulous of one another, and so refractory to commands, and so peeking in all punctillios of superiority, that it gall'd the poore old gentleman to the heart, who, having commanded abroad, and bene us'd to deale with officers that understood the discipline of warre, was confounded among those who knew not how to obey any orders, but disputed all his commands . . .[7]

Then again, at the siege of Sherborne Castle, Joshua Sprigge describes how,

The General [Fairfax] going to see the working of the Mine . . . and the making of the Gallery, escaped another great danger by his own souldiers, who encompassing some Dear, shot round, and killed one of their fellows, and missed the General (as he was passing by) narrowly.

At the same siege, Fairfax's siege guns were short of shot and,

the great adventurousness of many of our soldiers comes fitly to be remembered, who fetcht off the Bullets (that we had shot) from under the enemies Walls, and had six pence a piece for every Bullet they so brought off . . .[8]

Military engineers of any competance in this 'Fred Carno' atmosphere were clearly at a premium. Both sides felt the need to import a number of foreign engineers, mainly Dutch and French, but including a Swede, Diderich Beckman, and the German, Roseworm. The most illustrious of these experts was the Walloon, Bernard de Gomme, who arrived in Prince Rupert's following. By 1645 de Gomme was awarded the titles of Engineer-General and Quartermaster-General of the Royalist army. He was to return to England at the Restoration to be Charles II's Chief

Engineer. On the Parliamentarian side, the Dutchman, John Dalbier, became the Quartermaster-General of the Earl of Essex's army and, later, Peter Manteau van Dalem became the Engineer-General of the New Model Army. There were English engineers too: Captain Richard Steel, 'an Oxford Engineere', fortified Milford Haven in 1644; John Mansfield served under Prince Rupert at Bristol in 1645, and together with de Gomme signed the report of the state of the defences there. Occasionally, there are allusions to the engineering skill displayed by officers outside this professional discipline. Sir John Meldrum gained much credit for certain hornworks designed and executed by him at Portsmouth and Colonel Wemyss was described as 'that excellent engineer'.[9]

There was close association between the two technical arms of artillery and engineering. The trains of artillery were organised on the lines developed by Prince Maurice of Nassau a generation previously. The composition of the artillery train belonging to the Army of the North in 1639 and 1640 constituted a model for those raised subsequently during the war. Besides the master gunner and his various ranks of gunners with 30 or 40 pieces of ordnance, there were two engineers, each with a clerk, six conductors of the trenches and fortifications, one petardier with twelve assistants, one captain of pioneers, a master smith, a master carpenter and bridge-maker, each with six assistants, and finally a fireworker with an assistant. In addition, when conducting a siege, pioneers would be needed in great numbers since there was always a reluctance on the part of the ordinary soldiery to use a spade. In particular conditions, skilled miners, such as those from the Mendips, would be called in. On the Parliamentarian side, the supervision of engineering operations in the field seems to have been entrusted to the Quartermaster-General and this post, on either side, was often linked with that of Engineer-General. A chief engineer might be paid 10s a day, his clerk at 2s 6d; engineers could receive 6s, conductors of the trenches, 2s 6d, petardiers and a master pioneer, 4s; gentlemen of the ordnance, who might, in modern terms, be considered battery commanders, received 3s a day. It can be seen, therefore, that specialists could command a high price (the private soldier's pay was 8d a day).[10]

SIEGES AND SIEGE WORK

Maintaining a hold on territory and individual strongpoints, and, conversely, capturing those of your opponents, was the most common military activity during the war. Not everyone agreed with this approach. The Parliamentarian, Joshua Sprigge, resented the diversion of Fairfax's field army to relieve Taunton:

For such places are not able to hold out long; and then either there must be a loss of charge, arms, or of our friends, which would be a discouragement to our whole Party; or else an Army must be diverted from their principal designes, and besides the danger other places by its absence may be exposed to, expose it selfe also to the certain toyle, inconveniences, and hazardous chances of a long *March*, which is likely also to end in a *Fight*. And therefore it hath been held great wisdom by ancient and well experienced Souldiers, to have but *few Garisons*, and those very *strong*, which may hold out long without *relief*.[11]

Country houses figured alongside strategic towns and obsolete medieval castles as places to be defended. In some instances, entirely new forts were built to command lines of communication and landing places. Elsewhere, the defences ranged from the thorough to the makeshift. In the first days of the war hastily fortified country houses might consist simply of barricaded doors and windows, and make use of an adjoining church tower as a strongpoint for flanking the house itself. Such a case was Abbotsbury House in Dorset.[12] Elsewhere, the adaptation of old castles might take an idiosyncratic turn as at Rockingham Castle in Northamptonshire where the Norman motte was ringed by tiers of gun positions, some dug in and covered to form casemates.[13] Later, houses like Basing House in Hampshire or Donnington in Berkshire, might be entirely enclosed by regular, bastioned earthworks of advanced form, which required a formal siege to reduce them. Many old castles and houses, which might appear to be extremely vulnerable to guns, however, were able to hold out for a considerable time because of the ineffectualness of the opposing artillery. Siege trains of battering guns like whole cannon, demi-cannon and whole culverins were difficult to move about the country, particularly in bad weather, but the lighter, more manoeuvrable pieces were insufficient to break down thick masonry. At times the infantry went into the assault without supporting artillery fire. Sprigge relates how at the siege of Dartmouth, Devon,

> after the enemy had discharged once, our Men got under their Canon, and quickly possessed them, and turned them against the Enemy; for the Army had no Peeces at all of their own, the way and weather not admitting any to be drawn against that place, where there were an hundred Peeces ready mounted against them, (a strange and unparalleld undertaking).[14]

The fortification of towns, which might be under siege for months if not years, was a different matter. Where the town was already walled the defences could be brought up to date in the manner outlined by Venn in his *Military Architecture*:

> An ancient Rampar, if it be strong and surrounded with a wall and Towers, must not be demolished, therefore you must inclose it with a new fortification which must be Regular, if possible, or as near a

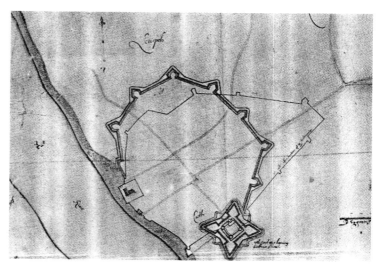

De Gomme's proposals for the defence of Liverpool. (Author)

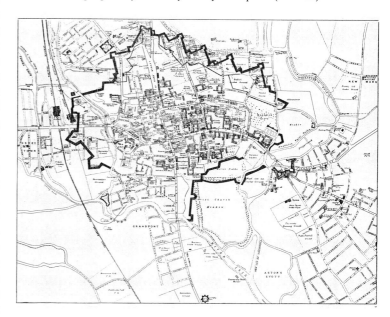

Oxford: de Gomme's plan of the defences, 1644, in relation to a modern map of the city. (*Oxoniensia* vol 1)

Regular as might be. Betwixt the New Fortification and the old Ditch there must be left a large Pomoerium [wide space or *terre-plein*] fit for military use.

The defensive strategy varied between the use of a continuous bastioned *enceinte*, and a ring of individual forts and sconces, perhaps connected by entrenchments. In the former category was Portsmouth, whose fortifications had developed during the previous century and were therefore already in existence at the start of the war. King's Lynn and Worcester had bastions added to their medieval walls as recommended by Venn. Reading possessed an irregular but continuous bastioned *enceinte* newly constructed, supplemented by advanced and detached works. Newark was similar, and is described later in some detail. At Liverpool, a

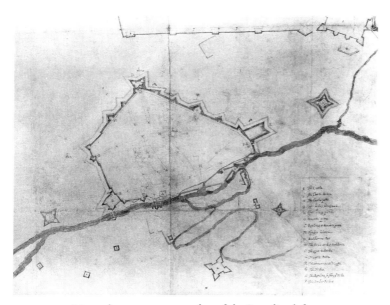

Newark: contemporary plan of the Royalist defences.
(RCHM)

scheme for a regular bastioned *enceinte* together with the medieval castle enclosed to provide a square, bastioned citadel, all designed by de Gomme, was intended to replace the irregular, ill-flanked enclosure constructed by the Parliamentarian forces, but the new design was never put into effect. The most accomplished plan of continuous fortification was that for the Royalist capital of Oxford. This provided a sophisticated double *enceinte* in the Dutch manner and was also probably designed by de Gomme.[15] Only part of that scheme was actually carried out. Elsewhere, at Bristol, Chester, Plymouth and London the pattern was for individual redoubts and self-contained bastioned forts linked by entrenchments. London was on the largest scale of all. The line of the defences extended on both sides of the river linking nine major bastioned forts and thirteen redoubts and hornworks.

In May 1643, London was visited by the Scot, William Lithgow, who made a tour round the defences and wrote a detailed description of the works, starting his tour at Wapping and working anti-clockwise:

> ... I found a seven-angled fort erected of turffe, sand, watles, and earthen work (as all the rest are composed of the like) having nine port-holes and as many cannons; and near the top round about pallosaded with sharp wooden stakes fixed in the bulwerkes, right out, and a foot distant from one another, which are defensive for suddain scalets, and single-ditched below, with a 'court du guard' within. Advancing thence along the trench dyke (for all the trenches are deep ditched about) which runneth through Wappinge fields to the further end of White-Chappell, a great way withoute Aldgate, and on the roadway to Essex, I saw a nine-angled fort, only pallosaded and single-ditched and planted with seven pieces of brazen ordnance, and a 'court du

guard' composed of timber and thatched with tyle stone, as all the rest are . . .[16]

The most comprehensively fortified, and the most consistently besieged, town was Newark in Nottinghamshire. It was garrisoned for the king towards the end of 1642 and served as a Royalist stronghold until it was surrendered in May 1646. During that time it withstood one assault and two sieges, all of which led to the creation of elaborate defences and opposing siege works. Contemporary plans remain of these works and many of the individual constructions survive as still visible earthworks. Surrounding the defences were two lines of circumvallation belonging to the besieging forces, together with their own sconces protecting their approaches as well as the defensible camps of their armies. Newark is as good an example as any to demonstrate that military engineering during the Civil War could match the professionalism displayed on the continent of Europe.[17]

But what of the sieges themselves? The contemporary descriptions throw a great deal of light on how these defences actually functioned. The best documented town is that of Bristol. Prince Rupert's chief engineer, Bernard de Gomme, described the attack and storm of the town by the Royalists in 1643, as well as providing a detailed description of the defences.[18] An alternative account of the siege from the opposite side is provided by the statements of the court-martial of the Parliamentarian commander, Colonel Nathaniel Fiennes, following his surrender of the town to the Royalists. There is a further eye-witness account from Sprigge, who was present when Fairfax invested and stormed Bristol in 1645 and received its surrender from Prince Rupert.[19]

More regular and painstaking forms of siege work might be adopted, though commonly attack was an impatient out and out storm. Newark in 1646 underwent the most elaborate siege of the war. Colonel Poyntz, the Parliamentary commander 'drew a line about the town, and made a very regular entrenchment and approaches in such a soldier-like manner as none of them who had attempted the place before had done.'[20] As the war progressed much more attention was paid to sufficiently equipped and mobilised siege trains. At Sherborne Castle, in two days, Fairfax's guns had made a breach wide enough for ten men to march abreast. Hugh Peters reporting to the House of Commons described how

> For the Castle of Winchester, we begun our Batteries upon Saturday morning, which wrought so effectually, that a breach, wherein 30 men might go abrest, was made . . . We plaid then with grenadoes from our Mortar-peeces, with the best effect that I have seen, which brake down the Mansion house in many places . . . The Lord's day we spent in preaching and prayer, whilst our gunners were battering, and at 8 a clock at night we received a Letter

Newark: Queen's Sconce, from the air. (RCHM)

from the Governour for a treaty.[21]

Since the various fortifications which were thrown up during the Civil Wars were essentially earthworks and therefore of a temporary nature, a surprising number remain and show great diversity. Almost all are in a very denuded and eroded condition so that only a general idea of their form can be appreciated from present appearance. Very little has been done in examining such works by archaeological excavation. Those fortifications which remain are mainly self-contained forts or sconces, either associated with town defences and various castles and houses, or isolated strategic strongpoints in the countryside.

Continuous defensive lines do not usually survive because the towns they protected have outgrown and overwhelmed the often inconspicuous earthworks. Short lengths of Oxford's former continuous trace can be found in the area of gardens and sports grounds to the north east of the city. At Newark-on-Trent, although only a fragment of the *enceinte* around the town itself remains, there are traces of various outworks, and also of the extensive and elaborate siege works beyond. Newark has benefitted from the comprehensive study of the siege works made by the Royal Commission on Historical Monuments (England) using all available historic and archaeological evidence.[22] In 1642 the Royalists constructed the first defensive circuit outside the medieval town walls. It

was not very professional, being without proper bastions, and flanking fire was only available from irregular projections from the curtain. After the first assault in 1643, which was nearly successful, a more regular *enceinte* was constructed. Even then, the size of the bastions was universally small, only partly compensated for by the hornworks at the principal angles of the *enceinte* (see illustration on p76). More substantial defences were erected outside the town rather later, notably the King's and Queen's Sconces, north east and south west of the town respectively. The Queen's Sconce survives. It is roughly 250 feet (76 metres) square, a regularly bastioned fort surrounded by a wide and deep ditch covering in all a little over three acres (1.25 hectares). The ramparts rise to a height of 25 to 30 feet (9 metres) above ditch bottom. The parapet still remains above the *terre-plein* on two sides and there are traces of the gun ramps in the gorges of the bastions. Close at hand there are also eroded remains of a Royalist sconce at Muskham Bridge controlling the access to the Island, a large area of pasture to the north east of the town. This is a small polygonal work with a central bastion and two demi-bastions. It was adapted later by the Scottish besiegers. Nearby, is a small, pear-shaped raised battery at Crankley Lane.

The besieging armies made use of the sur-

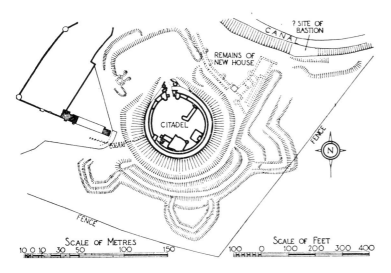

Basing House, Hampshire: plan of the earthworks.
(From B H St John O'Neil, *Castles and Cannon*)

rounding villages, and some were fortified. Traces of these bastioned defences have been located at Balderton, Coddington, Farndon and Winthorpe. In addition, there were the lines of circumvallation with individual sconces and redoubts at key points. Colonel Gray's Sconce terminated the northern line of circumvallation where it met the river Trent, and where there was a bridge of boats. It was square, with full bastions at the south and east angles and demi-bastions at the north and west. The curtains were 150 feet (46 metres) long. In 1958 the defences stood only 1 foot high with an external ditch up to 3 feet (1 metre) deep. Excavations showed that originally the ditch had been nearly 6 feet (2 metres) deep, and the rampart scarp had been revetted by timbers 2 feet apart. The original height of the rampart was probably 7 or 8 feet (2 metres). To the

Sherborne, Dorset: Civil War earthwork bastion flanking the western gatehouse of the medieval castle. (Author)

south of the town near the village of Hawton is a large, roughly rectangular redoubt adapting an earlier medieval moated enclosure. There are another half a dozen smaller redoubts recorded by the Royal Commission.

Other towns retain fragments of their defences. On Brandon Hill, Bristol, are bastioned earthworks of two distinct periods which may be part of the fort, or else possibly part of the continuous line. Part of the Royalist *enceinte* outside the medieval walls of King's Lynn can be traced on the northern side of the town. Carmarthen has a length of curtain and a mutilated bastion outside the line of the earlier town wall. Worcester had the quadrangular Fort Royal in a similar situation as Newark's Queen's Sconce, commanding the London road. There are slight remains at Barnstaple, and also in Devon are the Royalist outposts of Gallants's Bower and Mount Ridley outside Dartmouth and Kingswear respectively.[23] On the outskirts of Dorchester, Dorset, the Roman amphitheatre of Maumbury Rings was adapted to provide a parapet and *terre-plein* as well as a ramp for the movement of cannon.

The defences added to castles and houses are often better preserved and more numerous. Perhaps the most impressive, because they were among the most advanced technically, are the bastions around the ruins of Basing House, Hampshire. Donnington Castle, Berkshire, which also underwent a well recorded siege, was completely enclosed within an earthwork *enceinte* in 1644. One large bastion with an acute salient angle still remains north west of the gatehouse. Sherborne Castle, Dorset, whose storming is so graphically described by Sprigge, has a large earthen bastion outside the medieval ditch and flanking the western gatehouse. Raglan Castle, Gwent, which was one of the last Royalist strongholds to surrender has considerable remains

of its outer bastioned defences. The Royalist outworks of Pendennis Castle have, in recent years, been levelled to make a car park.

Isolated forts are not uncommon and sometimes survive in good condition. This is especially true of two Parliamentarian forts in Huntingdonshire, guarding the approaches to the territory of the Eastern Association. Horsey Hill is a bastioned pentagon. There are traces of a covered-way beyond the ditch and perhaps a redan before the entrance. The Earith Bulwark, guarding the approaches to Ely, is perhaps the most sophisticated of all. It is square, with the flanks of the bastions clearly at right angles with the curtains. Outside the ditch is a covered-way with glacis, while in the centre of each length of covered-way is a re-entering place of arms for the gathering of troops for active defence. Another example of this type of strategically placed strongpoint is Penrhos Camp near Caerleon, Gwent, which is another large quadrangular bastioned earthwork with the suggestion of additional bastions in the centre of two of the curtains.

There are other earthwork remains which are interpreted as batteries; not necessarily associated with siege works but whose role may have been in support of field campaigns and encampments. These are often simple rectangular raised earth mounds. O'Neil identified and published one such in Cornbury Park, Oxfordshire, on a low hilltop about 500 yards away from the castle gatehouse.[24] The battery has a slight rampart with silted ditch with a front and sides and no back. It is a type illustrated in seventeenth century military handbooks. Other raised mounds or mounts can be seen outside Raglan Castle, or at Braddock Down in Cornwall associated with Essex's ill-fated south western campaign.

THE ISLES OF SCILLY AND COMBINED OPERATIONS

It was the opinion of Bryan O'Neil, the British pioneer of artillery fortification studies, that nowhere can the course of a campaign in the Civil War be studied more closely on the ground than in the Isles of Scilly.[25] It was to Scilly that the Prince of Wales considered evacuating when Fairfax's army began to close in on the last major fortress in the south west, Pendennis Castle. The islands served as a valuable link between Jersey and Ireland. They were surrendered a few weeks after the capitulation of Pendennis but returned to Royalist control in 1648 when they served as a privateering base under Sir John Grenville's command. In 1651, a combination of piratical activity and the fear that a Dutch fleet under van Tromp might sieze the islands for the United Provinces, led Parliament to order Sir Robert Blake and Sir George Ayscue to Scilly with a substantial fleet.

The islands had been fortified over the course

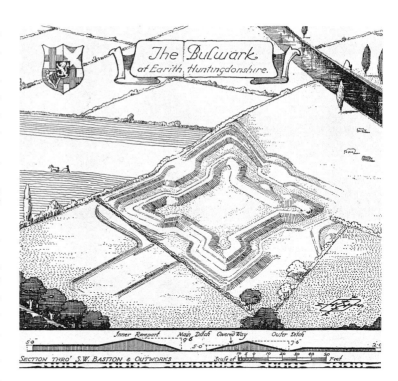

Earith Bulwark, Huntingdonshire: plan of a self-contained fort. (RCHM)

of the past century. The centre of gravity in defensive terms had moved from the largest island, St Mary's, to Tresco to the north in the mid-sixteenth century in order to protect the anchorage of New Grimsby, between Tresco and Bryher. King Charles's Castle, built in the 1550s was the principal permanent work. Towards the turn of the century, attention shifted back to St Mary's, and, in particular, to the headland behind Hugh Town, the chief town. A bastioned line cut off the neck of this headland, the Hugh, and on its highest point, Star Castle had been built in the 1590s, as the headquarters of the governor. A survey of Scilly in 1637 reported that

> the only strength that doth serve it at this present is a small castle (Star Castle) uncapable to lodge and accommodate of a garrison of 20 soldiers and so ill-contrived that the least assault of an enemy could easily carry it. There are several batteries placed at the foot of the hill beneath the Castle whose ordinance lie more convenient to command the harbour than those above but their platforms are not defended with any strength or works.[26]

This was what the Royalist garrison found, and then improved. Like Civil War fortifications elsewhere, the new works were entirely earthwork and therefore short-lived. Generally the improvements consisted of individual batteries and lengths of entrenchment. The batteries were mostly sited on promontories to command the navigational channels and anchorages. A breastwork seems to have been thrown up round much

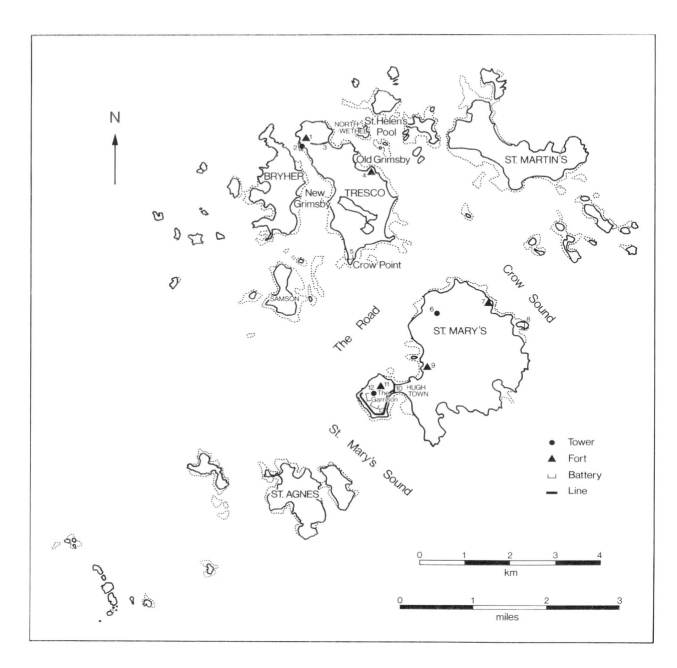

of the cliff top of St Mary's. In particular, the headland of the Hugh was given a continuous entrenchment.

The approach to St Mary's Pool both by Crow Sound to the north east and by St Mary's Sound to the south west was protected by batteries. Most of these defensive works are now rather shapeless mounds, since they were built of sand. Pellew's Redoubt on Toll's Island, just off the eastern coast of St Mary's, is much more defined and of considerable interest. The work may be described as composed of two demi-bastions set back to back to form a re-entrant angle. There is a gap in the rampart at the rear for an entrance. On Tresco, the emphasis was on defending New Grimsby harbour. King Charles's Castle, guarding the northern entrance, was refurbished and, it would seem, was given an irregular bastioned trace to protect the landward approach. The southern entrance was covered by a battery on Bryher. The harbour of Old Grimsby on the east side of Tresco was only protected by the stone blockhouse called Dover Fort, also of the 1550s.

Rather than risk a 'frontal' attack on St Mary's, the Parliamentary forces recognised Tresco as the key. Blake and Ayscue could establish there a base for their troops and the sheltered harbour of New Grimsby would allow their ships to ride in safety. Furthermore, as Ayscue later wrote,

> the gaining of these two islands will render S Maries useless to the enemy, for we have now the command of the Rode, as well as they, and enjoy a harbour, which they have not; so that I perceive they will or may be forced to a submission, for, the Men of War belonging to these piratical rocks, will be like mice that run from a falling house, and must be forced to seek a new Ren-dezovous; neither can S Maries subsist without them.[27]

The description of the attack on Tresco, the abortive landing on the island of Northwethel, the beating off of the first assault and the final successful night attack led by 200 seasoned sailors, is described in vivid detail by several of the participants. The attack was made in the vicinity of Old Grimsby where the defences were weakest. Following the establishment of a beach-head, the bulk of the Royalist garrison evacuated the island

for St Mary's that same night. Having established themselves on Tresco, Blake and Ayscue concentrated their forces at the southern end of the island where they constructed Oliver's Battery to command St Mary's harbour and a camp for their troops nearby. The situation of the Royalists was deemed hopeless, and rather than invite assault Grenville surrendered on 3 June 1651.

The capture of the Isles of Scilly brings out the necessity for coastal defences during the Civil Wars. It was a need felt chiefly by the Royalist forces because the navy had gone over to the Parliamentary side at the start of the war. There were sixteen men-of-war based on the Downs as the Summer Guard, two were in Irish waters and there were besides, twenty-four armed merchantmen. This was a factor which played a significant part in Parliament's eventual success. Strongholds like Hull, Lyme and Plymouth, which were otherwise deep in Royalist territory and under almost constant siege, were supplied by sea. Trade from Royalist areas was disrupted and, more particularly, the fleet could assist in the progress of military campaigns even to the extent of contributing towards combined operations. The siege of Bristol in 1645 employed the fleet to capture the fort on Portishead Point, and then advance its ships up the Avon into the city. A combined force of

Cromwell's Castle, Tresco, Isles of Scilly. (Author)

soldiers and sailors were detailed to take the Water Fort if need arose. Reprovisioning from the sea is frequently mentioned in contemporary accounts. Such combined operations could have their failures, as that which affected Essex's campaign into Cornwall in 1644. Bad weather and failure to secure the fortifications at the harbour mouth prevented the evacuation of the trapped Parliamentary army from Fowey and Lostwithiel and contributed to its capitulation.

Coastal defences therefore figure among the works constructed anew during the wars. One of the best surviving examples is Dennis Fort on the headland commanding the Helford estuary west of Falmouth on the one hand, and Gillan harbour on the other. Not only does it survive as a roughly square enclosure with sides of 25–30 yards (23–27 metres) long, bastions at each angle and scrappy remains of outworks across the headland further west, but the accounts of its building and garrisoning are among the papers of the Vyvyans of Trelowarren. Helford Haven could accommodate large ships, and as the description of the garrison's purpose said, 'that If the enemy should possesse this Harbour, they would not onely block up the Harbour of ffal-mouth, and indaunger the surprisall of Pendennis Cas-tell, but suddenly be masters of the west of Cornwall.'

Sir Richard Vyvyan claimed £859 7s 0d for building the fort. The captain was paid at the rate of 5s a day, the lieutenant, 2s 6d, two gunners and the porter at 1s a day each and twenty-four soldiers at 8d a day. At the time of its surrender the fort contained 22 guns, which included some heavy, long range pieces such as culver-ins and demi-culverins.[28]

The activities of hostile Dutch fleets early in the 1650s led to coastal defences being built by the victorious Parliamentarian forces. They strove to main-tain and improve the fortifications of Scilly by protect-ing the New Grimsby anchorage more effectively. This involved the construction of a strong gun-tower at the waters-edge below King Charles's Castle, and was subsequently to be called Cromwell's Castle. The tow-er is tall and circular with two floors of barrack accom-modation. The armament was designed to be mounted on the roof where there are six gunports piercing a high stone parapet. The associated lower gun platform was added towards the middle of the eighteenth century. A similar gun-tower was built at the same time as Crom-well's Castle on the promontory known as Mount Batten, Plymouth, covering the southern side of the entrance to the Cattewater and crossing fire with the predecessor of the Royal Citadel on Plymouth Hoe.

CHAPTER 5

Sir Bernard de Gomme: England's Vauban

Charles II's reign saw an expansion of permanent fortification on a scale not seen since the defensive measures of Henry VIII more than a century before. There were a number of causes. The naval and mercantile rivalry with the Dutch, which had led to war under the Commonwealth, revived with spasmodic intensity under Charles II. After some initial naval successes for the English fleet, conflict came to a humiliating head for England with the Dutch raid on the Medway in 1667. Linked to this disaster was Charles's personal enthusiasm for developing the navy, from which followed the need to strengthen the defences of the naval ports and dockyards. The disbandment of the standing army of the Commonwealth, which had been deployed less on home defence than on successful continental campaigns, meant that the Restoration army was steered into serving the state rather than representing the state. Finally, there was, most probably, an element of keeping up with Louis XIV and the widespread contemporary growth on a vast scale of permanent fortification in western Europe, especially in France and the Low Countries, and with which the names of Vauban and Coehorn, the most outstanding of military engineers, are forever associated.

The three Anglo-Dutch Wars were essentially maritime conflicts. They were both imperialistic and mercantilistic in conception. The Dutch had estab-

Late seventeenth century bastioned fortification, from Elements of Fortification *by Stephen Riou, 1746.* (Author)

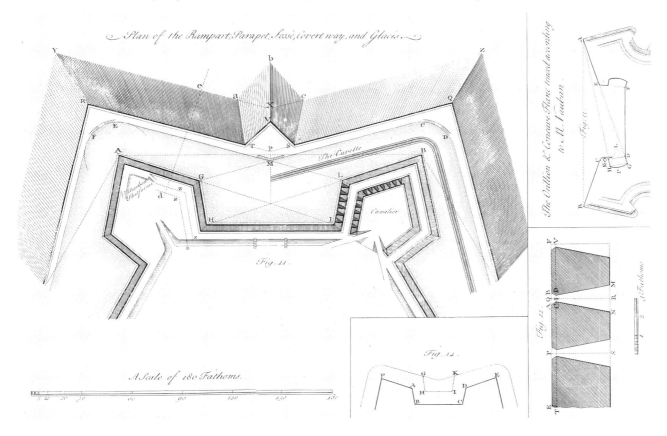

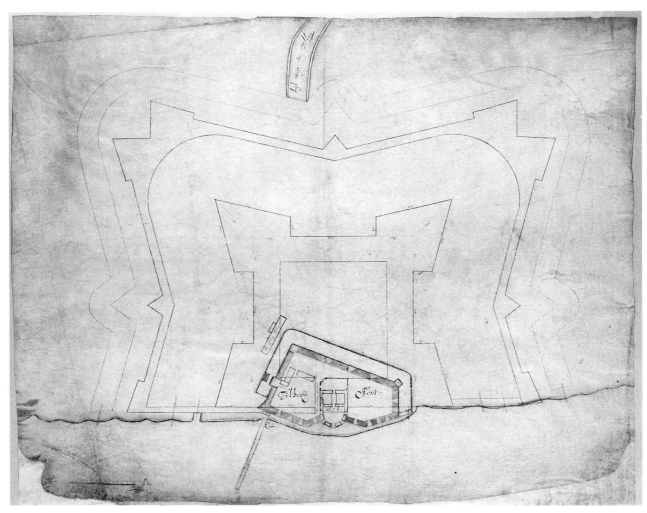

Tilbury Fort, Essex: de Gomme's scheme of 1661. (NMM)

lished themselves in the East Indies, North America and on the west coast of Africa. They had made themselves masters of the carrying trade and flouted English interpretations of maritime law. All this stimulated an intense commercial rivalry which spilled over into outright aggression as well as conflict of interest. This was especially so when leading naval and military administrators were personally interested in commercial and colonial expansion. The Second Dutch War of 1665 to 1667 was the most significant. It was basically a commercial war, with an emphasis on capturing places and possessions, particularly ships. On balance, the naval engagements went England's way but after a victorious sea battle in 1667 the government felt that there was little more to fear from the Dutch for the time being and decided to economise by putting the fleet out of commission, relying on the existing coastal fortifications including the new but unfinished fort at Sheerness at the entrance to the Medway. Against all expectations the Dutch put to sea again under the command of de Ruyter, not for invasion but a raid in force. A squadron appeared in the Thames and came as far as Gravesend,

then switched to attack Chatham and, as a preliminary, attacked and burnt the fort at Sheerness. The defenders in the Medway were put into a panic. The chain boom was in position between Hoo Ness and Gillingham and two batteries were thrown up, one at each end of the boom, and there was an ineffective attempt to block the channel. The leading Dutch ships, however, bore down on the chain. Whether it broke or was cast loose by a Dutch landing party is uncertain, but it proved no obstacle. The *Royal Charles* was carried off and other ships were burnt. If the attack had been pressed more vigorously more ships and the dockyard itself could have been destroyed. As it was, the raid represented an ignominious defeat. The diarist, Evelyn, visiting Chatham soon afterwards and looking at the burnt-out hulks, described it as 'a Dreadful Spectacle as ever any English men saw and a dishonour never to be wiped off.'[1] At least in the popular mind, Elizabeth's Upnor Castle, opposite the dockyard had acquitted itself well. Pepys said 'I do not see that Upnor Castle hath received any hurt by them though they played long against it; and they themselves shot till they had hardly a gun left upon the carriages, so badly provided they were.'[2]

An improvement of coastal defences was clearly in the mind of Charles II's government from the start of the Restoration. Individual reports in the 1660s indicated that the fortifications were often obsolete, and in nearly every case were in a poor condition. Preliminary sketch plans were produced for a radically new and enlarged design for Tilbury Fort as early as 1661, and new schemes were considered for Portsmouth and Plymouth. At Portsmouth in 1665 the governor was instructed to erect new fortifications about the town. At Plymouth in the same year a commission was issued to the governor, the Earl of Bath, directing him to build a citadel on the Hoe. Inevitably, the raid on the Medway stimulated greater activity in fortification, not just at Sheerness and the Medway but also in and around the established naval dockyard at Portsmouth and also at the developing yard at Plymouth. The construction work was to continue for the rest of Charles's reign well into the 1680s. The emphasis was less on preventing invasion than on protecting the dockyards and the approaches to London. The political and military climate demanded such safeguarding of the ships and naval stores, together with shipbuilding and repair capacity. The defences were not limited to the dockyards alone. Indeed, the actual fortified enclosure of the yards was generally very sketchy and slight. The new works covered the seaward approaches and the associated towns. While Charles II's coastal fortifications were nothing like as geographically widespread as those of Henry VIII, they were very much more concentrated about the object to be defended.

The policy of Cromwell during the Protectorate had been to intervene in continental wars and carry aggression towards potential aggressors. This had the effect of making England safe by making her dangerous. The creation of the New Model Army during the first Civil War was a landmark and the first acknowledgement of professionalism in British military affairs. The efficiency and conviction of the New Model Army was witnessed with some surprise by foreign commanders. Part of its success was appreciation of the balance between artillery and other arms. When the New Model was organised it was provided with a powerful artillery train though the details of its actual composition is unknown. It is clear that the field guns attached to it were principally demi-culverins and sakers. Its siege artillery was progressively increased in strength during the Commonwealth. The guns used were cannon, from 48- to 40-pounders, demi-cannon which were 24-pounders and 16-pounder culverins. Besides the battering pieces there were mortars, some weighing as much as 10 hundredweight and throwing shells 12 inches (304mm) and nearly 15 inches (380mm) in diameter. The restoration of the monarchy meant the disbandment of this well trained and disciplined standing army for this was one of the keys to a constitutional

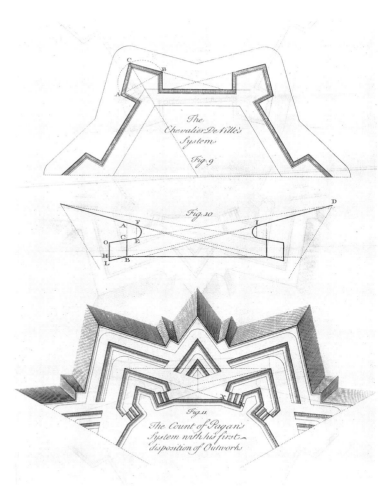

The Chevalier de Ville' system, and the Count of Pagan's system, from Elements of Fortification. (Author)

The citadel at Lille, designed by Vauban. (Author)

▲ *Coehorn's first system, from* Elements of Fortification.
(Author)

▼ *Naarden, Holland: fortified town designed by Coehorn.*
(KLM Aerocarto)

settlement. The alternative was intended to be a return to the traditional militia. The weakness of this arrangement became apparent in a time when there were still republican plots and two regiments of General George Monck's army were accordingly left intact. The Lord General's Regiment of Footguards still survives as the Coldstream Guards; the Lifeguard of Horse was merged into the Lifeguards. In the same year, the men who had guarded Charles II in exile were amalgamated into the First Footguards, which survives today as the Grenadier Guards. Other regiments were formed later in the reign but the standing army was deliberately limited in size and scope. This was a further reason for emphasis to be placed on fixed defences rather than an aggressive military policy.

Not that Charles II had the resources or the inclination for an aggressive foreign policy. The quarrels with the Dutch were over prizes and prestige. The Commonwealth's policies had been mainly directed against the failing power of Spain and with an alliance with France. Charles maintained an accommodation with France for most of his reign. Louis XIV was his cousin and, more to the point, Louis provided him with an annual subsidy. Later, the marriage of Charles's niece, Mary, to William of Orange meant a political break with France and the development of closer links with the Netherlands. Charles, from his long exile, had a deep knowledge both of France and the Low Countries. In political and military terms he was well aware of the degree to which permanent fortifications formed part of national posturing as well as the daily life of towns of any size. This was the period following the trauma of the Thirty Years War when bastioned fortification reached its apogee in Western Europe. It had a sophisticated theoretical base and a substantial literature. Probably the most influential French writer at this time was the Chevalier de Ville whose *Fortifications* went through many editions during the course of half a century from 1629. He believed in creating substantial outworks while, at the same time, simplifying the form of the bastions themselves. The bastion was the universal defensive system, and it had been brought to a peak of perfection first by Dutch and then by French military engineers. Fortification had contributed substantially to the survival of Dutch independence from the Spanish even if the defensive techniques had verged on the over-elaborate. Fortification was the preferred solution to the problem of France's highly vulnerable northern and north eastern frontiers. Perhaps the greatest achievement of defensive engineering of the later seventeenth century was Vauban's chain of fortresses which allowed France successfully to defy most of the rest of Europe armed in coalition against her.

Military engineering, which so fascinated contemporaries was, during the last quarter of the seventeenth century, dominated by two protagonists, one French, the other Dutch. Sebastien Le Prestre de Vauban was to be recognised as the greatest military engineer of this period, and the undisputed master of siege warfare. Not far behind Vauban, and probably his equal in the design of fortresses was Menno, Baron van Coehorn, against whom Vauban was often pitted. Vauban was cautious, methodical and thorough in attack, Coehorn sacrificed everything to surprise, speed and massed artillery bombardment. Coehorn indeed gave his name to a type of small mortar. Whereas Vauban demonstrated his genius by practical example, with the publication of his works largely in the hands of others, Coehorn published his three systems of fortification for Dutch low-lying sites in 1685.[3]

DE GOMME'S CAREER

In so far as England had an equivalent to Vauban and Coehorn, it was Sir Bernard de Gomme. Not English born, de Gomme nonetheless was a loyal and distinguished servant of Charles II and his father. His was the leading name in English military engineering both during the Civil War and after the Restoration, and certainly he had no rivals among British engineers. De Gomme was a practitioner and, as far as we know, no theorist. By continental standards he was probably not in the first rank but he was clearly in touch with the main changes taking place in the subject in France and the Low Countries. He was a Walloon and his work was grounded on his youthful experience in Netherlands water-based fortification. Ross repeats a tradition that he was born at Lille in 1620 and had served under Henry Frederick of Orange.[4] Dying in 1683, he was an older contemporary of Vauban (1633–1707) and Coehorn (1641–1704). De Gomme came to England in the entourage of Prince Rupert at the outset of the Civil War. He was responsible for the design of the elaborate defences of Oxford, and signed the plan for the proposed but aborted re-fortification of Liverpool. In 1645 he was appointed 'Engineer and Quartermaster-General'. He had also been knighted by Charles I during the course of the war.

With the collapse of the Royalist cause, de Gomme went abroad with his patron, Prince Rupert, turning up at Charles II's court at Breda in 1649 to have the post as Engineer and Quartermaster-General renewed. He returned to England at the Restoration in the royal entourage. Although the two engineer places on the normal establishment were already filled, the king granted to de Gomme the post of 'Engineer of all the King's Castles etc in England and Wales' with the fee of 13s 4d a day. Sir Charles Lloyd held the post of Chief Engineer for one year to 1661, and his brother, Sir Godfrey Lloyd, for less than three months after him. The Lloyds were succeeded by de Gomme, who held that post until his death in November 1685. In addition, de Gomme was made an Assistant Surveyor of the Ordnance Office in 1679, a post of some authority at the time. In 1682 he became Surveyor-General of the Ordnance.

De Gomme's career was an active one to the end, and did not fall away into bureaucratic posts and sinecures. Pepys records that:

Discoursing this 11th September, 1680 with his Majesty and Colonel Legg on board his new yacht upon this subject, viz how it comes to pass that England has in all time served itself with strangers for engineers; the King told me that England has never bred an able engineer of its own, no Englishman having given their mind to it, nor have we had occasion enough to invite any to the study of it; he never remembering any but two in all his time, viz Sir Charles (I think) Flud and Sir Godfrey Floud, the former of whom he said [was] worth very little and the latter was (at Sir John Duncomb and Sir William Coventry's urging him to encourage Englishmen) entrusted with the designing and managing the work at Sheerness, where after spending 2000*l* the King said he was forced to undo all that he had done and put it into the hand of Sir Bernard Degum, who and Beckman (another foreigner) are his present engineers; that there is very little mystery in the scientifical part of an engineer's trade – a small knowledge in geometry and particularly the doctrine of triangles, being sufficient for it – but that the only difficulty lies in judging and right laying out the ground for fortifications (which is not to be done but upon view of the place, where the ground is uneven) and the well-estimating beforehand the charge of a work which differs according to the nature of the soil rendering the labour of digging more or less easy; That the Germans, of all nations, have for a long time been esteemed the best engineers, but that now the French do go beyond all; So that if he had a work of

Plymouth, Devon: town and Royal Citadel by de Gomme. (NMM)

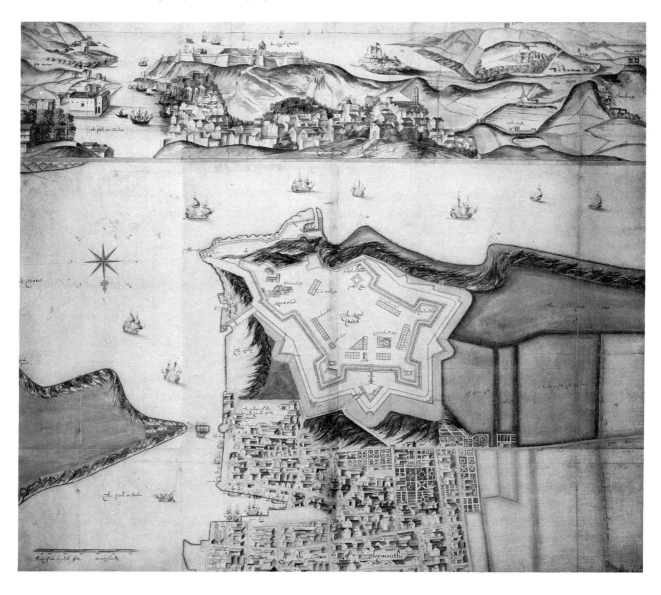

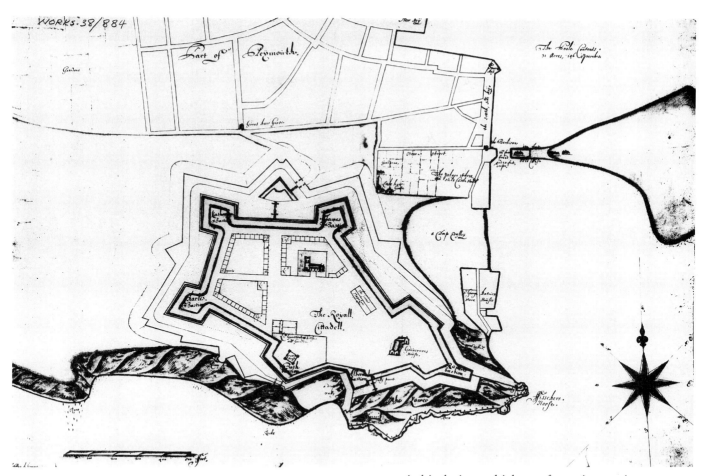

Plymouth Citadel: de Gomme plan. Public Record Office, Works 38/884.(PRO)

consequence now to do, we should be forced to employ engineers of that nation, and that men of that profession might be trusted, for they make it their business to keep up the credit of their profession with all princes.[5]

The foreign engineers, however, were not infallible. Lord Dartmouth, Master-General of the Ordnance, told Pepys that de Gomme had been influenced by the position of the Henrician blockhouse and Elizabethan fortifications at Tilbury into misplacing the new fort,

> as he showed me how much better it had been if we had placed the same at the point [Coalhouse Point, East Tilbury] above it where ships in coming up must have been upon the tack and so our guns have more play upon them whereas now the tide carry them away directly by us without half the opposition to be given them by our guns.[6]

How far de Gomme was obliged by political decision and superior instruction to remodel the existing defences it is impossible now to judge. He was, however, criticised by his junior colleagues. Thomas Phillips, the Third Engineer at the Ordnance Office, in a letter to Dartmouth accused de Gomme of committing 'several gross errors in his designs which you from time to time have corrected and much against his will', and opposing 'all things whatever is proposed by me letting the King suffer rather than he will admit of any man's judgement but his own'.[7] This sounds very much like professional in-fighting and the grievances of an ambitious junior. Yet, in his old age de Gomme does seem to have been a difficult character. Phillips again claimed that when he made designs and estimates de Gomme told him to mind his own business and had deliberately kept him in ignorance of the value of the work. John Duxbury, one of the clerks in the Ordnance Office, said that he would rather be sent 'against the great Turk . . . than be under the power and command of Sir Bernard or persons that will not be satisfied by reason.'[8] His successor as Chief Engineer, Sir Martin Beckman, commenting in terms of professional jealousy as late as 1693 on what he regarded as defects in the construction of the Portsmouth fortifications added

> . . . of which I often told the late King Charles and King James, but all what the late Chief-Engineer, Sir Bernard de Gomme, was pleased to do was approved of, as from an oracle, and I kept off from ever having anything to do with the fortifications, till I succeeded him, and then the fortifications were laid aside, and the army by land and the fleet were accounted the walls of England . . .[9]

Nevertheless, as we shall see, de Gomme's professional career was distinguished, his designs generally practical, and he demonstrated a flexible mind to changing fashions and an ability to put them into practice. When he died in 1685 he was buried in the Tower of London.

He left sizeable bequests in his will as well as a large personal estate. His long service to both Charles I and II did not go unrewarded.

Plymouth Citadel: main gateway. (RCHM)

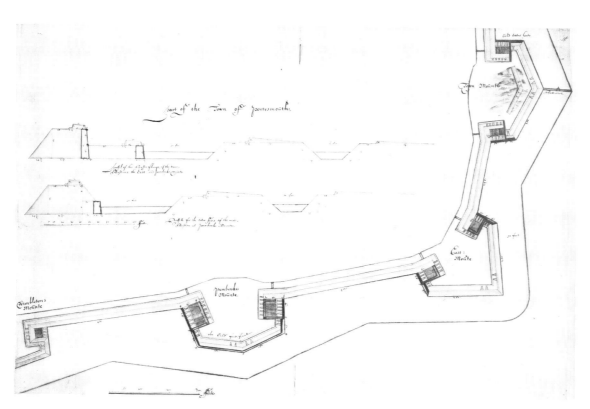

PLYMOUTH AND PORTSMOUTH

Portsmouth: 1668 plan, detail of bastions and 'base flanks'.
British Library, Add MS 16370. (BL)

In 1665, during the Second Dutch War, the governors of Portsmouth and Plymouth were commissioned to erect fortifications to the design of de Gomme. These were the first pieces of major, permanent fortification with which he was associated. At Portsmouth this involved bringing the Elizabethan town defences up to date, and later improving some of the outlying works such as Southsea Castle and devising new ones, particularly to protect the dockyard from the west. He was to be involved with Portsmouth for the rest of his life.

At Plymouth, there was no attempt to construct a continuous *enceinte* about the town as had been proposed by Genebelli. The Parliamentary defences, so successful during the Civil War were individual strong-points on the surrounding hills connected by entrenchments. Instead, the government decided upon a citadel which was an enlargement of the Elizabethan fort at the south eastern end of the Hoe, controlling the entrance to the harbour at the top of the Cattewater. According to the account of the governor, John, Earl of Bath:

> wee have thought fitt to strengthen and fortifie our Fort upon the Hoe of Plimouth and to secure it from any Foreign contrivance or Invasion with a New Cittadell and other workes according to a draught made by our chief engineer – 17 Nov 1665.[10]

This involved an *enceinte* of three regular bastions and two demi-bastions with two ravelins and a ditch cut out of the rock which strengthened the landward side, while the improved Elizabethan fort commanded the lower level and the sea approaches. The total charge in the fifteen years up to the close of 1675 was the colossal sum of £20,544 2s 4d.[11] Work was still going on in 1682–3, and nearly a hundred years later, General William Roy still considered the citadel incomplete, 'but is a reputable work'.[12] Technically the Citadel was a straightforward approach to a difficult and irregular site. The flanks of the bastions were at right angles to the curtain in conventional Dutch form. There were no elaborate outworks. Where the Citadel does show exuberance is in the detailing and ornamentation. The entrance gate is an eye-catching baroque frontispiece, quite the most ornamental of any fortress entrance in Britain. It is by no means certain that de Gomme was the designer but he certainly signed drawings and specifications for the sentry boxes or *guérites* at the angles of the bastions. Other elements of the granite ashlar details must have been designed as well as worked by local masons since they are in the architectural idiom of Tudor Gothic which was still in fashion in the south west well towards the end of the seventeenth century. The Citadel *enceinte* still remains little altered. Unfortunately the ravelins and the covered-way are all but lost under municipal gardening, and the rock-cut ditch has been converted into a road.

While Portsmouth involved de Gomme in a variety of projects – the defence of the dockyard, the improvement of Southsea Castle, Blockhouse Point and the new defences for Gosport, and batteries on two islands near the harbour mouth – it was the town fortifications which occupied him continuously. There is a plan of about 1665 which may have been one of de Gomme's preliminary sketches. It shows the existing Elizabethan bastioned trace with his own revisions of the bastions superimposed. The proposed bastion forms still had their flanks at right angles to the curtain and there were elaborate outworks envisaged with two moats and a covered-way with *tenaille* trace showing similarities with the trace of the Civil War defences of Oxford. A scheme for the fortification of Blockhouse Point on the opposite side of Portsmouth harbour was also advanced on the same plan. The revision of the town defences began straight away. The method of working was to divide the counterscarp and give a portion to each commissioner to attend to. Dutch prisoners were employed, receiving 3d a day in addition to the allowance of 5d to work extra hours.

Another plan was drawn up by de Gomme in 1668 which showed a radical change of thought and represented the influence of French engineers and, in particular, of the Comte de Pagan, over the now traditional Dutch methods. This involved strengthening the flanking cover by making the bastion flanks at right angles to the 'line of defence' rather than to the adjacent curtain, and therefore more direct in their effect. The employment of *fausse-brayes* was limited to the flanks of the bastions; 'base flancks', as de Gomme called them at Portsmouth, which had the effect of contriving a second tier of guns in the bastion flanks. The proposed 1668 outworks too were of unusual complexity with double moats and a ravelin in front of the Landport. The covered-way had small bastions opposite two of the salients and redans opposite the curtains. The vulnerable south eastern corner of the defences was modified later by de Gomme by the addition of a hornwork on the edge of 'the great morass', a marshy area of Southsea Common. The hornwork had a two-storey masonry redoubt in the re-entrant angle which was connected to the body of the place by a long caponier. The construction of eight sallyports through various parts of the town defences show de Gomme's concern with active defence.

In practice, the inadequate programming and financing of the construction led to the works being drawn out over decades. The effect of this was to build into the work its own sequence of delapidations. No sooner had one part of the defences been built than other parts, constructed some time before, began to collapse. This is clearly brought out in de Gomme's review of the condition of the Portsmouth fortifications in 1679.

The great Saluting Platform is very much out of repair. Counterscarp from Saluting Platform to the great Pallisados in good repair. The other counterscarp from the great Pallisados over against Wimbleton's Mount to the Mill Pond, the Breastworke almost in all places are fallen downe, and the Graft of the said counterscarp without is much with reades

and rushes growing in it and not in condition to defend the counterscarp unless the said counterscarp graft is cleared and filled with water . . . The face of Towne Mount where the old Towne Mount is slipped in the maine graft is a place of great danger: requires the Graft to bee repaired, the graft broader and a stone wall to bee built 15 feet high to the Traverse wall, and to raise the rampart again to his full height . . .[13]

The estimate for completion had risen from about £16,500 to over £45,000 in ten years. The survey continues in similar depressing vein. Yet, despite these deficiencies in construction and maintenance, the design of the new works was competent and Portsmouth was the best protected town in the country.

Elsewhere in the vicinity, various schemes were put forward for defending the developing dockyard but nothing substantial came of them. Southsea Castle was improved with the addition of a covered-way and glacis. A substantial battery, Eighteen Gun or Sallyport Battery was added beside the old Round Tower, matching the new battery at Blockhouse Point on the Gosport side, though the enclosing fortifications designed to protect the guns were not put into effect until some years after de Gomme's death. Additional harbour defences were provided on two islands near the harbour entrance, Forts Charles and James. These were essentially square masonry towers supporting open batteries at their bases.

In 1678 de Gomme put in hand the bastioned trace round the growing town of Gosport. As at Portsmouth, responsibility for the work was divided among a number of commissioners. Progress was slow and was still continuing into the 1690s. De Gomme's initial plan showed a formal bastioned land front. The trace was simpler yet more assured than some of his earlier work. Ravelins were adopted more freely, and the covered-way was made more regular. Careful use of water defences and of double moats was still his hallmark but, in practice, the outworks were not constructed till much later, and then to a different design.

THAMES AND MEDWAY

De Gomme had surveyed the Thames-side fort of Tilbury and superimposed his own ideas for its reformation as early as 1661. When the new fort at Sheerness was destroyed by the Dutch preparatory to the raid into the Medway in 1667, de Gomme was called in to put the defences of the south east to rights. At Sheerness he replaced the defences round the emergent dockyard with a conventional bastioned front across the narrow peninsula, two demi-bastions on either side of a curtain with a ravelin in front covering the entrance. Along the sea front was an indented trace, and the whole enclosed the small harbour of the dockyard (see illustration on p129). Chatham itself and the fleet anchorage, which had proved so vulnerable, he now protected with two powerful batteries on either side of the river, at Cockham Wood, well below Upnor, and Gillingham Fort opposite, beside the entrance to Gillingham Creek. Upnor Castle was now relegated to the role of powder magazine. Cockham Wood still survives in a very ruined state. It consisted of a brick revetted battery with two straight tiers of guns parallel to the river. Behind was a rectangular brick-walled enclosure and, in the centre of the gorge, was a three-storey brick tower. Gillingham does not survive at all. The fort was diamond-shaped in order to take a hostile fleet both from the front and rear. Inside was a similar square, three-storey tower with turrets and machicolations. De Gomme's two small forts in Portsmouth harbour were simpler versions of the Medway towers with two floors and gun platforms on the roof. De Gomme clearly set considerable store by towers whether as an additional tier of firepower or for observation.

Other batteries were sited further down the Medway later in the seventeenth century. They were

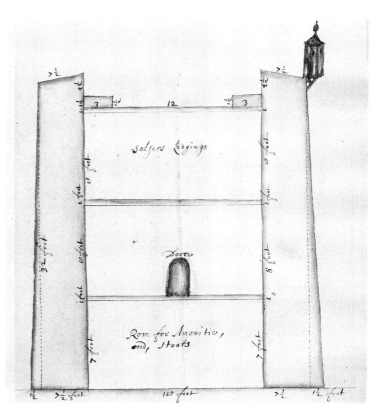

Cockham Wood: sketch elevation of the tower. (NMM)

The Medway and de Gomme's proposals for Gillingham and Cockham Wood forts, 1669. (NMM)

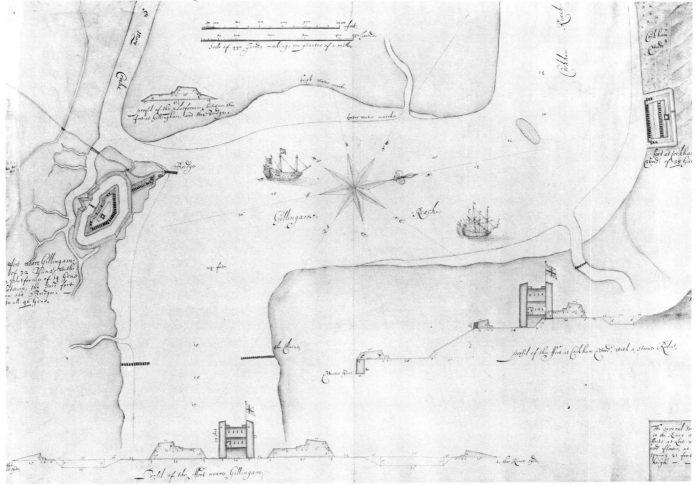

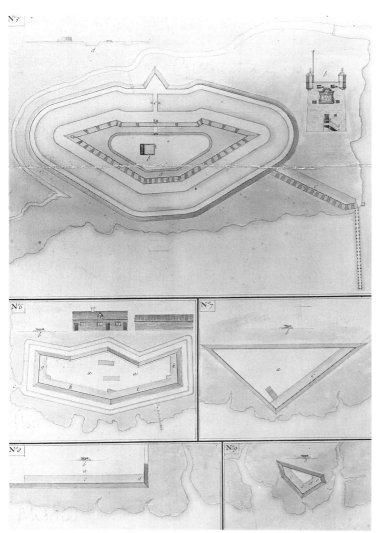

little more than platforms of timber for two or three guns with a small guardroom and magazine to serve them. Plans and elevational drawings of them remain to recall what must have been very short-lived establishments. They were however typical of many temporary defences.

The most significant of all de Gomme's designs and representing his development as a military engineer is Tilbury Fort. Tilbury is especially revealing of the changing fashion in bastion fortification because its conception was spread over the course of nine years.[14] It also has the merit of being the best preserved of all de Gomme's forts and, with Plymouth Citadel, the finest examples of seventeenth century fortification in the British Isles. De Gomme's project for Tilbury of 1661 was repeated almost exactly in 1665. The new fort, taking the Henrician blockhouse as its centrepoint, was to be nearly square, with two bastions on the landward side and two demi-bastions resting on the river bank. The flanks of the bastions were at right angles to the curtain in the usual Dutch manner and the outworks, on what was a marshy site, were very elaborate and included a double moat. The inner moat had the textbook width of 150 feet (46 metres). The design of the covered-way with its *tenaille* trace and *tenaille* heads was distinctly reminiscent of the Royalist defences of Oxford with which de Gomme probably had a hand.

Sheerness: de Gomme's northern trace with the corbelled base of a guérite at the angle. Garrison Point Fort in the background. (DOE)

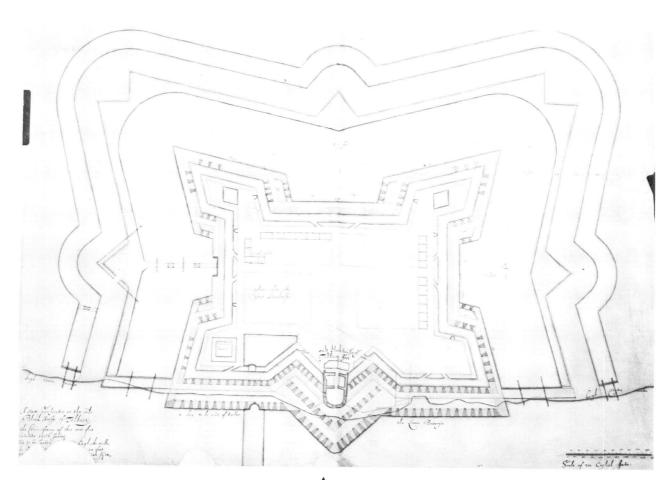

Tilbury Fort: de Gomme's 1668 proposals in the form of a pentagon or parallelogram. (BL)

At either end of the covered-way, where it met the river, there were fussy, turreted, brick or timber re-doubts, which were to reappear again in de Gomme's later designs. The 1665 scheme, while paying close attention to the land defences, seemed to play down the main function of the fort which was to provide a strong riverside battery to block the approaches to London.

The deficiency was not repeated in the next surviving plans which were dated 1668 and were a response to the success of the Dutch raid the year before. There were two alternative schemes, one based on a parallelogram, the other on a pentagon. Both strongly emphasised riverside batteries, and in each case, three tiers of guns were proposed. Although both schemes were rejected, they show a marked degree of influence from the French school of bastion fortifica-tion which was not to be seen in de Gomme's previous plans for Tilbury but had begun to be adopted at Portsmouth. The bastion flanks were now perpendicu-lar to the 'line of defence', that notional line from the angle made by the flank of one bastion with the curtain, and the salient angle formed by the meeting point of the two faces of an adjacent bastion. This change moved the weight of the defence away from the curtain and its ditch and achieved direct fire over the face of the

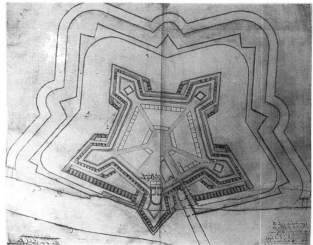

adjacent bastion, and therefore kept the besiegers that much further from the walls themselves. As at Ports-mouth, the use of the *fausse-braye*, so common in Dutch fortification for covering the moat with hori-zontal fire, was adapted to something very similar to a type of *tenaille* which was to be used by Vauban and later engineers. De Gomme referred to the feature as 'lower flancks or faucebray'. The Dutch had found *fausse-brayes* very useful when broad wet moats were present as it was difficult for the guns on the bastions and curtains to be depressed sufficiently to cover the moat once the covered-way had been taken. While de

Tilbury Fort: from the air. (English Heritage)

Gomme eliminated the *fausse-braye* in front of the curtain, he adapted it for additional firepower at the flanks of the bastions. De Gomme may have picked up these new ideas from professional colleagues but a written source likely to have been available at the time was the writings of Le Comte de Pagan. Pagan's main treatise was published in 1645 in France, but in 1666 *The Count of Pagan's method of delineating all manner of Fortification (regular and irregular) from the Exterior Poligone reduced to the English measure* was published in London. Pagan's main proposition was to bring powerful artillery fire from the flanks to defend the faces of the adjacent bastions (see illustration on p85). This was to be the chief element of the defence to which all else should be subordinated. His ideas had wide influence and Vauban derived his 'first system' from Pagan. In other respects de Gomme's 1668 plans show a much more restrained trace for the covered-way, with *places d'armes* in the re-entrant angles. An interesting feature in the 1668 proposals, which can be paralleled in some Dutch towns, is the provision of a small harbour within the fortifications approached from the river by a tunnel under the ramparts.

In 1670 de Gomme produced another plan for the new fort at Tilbury. This one seems to have been the basis for what was actually carried out. As in the previous proposals, the Henrician blockhouse was re-tained as the centrepiece, but the riverside batteries were simpler on account of the restricted space on the bank. The geometrical figure employed was an irregular pentagon, with one of the five bastions enclosing the blockhouse and projecting into the river, almost to low-water mark. The French fashion in flank defence was repeated but there was a return (though not carried out in practice) to a more conventional Dutch continuous *fausse-braye*, nevertheless with artillery embrasures only located below the bastion flanks. The land entrance from the road to the north required a covering ravelin in the wet moat opposite the Landport in the north curtain. The outer moat had declined in width since the earlier schemes to a very narrow ditch, compensated perhaps by provision for flooding the surrounding marshes. The cross sections on the drawing show the fort's ramparts as unrevetted.

Construction began in the first quarter of 1670. Although the 1670 plan may have been the basis, the actual fort showed a number of divergencies by the time of its completion in the 1680s. The most notable omission was the water bastion. It was begun, however, and the close-set piles and timber framing intended for its foundation can still be seen in the mud at low water. In 1676, a decision to include the water bastion in the contract was postponed, and whether because of the structural difficulties of building in a strongly tidal river or because of economy, it was not completed. The lack of the fifth bastion in such a vulnerable position led to a continuing weakness in the design. The *fausse-braye* was also omitted entirely. The covered-way, however, was given a stronger trace, with the north east and north west salients developed into a star trace instead of the original *tenaille*. The outer moat was also cut to a respectable width. Guarding both the landward approach and the extreme western end of the riverside batteries were two, two-storeyed machicolated redoubts, triangular in plan, with the upper floor constructed in timber and with turrets jutted out at the angles. Both resembled the redoubts proposed in the plan of 1665. The existence of the landward redoubt has been confirmed by recent excavation.[15] The bastions in the body of the place were large and the curtains short, only 230 feet (70 metres) at most. The flanks of the bastions were at least 85 feet (26 metres) long and the salient angles were of 69°. Like all the defence works of the day the building of Tilbury Fort took a prodigious time to complete, over fifteen years. It marks a simpler yet more solid statement of the way in which fortification had developed during the seventeenth century and remains a monument to the heyday of the bastion system of defence.

Military architecture: ideal gateway and guardhouse, from Elements of Fortification. (Author)

THE ORDNANCE OFFICE AND FORTRESS CONSTRUCTION

In many matters military the Restoration of 1660 was a point of re-ordering and radical change in an army structure which was both administratively undeveloped and, at the same time, frighteningly efficient on the battlefield and as a political force. A case in point was the Office of the Ordnance.[16] The Office owed its origin as the supplier and storekeeper of weapons and military materiel. As a builder of fortifications and with responsibility for the maintenance of all kinds of garrison buildings, the Office was a latecomer. It was not until 1635–6 that a connection between the Office and defence works can be traced. Then a Lieutenant-Colonel Francis Coningsby was nominated as Commissary-General of all His Majesty's castles in England and Wales. The staff commanded by the Master-General and the Principal officers were numerous and widespread. As well as the clerks and storekeepers, there were significant groups of specialists: fireworkers, bombadiers and petardiers besides the gunners and engineers. The duties of the Chief Engineer were set out at great length:

He ought to be well skilled in all the parts of the mathematicks, more particularly in Stereometry, Altimetry, and Gedosia . . . and to cut any part of

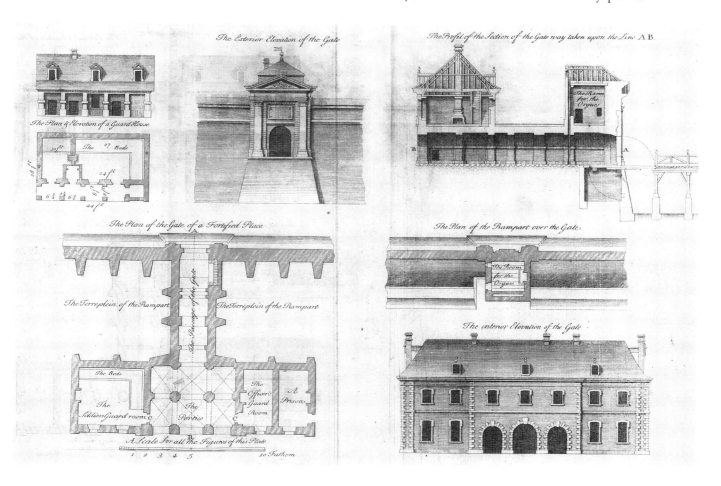

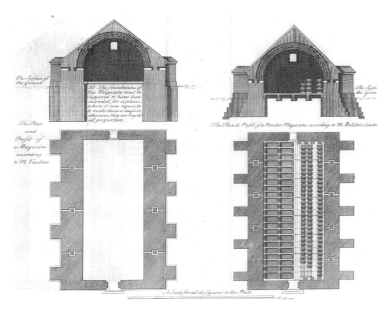

Military architecture: powder magazine, from Elements of Fortification. (Author)

Military engineer: pegging out the enceinte *from the engineer's plan, from* Les Travaux de Mars. (Author)

ground to a proportion given, to be well skilled in all manner of foundations, in the scantlings of all timber and stone and of their several natures, and to be perfect in Architecture, Civil and Military, and to have always by him the descriptions or models of all manner of Engines useful in Fortifications or Sieges, to draw and design the situation of any place in their due prospects upright and perspective, to know exactly the rates of all materials for building of fortifications, thereby to judge of any estimates proposed to him to examine. To keep perfect draughts of every the fortifications, forts and fortresses of our Kingdom, their situation, figure, and profile, and to know the importance of every one of them where their strength or weakness lies, whether the lines be drawn to a due length or the chief angles truly formed.[17]

He was to make plots or models of all manner of fortifications, to visit all the forts in the Kingdom as commanded, to supervise the construction of new works, to provide sufficiently capable engineers and to supervise the setting out and conduct of siege works in wartime. The instructions for the duties of the Inferior Engineers can be summed up as improving their knowledge in all things belonging to an engineer, and to carry out the instructions of their Chief Engineer, who ultimately had to report on the condition of the fortifications to the Master-General, who in turn presented them to the king.[18]

'All the later Stuart kings were greatly interested in the science of fortification and its practical implementation by the Ordnance Board.'[19] In this respect Charles II was much like Henry VIII, even to devising new details himself, and Clarendon noted that the king supervised the initial building works at Sheerness Fort. Both Charles and his brother, James, made frequent visits to the coastal defences.

An aspect of this re-ordered department of the Civil Service was that it produced a great deal of paper and this in turn has been a great boon to the later historian. An immense quantity of information relating to the building of Charles II's forts has come down to us, and much of it of a very detailed kind. It ranges from the engineer's sketches, his worked-up proposals, estimates and specifications, to the day-to-day instructions and drawings for the work force on site. There are the reports on progress and costings for the Ordnance Office and the Privy Council, dealings with contractors, large and small, with the direct labour force and with the presentation of regular accounts. It is possible to follow the whole course of the building operation, whose problems were little different from those of today. The accounts are a mine for those social historians wishing to compare the wage rates and costs of materials with those of other periods. In short, they provide a very clear picture of the life of a military engineer.

Tilbury Fort: gatehouse. (Author)

The work of Sir Bernard de Gomme provides good examples of the engineer's duties. A common situation for him was to be left high and dry without instructions. On 12 February 1677/8 de Gomme wrote:

> Sir, His Majestie having commanded me to repaire to Portsmouth to sett & steake out the new Intended Fortifications att Gosportt, which I have performed all what there is to be don, both in steaking and keilespitting the same, and devided the said workes into severall companyes according to his Majesties command, but the Governer here in Towne has not received any orders to breake ground, neither are there any Materialls here in store, nor money sent downe, soe yt I shall humbley desier to know his Majesties commands how to dispose of my sealfe, to stay here longer or to returne to London . . .[20]

When able to begin operations, the works at Tilbury, in particular, demonstrate the nature and variety of an engineer's task.[21] Construction began at Tilbury towards the end of 1670. Almost from the start, large numbers of workmen, presumably for digging the ditches and throwing up the rampart, were pressed into service. They came from all the neighbouring villages in Kent, as well as Essex, and from places as distant as Barking and Sittingbourne. Other labour, particularly skilled men, such as carpenters and watermen, was supplied by local contractors. The total number of men employed during 1671 varied from 158 to 265. They were supervised by five to seven 'officers' who acted as overseers and surveyors, a storekeeper, a tallyman, and a 'clerk of the cheque'. De Gomme himself supervised the works and was involved in much travel as he simultaneously supervised similar works at Plymouth, Portsmouth, Sheerness and the other defences in the Medway. In 1661, he was entitled to a salary of 13s 4d a day and a travelling allowance of 20s a day for riding charges. He was involved in much of the detail which a subordinate might have been expected to perform, dealing with petty contractors, paying out small bills, and signing many accounts. The actual work at Tilbury involved the removal of the ferry house westwards to the site now occupied by 'The World's End' public house, levelling the ramparts and filling the ditch of the old fort, cutting the two moats, throwing up the new ramparts, and raising the general level of the ground within to prevent flooding. The earth ramparts required to be revetted in brickwork, and this, together with all the buildings inside, had to have their foundations well piled. Piles were so essential to this marshy site that, when in 1672 de Gomme was asked to supply some of his stores to another construction site, he replied that to do so would entail a stoppage of the work at Tilbury; 2000–3000 piles were needed there immediately besides those in stock, and he had sent three ships to Norway for them.

By 1676, with so much work going on at all the other fortifications, progress at Tilbury declined. The buildings within were sufficient to house a considerable garrison, but the fort was far from being in a satisfactory state of defence. The ramparts were not much more than half-completed and for long stretches the pile and frame foundations for the revetment had not even been started. It was evident that too much was being attempted at too many places. A meeting of the Privy Council resulted in a decision that, wherever possible, greater use of contractors should be sought. Accordingly, an agreement for the completion of Tilbury Fort was made between the officers of the Ordnance and Sir William Pritchard, an alderman of the City of London, who had in 1672 and 1675 contracted to supply timber, laths, deals, tiles, bricks, lime and sand. De Gomme still maintained general supervision and drew up the contracts, but he seems to have been less concerned with the day-to-day management. By 1680, the fort was already armed; but in a survey of its condition de Gomme found much still to be done, and in the next year he prepared an estimate for over £14,500 for its completion. Another agreement was made with Sir William Pritchard for completing the brickwork and the two gates, also for the provision of such things as palisades and sentry boxes at the salients of the bastions. Agreements were made with small contractors, generally for carpentry and the carriage of earth and chalk, work mainly concerning the covered-way. In a survey of work completed in 1682, de Gomme notes, 'for ye front of ye Water Gate being wrought with Portland Stone carved with Trophies and other ornaments, 476-16-0'. Another £785 6s 2d was required to complete both the gates and by the following year work on the facades had virtually finished. The Water Gate, as its name implies, was the entrance from the river near the wharf and slip. It is the finest piece of architecture in the fort, an ornate frontispiece in an otherwise functional structure. It is more restrained than the other monumental gateway at Plymouth Citadel. There is no direct evidence in the accounts for it being of de Gomme's design, but he clearly superintended the details of its gradual construction by Sir William Pritchard without any other name being associated with it. There seems no cause to doubt the authorship and it would fall into place with the contemporary continental fashion for military engineers to complete their fortresses with such a piece of embellishment. It is probably impossible to assess the total cost of the work, which was spread, without a break, over more than thirteen years. It is certain that it far exceeded the £47,000 which de Gomme originally estimated. The building of the fort created a great impress-ion among contemporaries. Pepys and John Evelyn visited the works, the latter describing it as 'a Royal work indeede and such as will one day bridle a greate citty to the purpose before they are aware.'[22]

Despite royal enthusiasm and an improved bureaucracy, the late Stuart fortifications were an expensive and only partially completed enterprise. What emerges is that everyone involved with the building of permanent fortification hopelessly underestimated the cost and, more particularly, the time these works would take. The moment of national crisis which required the building of new defences, as happened so often, passed before the first stones had been laid. Those organising their construction failed to appreciate that, just like medieval cathedrals, large fortifications could take decades to complete. As a result, the building process was made the more expensive by a chronic shortage of money which meant that contractors could not be kept to their contracts for men and materials. Because the work was drawn out, and because much of the nature of the work involved earthwork, the earlier efforts deteriorated over time, and demanded repair or renewal before the other elements of the fort had been started. Other factors were changes of personnel: the latest engineer always finding fault with the work of his predecessor, and therefore changing the design and making 'improvements' at great expense, coupled with their prevailing optimism over estimates. As one surveyor wrote:

> it is more use to a prince to have an engineer that is knowing in the measures of a country and in the rate and values of works than in one that can vapour and talk of the forms and lines and be ignorant otherwise; for one may lay down more forts in an hour upon paper than all the Christian princes joined together shall make in ten years.[23]

SIR MARTIN BECKMAN

Sir Bernard de Gomme was involved with other projects besides Plymouth, Portsmouth, Tilbury and the Medway. There was also Harwich and, furthermore, he produced an elaborate scheme for the defence of Dublin which would have been prodigiously expensive and was not taken up. He was also concerned with the fortifications of Tangier. The dowry of Catherine of Braganza included Tangier, and thus England briefly acquired this North African foothold. In order to use the port as either a naval station or a commercial post for the Levant trade, a large garrison was needed to protect it from the Moors of Barbary. The English garrison had established a double ring of detached redoubts and batteries on the high ground above the town. Some later additions were made by de Gomme. He made periodic visits to Tangier to supervise the construction of his designs during the late 1660s and early 1670s. His efforts to make improvements, and of those responsible on site for carrying them out, achieved him no credit. The defences were considered so bad both in repair and plan that a commission appointed to inspect them in 1683 estimated that £4,798,561 16s 6d would have to be spent in order to make Tangier defensible.[24] There were other defensive programmes along the north east coast of England underway simultaneously, but these were the responsibility of Martin Beckman, the Second Engineer.

Sir Martin Beckman (he was knighted in 1685) was Swedish in origin. Captain Beckman, one of the number of foreigners on the Royalist side, was an older brother. He was described by Lord Digby as 'our incomparable engineer'.[25] Part of Captain Diderich Beckman's duties involved having a hand in the fortifications of Oxford, where he must have known de Gomme. After the Restoration, Martin also came to England and was employed at Tangier. He was recalled to England in 1670, and from then on he served as Second Engineer until 1685 when he succeeded de Gomme in the post of Chief Engineer which he held until 1702. From 1688 to 1702 he also held the office of Comptroller of Fireworks.

Beckman's main work was in the north east, at Tynemouth, Holy Island and Hull. His most significant work was Clifford's Fort at Tynemouth, and is the only surviving, but much altered, example of his contribution to England's coastal defence. It was essentially a central redoubt defended to landward by a bastioned trace associated with batteries on the banks of the Tyne. In 1681, Beckman described at length the deficiencies of the defences of Hull. He was commissioned to repair the Henrician blockhouses and castle and to strengthen them with a new fortification which he designed in the form of an *enceinte* of demi-bastions. By 1685, Major Beckman was reporting that Hull needed a citadel. Work on this was put in hand with Richard Wharton, one of the junior engineers, actually on site. By 1690, Beckman reported that the main ramparts were completed apart from a facing of brick.

His estimate of cost when finished was £74,425 0s 0d in 1699, but in about 1705, the citadel was still unfinished with no embrasures towards the Humber. The ravelin and counterscarp was staked out but nothing more done to them.

This is a familiar story. In fact Beckman possessed the failings of contemporary English engineers in their inability to complete work in good time, and to something close to the original estimates. Nor did he have the flair for design whch was de Gomme's great strength. Whether or not de Gomme's fortresses were of the top quality, he had the breadth of mind to put his personal stamp on English late seventeenth century fortification. Beckman seems to have had an eye towards improving the work of others. After de Gomme's death he added a redan to the landward approaches to Tilbury Fort, and remodelled the covered-way at the south east corner of the Portsmouth defences, eliminating de Gomme's hornwork. His work on Holy Island was that of improving the recently built batteries. Beckman was, of course, especially scathing about the qualities of his senior. In 1699, he estimated that the repair of the existing fortifications at Portsmouth would cost at least £150,000,

the foundation of the whole works not being laid deep enough by 10 foot so that instead of 12 foot [of] water there is not at present in most places above 2 foot and to make the moat deeper without the foundation be made lower is directly to undermine and demolish the whole fortification.[26]

Beckman and de Gomme were the last of the Civil War generation of military engineers. They had developed their skill and professionalism over the Restoration period, and, within the limits of the system for building forts, they produced works which to a considerable extent still exist today. Between them, they saw out the seventeenth century and what was to be the high summer of bastion fortification.

CHAPTER 6

Scottish and Irish Insurgency

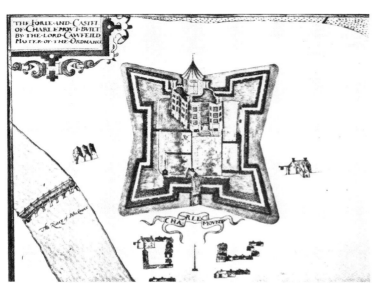

Charlemont, Co Armagh: view in 1624. (BL)

As Scotland and Ireland came more and more under the political and military influence of England from the late sixteenth century onwards, so did the nature of the fortifications constructed in those countries change. The castles and defensible towers of wealthy land-owners, as well as those of leading magnates, which owed their being to medieval conditions, ceased to be either effective defensively or politically necessary. Centralised power was now more pervasive and effi-cient, and military threat became external or a matter of internal revolt on a large scale, rather than that of local banditry. Scotland's kings, despite serious problems with their vassals, had struggled, generally successfully, to maintain their independence from England until the Union of the Crowns in 1603 in the form of James VI and I. Even the civil war which followed the abdication of Mary Queen of Scots and the proclamation of James VI was finally determined by the capture of Edinburgh Castle by English guns in 1573. The repair of the damage resulting from the siege was the construction of the Half-Moon Battery enclosing the damaged David's Tower. Many of the castles and later artillery defences

had half an eye on the likelihood of incursions from the south as much as a response to internal politics and insurrection. The Union of 1603 was the beginning of still closer integration, if not to say eventual dominion from London. Future defensive priorities therefore shifted elsewhere, away from the Border, and were largely dictated by English need. These often enough, in the seventeenth and eighteenth centuries, meant holding down parts of Scotland by force against inter-nal rebellion and the possibility of French intervention. The English civil wars served as a catalyst for a military control of Scotland more effective than before.

In the case of Ireland, the unremitting col-onisation of the country by the medieval English baronage had produced few 'national' fortifications. Apart from some walled towns, defensive provisions were virtually personal and local until the end of the sixteenth century. They reflected a chronic state of domestic turbulence. 'Every petty gentleman lives in a stone tower, where he gathers into his service all the rascals of the neighbourhood (and of these towers there is an infinite number)' is how a Spanish agent reported on social conditions to Philip II in 1579.[1] From the decisive defeat of O'Neill's rebellion at the turn of the seventeenth century, and the increased plantation of parts of Ireland (first begun under Mary Tudor by Scots and English thereafter), the pattern of fortifica-tion changed. The defence of castles and houses was enhanced by the need to defend the new plantations. Settlers from Scotland brought with them a distinctive style of defensive building. Here the still imperfectly understood precepts of bastioned fortification came to rule, especially in Ulster. Often the individual settle-ments consisted of a strong house and fortified bawn. That of Charlemont, built in 1622–4, was one of the most accomplished. The house was a purely domestic building in contemporary English style, of three storeys with large windows on each floor. There was nothing military about it except for decorative battle-mented parapets, but it stood within a square earth-work enclosure with regular bastions at each angle and a palisade on the counterscarp of the ditch. By contrast, some of the strong houses and bawns of various London City companies of the same time could be a simple rectangular loopholed walled enclosure, with the house occupying one side, the bawn the remainder and two round tower flankers at alternate angles. Elsewhere, during the first fifteen years or so of the century the established towns such as Londonderry, Belfast, Carrickfergus, Coleraine and others acquired bastioned defences of some competence. An angle bastion replaced a corner tower of Limerick Castle in 1611.

The dangers of a combination of an Irish revolt with an invasion force from a foreign power was demonstrated in 1580 at Smerwick Bay, and more substantially in 1601 by the Spanish landing at Kinsale. Castle Park (James) Fort was the result of the latter with other new works constructed elsewhere. The need for better coastal defences was obvious, and there was renewed fear of a Spanish landing in 1625 when more work was put in hand. A citadel, also called St Patrick's Fort, was designed by the engineer, Nicholas Pynnar, and added to the defences of Waterford. Elizabeth Fort, Cork was rebuilt, and another fort was built on Haulbowline Island in Cork Harbour. Pynnar, also in 1625, prepared the plan for the West Citadel at Galway.

Such were the preparations of the occupying English forces. Among the native Irish there was growing awareness of continental military matters during the early decades of the seventeenth century, following the failure of the O'Neill rebellion of 1601 and the disaster to their cause at Kinsale. This awareness came in a practical form as a result of Catholic Irish soldiers returning with front-line experience of the Thirty Years War. Many of the leading commanders of the rising of 1641 and the Confederate Wars had had this experience. In 1642, Owen Roe O'Neill, a veteran from the Spanish service, landed in Ulster bringing with him other Irishmen from the Continental wars. Many would have acquired knowledge of military engineering. One such was Captain Gerat Barry whose *Discourse of Military Discipline* was published at Brussels in 1634, and is thought to be the first military manual to come from an Irish author. It includes a well illustrated discussion on fortification.

CROMWELL IN IRELAND AND SCOTLAND

The Irish rebellion of 1641 led to the investment of many fortified places, the construction of many more, and a massacre of English settlers. Despite this, during the English civil war the various factions in Ireland were brought together into an alliance in favour of the Royalist cause. The presence of Irish Catholics in Charles's army was the greatest iniquity in Parliament's eyes. The Parliamentarian port of Duncannon was besieged and captured in 1645. By 1649 the Earl of Ormonde had further advanced the Royalist position,

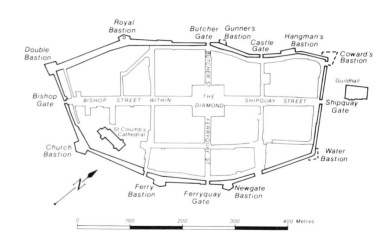

Londonderry city walls. (DOE, Northern Ireland)

besieging Dublin, Derry and Dundalk. There was therefore a political and military situation which demanded a response from the English parliament. Cromwell was instructed to lead the New Model Army on the first of its operations outside England which was to crush the Irish rebellion with the ruthless storming of Drogheda, Wexford and Clonmel and whose ferocity has had a lasting effect on Irish folk memory. It was characteristic of the generals of the New Model that they preferred to storm fortified towns whenever there was the least chance of success rather than adopt the conventional but gradual system of circumvallation and approach trenches. The siege of Limerick was the exception to prove the rule in that General Ireton built a number of detached forts linked by a line of entrenchments and succeeded by a combination of battery and blockade. Again, the collaboration of navy and field army that had been developed in the English civil wars was an important factor in the New Model's success, as well as good organisation and an effective siege train. Although Cromwell returned to England soon after his initial success, a war of sieges and forays lasted until the surrender of Galway in 1652. The Irish factions were then so divided there was no field army to oppose the English forces. Nevertheless, town walls were repaired, citadels added at Galway, Limerick and Clonmel, as well as some coastal defences of small size. It was, however, a period of considerable consolidation. The policy of plantation, often as a reward to the English soldiers, together with transplantation of the native Irish and the establishment of garrisons in many small forts and castles spread across the country at strategic points, such as crossings of the river Shannon, were sufficient to establish the Cromwellian settlement. The isolated forts were generally built to a similar plan, usually rectangular or square (140–250 feet, 43–45 metres), with a bastion at each angle, such as that at the Green Fort, Sligo, or Fort Cromwell at Bellahy. The

Oliver's Fort, Inverness, citadel founded by Major-General Deane in 1652. (From Stewart Cruden, *The Scottish Castle*)

Ayr citadel. (From Quentin Hughes *Military Architecture*)

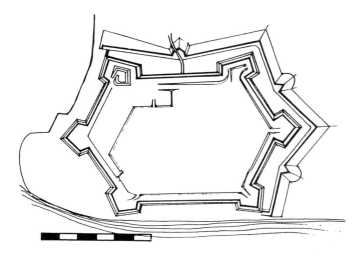

length of the curtain from bastion to bastion flank varied from 75 to 100 feet (23–30 metres).[2]

In Scotland in the meanwhile, six days after the execution of Charles I, the Scottish Estates proclaimed his son, King of Great Britain, France and Ireland. This maintenance of monarchical legality had serious political consequences for the English Commonwealth. In 1650–1, Cromwell next had to deal with Charles II's attempt to use the Scots to re-establish the monarchy during what became the Second Civil War. One Scots army was defeated at Dunbar, another was

lured deep into England and crushed at Worcester. As an aftermath of Dunbar, Cromwell and General Monck, a former Royalist officer and now Lieutenant-General of Ordnance, rapidly reduced the traditional Scottish fortresses of Edinburgh Castle, Dirleton, Borthwick, Tantallon and Stirling using mortars and heavy cannon supplied by the navy. Later, in 1654, Monck, now commanding the Commonwealth forces in Scotland set about planting garrisons and forts across the country linked with a system of mobile columns. Scotland, like Ireland, was now controlled by England but, unlike Ireland, it still posed a potential military threat.

The forts used to pacify Scotland mark an important technical stage in engineering development in Britain.[3] They represented for the first time a co-ordinated programme of fortress building against an internal rather than an external threat. Unlike the forts of the civil wars, which were in the main temporary field works, these were forts of conquest. The five most important Cromwellian fortresses at Ayr, Leith, Perth, Inverlochy and Inverness were permanent works designed by expert military engineers. Elsewhere there were also twenty smaller forts, supplemented by a police system.

The form and function of the five major works was entirely alien to Scotland, and in some respects to England too, in that they were bases for a military government and not coastal defences. None is now complete since they were mostly swept away at the Restoration, but traces of the citadel at Ayr and a little of Leith can be seen. Fortunately, there are a number of contemporary plans and further drawings made by government draughtsmen after the Jacobite Risings of 1715 and 1745. The preliminary fort at Inverlochy, later known as Fort William, was of turf and wattles. Its replacement was dominated by a defensible barracks surrounded by a stone enclosure with one full bastion covering the landward side and demi-bastions at the other four angles of the irregular *enceinte*. The site has been almost entirely destroyed by railway yards and sheds.

Monck's strategy involved another fort at the opposite end of the Great Glen. This was the citadel of Inverness, known as 'Oliver's Fort' and founded by Major-General Deane in 1652. The fort was intended for a garrison of about 1000 men. In plan it was a large regular pentagon on the east bank of the river Ness. Internally the fort was most spacious with broad streets, avenues and parade grounds, an element of internal planning which had not been seen before in Britain. The fort, however, did not last ten years, being slighted in 1661 by Act of Parliament upon the Stuart Restoration. The three forts in the south were of comparable scale. Ayr was designed in 1652 by the chief engineer of the New Model Army, Hans Ewald Tessin, and was a most accomplished work. It was a symmetrical elongated hexagon with a bastion at each angle, an outer ditch, counterscarp with covered-way and a long glacis. The fort, like Inverness, was large enough to have a spacious 'market-place' in the centre with three ranges of buildings on each side of it. The surviving bastion near the harbour has at its salient angle a sentry box corbelled out from it somewhat dramatically and in good continental style. The fort at Perth was a simple square also regularly bastioned. Leith was held to be 'one of the best fortifications that ever we beheld, passing fair and sumptuous' and perhaps the greatest of the five, replacing an earlier and unsatisfactory fortification on the same site.[4] It was designed to be easily accessible from the sea. The Scottish Cromwellian forts were on an entirely different scale from the English southern coastal forts and had clear social functions implied by their internal planning. Their design reflects the Low Countries origin of the Commonwealth's engineers in the matter of their detail, but in their overall concept of planned settlement they perhaps owe something to renaissance ideas of urban planning.

CHARLES FORT

The Restoration of Charles II did little to alter military circumstances in Ireland. In 1666, a list of master gunners on the establishment pointed to the main fortifications existing at Dublin, Duncannon, Athlone, Galway, Sligo, Isle of Aran, Inishboffin, Waterford, Limerick, Cork, Haulbowline, Youghal, Kinsale, Crookhaven, Inisherkin, Valentia, Londonderry, Culmore and Carrickfergus.[5] Indeed the recognition that Ireland's geographical position could represent a source of danger for England led to continuing attention to coastal defence. During the first Dutch War of Charles II, when the French were allied to the Dutch, the idea had been floated by Irish Catholics that Ireland might become a dependency of France should the fortunes of war go against England. There were nevertheless the customary complaints of neglect of the defences there were. The Earl of Orrery complained in 1666 that the south western forts of Valentia, Bantry, Sherkin Island, Crookhaven and Kinsale were in a poor condition. Then, with the successful Dutch raid on the Medway the next year, there followed a flurry of activity, and earthworks were thrown up at Ringcurran, Kinsale, opposite the existing fort of Castle Park. A two-tier battery was created to cross fire with the guns at Castle Park thereby commanding the harbour entrance. The new fieldworks were enclosed by a *tenaille* trace on the site later to be occupied by Charles Fort. There were also proposals to enclose Dublin with earthworks, and build other defences in Dublin Bay. These ideas may have eventually led to the instruction to Sir Bernard de Gomme in 1673 to produce a design for an elaborate citadel at Ringsend, Dublin. It was a scheme which came to nothing despite some nervous-

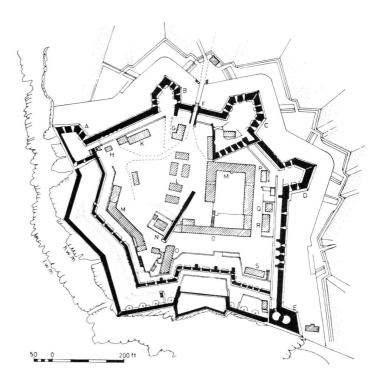

Charles Fort, Kinsale (as in 1870 with later barrack buildings):
A   Devil's bastion
B   North bastion
C   Flagstaff battery
D   East bastion
E   Charles bastion
F   Gateway
G   Guard room
H   Engine house
K   Barrack stores
L   Wooden huts
M   Soldiers' quarters
N   Magazine
O   Officers' quarters
P   Cook house
Q   Royal Engineers' stores
R   Hospital
S   Officers' quarters and master gunners' quarters
T   Gun shed.
(Paul Kerrigan)

ness about coastal threats which had led to the improvements at Ringcurran in 1672.

In 1678, work began on converting the earthworks of Ringcurran into a permanent fortress. It is not clear what spurred this decision, which seems to have been made in Dublin. On this occasion, neither Sir Bernard de Gomme nor anyone else from the Ordnance Office was given the job. Instead, William Robinson, 'engineer and surveyor general of all fortifications, buildings etc, in Ireland', was put in charge. He was to be assisted by Captain James Archer, which was just as well because, although Robinson was to acquire a justly deserved reputation as an architect, his strength was not in military engineering. Archer was responsible in fact, with the Earl of Orrery looking over his shoulder.

Charles Fort, from the air in 1966. (Cambridge University Collection)

Charles Fort, as Ringcurran later came to be known, is well documented and survives well nigh complete. It is also the outstanding example of seventeenth century fortification in Ireland.[6]

The principal element of the fort was the original two-tiered sea battery, which was now fossilised in stone. The preliminary plan, probably conceived by Robinson, was a conventional bastioned pentagonal trace. It was a drawing office plan, which had little regard to the nature of the site, and was not adopted. An interesting feature on this drawing was the appearance of a small harbour in a narrow re-entrant between the two waterside bastions, which could have been a feature in the original works, very reminiscent of one of de Gomme's early designs for an internal harbour at Tilbury Fort. Today, along the seaward face is what appears to be a walled-off large cavity extending under the fort and which may be such a harbour.

Behind the sea battery and facing landward, was an irregular figure which was intended by Orrery to be no more than a crownwork for a large pentagonal fort occupying higher ground to the rear. In the event, the pentagonal fort was not built, and the 'crownwork' was completed with a bastioned trace to landward, suffering the drawback of being commanded by higher ground. The curious internal triangular projection at the gorge, which might be interpreted as a small citadel is more likely to have been the salient of an unfinished ravelin at the gorge of the intended crownwork. Certainly, the three bastions now applied to see landward face look like afterthoughts, of different sizes and unusually small for the period. Only the *tenaille* trace of the covered-way looks conventional.

In 1683 money was being applied to finishing the work, but in 1685 Thomas Phillips, then Third Engineer to the Ordnance Office visited Ireland to carry out an inspection of the chief harbours, forts and fortifications. At Kinsale he found the earthworks of Castle Park Fort 'ruined and decayed' and recommended their revetment in brick or stone. As for Charles Fort

> . . . I must needs say, is well built as to materials, and workmanship; but as to the strength to landward or its terror to sea I can say nothing. For it being so very ill situated under the command of hills, that is a very hard matter to cover the inhabitants thereof, on any occasions that they shall have to stand by the guns, or the sea batteries . . .[7]

Phillips proposed making good the landward deficiencies by a much larger front of two bastions with a hornwork, extending the defences to an area almost as large again as the fort itself. His advice was not acted upon. Despite its monumental impressiveness today, Charles Fort was both a botched job and an anachronism. The design clearly suffered from lack of single direction and over ambition.

Phillips's report detailed the state of the defences elsewhere in Ireland, and most usefully was supported by many maps and plans, particularly of seaports and harbours. He proposed that Dublin should have a citadel on higher ground than that suggested by de Gomme. As with Charles Fort, he was critical of Duncannon Fort because it was overlooked by higher ground. He commented that many of the inland garrison centres had lost their strategic importance since the Cromwellian settlement. He recommended instead that the six principal towns should be strengthened and fortified so that each was strong enough to resist a considerable army. As so often happened, such advice fell on deaf ears.

The 'Glorious Revolution' of 1688 which was bloodless as far as England was concerned, was in fact fought out in Ireland over the course of three years between the largely professional armies of James II and William of Orange. It involved many inland towns with investment and capture. The larger towns had residual medieval walls which required improvement in terms of artillery, such as Limerick and Galway. Newer towns such as Londonderry were already provided with artillery fortifications. On the line of the Shannon, James's French engineers improved the defences of major crossing points such as Athlone and Limerick. Some of these earthen fieldworks of the Williamite war still survive, such as those at Enniskillen.

The deficiencies of Charles Fort, identified by Phillips, were confirmed in action. The Williamite army under John Churchill (later Duke of Marlborough), and the Duke of Wurtemburg, attacked the fort in 1690. Batteries were placed on the high ground to the north. Castle Park Fort was attacked and taken, and simultaneously siege trenches were opened before Charles Fort. The weight of the attack was concentrated on the central bastion, and the adjoining curtain was breached; at which point the garrison sued for terms.

After the treaty of Limerick in 1691 the Irish spirit of resistance was temporarily crushed. Major fortifications were not needed. The settlement of the country was enforced with 'redoubts', or small defensible barracks, together with more substantial barracks sited in the larger towns. As well as the needs of internal security, it was very convenient for the English government to have an army establishment in Ireland. Not only was this army paid for by the Irish exchequer but it also avoided maintaining a standing army in England with all the political difficulties that came with it. The 'Irish' army provided a large and flexible pool of regiments, both horse and foot.

THE JACOBITE RISINGS OF 1715 AND 1745

The landing of William of Orange at Brixham in 1688 demonstrated that it was possible to mount a successful invasion of England without total command of the Channel. There were, however, special circumstances.

Lord Dartmouth, as Admiral of the Fleet, had stationed his defending fleet off the Thames Estuary rather than in the Downs, whether out of treachery or incompetence, leaving the Channel and the south coast open and vulnerable. Although Dartmough got as far as Spithead in pursuit, the political balance swung against James II, and Dartmouth switched to the winning side. The next year, France was able to land an army in Ireland unopposed in support of James II, and in 1690, Admiral Tourville defeated the combined English and Dutch fleet off Beachy Head, creating a wave of panic in London. With the Channel in French hands an invasion seemed certain, but all that was attempted on this occasion was a destructive raid on Teignmouth. Nevertheless, it did stimulate a more serious invasion attempt in 1692 which was only forestalled by the allied sea victory of La Hogue. However, 1692 was the military turning point for the 'Glorious Revolution', and for the next fifty years England was not to be seriously threatened with invasion.

Although the 1688 revolution did not have the same consequences for William III in Scotland as occurred in Ireland, his authority in the Highlands had to be reinforced by military activity. The Cromwellian citadels had been slighted twenty-eight years before, so that the fort of Inverlochy at the southern end of the Great Glen had to be rebuilt by General Mackay, who called it Fort William after the king. The fort at the northern end at Inverness remained in ruins, and instead Mackay strengthened the old castle beside the bridge over the river Ness. The death of Queen Anne in 1714, produced further political upheaval with a strong Jacobite movement for the maintenance of the Stuart line, as opposed to the Hanoverian succession to the Union of the two crowns of Scotland and England. The most serious military threat to George I came in Scotland. In 1715, without any foreign military support, the Highland Jacobites under the Earl of Mar rose, but were dealt with at Sheriffmuir by the pro-Hanoverian forces under the Duke of Argyll, securely based on Stirling Castle. The Lowland and Northumbrian Jacobites moved south into England and eventually surrendered at Preston. The 1719 attempt might have been more serious when Spanish troops did land in Scotland, but this was a diversionary force to assist an attack on south west England which foundered in heavy seas off Finisterre and was not exploited by the Jacobites.

The aftermath of the '15' was an enhanced garrison policy for disarming and controlling the Highlands. This repeated the Cromwellian military strategy based on Inverness and Fort William at either end of the Great Glen. These forts were supplemented by the building of four infantry barracks, a policy which had been considered earlier, in 1699, when a report of a parliamentary committee recommended 'that a garrison be established at Ruthven of Badenoch consisting at least of thirty Sentinels with a Captain and Sub-

▲ *Ruthven Barracks.* (HBM)   ▼ *Corgarff tower-house and barracks.* (HBM)

Stirling Castle, remodelled by Captain John Romer after 1715. (HBM)

alterns, two Sergeants, two Corporals and a Drum.'[8] Other posts were to be established at Ardclach and at Invermoriston. They were not carried through immediately, but the proposal was revived in respect of Ruthven in 1719.

The four defensible barracks built as part of the 1717 scheme were at Bernera and Kiliwhimin in Inverness-shire, Inversnaid, Stirlingshire, as well as at Ruthven. The largest of them was at the south end of Loch Ness, Kiliwhimin, near the site where Fort Augustus was later built. Otherwise the defensible barracks share common design features.[9]

The smallest and best preserved is that at Ruthven. It is set on a substantial mound on which had been an earlier castle. The barracks consisted of two large three-storey blocks occupying two sides of a square, loopholed and high walled enclosure. Each barrack block contained two rooms on each floor with a central staircase. At two diagonally opposite corners were projecting bastion-towers providing all-round flanking cover but, again, for nothing more substantial than musketry. It was proposed to add towers on the other two corners but there were insufficient funds. At Kiliwhimin, the barracks were larger, of double tenement size with six rooms on each floor and two staircases. Likewise, only two of the corner bastion-towers could be afforded. At Inversnaid, Bernera and Kiliwhimin, the rectangular masonry enclosures were further surrounded by a regular star-shaped covered-way, which were probably added in 1749. The old tower-houses of Braemar and Corgarff were also surrounded

by star-shaped and loopholed curtain walls.

Despite these measures, lawlessness and Jacobite disaffection continued. In 1724, General Wade was instructed to report on the condition of the Highlands and suggest remedies. As a result, a new fort was built at Inverness Castle; this first Fort George was designed by the engineer John Romer, who was on the strength of the Board of Ordnance and accompanied Wade on his mission. Romer also designed a new fort in the middle of the Great Glen, Fort Augustus, which succeeded the short-lived barracks of Kiliwhimin. Fort Augustus was to serve as the focal point for all the Highland garrisons. It was designed as a fortified residence and and administrative centre, as much a seat of civil power as a military barracks or even a fully fledged fortress. The plan gives all the appearances of a fort: four-square with prominent and large bastions at each angle, but each curtain was dominated by splendidly architectural ranges, three storeys high with attics. The defensive capabilities only came from the bastions, and even then they were limited. Each bastion contained just two embrasures in each face and one in the flank, and internally had a circular building with pitched roof rising above the parapet; one contained the well, another the necessary house, another the magazine! Clearly, this show of defensive strength did not envisage an attack by trained soldiers armed with a siege train. The inscription on a surviving plan describes Fort Augustus as a 'modern fortification' begun in 1729 and finished in 1742.[10] In practice it was a 'toy fort' whose defence, when put to the test, only lasted two days, after a shell fired from Kiliwhimin half a mile away scored a direct hit and detonated the exposed powder magazine. Romer's other fort at Inverness also had a

Edinburgh Castle with the Half-Moon Battery built in 1574 in the foreground. (HBM)

superficial warlike appearance and contained barrack blocks of the Fort Augustus style. Elsewhere, established castles like Edinburgh, Dumbarton and Stirling were reformed in an up-to-date military manner.

Of lasting significance were Wade's military roads into the southern edge of the Highlands from Crieff and Dunkeld. These were part of the overall strategy providing links with the forts in the Great Glen. In 1727, Wade recommended that a military way should be constructed between Loch Ness and Ruthven-in-Badenoch, and also

> That a stable for 30 horses be erected at the Barrack of Ruthven which, being over the middle of the Highlands and on the road proposed in the preceding article, I conceive to be a proper station for a party of dragoons to serve as a convoy for money or provisions for the use of the Forces as well as to retain that part of the country in obedience.[11]

The ruins of the stables are still there. They were built by 1734 and are described as 'Erected and built in a workmanlike and substantial manner . . . within the compris of the Barracks of Ruthven where three of the roads lately made through the said Highlands do meet.'[12]

These military works had only a value as police posts. When a substantial military crisis occurred such as the Jacobite rising of 1745, they contributed nothing. They were ignored in the first stages of the rising. Later, in 1746, Prince Charles Edward's commanders decide to reduce the forts in order to allow greater freedom of movement during the prolonged Highland campaign which was contemplated after the Jacobite withdrawal from the expedition into England. At Inverness, a mine was begun under cover of the nearby houses in the town, and a battery of the few guns the Jacobites did possess was mounted commanding the interior of the fort. Defence was judged impossible, and the fort was surrendered only to be blown up by the Highlanders. Fort Augustus, as we have seen, fared little better. Fort William put up a more creditable defence, and was the only fort not to be taken before the final annihilation of Charles Edward's cause at Culloden.

FORT GEORGE

The ruthless pacification of the Highlands, and near destruction of clan life which followed Culloden demanded the maintenance of a large military presence. The ruins of the two northern forts presented a humiliating and cautionary spectacle. The shattered pieces of garrison control had to be picked up, and care taken that such disasters did not happen again. The Duke of Cumberland urgently asked that Fort Augustus and Fort George at Inverness should be replaced by new works. Plans were drawn up for a replacement for Fort Augustus but they were not executed. Instead, Wade's fort was rebuilt with minor improvements. A new plan was presented for Fort George but claims for compensation from the Burgh Council of Inverness for loss of use of a recently developed harbour led to the search for another site.[13] Elsewhere, the construction of the outworks about the barracks of Inversnaid and Bernera probably belong to 1749. Corgarff and Braemar tower-houses were also remodelled as small barracks. At Corgarff, single-storey wings were added to each end of the tower, and the whole was enclosed by an angular curtain wall, well loopholed for musketry. Corgarff, by Cock Bridge at the foot of the Lecht Road, commanded the crossings of the Dee, Avon and the Don, and was a site of considerable strategic importance. It was proposed that it should be given up as a military post in 1802, but it was re-garrisoned between 1827 and 1831 by a captain, a subaltern and fifty-six troops as a deterrent to smuggling in Strathdon. At about the same time, there was a detachment of the 74th Foot accommodated for the same reason at the similarly fortified Braemar. The system of military roads was also greatly enlarged after Culloden. By 1767 there were over a thousand miles of them. A memorial of their construction remains at the Well of the Lecht, south of Tomintoul, beside the military road from Blairgowrie to Fort George. Dated 1754 it reads: 'Five companies the 33rd Regiment Right Honle Lord Chas Hay Colonel made the road from here to the Spey'.

The seal was set to the chances of future Highland troubles by the second Fort George on the promontory of Ardesier, nine miles east of Inverness, and only a few miles from the battlefield of Culloden itself. Here is the finest example of eighteenth century military engineering in the British Isles, and in its state of preservation, virtually unaltered since its completion even though it has remained in use as a barracks ever since. It is one of the outstanding artillery fortifications of Europe.

Fort George from the air: the ravelin and covered-way of the land front is particularly prominent. (HBM)

The new Fort George was designed by William Skinner, the newly appointed engineer for North Britain.[14] Given the limitations of the narrow peninsula of Ardesier, it is a bastioned fort of regular construction. The landward defences were concentrated on one front towards the east, consisting of two bastions, a ravelin before the main gate in the middle of the curtain, covered-way and glacis. The two long sides of the fort were each flanked by a large flat bastion in the centre of the curtains, and a powerful sea battery occupied the tip of the promontory. Small ravelin-like places of arms covered the sallyport on each of the long sides.

Comparison must be made between the regular bastioned land front of Fort George and the *enceinte* of Tilbury Fort, seventy-five years or so earlier. Between the two can be seen the changes that had affected military engineering in that time, and especially the influence of the ideas of the innovatory French engineer, Cormontaigne.[15] There is no difference between the two forts in terms of flanking angle within the bastions; the contrast chiefly lies in scale. The bastions, and in particular, the ravelin, of Fort George are considerably larger and more elongated than those at Tilbury. The faces of the bastions are almost half as long again, though the length of the flanks, 125 feet (38 metres) to 95 feet (29 metres) is not so marked. The

salient angles differ to the extent of 10° (60° to 70°), and the internal width of the gorge is a little shorter at Fort George. The bastions of Fort George are solid, unlike Tilbury, giving more room for working the guns and allowing greater scope for retrenchment under siege conditions. The ravelin is overwhelmingly larger than at Tilbury (it is in fact larger than the individual bastions at Fort George!) and emphasises the contrast between the two forts. The faces of the ravelins differ from 320 feet (97 metres) to 180 feet (55 metres) and the width of gorge is between 200 feet (61 metres) and 120 feet (36 metres). Indeed, it is in the design of the outworks of Fort George which point to the greatest changes in engineering practice. This is borne out especially in the differing treatments of the covered-way. Where the trace of the covered-way at Tilbury is fussy, with many changes of angle, extremely short flanks and with little attention to enfilade, Fort George is simple and over 38 feet (12 metres) wide, with just the two re-entering angles on the long sides, extruded to form places of arms, within which are lunettes to resist penetration of the covered-way. The covered-way itself is provided with stone revetted earthen traverses which act as a check to the attackers enfilading the covered-way with gunfire for the whole of its length. In the salient angles there are crochets in the glacis which allowed access round the end of the traverses. These features were very much in keeping with the now more

Fort George: covered-way and bridge into the ravelin. (Author)

Fort George: reconstructed soldiers' barrack room. (Author)

active nature of defence, which encouraged sorties from the fortress on the besiegers and required the means of movement in and out of the defences. The glacis was more carefully formed to shield the masonry scarps of the fort rampart, and the ditch, while usually dry, could be flooded by means of sluices and the water retained by *batardeaux* closing each end of the ditch. De Gomme's Tilbury was essentially a fortress and river battery with little attention to the needs of a large

garrison. Skinner's fort was also intended to be a major barracks, designed to hold two infantry battalions (1600 men), and an artillery unit besides, all housed in symmetrically planned barracks. There were additionally casemated barracks below the north east and south east curtains, which were proof against mortar bombs and were available in times of siege.

Fort George is remarkable, since despite its continued use as a military establishment, it has remained in all essentials, unaltered. The embrasures of the bastions remain. At the salients of the bastions of the main front the *terre-plein* is raised for long range guns firing *en barbette* over the parapets. Two of the stone platforms for mortars are still intact. The surviving details of the outworks are particularly impressive, and some of the features are worth describing since they provide the most complete range to be seen in Britain. The ravelin, which was among the first elements of the fort to be built, was used as a self-defensible redoubt while the main works were building. It had its own guardhouse and a gate leading by a tunnel to the outer defences. The ditch counterscarp was revetted in masonry with flights of steps at its angles providing access from the ditches to the covered-way and also the ravelin. Lifting bridges connected the covered-way with the ravelin, and thence with the body of the place. The covered-way itself had a brick parapet, and between it and the earth firing step there was a slot for a continuous wooden palisade. Equally,

Fort George: drawbridge and main gate. (Author)

the lunettes in the places of arms had their own fighting platform and firing-step, and so had the traverses, also with provision for a palisade. The covered-way, it should be noted, was not equipped for artillery, unlike that at Tilbury, and was solely for infantry defence and offence. The simplification, and yet more effective use, of the outworks in the eighteenth century was also matched by greater provision for defensive mobility. As well as good internal access, Skinner provided opportunities for the defenders to counter-attack, not only from the sallyports in the north and south cur-

tains, already mentioned, leading to the detached places of arms and from there to the shore, but also in the main front by means of two cuttings in the glacis leading from the eastern places of arms.

Fort George remains the most accomplished of British eighteenth century artillery fortification, and besides is the best preserved and least altered of any major fortress in Britain of any date. Fortunately it is both a living garrison fort and a monument accessible to the public.

CHAPTER 7

Eighteenth Century Coastal Defence

CONFLICT WITH LOUIS XIV

Although James II endeavoured to regain power after the Revolution of 1688 with military campaigns in Ireland and political pressure in Scotland gauged to incite and draw on internal disaffections with the Dutch king, England was more at risk from attack by Louis XIV of France. The accession of William of Orange compelled a decisive change in foreign policy. England became ranged among the opponents of France in alliance with the Dutch and other northern European powers. It was a foreign policy which with varying intensity was to last for much of the next two hundred years. The years immediately following the 'Glorious Revolution' included two European wars: the War of the Grand Alliance (1689–97) and the War of the Spanish Succession (1702–13). The campaigns and great victories of the Duke of Marlborough in Germany and the Low Countries, and the inglorious English participation in Spain during the course of the latter war, concentrated attention on the continent of Europe. Domestic military considerations were still important, especially in the early years of William's reign. It was not until the British navy's great victory over the French at La Hogue in 1692 that the risk of invasion was greatly reduced.

The defensive measures inaugurated under Charles II were continued at Portsmouth, Plymouth and Tilbury Fort. But these were only the two principal naval bases and the main outpost in the defence of London. There were many batteries or minor forts scattered along the coasts, mostly erected by townsfolk anxious to protect their harbours and trade. An example of this initiative is that of the town of Newhaven in Sussex which had asked for carriages and munitions in 1702 for their fort at Seaford which commanded the bay as 'a security to them against the insults of the enemy and a refuge for ships and vessels forced in by them or the weather'.[1] Such defences were mostly ignored by the Ordnance Office, except perhaps in time of war, when the Office was petitioned for money for repairs, guns and ammunition. Exceptions could be

made if the place was 'open to the sea over against the French coast'.[2] There were, however, long stretches of coastline, even in counties like Kent, without any protection. This was particularly true along the east coast. There was no major fortification between Landguard Fort at the mouth of the Orwell and Hull, or between Hull and Tynemouth, although there were minor works at Great Yarmouth, Bridlington and Scarborough. On the western coasts of England and Wales there was virtually nothing, though Beckman surveyed Milford Haven and made estimates and designs for its defence in 1691. He also surveyed the Avon at Bristol, but there were no new initiatives of any substance during the 1690s. Various improvements were always being suggested at the principal fortresses because these were the places where engineers were concentrated. So a number of plans appeared for the protection of the developing dockyards themselves, especially at Plymouth where the new dock on the Tamar side of town was without defences. Several plans appeared at this time for fortifying St Nicholas (now Drake's) Island to this effect. There was, however, sufficient general concern in the government for there to be a survey of armaments across the country in 1691, and another on the condition of coastal fortifications in 1698. When temporary coastal batteries do appear, such as those in the lower reaches of the Medway, which were recorded in detail both in plan and elevation, they were such that their rapid decay was inevitable without regular maintenance. They were little more than timber gun platforms with slight earthen breastworks and a small weatherboarded shed to house munitions and perhaps a caretaker gunner (see illustration on p94).

The renewal of war in 1702, after a brief lull of five years, was a further stimulus to the Ordnance Office to take note of the repeated complaints from its engineers. The deteriorating situation was so bad that a royal warrant was issued in 1703 to the Master-General to survey all the forts and batteries in England. The estimates for repairs which resulted were so astronomical that little was done. Although there were alarms and dangers of piratical raids – as in 1707 when the

French landed in Anglesey and plundered the inhabitants – there had previously been little incentive to continue expenditure on fortifications, since the immediate danger of invasion had receded, especially after the naval victory of La Hogue in 1692. The main military effort and expenditure was directed towards the field army on the Continent. As usual, when the danger of attack diminished existing fortifications were allowed to deteriorate.

Further invasion alarms came in 1707 and 1708. An ill-assorted French force assembled at Dunkirk with the intention of capitalising on the supposed unrest arising from the Act of Union in Scotland and England. The enterprise was a fiasco but it did stimulate more determined action by the government that year when an Act of Parliament was passed for securing the docks at Harwich, Portsmouth and Chatham, and large sums of money set aside for buying land for new defences. But this activity was largely illusory. Apart from buying land at Dock (Plymouth), Portsbridge on the approaches to Portsmouth, and at Gosport, little substantial work was done. For example, the engineer, Talbot Edwards, recognised that de Gomme's defences of Gosport on the western side of Portsmouth harbour had never been finished: 'The moat therefore wants to be broader and deeper, set with palizadoes and two sluices to it; the breaches made up, the ramparts enlarged, the parapetts raised and gunns planted on all the flankes; also a new gate, a bridge and ravelling. Likewise a covered way. This what's necessary on the land side.'[3] Forty years were to elapse before these fundamental recommendations were to be put into practice. As for Portsmouth itself, Talbot Edwards wrote that the town ought to be as well fortified as Toulon, since it was not inferior. Yet the moat was fordable in several places, the ramparts were narrow and the parapets low. The whole fortification was very irregular 'being after the old way' with short flancks and 'sad' proportion in every part. Portsmouth should be fortified after the modern manner abroad as it deserves.[4] Talbot Edwards did in fact make some alterations to the outworks. The double moat was abandoned, and the two covered-ways merged into one. The old places of arms were converted into ravelins. De Gomme's hornwork was demolished and the total defence made more manageable.

The most substantial result of the 1709 Act was the rebuilding of Landguard Fort at the mouth of the Orwell in the seaward approach to Harwich. The new fort was larger than the old and on a site closer to the estuary. It was bastioned and capable of mounting twenty guns. It was however not begun until 1717 and finished in 1720. In 1750, the fort was said to be surrounded by a very good covered-way and glacis, and the scarps were brick faced. Although the bastions and curtains were then considered too small, the rampart, being 30 feet (9 metres) wide was of sufficient

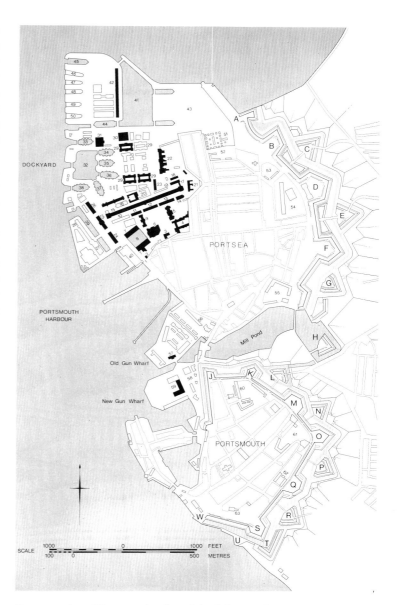

Portsmouth and Portsea: the plan of the defences of Portsmouth reflects the changes made by Talbot Edwards to de Gomme's lines. (RCHM)

breadth for the recoil of great guns. A battery was established at the foot of the glacis to seaward.[5]

Elsewhere there was the familiar story of delapidations. This is well brought out by the Ordnance Office's Third Engineer, Christian Lilly, who, in response to general instructions for a thorough survey of the condition of coastal defences from the Duke of Marlborough, as Master-General of the Ordnance, produced a well illustrated survey of the forts in the south west. The earthworks of Pendennis Castle were 'in a very ruinous condition there being but little of the parapets remaining, and there is several places on the outside of the ramparts where men may without difficulty climb up. Also the breastworks and intrenchments of the outworks are in many places filled up and entirely covered with furze and brambles.' The sea had

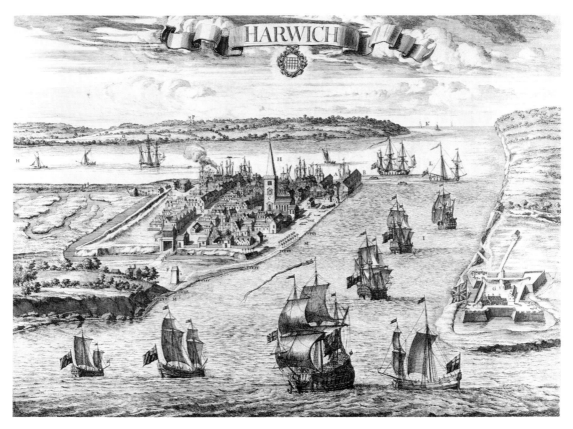

Harwich, Essex: view of the mouth of the Orwell with the newly built (1716) Landguard Fort on the right and the decayed earthen defences of Harwich on the left. British Library, King Top Coll xiii.15.4a. (BL)

breached a space of 112 feet (34 metres) in the foundations of Portland Castle. The lower fort of Plymouth Citadel had parapets entirely destroyed and the platforms ruined.[6]

THE WAR OF THE AUSTRIAN SUCCESSION AND THE SEVEN YEARS WAR

In the years after 1715, changes in the composition of the army affected the manning of coastal fortifications. The artillery found themselves in a comparatively subordinate position to the engineers, and Michael Richards, the Chief Engineer, proposed a scheme for the separation of the artillery and the development of his own branch of the service. These views tallied with the current spirit of military reform. The Royal Regiment of Artillery was constituted in 1716 with two 'marching companies' stationed at Woolwich. The regiment, as with the engineers, came under the Master-General and the Board of Ordnance. At first, this did not affect the permanent detachments of artillerymen quartered in the coast defences. From 1722 onwards, the manning of the forts gradually was found from companies of the Royal Artillery. The garrisons, such as they were, still consisted of a master gunner with two or three gunners to take charge of the fort on a care and maintenance basis, and to act as a trained nucleus which would instruct the local militia, seamen from the fleet, or an infantry garrison in times of crisis. Only the

major establishments had a garrison of gunners whose numbers were in double figures. During the late war, the government discovered a way both of providing infantry garrisons for the home forts and sending trained troops to serve overseas. This was by creating companies of Invalids (soldiers who were either too old, or not physically fit to stand the strains of active service). By the time of the Jacobite Rising of 1745 there were infantry Invalid Companies in garrison at all the main ports and bases in the country.

In his arguments for the improvement of the Engineers branch, Michael Richards wrote:

It is fit to take notice that whenever anything has been done in our Fortifications it has been from pure necessity and the performance in a hurry, whereas these being works for the Safety and Honour of Princes and Nations they require the most mature deliberation . . . The Engineers in Ordinary ought to be appointed to reside at the several Fortifications and to employ themselves in making actual Surveys, Plans, &, whereby they will be perfectly acquainted with all the circumstances of the place they are encharged with . . . As for the Practitioner Engineers they may be educated in the several [Artillery] Companies amongst the subalterns, by which means they will be distributed in the several Garrisons and have the proper opportunity of employing their genius in seeing what works are carried on . . .[7]

This memorandum had its effect. At the same time as the artillery was being put on a proper footing in 1716, a regular corps of engineers was formed consisting of a Chief Engineer paid at 27s 6d a day, three Directors at 20s 6d, Engineers in Ordinary at 12s 6d, Engineers Extraordinary at 8s 6d, Sub-Engineers at 5s, and six Practitioner Engineers at 3s a day. The next step was the formation of establishments not only for Great Britain but also for Minorca and Gibraltar. Indeed the considerable growth in the numbers of engineers reflected the extensive continental campaigns and the steady acquisition of overseas possessions.

The aftermath of the Scottish rebellion in 1715, and the disarray of the forts in the north led the Duke of Marlborough to order complete surveys and reports to be prepared of the fortifications, barracks and storehouses in the kingdom. Engineers were appointed to carry out this review, which was the first systematic survey to be carried out on a national scale. The Second Engineer, Captain Talbot Edwards, was responsible for the Portsmouth Division which consisted of: Portsmouth town, Southsea Castle, Blockhouse Fort (Gosport), Charles Fort, James Fort, Gosport, The Dock; on the Isle of Wight, Yarmouth, Sandown, Carisbrook and Cowes Castles; and in the western approaches, Hurst and Calshot Castles. Colonel Lilly, the Third Engineer, was responsible (as mentioned above) for the Plymouth Division: Portland Castle, Plymouth, St Nicholas Island, Pendennis and St Mawes Castles at Falmouth, and the Isles of Scilly. Captain Theodore Dury covered North Britain which included the castles of Edinburgh and Stirling, Dumbarton and Blackness Castles, and Fort William. Captain Thomas Phillips was responsible for Scarborough Castle, Berwick, Holy Island, Tynemouth Castle and Clifford's Fort, Hull and Carlisle. The Medway river and Chatham fell to Captain John Greuil. This included Sheerness, Hoo-ness, Gillingham Fort, Cockham Wood Fort, James Battery, Middleton Battery and Upnor. Lieutenant John Romer was given the task of Tilbury Fort and Gravesend. John Brookes had the Cinque Ports: Dover Castle, Moats Bulwark, Archcliff Fort, Sandown, Deal and Walmer Castles and Sandgate Castle near Folkestone. This list demonstrates that the defences of Britain still rested substantially on the strategic castles of medieval origin, and the fortresses built by Henry VIII and those of Charles II.

After 1715, there was a period of peace until the War of the Austrian Succession in 1739. In 1716, the Board of Ordnance instituted a reduction of coast defence armaments which left establishments with, at best, half their complement of guns, and often only a quarter. As usual the defences listed above and the lesser works had fallen still further into decay as expenditure on new works and maintenance dwindled to

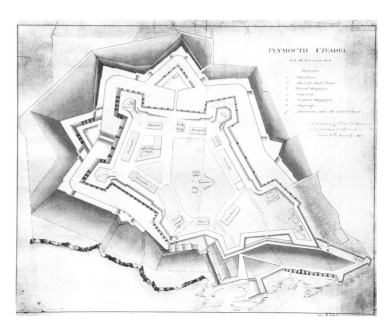

Plymouth Citadel in the eighteenth century. Public Record Office, MPH 232/2 (PRO)

almost nothing. In the 1730s, the House of Commons began to enquire what had happened to the lands bought for new defences at Portsmouth, Chatham and Harwich at a cost of £40,000 in 1709. Even ground which was acquired at Portsmouth and Gosport as part of de Gomme's schemes was still to be developed for the defences. Instead, numerous encroachments had been made by local civilian interests. With the onset of the new war, a survey of all likely landing places from Lowestoft to Land's End was ordered. Along the south coast the chief areas of concern were Falmouth, Portland, Stokes Bay to the west of Gosport, Southampton Water, Pevensey Bay, Rye and the stretches of coast between Dungeness and Folkestone, and around Sandwich. The East Anglian coast between Hollesey Bay and Lowestoft was considered to be vulnerable. The lack of defences in Milford Haven and in the Bristol Channel was also noted. Such fears were not fanciful. In 1743–4 the French, in an attempt to put pressure on British forces on the continent, made use of Jacobite ambitions, and planned supporting action on behalf of Prince Charles Edward Stuart. Marshal Saxe, the renowned French commander, assembled a force of 10,000 men which was to cross from Dunkirk to land near Maldon on the Essex coast, and march on London. While the French fleet, concentrated on Brest, would blockade the British fleet in Portsmouth, some additional warships would sail up the Channel to escort Saxe's transports. The British government, however, had intelligence of the plan. Preparations were made and troops assembled. Yet again it was the weather which scotched the attempt: gales drove the transports ashore with much loss, and the Brest squadron was dispersed when up-Channel of Brighton. A 'Protestant

The Garrison, Isles of Scilly: Redan 'B' on the lines north of Woolpack Bastion. (DOE)

wind' once more had come to the rescue.

During this time of uncertainty, local initiatives were being taken, and not necessarily in the most vulnerable south east. An example comes from the Isles of Scilly. Colonel Christian Lilly's report of 1715 described the headland of the Hugh as fortified but only that part which faced the isthmus towards Hugh Town was strongly built, 'all the rest of it being but slight intrenchments near the seaside with several platforms or batteries on the promontories.[8] Many of these works were in a damaged state as were the defences of Tresco. Between 1715 and 1746, the resident master gunner, Abraham Tovey, changed the character of the Hugh until it was rightly known as the Garrison. The line round the headland was, for the most part, revised and translated into permanent stone. The navigable channels were covered by batteries placed in large bastions connected to each other by a long curtain wall interrupted by redans which increased the flanking capabilities. A new rectangular battery was added to the tower of Cromwell's Castle on Tresco, and barracks, guardroom, storehouse, and a handsome house for himself, were built inside the Garrison at St Mary's.

Additional works were conceived at the more usual locations. The bridge onto Portsea Island had been protected by a redoubt since the seventeenth century. In 1747, a small fort, begun the previous year, was completed. It was entirely earthwork except for gateways of masonry, and a breastwork revetted in brick. At the same time, the eastern flank of the Island and the entrance to Langstone harbour was protected by an irregular star-trace earthwork fort, known first as Eastney Fort, but later to be rebuilt as Fort Cumberland. The design of the first fort was the responsibility of John Peter Desmaretz, Clerk in Ordinary to the Chief Engineer. By 1748, thirty-four guns had been mounted and there was a barracks for 100 officers and men. Works and improvements continued throughout the 1750s.

The opening phase of the Seven Years War saw a repeat of the French tactic of threatening invasion. The movement of French troops towards the Channel ports early in 1756 produced a panic among the population of south east England. All horses, cattle and sheep, together with provisions and forage were intended to be removed inland for a depth of at least twenty miles from the coast. Concentrated between Dunkirk and Cherbourg were some 50,000 troops under Marshal Belleisle, but, without command of the Channel, an attempted invasion would have been extremely risky. A military assessment at the time suggested that the most probable areas for enemy landings would be around Sandwich and Deal, between Hythe and Rye, between Pevensey Bay and Eastbourne and between Brighton and Chichester. However, invasion depended on a diversionary tactic of an assault on Minorca to draw off British naval reinforcements from the Mediterranean fleet. In fact, slow British reactions

Portsmouth: the Landport gate before the removal of the ramparts. (DOE)

meant that the Channel command was retained but Minorca lost. The early disasters of this war were sufficient to carry a militia bill through Parliament in an attempt to create a more effective home defence force. Inherent opposition to anything approaching a standing army was still enough to delay its full implementation, and it took a new invasion scare in 1759 to bring the reformed militia into being.

Although this invasion threat of 1756 was marked by the attack on Minorca, the perhaps more serious invasion threat of 1759 was also designed to distract Britain from its successful colonial campaigns. This made 1759 a year of prolonged tensions. The duc de Choiseul committed greater numbers of men than ever before to the invasion project. In all, 100,000 veterans were to be withdrawn from Germany in a scheme whose objective was the capture of London and the resulting restitution of all the French colonial possessions lost since 1756. Together, these threats produced the most coherent programme of coastal defence since that of Charles II. The response took two forms. The first was the construction of nine 'sea batteries' 'to oppose an enemy landing at the most exposed places on the sea-coast of Sussex and Kent.'[9] The second was better protection of the dockyards of Plymouth, Portsmouth and Gosport, and Chatham by continuous bastioned lines of enclosure. Milford Haven was also considered but Colonel Bastide's recommendations

were not taken up. In some instances this new work was a fulfilment of the land purchases of 1707.

The batteries of 1759 were substantial structures. The smallest was at Folkestone where there were just six 9-pounders. At Hythe there were six 18-pounders. Rye had ten 24-pounders, and five others of different natures. At Hastings there were eleven 12-pounders. Seaford had two batteries, one for five 24-pounders, and the other for five 12-pounders. Newhaven also had five 12-pounders. Brighton was the largest with twelve 24-pounders, Arundel Haven just seven 18-pounders. This last, now known as Littlehampton, still remains on land which had been purchased for £7 from the Duke of Norfolk. The plan is that of a flattened, obtuse-angled bastion set at right angles to the river bank so that the two faces covered the river mouth and the sea front respectively. The battery was open with the seven guns mounted on a timber platform, firing over a parapet. The steep ramparts which enclosed the battery were faced with turf. To the rear was the magazine with a protective cover of five feet of earth, and stables, artillery store and quarters for the master gunner. These were enclosed only by a palisade, and were vulnerable to attack from the rear. One master gunner and one gunner were to be allowed for each battery, who were to 'teach such of the inhabitants as shall be inclinable to learn how to load, point and fire the guns placed there for their defence'.[10]

The enclosure of the dockyards by regular, bastioned lines was more substantial work. Plymouth Dock at Devonport involved the enclosure of 77 acres

Berwick-upon-Tweed: powder magazine. (Author)

Gosport, Priddy's Hard, Portsea and Portsmouth: full extent of the lines protecting the dockyard, associated naval installations and the attendant towns. (RCHM)

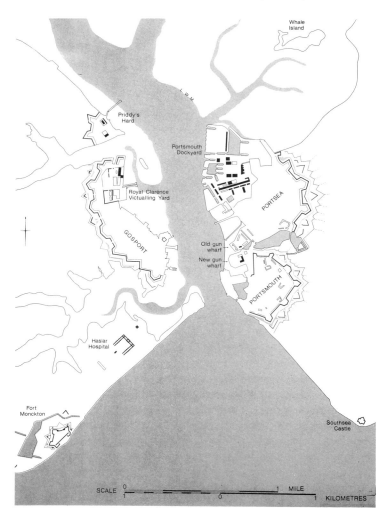

after land purchase in 1759. The lines were described as of slight strength and only thirty guns were mounted. The land was subsequently given up to the Navy Board in about 1772 for enlarging the dockyard itself. Barracks were built to accommodate twenty companies of foot.

At Gosport, the rebuilding of de Gomme's lines had begun somewhat earlier in 1748. Associated with the work and with projects elsewhere in the Portsmouth area was the engineer John Peter Desmaretz. By 1751 the ramparts and moat had been enlarged and improved northwards. The impetus which came in 1757–8 saw a substantial enlargement of the original enclosure. This provided a covered-way beyond the earlier line and a projection of the new bastioned trace to enclose Priddy's Hard. The dockyard across Portsmouth harbour at Portsea was enclosed at the same time.

One of the major products of the 1755 building programme was the Brompton Lines at Chatham. The earliest protective work for the dockyard was a brick walled enclosure built in 1634. Early in the eighteenth century there were various proposals for defensible lines, but it was not until 1755 that Hugh Debbeig's design was adopted. The lines crossed the high ground above the dockyard itself and took in the barracks at Brompton. The system was one and a half miles long, and consisted of unrevetted ditches with bastions at regular intervals. The bastions and curtains were fraised with pallisades. The works were supervised by Captain Desmaretz, and by 1756 the southern three bastions and one demi-bastion were complete.

The purposeful response to this period of danger owes much to John Ligonier, future Field Marshall, whose many responsibilities included that of Chief Engineer and Master-General of the Ordnance.[11] He took the initiative in creating the south coast batter-

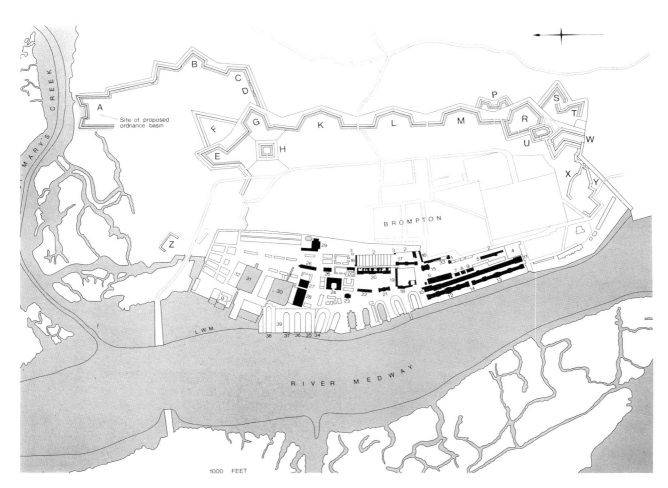

Brompton Lines and Amherst Redoubt at the southern end above Chatham. (RCHM)

ies, and putting Plymouth and Portsmouth into a better state of defence. He was also better able to furnish garrisons and field reserves for the coastal defences without drawing excessively on the regular regiments by virtue of the new militia. By mid-summer 1759, a force of more than 11,000 men was under arms, and other units totalling over 7000 men were sufficiently advanced to have received their arms by the end of the year. The French invasion preparations for the autumn of 1759 were of the classic model for all the great plans for invading England. A landing fleet capable of conveying a force of 48,000 men was to be constructed together with supply and store ships. The troops were concentrated on Le Havre and, on this occasion, the objective was to secure a beach-head in the Portsmouth area prior to a march on London. Another force, embarking at Brest, was to be put ashore near Glasgow. The main part of the Brest squadron was to escort the principal invasion force from Le Havre to Portsmouth. However, the Toulon fleet, coming up in support and having passed through the Straits of Gibraltar, was convincingly defeated by Admiral Boscawen at Lagos off the Portuguese coast. Despite this disaster, the French eventually began their move in November, and

the Brest fleet sailed in order to link up with their transports in Quiberon Bay. In terrible weather Admiral Hawke attacked the French fleet on a lee shore within sight of the tranports; the French force was shattered, and the gale destroyed all hope of recovery.

THE 'OTHER ARMADA' OF 1779

If we put to one side Skinner's achievement at Fort George, Ardesier, the coastal defences built in southern England during the first half of the eighteenth century were simple and unsophisticated bastioned lines, and a scatter of isolated open batteries. No innovatory flair can be perceived, perhaps because these fortifications were the best that a grudging government could afford. The last quarter of the century, however, saw a measure of innovation in design, and a better awareness of wider strategic considerations. In particular, greater attention was paid to the weaknesses of existing bastioned lines, and evidence of internal retrenchments appears, notably at Chatham.[12] The role of individual batteries was given greater prominence. They became more widely distributed geographically, and while few were properly self-defensible, more care was taken to ensure that the batteries were better protected from gunfire from a landing force. The value of gun-towers for beach defence was becoming more appreciated. Perhaps most significant of all was the realisation that the two main south coast naval dockyards were less liable to direct attack than they once were but more vulnerable to bombardment and being outflanked by an invading force that might have come ashore some distance further along the coast. This factor stimulated the process of an outward expansion of the defensive works around the dockyards, which took in the strategically important features of the immediate hinterland, and aimed to secure the likeliest adjacent landing places and approaches. It was a process which was to be vastly extended over the next hundred years. In addition to those parts of the coasts where there had been long continuity of defensive works, there was now a much greater need for protection along the whole seaboard of the British Isles, and the east coast especially. In the face of the dangers arising from the activities of American privateers, in addition to threats from traditional enemies, Scotland and the north west of England also needed to be prepared.

Elimination of French power in North America had been the chief result of the Seven Years War. It had unexpectedly meant a huge and continuing financial burden for Britain, and one which the American colonists had little will to share. Pressure from London for increased taxation to cover the costs of the war and providing continuing security led to developing tensions which ultimately, in 1775, led to military conflict. The war did not go well for Britain, and the disaster of Burgoyne's surrender at Saratoga in 1778 led France to the conclusion that the cause of American independence provided the means for striking back at Britain. France signed an alliance with the newly created United States, and a colonial quarrel became a general war. In the following year, Spain, and later in 1780, Holland, joined in against Britain. Suddenly the Royal Navy was outnumbered and no longer had command of the seas. It was stretched from the West Indies to the Indian Ocean, and temporarily lost control of the English Channel.

Such a state of affairs had largely come about from the usual economies and neglect of matters military and naval which accompanied a period of peace. The French on the other hand, under the great war minister, the duc de Choiseul, had spent the 1760s reforming French military capacity. By 1767, Choiseul was considering plans for a surprise landing in south eastern England with the immediate objective of capturing London. Deal was picked as the place to land. The three Henrician castles of Deal, Walmer and Sandown were reported to be easily takeable as they were very old and little more than gun platforms. The quality of the militia was held to be very low, and it was expected that the decisive battle would be fought on Blackheath. An alternative plan was a return to the earlier scheme for the seizure of Portsmouth, and a march on London which aimed at the prior capture of

Fort Amherst, in the course of restoration. (Author)

the northern heights of Hampstead and Highgate.

The year of 1779 was therefore one of acute crisis. In May, 5000 French troops under the Prince of Nassau unsuccessfully attacked Jersey. In the following month, the British prime minister received intelligence of French plans to attack Portsmouth and Plymouth, with a diversionary raid on Ireland. British military advice, in the person of General Roy, took the view that the French could probably effect a landing in the south east, and considered that landings elsewhere were unlikely because of the distance from the essential target of London. The actual appearance of a huge combined French and Spanish fleet off Plymouth in August, and the report that a French force of some 50,000 was being massed in Normandy and Brittany, caused a panic. In fact, the great fleet, the 'other Armada', in the face of easterly winds, gradually fell away and danger receded, but regularly every year until 1782, a projected invasion was conceived as a possibility. This was bound to be so while Britain was unable to concentrate sufficient warships to resume control of the Channel. At the same time, there were the embarrassments caused by American privateers raiding shipping and hazarding coastal ports in England, Scotland and Ire-

Elizabeth Castle, Jersey: guérite *on the south-west bastion of the outer ward.* (DOE)

land. The most notorious of them, John Paul Jones, raided Whitehaven, spiked the guns in the battery and burnt many ships. In the face of all these threats and emergencies, the militia was mobilised in large numbers, and greater attention paid to land defence which, like the navy, had been allowed to deteriorate.

At the beginning of June 1779, the Board of Ordnance warned commanders of all coast defences on the south and east coasts to be at readiness. At Hastings, Seaford, Newhaven and Brighton many of the wooden gun carriages had rotted, and gunpowder was suspect. Matters were rather better further west but the bores of the 6-pounder battery at Dartmouth were much damaged from having been exposed to the sea spray for twenty years past! New batteries were constructed. The east coast batteries ranged from Caister Heights near Great Yarmouth, Gorleston Hill, Lowestoft and South Lowestoft, Parkefield Battery, Harwich Battery and New Tavern Fort at Gravesend. In Kent there were new works at Margate, Broadstairs and Dover, and at Blatchington in East Sussex. Further west, Swanage and Lyme Regis were provided for. There were four batteries apiece at Poole and Torbay, and others at Looe, Mevagissey and Fowey in Corn-

wall. The armament varied from 6-pounders to 32-pounders with the balance of heavier calibres in the south eastern batteries and lighter guns allocated to the south west.

Thomas Hyde Page was the engineer responsible for the east coast defences. Apart from the brand new works, his concern was to recommend improvements to the firepower of existing positions. At Landguard Fort, substantial batteries were added to the covered-way and glacis to cover the channel approaching Harwich. In addition, the promontory on which the fort stands was defended by an entrenchment flanked by twenty-seven guns with a further battery covering the seaward approach. This additional work was later described as 'a very good rentrenched camp without the Fort' and was thought to be sufficient for the quartering of 1000–2000 men.[13] Similar strengthening was done at Tilbury, where a six-gun battery was created on the downstream end of the covered-way. This was intended to cross its fire with a new work at Gravesend opposite, New Tavern Fort. Despite its irregular bastion trace, New Tavern was designed to provide the greatest possible offensive fire rather than achieve all-round defence. Although there was a wide, flat-bottomed ditch with palisades towards the main front, the earth rampart was unrevetted and there was no provision for the protection of the gorge.[14]

Hyde Page was also responsible for substantially strengthening the Chatham lines. Each end of the Lines was retrenched on the basis of two rectangular redoubts, Amherst and Townshend, to the south and north respectively. At the same time the southern end was improved by the building of two outworks: the Spur Battery and a hornwork. The remarkable complex of defensive devices that was formed on the cliff edge above Chatham town became known as Fort Amherst and is currently in the course of restoration.[15]

At the two main naval bases major works were also in hand. The town of Portsmouth had long been enclosed by bastioned lines. The dockyard and its attendant town of Portsea had never been properly protected. Continuous lines were begun at Portsea in 1770 extending nearly two miles. Major John Archer was the engineer responsible. The lines followed a conventional bastion trace with ravelins, *tenailles* and lunettes. The design of the bastions reflected the mid-eighteenth century preference for larger size than those in the old Portsmouth Lines (see illustration on p115). But the most significant step in Portsmouth's defences was the extension of concern to the long stretch of beach in Stokes Bay, west of Gosport. A pair of French spies had reported that Gosport was 'virtually without defence, protected on the landward side only by an ill-maintained entrenchment . . . which would fall at the first assault and by a feeble *enceinte* much too extensive for its garrison' of one militia battalion.[16] In August 1779 Lieutenant-General Monkton directed

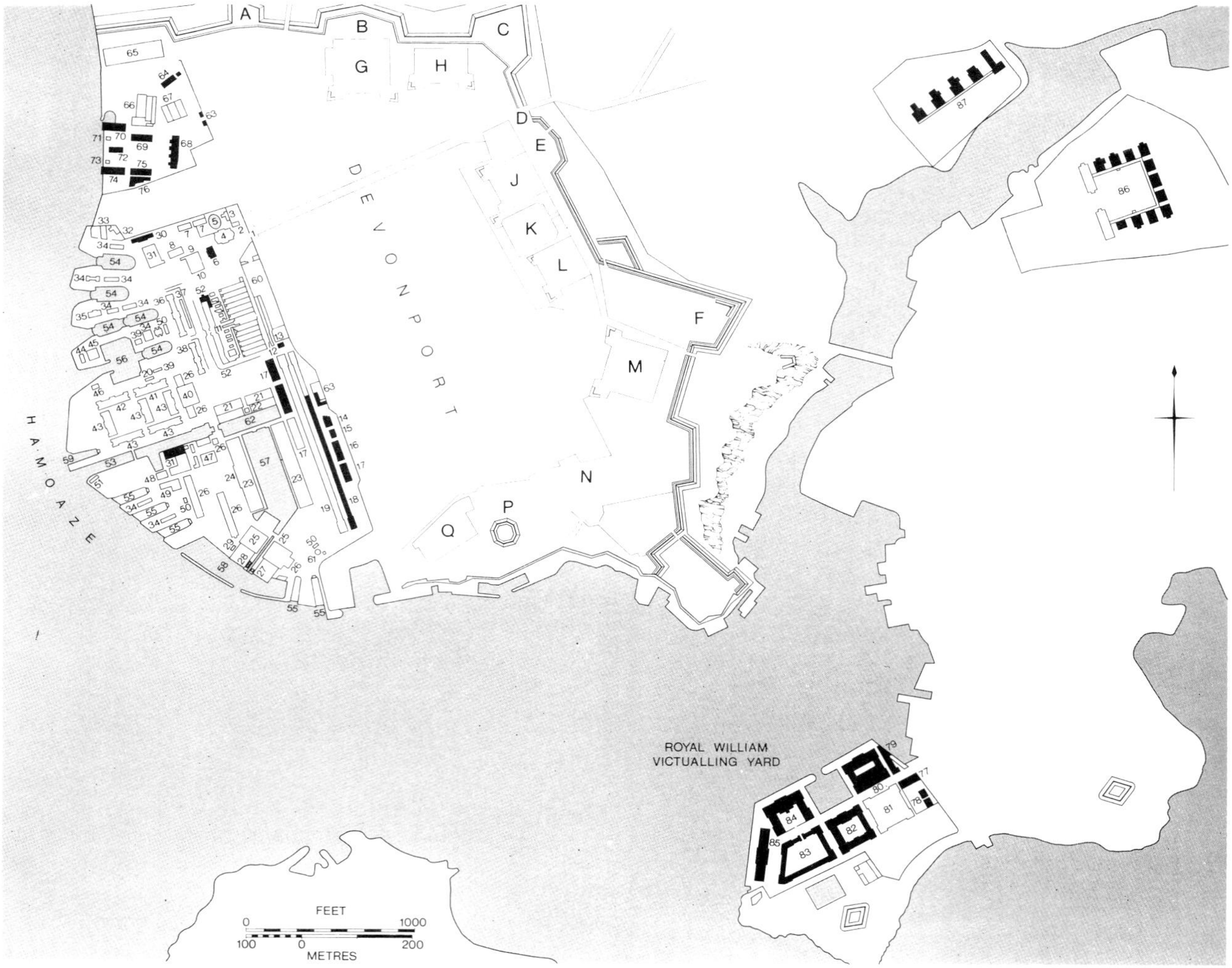

Devonport Lines. (RCHM)

Archer to throw up a temporary fort at Gilkicker. This was basically triangular with the long side and principal battery along the beach. The *enceinte* was flanked by three bastions. In 1780 a plan was approved for the building of a triangular, defensible barracks in the centre of the fort. This was the beginnings of what was later known as Fort Monkton.[17]

Similar activities were taking place at Plymouth. The Devonport Lines were commenced in 1756, but they were of a slight nature mounting only thirty guns. During the parliamentary debates of 1785 it was said that 'the construction of the lines is not calculated to resist a regular siege'.[18] In 1779 Lieutenant-Colonel Matthew Dixon of the Engineers proposed simple improvements to the bastioned lines by repairing the parapet, widening and deepening the ditch, and fixing palisades in the ditch and *fraises* in the scarp. The real weakness lay beyond the lines. The works could be commanded from high ground in many places, and an enemy landing to the west could bombard and completely control the dockyard from the Cornish side of the river Tamar. Dixon proposed a chain of blockhouses or redoubts to forestall such an event. The topographical situation of Plymouth lent itself to the provision of detached works to command the three hilltops immediately in the vicinity of 'the three towns' and the dockyard: Mount Pleasant, Mount Wise and Stonehouse Hill. There was no uniformity in the design of these three redoubts other than the employment of earthwork. Mount Wise was an octagonal work enclosed by a ditch, Stonehouse was rectangular with two square bastions at alternate angles with an oblong guardhouse in the centre, and Mount Pleasant was square with a square blockhouse set diamond fashion inside it. The anticipated French landing point was Cawsand Bay in Cornwall. It was decided to construct three redoubts here so sited to cover the foreshore with grapeshot. In 1779 Dixon did not consider the Maker Heights behind Cawsand a very important position. This opinion was to alter five years later. Other new batteries along the waters-edge for 18-pounders were Eastern King, West Hoe and Passage Point.

The invasion crisis also revived interest in Dover. In 1778 Lord Amherst received unfavourable reports on the effectiveness of the ordnance there, and the next year £4100 was allocated for new works. Some of the money was spent by Hyde Page on the castle, the rest was divided between the construction of three batteries along the beach protecting the harbour (North, Amherst and Townshend), and fieldworks on the Western Heights.[19] The latter appear to have taken the form of an irregular bastioned fort on the site of the present Drop Redoubt on the eastern end of the hill, a series of earthwork batteries, and, on the western end of the broad plateau, was a bastioned work on the site now occupied by the Citadel. Like the new works at Landguard Fort, these seem to have been intended as an entrenched camp for field forces kept in reserve against the anticipated invasion. If this is so, it represents a shift towards a more mobile defence than the previous policy of fixed positions around a focal point.

The other novelty in the military response to 1779 was the systematic use of gun-towers for beach defence in the Channel Islands.[20] Gun-towers were nothing new, and had been employed occasionally during the seventeenth century, as at Cromwell's Castle in the Isles of Scilly and at Mount Batten at Plymouth. The initiative here came from General Conway, Governor of Jersey, who in a report of May 1778

> proposed the erection of 30 Round Towers for the defence of the island. Towers to be of masonry, 30–40 feet high and about 500 yards from each other – to be absolutely solid for 10–12 feet from the bottom. Wall above to be strong, pierced with loopholes for musketry in two stages and on the top, where it is proposed to place cannon, a parapet of brick . . .[21]

The towers, however, took some time to be built. Captain Mulcaster appears to have completed four during 1779, but in a letter from General Conway of 1794 only twenty-two of the intended thirty-two had been built. Some of the towers, which were intended for 'all the most accessible parts of the coast' were associated with batteries. The Seymour Tower is the exception from the rest in being square in plan. These towers anticipated by fifteen years the naval action off Cape Mortella, Corsica, which gave its name to the familiar Martello Towers. The fifteen towers on Guernsey were slightly different from those on Jersey. They were loopholed for musketry, capable of housing 20 men and mounting a 6-pounder cannon on top, and were built at the likely landing places.

THE DUKE OF RICHMOND, 1782–6

The 'Other Armada' of 1779 dispersed, but British fear of invasion and disaster remained until 1783 when peace was concluded with France, Spain, Holland and the rebellious American colonies. Dissatisfaction with the condition of the coastal defences continued for even longer. Jersey had been attacked again in 1781 in a more determined manner than two years before, and only a

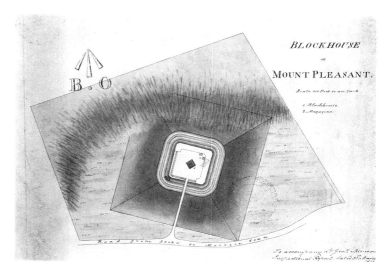

Mount Pleasant blockhouse, Devonport. Public Record Office, MPH 233/4. (PRO)

Tower at Greve de Lecq, Jersey. (Author)

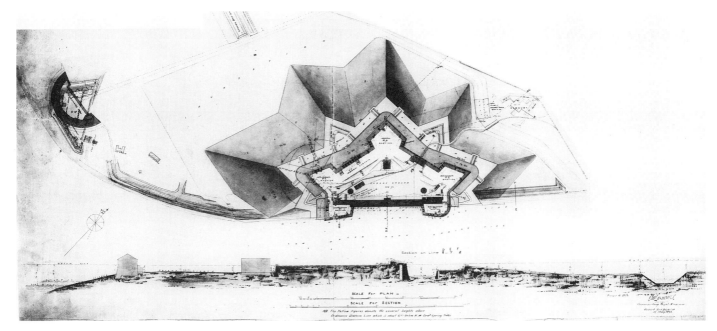

Fort Monkton, Gosport: plan and cross section. Public Record Office, MPHH 226. (PRO)

fierce hand-to-hand struggle in the market place of St Helier finally led to the abandonment of the French attempt to seize the island. The defensive preparations carried out in 1779 on the south and eastern English coasts were conscientiously maintained and, indeed, developed more emphatically and with continuing improvement. They would have been even more extensive and technically advanced if the programme adopted and pressed by the Duke of Richmond had been supported by Parliament.

The change of government which followed the Peace of Paris in 1782 brought the Duke of Richmond to the office of Master-General of the Ordnance with a seat in the Cabinet. He was a remarkable reformer, reorganising the engineers' establishment and re-instituting competitive examinations for prospective engineers. He was responsible for the creation of the Corps of Royal Military Artificers and Artillery Drivers and for the founding of the Ordnance Survey. The Duke had been a controversial figure in 1780, asking for a committee of inquiry into the neglect of the defences of the south west. Now in power, he pressed for the substantial re-fortification of Portsmouth and Plymouth. His views were developed by a high-powered military committee including Colonel Dixon, Chief Engineer, Major-General Roy and Lieutenant-Colonel Moncrief. Their objectives were to expand the defensive systems well beyond the immediate continuous lines around the towns and dockyards, bearing in mind the risk of attack from an enemy landing some distance from their main objective. At Portsmouth this meant defending the whole Stokes Bay area to the west, the land approaches to Portsea Island from the north at Hilsea, and the eastern flank adjacent to Langstone

harbour. To meet these objectives a more permanent version of Fort Monkton was proposed, a pentagonal fort further west along Stokes Bay, another at Frater Lake and one at Hilsea to the north, substantial improvements both to Southsea Castle and to Fort Cumberland, and the building of six gun-towers between the last two forts along the intervening beach. At Plymouth, a similar policy envisaged substantial forts on Maker Heights, and at Merrifield near Torpoint, both on the Cornish side of the Tamar. The Devonport Lines were given greater emphasis. Elsewhere, at Dover Richmond supported the development of the works on the Western Heights for the same purpose of establishing wider defensive zones. If Richmond's grand design had been allowed to proceed to completion it would have been on a scale comparable only with the defensive programmes achieved by Henry VIII and Charles II.[22]

The costs of such schemes would have been enormous, not just in cash but also in the numbers of troops required to garrison the new lines. It was as much the political charge that Richmond was seeking to enlarge the army that stimulated the opposition, as the cost of the fortifications. The fortresses could be 'termed seminaries for soldiers and universities for Praetorian bands', said one opponent. Another argued that the proposals would take thirty-five years to complete and cost around £2,000,000.[23] By 1785 the opposition had grown extremely vociferous. The traditional 'blue water' argument was brought out, regardless of the all too recent experience of the navy losing command of the Channel. Richmond's supporters riposted that the maintenance of a squadron permanently in the Channel was more expensive than building forts. John Courtenay, a persistent critic, stirred inherent prejudice by foretelling that soon 'the

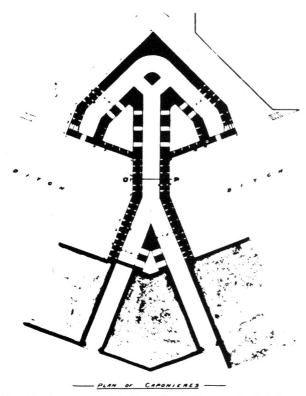

Fort Monkton: plan of the lower level of a caponier. Public Record Office WO 78/5011(3). (PRO)

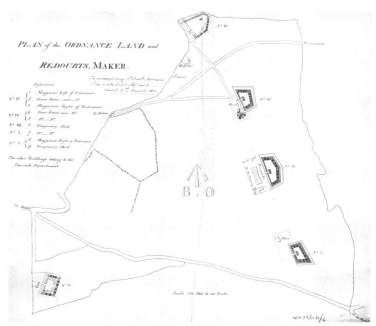

Maker Heights, Cornwall: line of detached redoubts. Public Record Office MPH 233/6. (PRO)

Maker Heights: redoubt at the northern end of the line. (Author)

country gentlemen would find their terraces converted into bastions, their slopes into glaces, their pleasure-ground and shrubberies into hornworks and crown-works, to which they have hitherto born an irreconcilable aversion.'[24] In the event, the voting over the necessary supply legislation resulted in a tie, and the Speaker cast his vote against the government's proposals. Richmond subsequently drew up revised plans, cutting the estimated expenditure by nearly half. Plans for erecting new forts at Stokes Bay and Maker Heights, together with the six brick gun-towers at Southsea, were included, but the more controversial detached works at Frater Lake, Hilsea and Merrifield were omitted. This was a poor tactic, and the bill was withdrawn because the principles of the rejected measure were still present. It was, however, subsequently agreed that the improvement and completion of the old works at Portsmouth and Plymouth should be carried through, and a few years later, limited works were erected at Stokes Bay and Maker Heights. Despite the failure of Richmond's grand design, the ideas which he had received from his professional engineer colleagues were not lost. The concept that major defended complexes could be outflanked and bombarded from a distance beyond their limits was recognised in future defensive measures. The 1780s was therefore a period of much novel construction as well as the consolidation of permanent defences.

Archer's bastioned lines around Portsea had been under construction through the 1770s. In 1782,

the Duke of Richmond demanded to know the exact state of the dockyard defences, what works could be erected for immediate security, and the length of time they could resist a force of 20,000–30,000 men. In 1786, £60,000 was voted towards the completion of the old works at both Portsmouth and Plymouth. The Portsea Lines no longer exist, but plans show them to have consisted of a continuous line flanked by three large bastions, with a moat which could be flooded, and

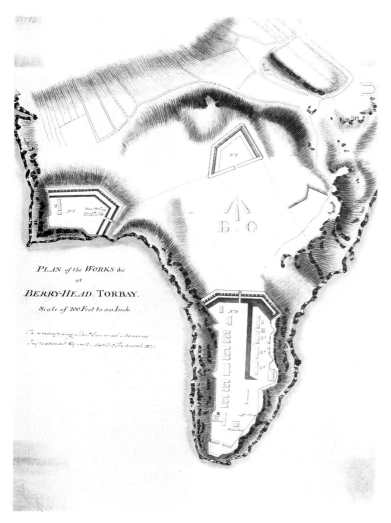

Berry Head, Brixham: detached batteries. Public Record Office, MPH 233/11. (PRO)

remained constant, the main armament was more frequently protected by mounting the guns in casemates. Traditional flank defence from the bastions was now clearly not sufficient, and additional ditch defences were provided often in the form of caponiers.

At Plymouth, it had already been appreciated that the Devonport lines could be commanded from high ground beyond, and an enemy landing to the west could bombard and completely control the dockyard from the Cornish side of the Tamar. Although the major fort on Maker Heights in the Richmond scheme to counteract this risk did not materialise, 103 acres were bought in 1784 and five detached earthen redoubts were thrown up across the peninsula. They were permanent works with masonry revetted scarps and deep ditches, rectangular in plan without flanking bastions at the angles. They were essentially batteries with only a minimum provision for self-defence in the form of a drawbridge and a loopholed gorge wall. Nor were the redoubts entirely mutually supporting. By 1804, a barracks had been erected for the men manning them.

This use of detached works instead of a continuous bastioned line was new in Britain. Something similar to the Maker redoubts had been adopted for Berry Head, where it was thought advisable to guard the much used anchorage in Torbay, South Devon. But here the three detached batteries armed with a total of twenty 20-pounders were protected by an entrenchment cutting off the headland, in a way similar to the enclosing earthworks at Landguard Fort, a few years previous. Although substantially improved later, the batteries at Berry Head were in existence by 1783.

Away from the two major dockyards, proposals for improvements at Sheerness were drawn up by Captain M Pitts in 1783; these led to a new line of bastioned earthworks including a wet ditch enclosing the dockyard and the associated Blue Town, which had grown up outside the former in much the same way as Portsea and Devonport had developed. Sheerness was to remain, until about 1970, as the last English town, other than Berwick-upon-Tweed, to retain its complete bastioned defences.

The 1780s also saw the building of two self-contained fortresses at opposite ends of the kingdom. Fort Charlotte was the most northerly, built to command the Bressay Sound at Lerwick in Shetland. It was originally built in 1665 against the Dutch threat by John Mylne, Charles II's master mason in Scotland. This fort was burnt by the Dutch in 1673, and had been left derelict ever since. It was rebuilt in 1782 and renamed in honour of the Queen. It has since been encroached upon, and is now surrounded by modern Lerwick. The plan is an irregular pentagon and is dictated by the concentration of the armament along the sea front. The three full and two demi-bastions are small, and are a survival of the late seventeenth century design. Inside, there are three barrack and administra-

containing four ravelins opposite the intermediate lengths of curtain.

Fort Monkton does survive but it is not available to the public. The Duke had visited the earlier work here and disapproved of what he saw. New plans were approved in 1783 for a symmetrical work, triangular in plan with its base along the shore containing the main armament of thirty-five heavy guns, for the most part mounted in stone-built casemates with rather vulnerable barrack accommodation built over the top of them. At either end of the casemated battery was a pair of demi-bastions, and from their re-entrant angles sprang elaborate arrow-shaped, brick caponiers covering the seaward ends of the moat. A bastion at the salient covered the two landward sides. Beyond the moat was a conventional covered-way. Lieutenant James Glenie was in charge of the work in its early stages, and the fort was built with civilian labour using locally produced bricks. Fort Monkton is a good example of the new ways in which fortress design was moving in the late eighteenth century. While the bastion theme

tive blocks ranged round a central parade.

The other new fort was Fort George on Guernsey above St Peter Port, but this has now been almost entirely removed for modern housing. It was begun in 1782 and remained under construction until 1812. The nucleus was a regular bastioned fort casemated throughout with barrack accommodation for 13 officers and 250 men. It served as a 'keep of last resort'

Sheerness, Kent: de Gomme's tightly drawn enceinte with bastioned front and ravelin was superseded by the development of the dock and its associated town, Blue Town, which was given its own bastioned defences in the late eighteenth century. (RCHM)

for a complex of batteries and other works which developed during the early years of the nineteenth century, and which replaced Castle Cornet as the main protection for the harbour of St Peter Port and its approaches. Leading from Fort George were the Queen's and Prince's Lines which enclosed subsidiary works along the cliff, such as Fort Irwin, Charlotte Battery, Clarence Battery, Town Point Battery, Adolphus, York and Kent Batteries. Fragments still remain along the cliffs. The most interesting survival, and unique in the British Isles, are the three *fleches* open at the gorge which lie in advance of the glacis on the west front of Fort George.

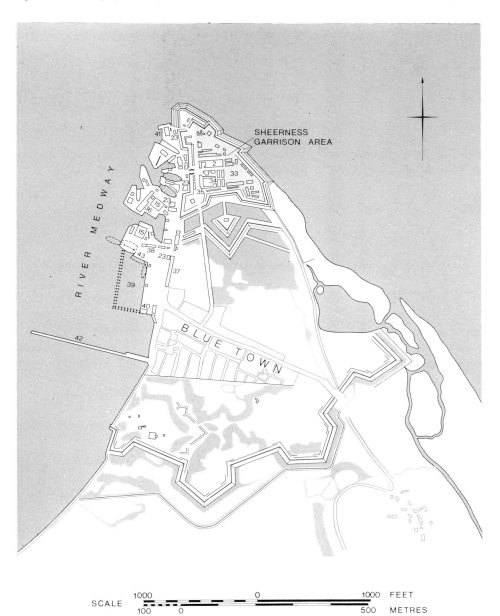

SHEERNESS GARRISON AREA

RIVER MEDWAY

BLUE TOWN

SCALE

1000   0   1000 FEET
100   0   500 METRES

CHAPTER 8

The French Revolutionary and Napoleonic Wars

FULL SCALE WAR, REAL DANGER

The next war with France, beginning in 1793, was unlike any that Britain had fought before, or, indeed, any that Europe had previously experienced. While it did not have the moral fanaticism of the religious wars of the previous century, it possessed an ideological strain as well as a drive for autocratic domination which demanded the submission of whole peoples, and the imposition of foreign standards, if not an aim of world conquest. At first, the revolutionary aspirations of liberty, equality and fraternity which caused the overthrow of the corrupt and oppressive monarchy and nobility in France, gained sympathy on some scale among intellectuals and the working classes in Britain as elsewhere. The excesses of Jacobinism, however, and the rise of the despotic ambitions of Napoleon Bonaparte quickly turned feelings in Britain to their traditional hostility towards France. Britons were accustomed to wars in which campaigns were fought in remote places, by small professional armies whose objective was to avoid major battles and bloodshed as far as possible, unless it involved those of other races and colours. Warfare now came closer to the ordinary citizen. Only Prussia, Austria and Russia, among European states, had the resources and ability to replace heavy losses of men and could therefore engage in repeated pitched battles. Even they followed a campaigning regime which relied on a provisioning system of regularly spaced magazines, without making undue demands on the local populations, and thereby, except at the point of fighting, separated the military consequences of warfare from civil society. The European wars of the earlier part of the century were those where armies manoeuvred, counter-marched, laid siege to strategic strongpoints, sought out their opponent's magazines in order to reduce their campaigning powers and, in short, conducted military engagements with some style and convention. After the French Revolution, the pattern of warfare was to change from the often artificial and stilted to something more ruthless and committed. War was no longer an 'art'. The French armies were now armies of mass, whose cost could only be met by making subject territories pay for their needs, and encouraging the troops to live off the country in places other than France. These were wars which involved all Europe, and attempted to impose a Bonapartist vision on whole nationalities, which spilled over into Africa and even engaged the new United States of America. Grand strategy involved blockade and restriction of trade on a scale never before effected, as well as military campaigns which involved whole nations, and not just the armies themselves. They were a foretaste of the realities of 'total war' which were to become familiar to the generations of the twentieth century. As a result of this novel enlargement of the effects of war, there grew up in Britain a popular involvement in what was a truly national struggle involving economic hardships which could be related to Napoleonic embargos, as well as self-defence against an even more obvious threat of invasion than had been apparent before. The collective impression caused by the Napoleonic Wars has remained in the British folk memory, and still has its physical manifestation in the Martello tower, which remains the one monument of this era that has immediate popular recognition.

The overthrow of its neighbouring maritime rival had always meant for France the preparation of an invasion of the British Isles. The direct approach which would lead to a quick kill was, of course, a descent on the south east coast of England with the objective of London. There was also an alternative strategy which might involve capturing off-islands to embarass British naval strength, or landing in Ireland, Scotland or Wales in the hope of gaining support from political or religious dissidents. Earlier invasion plans were dusted down as soon as hostilities were resumed, and it has been shown that some invasion projects antedate the declaration of war by France in 1793. The possibility of attack was well known to the British government and that, even if it was not a full-scale invasion, there might

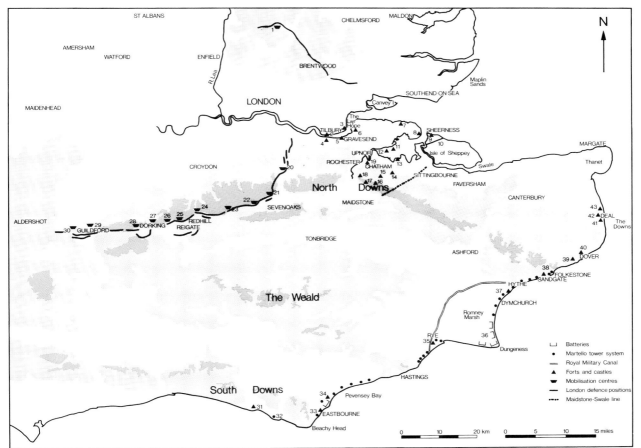

come a raid in force on a limited objective such as one of the naval bases.

There was an immediate response to the declaration of war from the Board of Ordnance in the form of a comprehensive report on the state of defences prepared early in 1794. Only those permanent defences at Plymouth, Portsmouth and Chatham were thought to be in any way adequate. French seizure of the Flemish ports in 1795 made the threat greater, since an invasion could thus be planned from a wider offensive base. One of the French schemes, from the many that were considered, was carried out early in 1797 by a

force of 1500 released convicts under the command of an elderly American soldier of fortune named Tate, which was to be carried up St George's Channel to seize and destroy Bristol. Having anchored off Lundy, easterly winds drove the four ships carrying the troops to their secondary objective in Cardigan Bay where they hoped to enlist the Welsh in an insurrectionary movement. The French troops came ashore just west of Fishguard and established themselves on a nearby hill, but the prompt action of the local volunteers and militia under Lord Cawder led to their surrendering without a shot.[1]

Rather more serious was an attempt to land a force of 15,000 men under General Hoche in the south west of Ireland at Bantry Bay during the same winter of 1796–7. It failed not through any action on the part of the Royal Navy or military but because an effective landing was prevented by bad weather. Bantry Bay, at the time, was completely undefended! In May 1798, rebellion in Ireland broke out, and there were further French preparations to take advantage of the unrest. Two armies were dispatched, but only after the revolt had been suppressed. General Humbert, Hoche's former second-in-command, landed at Killala Bay in north west Mayo, but after initial success, failed to stimulate renewed insurrection in his support. He was eventually cornered and captured at Ballinamuck. The other French force was intercepted at sea and captured in Lough Swilly.

England itself was seriously at risk from direct invasion in 1797–8, when Napoleon only drew back because of lack of confidence in obtaining even temporary command of the narrow seas. The next major crisis came in 1801 when an army of invasion was concentrated along the Channel coast. This was perhaps more a means of putting pressure on the British government to come to terms, which it did under the temporary Peace of Amiens of 1802. The resumption of war the next year saw Britain at her most vulnerable, alone against France, with Napoleon's Grand Army distributed among the western ports from Hamburg to Bordeaux, and concentrated in the immediate area of departure between Flushing and Le Havre. Napoleon's resources included the 12 million dollars received from the United States for the sale of Louisiana, and with no other campaigns in view, he engaged upon the preparation of an invasion fleet on a gigantic scale to the extent of creating vast new harbour facilities at Boulogne, Etaples, Ambleteuse, Wimereux, Calais, Dunkirk and Ostend. Along the coast were massed 80,000 veterans with over 2000 barges, pinnaces and gun-boats in support, waiting for the moment when French naval forces would have at least temporary control of the Channel. The crisis lasted twenty-seven months, until August 1805, when the Grand Army marched off to the Danube to overwhelm the combined forces of Austria and Russia at Ulm and Austerlitz. Then, in October, came the defeat of the combined French and Spanish fleet at Trafalgar. Even so, Nelson's victory and the departure of the Grand Army only postponed the immediate danger of invasion. It did not remove it. Napoleon, for the remainder of the war never lost sight of his aim to build up a naval force of such overwhelming strength to seize control of, at least, the Dover Straits for a crucial period.

Just as the French had a well-matured range of plans for invasion and strategies for advancing towards London once on English soil, so there were British defensive schemes of long standing, many of some ingenuity based on sound deductive reasoning. Some were even published, such as Colonel George Hanger's *Reflections on the Menaced Invasion and the means of protecting The Capital by preventing the enemy from landing in any part contiguous to it* of 1804. In 1795 he had published another tract entitled *Attack and Defence of the City of London*. Others, especially disaffected French officers, had had experience of the French invasion plans of 1776–9. Most notable of these was General Dumouriez who had defected to England, and recommended to the government the counter-invasion measures he thought necessary.[2] The man, however, who had most practical responsibility for defensive preparations was the Quartermaster-General of the Forces from 1796 to 1803 and commander of the Southern District from 1803 to 1805, General Sir David Dundas.

It was recognised that to attempt to defend the whole coastline was impossible. Instead it was necessary to identify the most likely landing places, station troops there, and have more in reserve two or three marches to the rear. Everyone was agreed that a descent north of the Firth of Forth was improbable. The many places on the east coast where landings were at all possible were Berwick, Alnmouth, Blyth, Seaton, Tynemouth, Sunderland, Teesmouth, Whitby, Scarborough, Bridlington, Hornsea and the Humber, Great Yarmouth, Lowestoft, Southwold, Hollesley Bay, Harwich, the Mersea, Blackwater and Crouch estuaries and Rochford. However, the coast between Great Yarmouth and the Thames was covered by shoals which would make landings difficult, and the Yarmouth naval squadron protected the coast south of the Humber. The western half of the south coast of England had practicable beaches at Studland, Poole, Weymouth, Portland, Whitsand Bay, Falmouth and Mounts Bay, to identify the most likely. This stretch of coast was, however, protected by the Plymouth squadron. Elsewhere on the western coasts of England, access to the chief ports was difficult and often dangerous. It was felt therefore that major defences in these areas could be confined to the Forth, the Humber, Plymouth and Falmouth.[3]

Yet these locations on the east and western coasts represented secondary objectives. Any invasion with London and the seat of government as its object would occur between the Thames Estuary and the Isle of Wight. It was this area that was most heavily fortified. Even here, the naval squadrons based on the Downs and Spithead were well placed to give a warning and to take early action against an invasion fleet. The most vulnerable locations were defined as East Wear Bay near Folkestone, Hythe Bay, and on either side of Dungeness, depending on whether the wind was westerly or easterly. Further west were the beaches near Rye, Pevensey Bay and Eastbourne. West of Beachy Head, Seaford was considered suitable for a landing, as were the beaches of Brighton and Hove.

The French having landed, opinions on their next moves varied. There had been earlier thoughts that the capture of Portsmouth would lead to an attack on the capital from the west. But the possible invasion beaches were now more narrowly identified. Dundas took the view that because of the lie of the North and South Downs, the enemy would encounter fewer obstacles the further east he was. Canterbury he thought to be the key in this approach, although this could mean the invader taking a chance and leaving an untaken Dover Castle and Western Heights in his rear. In this scenario, however, the enemy could use Ramsgate as a supply base and for landing his siege train. Whatever the approach on London from the south east, the invading army would have to force the Medway, and with it, the Chatham Lines, unless it faced the time-consuming march by way of Maidstone. If an eastern advance on London was favoured, Dover and Chatham assumed a vital strategic importance. With a garrison of 4000 men, Dover might hold out for three or four weeks; Chatham was less predictable.[4]

As well as fixed defences, other precautions were taken to gain advance warning of enemy movements and forestall the build up of his forces. Some indication of the general direction of a French attack could be anticipated from noting the port from which the invading force sailed. A force setting out from Texel might imply a landing in Scotland or Ireland; one from Brest suggested a destination in Cornwall or Devon or the west of Ireland. Cherbourg was the nearest base for attacking Portsmouth or the Isle of Wight. The ports of the Seine, Boulogne, Calais, and the Flemish coast threatened Kent and Sussex. In addition to a network of informants and spies reporting through smugglers and fishermen, a semaphore signalling system which linked the navy with London in a matter of hours was developed. There were also a number of pre-emptive combined operations on French ports which were designed to break up concentrations of shipping. The first to be carried out was an attack on Ostend. That on Copenhagen effectively deprived Napoleon of the Danish fleet, and the Peninsular War began with the same objective.

DISENCHANTMENT WITH THE BASTION SYSTEM

Military engineering, like warfare itself during the eighteenth century, followed conventional and familiar lines. The pattern of defensive systems was dominated by the bastion, and the methods of its application were strongly influenced by the works of Vauban. Although Vauban's main innovations were in the techniques of siege work, it was in his fortress designs that he achieved his most lasting fame. His many fortresses served as models for subsequent engineers, and

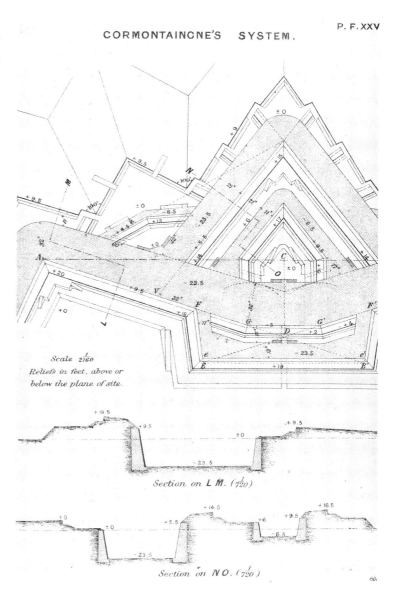

CORMONTAIGNE'S SYSTEM.

Scale 1/2160
Reliefs in feet, above or below the plane of site.

Section on L M. (1/720)

Section on N O. (1/720)

Cormontaigne's bastion system. An adaptation of Vauban's methods. An unauthorised version of Architecture Militaire *appeared in 1741. He stressed the concept that a straight line of defence is most easily held. From E M Lloyd's* Textbook of Fortification and Military Engineering *1887. (Author)*

appeared in all subsequent textbooks. As late as 1851, Lieutenant Henry Yule in his *Fortification for Officers of the Army and Students of Military History* was writing:

The system of permanent fortification usually taught is called the 'First System of Vauban'. It was never laid down by that illustrious soldier methodically as a system but it has been deduced by the engineers who succeeded him from an examination and comparison of the numerous fortresses which he constructed or renovated, such as Lille, Strasburg and Givet.

Vauban's influence was perpetuated longer and most rigorously within the future French engineering estab-

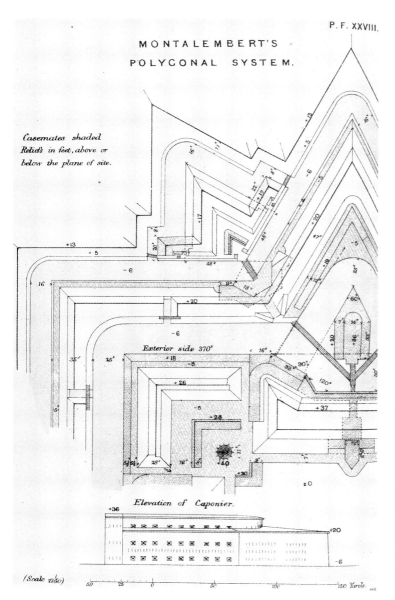

P. F. XXVIII.

MONTALEMBERT'S
POLYGONAL SYSTEM.

Casemates shaded
Reliefs in feet, above or
below the plane of site.

Exterior side 370ˣ

Elevation of Caponier.

(Scale ⅟₂₁₆₀)

Montalembert's polygonal system. From E M Lloyd's
Textbook of Fortification and Military Engineering *1887.*
(Author)

lishment. So much so that Fourcroy, its supreme head for much of the eighteenth century, described any ambition to improve on the doctrines of Vauban as 'one of the distinctive characteristics of a man who is ignorant of the engineering art'.[5]

With attitudes like this, military engineering stagnated among those who had become its leading exponents. Indeed Fourcroy designed an 'authorised French trace' based upon Vauban's methods. Departures from this regularity either became more and more complicated and extravagant, or, at the other extreme, some commanders were led to deprecate the effectiveness of permanent fortification altogether. The Marshal de Saxe, conqueror of the Netherlands in the 1740s, was sceptical of elaborate defences around towns and

claimed that it would be more sensible to set the army on entrenching strategic points in open country.[6] The success of the French *places du moment* stimulated an interest in improvised fieldworks as a valid alternative to permanent fortification. There were also those who even challenged the bastion system itself. A particular sceptic, admittedly of a later century, wrote:

> The geometrical foundation of the Vauban systems was the bastioned trace. Draw a polygon round the area to be defended, make each side a bastioned front, obtain saliency and a cross-fire over the front by ravelins. This was the foundation to which Vauban, in his so-called first system added little. Supplement this trace by any number of counterguards; place an independent reduit – in England to be erroneously termed a 'redoubt' – in every available angle; build high cavaliers to give simultaneous lines of fire; retrench everything retrenchable; throw out hornworks, crownworks, tenaillons, demi-tenaillons, etc to the front, thus indefinitely increasing geometrical possibilities; finally, build a 'citadel' in which most of the above artifices could be repeated inside the main line, and one arrives at a fair idea of what may be termed the linear method of fortification.[7]

Engineers across Europe began to adapt their own or inherited methods to particular circumstances. Cormontaigne devised his 'scale of comparison' whereby the number of days a fortress could be expected to hold out under siege could be calculated by according to it the perceived merits of the defensive system employed. Simultaneously there were improvements in the mass production of artillery with greater availability of cast iron pieces, which could be turned out more quickly and more cheaply than brass. Innovations in carriage design also improved firepower. The invention of the Gribeauval carriage allowed guns to fire over the parapet as well as through the limited number of embrasures (an example of a traversing Gribeauval mounting survives in the lines of Garrison Walls, St Mary's, Isles of Scilly). There was a move in Britain, as we have seen at Fort George, near Inverness, towards a simpler trace with fewer outworks, larger bastions on which to mount more guns, and, at Portsmouth, an increasing use of casemates, both for shielding guns and also for protecting the garrison.

The formulation of radical change came from Marc-Rene, Marquis de Montalembert, whose first volume of *La Fortification Perpendiculaire* was published in 1776. Montalembert identified some of the disadvantages of the bastion system: the weakness of the curtains and of the flanks of the bastions, which restricted the degree to which a bastioned front could be effective and provide offensive fire towards the field. He substituted a *tenaille* system on the grounds that a long flank is better than a short one. Essentially, he stressed that the best way of opposing the enemy's

Fort Cumberland, aerial photograph. (Airviews)

breaching batteries was to effect their destruction by means of overwhelming fire. The rampart should be organised to hold as many guns as possible, and to complement the offensive objectives, the ditch defence should be strengthened by placing a strong keep in the re-entering place of arms with casemates for flanking fire. Superiority of firepower was an objective defenders should seek, with guns preferably housed in casemates and not left exposed on the open rampart. The revival of casemates after a lapse of two centuries or so surprised some engineers, who argued that difficulties of ventilation would make them unusable for the defenders, and accurate fire into the gunports could be all the more destructive as a result of splinters struck from the stone cheeks of the embrasures. The advantages of casemates, however, were the protection they gave against enfilade, ricochet or vertical fire. Montalambert proved experimentally that casemates could be efficiently ventilated, and the improvements in powder charges by the latter part of the eighteenth century reduced the amount of gases coming back into the casemates after firing. For coastal defence, Montalambert advocated high, multi-tiered towers with casemated guns in order to deliver a great weight of fire over a short space of time. He anticipated the development of the future 'polygonal' trace by proposing long straight curtains without bastions, often with multistorey casemates, for greater offensive firepower, and with projecting caponiers of great strength in the ditch to give close defence. Montalembert's third principle related to defence in depth by means of isolated forts of no standard shape but suited to the terrain.

The effect of these ideas has been seen in some of the British works begun during the crises of the 1770s and 1780s. The use of coastal towers in the Channel Islands, detached works on Maker Heights, the use of casemates and caponiers at Fort Monkton, all show that British engineers were aware that the traditional bastion system could be improved. This ability to change and keep up with new trends developed more emphatically during the programme of coastal defences stimulated by the threat of Napoleonic invasion. It can also be seen in British military engineering abroad, for example in the highly effective detached redoubts and fieldworks which constituted the Lines of Torres Vedras with which Wellington defended his base at Lisbon during the Peninsular War.

COASTAL BATTERIES AND REFURBISHMENTS

The work carried out during the 1770s and 1780s, especially under the Duke of Richmond's aegis, had ensured that the major naval bases were comparatively secure. Only in the environs of Portsmouth was there need to close the eastern side of Portsea Island, and control the entrance to Langstone harbour. Although plans for a replacement for the fifty-year-old Fort Cumberland were in existence in 1788, work does not seem to have begun on the new fort until 1794.

Fort Cumberland, casemated flanks in the bastions. (Author)

Lieutenant-Colonel John Evelegh, the Commanding Royal Engineer for Portsmouth, and famous for his part in the siege of Gibraltar, was in charge of its construction and may have designed it. The second Fort Cumberland was the last self-contained fully bastioned fortress to be built in England. Fort Regent, Jersey, and Fort Westmoreland in Cork harbour were begun a few years later and marked the end of this type of fortress in the British Isles and Ireland. Although complementary to Fort Monkton on the western extremity of the Portsmouth defences, Cumberland was more conventional in design. It was of a regular, pentagonal plan enclosing 24 acres, which made it larger than Tilbury but not so extensive as Fort George, Ardesier. The bastions were large and commodious, the salients varying from 73° for the landward bastions, 80° for the north and south east bastions, with the salient of the central bastion, whose right face covered the approaches to Langstone harbour, of 90°. The outworks were simple: a wide, dry ditch, covered-way and glacis, with a large ravelin covering the landward approach and the main gate. Fort Cumberland did not share the elaborate caponiers of Fort Monkton. Its ditch defence was provided by gun casemates in the bastion flanks. Emphasis was also placed on an active defence. The curtains, except for the one which contained the main gate, were pierced by sallyports into the ditch. In each of the re-entering angles of the covered-way was a place of arms protected against enfilade fire by traverses, and each was reached by two flights of steps from the ditch. The fort was built by convict labour, and was brick faced, the bricks being burnt on site. By 1809 the body of the place was said to be complete except for the paving of the four sallyports, oak palisading, sodding the glacis and the oak stockade to enclose the gorge of the ravelin. Work, however, was still going on until 1812.

Both Forts Monkton and Cumberland, more than anything elsewhere in the British Isles, demonstrate the important modifications which had taken over bastioned fortification towards the end of the eighteenth century, and the influences derived from the writings of Montalembert. The move towards separating offensive fire from defensive, which implied the conscious identification of ditch defences, was the main characteristic of both forts; also, the adoption of the bombproof casemates for guns as well as for barrack purposes. The outworks were to be the springboard of active defence as well as incorporating the function of the glacis to protect the rampart scarp from direct fire. This last aspect can be seen most dramatically at Fort Regent, Jersey and at the Shannonbridge *tête-de-pont* in Ireland which will be discussed separately.

The extensive vulnerability of the coastline outside the main naval ports, led to an unprecedented demand for batteries to be built at almost every harbour. By 1803, the Firth of Forth had guns mounted at Blackness Castle, Leith Fort and at Queensferry, Inchcolm and Inchgarvie. Dumbarton Castle, commanding the Clyde, was well armed. In north eastern England there were batteries at Berwick, Bamborough Castle, Blyth, Seaton Sluice, Tynemouth, South Shields, Hartlepool, Whitby, Scarborough, Hull, Paul's Cliff, Stallingborough and White Booth. Further south, along the east coast, there was a battery at Cromer, considerable numbers of guns at Great Yarmouth and Lowestoft, then smaller batteries at Southwold, Gorleston Cliff and Aldeborough. Landguard

Fort mounted forty-two guns of varying calibres. On the Essex coast were small batteries at Harwich, around the mouths of the Stour and Colne. In Kent, away from the main concentrations of firepower in the Thames and Medway, there were minor batteries at Whitstable, Margate, Ramsgate and Pegwell Bay. South of the three Downs castles were three 32-pounders at St Margaret's Bay. Moving west beyond Dover into the danger area, there were two batteries at Folkestone, one at Copt Point, at Eastware, Sandgate Castle, Shorncliffe, and three at Hythe, each dignified by the title of 'fort', and named after Twiss, Sutherland and Moncrieff, with a smaller work on Saltwood Heights. There was a battery at Lympne, New Romney and Dymchurch Sluice, a redoubt and four batteries at Dungeness and a battery at Lydd. The Sussex coast had ten batteries: Rye, Hastings, two at Langney Point, Eastbourne, Seaford, Blatchington, Newhaven, Brighton and Arundel Haven. West of the concentration of defences around Portsmouth, the Solent and the Isle of Wight, the Henrician works at Weymouth and Portland remained armed, and Swanage and Bridport had three guns each. Into Devon, Seaton had a few guns, but the Berry Head batteries and Dartmouth were well equipped. West of Plymouth, and also excluding the Falmouth fortress, the minor harbours of Looe, Fowey, Charlestown, Mevagissey, St Anthony's Head, Mount's Bay, St Ives, Portreath, and up the north coast into Devon, Ilfracombe, all had their batteries. The Bristol Channel was not well armed at this time. There were four guns apiece at Portishead Point and Avonmouth. Swansea had two 9-pounders and Fishguard six. There were three batteries at Liverpool: the North Batteries, Red Noses and Rock Channel. Further up the north coast was a well stocked battery at Whitehaven. The calibre of the armament varied enormously at all these locations. The most frequently mounted pieces were 24-pounders followed by 32-pounders. The larger concentrations of fortifications tended to have large numbers of smaller pieces as well as a few of the heaviest calibre at 42-pounder.

Many of the long established fortresses were augmented by additional batteries alongside the main works. At Landguard Fort, the entrenched camp and batteries outside the fort, constructed twenty years before by Hyde Page, were removed. Instead, the south facing ramparts of the fort itself were improved and fitted with traversing platforms, and Beauclark's Battery, built on the top of the glacis, now became the strongest element with its eleven 42-pounder guns. The newly improved Thames defences at Tilbury and Gravesend were further strengthened by advanced batteries for four 24-pounders downstream, at Coalhouse Point, East Tilbury on the Essex bank and at Shornemead and Lower Hope Point on the Kent side.[8] These were semi-circular in plan, having a wide rampart with traversing platforms behind. A triangular-shaped en-

A 24-pounder smooth-bore gun on a sliding traversing carriage. (Author)

The Thames-side 1799 battery of East Tilbury. (V T C Smith)

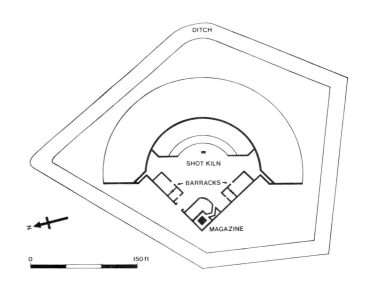

closed area to the rear, containing weatherboarded barrack buildings and a magazine, was defined by a brick wall. Likewise at Hurst Castle, controlling the Needles Passage, the arrangement of guns on the semi-circular bastions of the Henrician castle offered an insufficient concentration of firepower. Early in 1795, two six-gun batteries were sited on the shingle bank outside the castle. Like many batteries at this time, they were each to have a shot-heating furnace, red-hot shot being an effective weapon against wooden ships. By 1803, more work was planned at Hurst which entailed inserting a vault in the central tower in order to mount heavy guns on the top.[9] This involved gutting the interior of the tower, and inserting a central pier containing a staircase and supporting the vault which

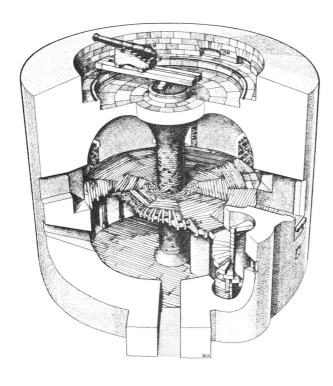

Sandgate Castle, Kent: a reconstruction of the keep as a Martello tower. (From Edward C Harris, 1980; drawn by Simon Hayfield)

carried the six 24-pounders mounted on traversing carriages above. The central tower of Sandgate Castle was similarly converted into a substantial gun-tower between 1805 and 1808.[10]

The batteries erected at this time of emergency were mostly of a temporary and simple nature. The guns were often mounted on platforms which together formed segments of a circle in plan. The guns were protected by a rampart of earth but often were mounted to fire over it, *en barbette*. The interior of the rampart would be revetted. At Hurst Castle, Evelegh proposed using earth-filled barrels to serve as revetment. Unless the batteries were adjuncts of a substantial work, they were enclosed at the gorge, usually by stone or brick walls, meeting at a salient angle. The larger batteries in Hythe Bay also followed much the same arrangement. The four batteries at Dungeness were more ambitious. They were enclosed and roughly hexagonal in shape with barracks and magazine. The parapets were 20 feet (6 metres) thick, revetted by a low scarp wall 4–7 feet (1–2 metres) high, without a ditch or counterscarp. The gorge was enclosed by a loopholed wall, only 1½ feet (450mm) thick and 10 feet (3 metres) high, flanked by two square, loopholed, two-storeyed bastions at the rear angles. There was barrack accom-

modation for as many as 3 officers and 50 men. Because of their construction few of these Napoleonic batteries remain today; as early as 1816 many were described as shapeless earthworks. Probably because they were more substantially revetted than most, those at Dungeness are the best survivors.

Dover was given much attention, and between 1793 and 1815 close on half a million pounds were expended its defences.[11] More than half of this was devoted to the Western Heights and the fieldworks there. Much smaller sums were spent on the castle and on the Grand Shaft, the securing of the town and harbour 'against *coup de main* from the sea', and repairing Archcliffe Fort. By 1798, the then Secretary of State for War, summed up the importance now placed on Dover:

> Without Dover Castle the enemy can have no certain communication; and always supposing that on our shore he finds no means to advance his purpose, the bringing up and placing sufficient artillery to reduce it is a work of slow process and would give time to relieve it, whether he remained in east Kent and made that his chief object or whether he found himself sufficiently strong to press on to the Medway and there wait the result, if in the meantime he could depend on subsisting in the country. The possession to an enemy of Dover Castle, of the opposite Entrenched Height and of the town and port, fortified in the manner that he would soon accomplish and defended by 6 or 7000 men would establish a sure communication with France and could not be easily wrested from his hands. The conquest of this alone would be to him a sufficient object could he arrive with means of immediately attacking it. Its preservation to us is most important . . .[12]

The initial impetus was directed to Dover Castle which underwent the most radical changes of its existence since the Middle Ages. The commanding engineer of the southern district from 1792 to 1809 was Lieutenant-Colonel William Twiss, an engineer of great inventiveness, which he demonstrated during his career in Canada as well as against French invasion at home. His first objective at the castle was to strengthen the eastern defences. This involved reducing the height of the medieval outer curtain, backing it with a massive earth rampart, widening and deepening the ditch, and constructing four powerful outworks beyond the counterscarp bank. East of Avranches Tower was Horseshoe Bastion, next was Hudson's Bastion and on the cliff edge was the East Demi-Bastion. Further down the slope from the last two works was the detached East Arrow Bastion. Although described as bastions, these bore no relationship in plan or function to the angle bastions of Vauban and before. They were enclosed, rectangular, independent earthworks in advance of the main line of the castle defences giving command to the

Dover Castle eastern defences: Hudson's bastion. (Author)

Dover Castle: the re-formed Spur connected by a caponier to the circular St John's Tower. (Author)

slopes below the castle, thereby allowing the heavy guns on the new rampart to cover the far side of the valley and beyond. These outworks were connected to the castle by underground passages which themselves were protected internally by drawbridges and musketry loops. The western side of the castle, nearest the town, was given better communications in that direction with a new entrance at Canon's Gate wide enough for a column of troops and artillery. The gateway passed below a bombproof vault, one of a line of five casemates. Below the drawbridge was a caponier across the ditch. There was another caponier at the medieval entrance of Constable's Gate. The weak northern side of the castle, which had always caused the defenders' trouble, was given 'a sort of Redan', according to Twiss, on the medieval Spur, in an attempt to command the higher ground beyond. Covering the approaches to the redan were the most elaborate local defences imaginable. Not only was the ditch elaborately covered by caponiers, but anyone who had managed to get into the underground system could be trapped behind dropping doors or doors operated by remote control, and all the while be under fire from internal musketry positions. The mutilation of the medieval castle was completed by the insertion of massive brick vaults within the keep to provide a bombproof magazine and gun positions on the roof.

Comparatively small sums were spent on the earlier fieldworks on the Western Heights between 1793 and 1803. Then, with invasion seemingly imminent in 1803, General Sir David Dundas and Twiss

spent two days examining the Heights. Twiss felt that they could be held by 'detached Redoubts with small garrisons'. Twiss had appreciated that the fieldworks could be improved, 'to form this position into an entrenched camp where a corps of five or six thousand men might remain in security and with tolerable convenience and in readiness to move against an enemy wherever required.'[13] The engineer on the spot, Captain William Ford, saw the answer requiring three

Dover, Western Heights: the fieldworks as remodelled by Twiss in the first decade of the nineteenth century and further refined in the 1860s. (DOE)

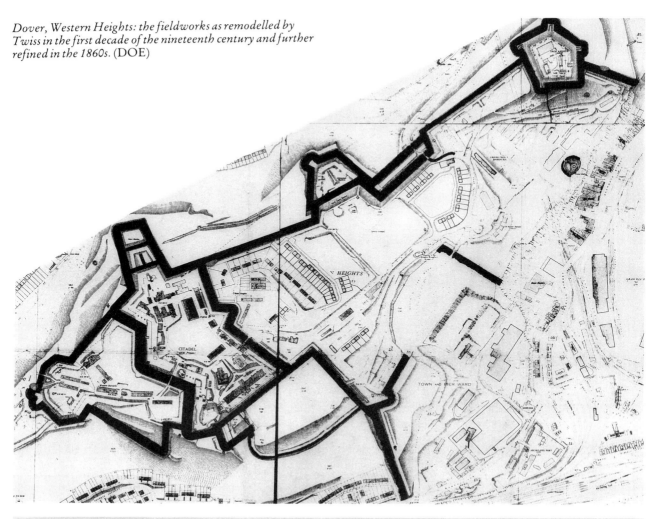

Dover, Western Heights: North Centre Bastion. (DOE)

major detached works. The eastern end of the downs was given over to the polygonal Drop Redoubt. At the western end, and the key to the position, was the Citadel, and between the two was the square-fronted, North Centre Bastion. These separate works were connected by the reformed earlier lines. Despite the colossal sums expended on developing the system of fortifications with their underground works and massive barracks, they remained unfinished at the end of the war. They were not completed until another Napoleon caused a new invasion scare in 1859. Even then, the improved defences did not fulfil Ford's ambition of linking the Western Heights with the castle by means of an earthwork which would close Dover to the north.

Associated with the works on Western Heights was a need to refurbish Archcliffe Fort above the harbour, which now served as a flank position for the Drop Redoubt. There was also a requirement for rapid communications between the barracks and defences on the Heights and the town and harbour below. This was solved most ingeniously by Twiss who built the Grand Shaft to connect the two. The Shaft contained a triple staircase winding round a central light-well, enabling a large body of troops to move simultaneously. The story of separate stairs for officers, NCOs and privates is, alas, a myth![14]

MARTELLO TOWERS AND DEFENCE IN DEPTH

The defensive preparations proposed or carried out before 1803 were largely conventional in strategic conception, if somewhat innovative in practical application. They were principally coastal batteries intended to deter shipping from approaching landing places, harbours and anchorages. They were not specifically designed to repel the landing and subsequent deployment of an invading force. Indeed, it had long been accepted that an enemy could not be prevented from landing, and if he did, the local population was to adopt a 'scorched earth' policy, for example, by flooding Romney Marshes, and he was to be confronted by a field army as soon as possible. This was why so much store was placed on the establishment of entrenched camps, such as that on the Western Heights, Dover, enabling a mobile force stationed close to the expected danger points to move on the invasion beach-head wherever it occurred.

The presence of a very obvious invasion army across the Channel in 1803, and in the two years immediately following, stimulated a defensive response quite novel in this country, and only paralleled by the preparations made in similar circumstances in 1940. The new strategy was to require beach defence against actual landing, combined with defence in depth, whether to contain the landing force until the field army could arrive, or which would envisage lines of

South coast Martello tower 24 at Dymchurch with its 24-pounder gun. (DOE)

defence in commanding positions well to the rear, and inevitably protecting London. This involved the creation of a barrier fortress at the main crossing of the Medway.

Beach defences were to be in the form of interdependent gun-towers. This was a development on the earlier use of towers built to defend beaches in the Channel Islands about twenty years before. Undoubtedly, the use of towers was further stimulated by descriptions of the effective deployment of a tower at Cape Mortella in Corsica against a British naval squadron in 1794. It was an action which was to give its name to this particular type of defensive work. At about the beginning of 1797, Sir David Dundas, who had commanded in Corsica at the time of the frustrated naval action at Cape Mortella, proposed in a memorandum on coast defence, the desirability of 'disconcerting' an enemy fleet while still at anchor, of preventing him from settling in any roadstead, and of delaying his landing for 24 or 48 hours. He favoured the construction of

strong stone towers, favourably situated, not commanded, mounting two or three large guns and

Dymchurch Redoubt: internal parade surrounded by casemated barracks with the gun platform on top. (Author)

protecting as long as proper an outward battery of two more guns, bomb-proof, garrisoned by about thirty men, about 30 feet in height and 12 of interior diameter, entered by a ladder . . . would answer this purpose better than larger batteries and expensive low works. Supposing such a tower to cost £700, one hundred of them properly disposed in the different bays most inviting to an enemy would give great security to a very extensive range of coast.[15]

This idea was given support by a memorandum from a Major Reynolds in the following year. Reynolds, having observed the ineffectiveness of the south coast defences, listed sites for 143 'Martella Towers' between Littlehampton and Yarmouth. Of these he considered 73 urgently necessary, 48 necessary and 22 desirable.[16]

The idea of extensive deployment of gun-towers was not immediately taken up, and not revived until the critical days of 1803. Dundas found Brigadier-General Twiss equally enthusiastic about towers. Captain Ford, on Twiss's staff, produced alternative designs for square or circular towers. Like Reynold's proposals, they were to be sited at close intervals so that they could cross fire with their neighbouring towers. The circular form gained acceptance for reasons of cost among military circles but official and political acceptance was another matter. After prolonged delay and obstruction, 'the expensive and diabolical system of tower defence' was finally agreed but the delays meant

that building could not begin until 1805.[17] The south coast towers were more or less completed by 1808. Those on the east coast were not finished until 1812.

Seventy-four towers were built between Folkestone and Seaford, including the conversion of the keep of Sandgate Castle, along with two eleven-gun circular redoubts, one at Eastbourne, and the other at the eastern end of Dymchurch sea wall. The towers were generally spaced 500 to 600 yards (457–548 metres) apart. Some, like those at Dymchurch, were set closer together in order to defend the sluices which drained Romney Marsh. Work on them was under the direction of the Board of Ordnance and the Royal Engineers. The main contractor was a William Hobson, who sub-contracted work to local builders. He arranged for a large proportion of the huge quantity of bricks required to be bought up discreetly to avoid stimulating price rises among the London brickmakers, and then to ship them down the Thames.[18]

The south coast towers were all of identical plan. Although superficially circular, they were elliptical in plan with the inner and outer wall faces arranged eccentrically so that the thickest part of the wall faced the most vulnerable seaward side. The towers stand 33 feet (10 metres) high, and taper from a thickness of 13 feet (4 metres) at the base of the seaward side to 6 feet (1.8 metres) at the parapet. They were built throughout in brick, bedded in hot lime mortar (a mixture of lime, ash and hot tallow), intended to increase the tower's resistance to bombardment. Entrance to the towers was at first floor level, by moveable ladder if there was no

Harwich Redoubt, from landward. (Author)

surrounding ditch when access was from a drawbridge. The first floor was divided by timber partitions to form living quarters for the garrison of 24 men and 1 officer. The ground floor was a space for the magazine and stores, with water cisterns below. The flat roof formed the gun platform and was carried on a brick vault supported by a central pier from the base of the tower. The gun platform was reached by a stair in the thickest portion of the wall. Ventilation shafts and chimney flues exited through the parapet. The main armament was a single 24-pounder gun mounted on a traversing carriage pivoting centrally to provide all-round cover. Originally, it was intended to mount two carronades of the same calibre as well, all three guns traversing from the same pivot, but this ingenious device does not appear to have been carried out. Those towers on the high ground at the eastern end of the chain were equipped also with 5½-inch (140mm) howitzers. The garrison was armed with muskets.[19]

The east coast towers followed. Here 27 three-gun towers of a similar but improved design were built between 1808 and 1812 between St Osyth Stone and Aldeburgh.[20] The latter, at the northern limit of the chain, was unusual in being larger and intended for four guns. As on the south coast, the system included a 'circular casemate redoubt' at Harwich; this time for ten guns, though eight was the original plan. This was self-contained and intended for all-round fire, with casemated barrack accommodation below the gun plat-

forms, and the whole surrounded by a deep ditch with revetted counterscarp and glacis. It had been conceived in 1806, begun the next year, and completed in 1810. Originally a similar redoubt was intended for Aldeburgh but economy demanded the compromise of the present unique tower.

While the Martello tower system was being debated, a significant decision was taken by government to accept Lieutenant-Colonel John Brown's plan for a defensive canal from Hythe to the river Rother at Rye to isolate Romney Marsh from the high ground to the rear. A western extension from the river Brede to Cliff End cut off Pett Level and Winchelsea Beach (see map on p131). Three substantial military advantages were provided by what was to be known as The Royal Military Canal. It formed a physical barrier separating the marshland from the rest of the country, thus avoiding the need to take the damaging and unpopular step of flooding Romney Marsh when invasion threatened. Barges could provide easy transport of troops and supplies behind this very vulnerable stretch of coastline. The provision of gun emplacements and a road along its bank, which was raised into a parapet, together with the canal acting as a wet ditch made this feature a 'retrenchment' in military terms. Its clear defensive value led to the construction of the canal without delay. The civil engineer Rennie was put in charge and mainly navigator labour was used. It was more or less completed in the summer of 1805.[21]

Other internal defensive lines and measures for hampering any invaders were prepared. In the

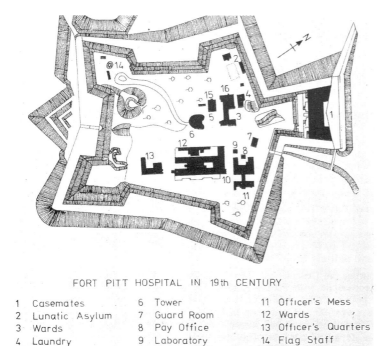

FORT PITT HOSPITAL IN 19th CENTURY

1	Casemates	6	Tower	11	Officer's Mess
2	Lunatic Asylum	7	Guard Room	12	Wards
3	Wards	8	Pay Office	13	Officer's Quarters
4	Laundry	9	Laboratory	14	Flag Staff
5	Library	10	Offices	15	Museum
				16	Purveyor's Store

Fort Pitt, plan. (K R Gulvin, Medway Military Research Group)

Eastern District, the two entrenched camps, one near Colchester between the rivers Colne and Stour, the other on the high ground above Chelmsford, which had been identified during the American War, were brought back into use. Additional works were prepared between Sudbury and Gun Hill (Langham) to cover an enemy's line of approach from the direction of Harwich. Since London was reckoned to be the principal objective, a defence line was planned which ran from the north bank of the river Lea as far as Stamford Hill, through Highgate and Hampstead to Willesden Green then on to Holland House and down to the Thames at Chelsea. This northern line was to be strengthened by flooding the Lea Valley. On the south bank, fieldworks were thrown up on Shooter's Hill and Blackheath to serve as outworks to the main line of defence. This ran from Deptford through Sydenham and the Norwood Hills, and back to the Thames at Wandsworth. To improve communications north and south, a floating bridge was constructed between Blackwall Stairs and Greenwich Marshes, almost exactly on the line of the present Blackwall Tunnel.[22]

Between London and the south coast lay the North Downs. Along this line a military road was established, known as the 'Chalk Ridge Communication', running from Guildford to Rochester. This was designed to give support to the camps which had been, or were to be, established at the gaps in the North Downs. As well as the naval semaphore system, warning beacons were erected on prominent heights, such as

Fairlight, Firle and Chanctonbury. The establishment of the Board of Ordnance depot at Weedon, Northamptonshire, on the Grand Junction Canal was a major strategic move, and was described as one of the most magnificent establishments of its kind in Europe. Apart from serving as a refuge for the royal household and government, the depot was intended as point for the collection and finishing of arms manufactured in and around Birmingham, and removing the country's principal ordnance store from the dangerously exposed arsenal at Woolwich.

Associated with this counter-invasion strategy was the creation of a barrier fortress on the most likely line of advance from a beach-head in Kent or East Sussex, the Roman road from Canterbury to the main bridge-crossing over the Medway at Rochester. The earlier defences at Chatham were primarily intended to protect the dockyard, and, although recently retrenched, were continuous lines from the cliff edge above Chatham town across the Brompton heights to the river near the old Gillingham Fort. The new emergency meant that the lines were further remodelled and revetted in brick throughout. At the northern end the lines were realigned completely. There had been a scheme for an extension of these continuous lines to take in Rochester to the south. Instead, the new defences were detached works ringing Rochester. They guarded the flank of the Chatham Lines, but they also provided greater protection for the river crossing, and blocked the approaches from the south and east.

The principal work was Fort Pitt on a spur overlooking the river, and with good command to the south. Work was begun in 1805, though the fort was not completed until 1819. The plan of the fort was superficially of bastion form, but its dominating characteristic was a large, casemated, defensible barracks and multi-tiered gun-tower, something of a hornwork in plan, placed on the north side where the principal armament was mounted. In the centre of the fort was a detached, two-storey tower with a gun platform on its flat roof. The landward front was of regular bastioned form complete with a ravelin in the ditch, entered by means of a caponier, and, behind the curtain were two large cavaliers. Fort Pitt was a remarkable hybrid at a time when the bastion system was already out of favour, and brick gun-towers becoming all the rage. It is regretable that only a partial outline of the fort now remains, and its significant features long demolished. Something of its flavour can be seen at the next defensive work to be built south of Rochester, Fort Clarence. This was begun in 1808 and not completed until 1812. The principal element of what amounted to a substantial road block controlling the access from the Maidstone road to the Medway, remains a large, three-storey, brick tower. It resembles nothing so much as a late medieval tower house, complete with round turrets and machicolations. Its main function was to flank a

Fort Clarence, Rochester. (Author)

long, brick-revetted ditch with guns firing from case-mates in its basement. The height of the tower must have been more for observation than as a lofty gun position. At either end of the ditch were smaller works, the Medway Tower and the Maidstone road guard-house, adding to the flanking capability. Behind the long ditch and rampart were the barrack and ancillary buildings extending in a lightly enclosed strip. Also controlling the north–south roads between Fort Clarence and Fort Pitt was Delce Tower, armed with two 18-pounder carronades. Another isolated brick tower or defensible guardhouse, Gibraltar Tower, was sited between Fort Pitt and Chatham. Both Gibraltar and Delce Towers were two storeys high, with magazines and stores below the ground floor, and walls loopholed for musketry.[23]

IRELAND: A SECOND FRONT

Ireland was the one part of the then British Isles to have experienced potentially serious invasion. Between 1793 and the end of 1798, there were five attempted expeditions with the intentions of assisting and equipping the United Irishmen in an armed rising which would set up an Irish republic. It was only lack of synchronisation with local rebellion that doomed Humbert's force to early defeat at Ballinamuck in 1798. On the eastern side of the country, Michael Dwyer and his band kept up guerilla activities in the Wicklow mountains until the end of 1803, in the hope of French aid. Dwyer's actions

were enough to demand the construction of the military road, associated with a line of barracks, through the mountains from Rathfarnham to Aughavanagh.[24]

For all the potential danger, Irish coastal defences were nevertheless ineffective. Irish fortifications were as much inward looking as geared to a foreign threat. The major harbours and coastal towns had fairly orthodox defences, but with the build-up of a French expeditionary force, radical regard had to be paid to the coastline of the south and west. While the main thrust of Napoleon's ambition lay in the direction of London, the possibility of the capture of Ireland would have been a shrewd move to wearing down the British economy and fighting potential, without the risks of a more dramatic assault on the heavily defended coastline of Kent and Sussex. The establishment of a second front in Britain's western flank was a serious consideration. French plans for an invasion of England between 1803 and 1805 included sending a large force to Ireland. Napoleon noted in 1804 that 'With only 18,000 men in Ireland we would run great risks; but whether they be increased to 40,000 or myself be in England and 18,000 in Ireland, the gain of the war would be ours.'[25] The several commanders-in-chief in Ireland drew various conclusions on maintaining a defensive policy. Officers, like Lieutenant Henry Keating in 1795, published pamphlets on the subject.[26] In addition, with the advantage of inside knowledge, General Dumouriez followed up his report to the British government on the 'Defence of England' with a detailed 'Military Memorandum' on the defence of Ireland.

From the many conflicting opinions certain broad principles emerged. The east coast was a most

Sandymount Martello tower, Dublin Bay. (Author)

unlikely place for a landing. However, if Dublin was to be the main objective then the shortest route to the capital would be achieved by a landing in Galway. After Dublin as the political prize, the place of the greatest military concern for the defenders was the security of Cork, whose magnificent harbour was the Royal Navy's base in Ireland. Limerick and Waterford were considered next in importance. As for landing places, an enemy could shelter only in Belfast Lough, Lough Foyle or Lough Swilly in the north. In the south, there were Kinsale, Cork and Waterford harbours. The most favourable and numerous anchorages were on the west coast, the more obvious being Galway Bay, the Shannon estuary, the Kenmare estuary, Bantry Bay and Crookhaven. While Berehaven in Bantry Bay was 'one of the noblest harbours in the world', Galway Bay 'admits the enemy at once into the centre of the kingdom and seems calculated for almost every purpose he might think worthy of a great armament.'[27]

Robert Emmet's rising in July 1803, coinciding with Napoleon's build-up of naval and military might on the Channel coasts, renewed fears of another French invasion of Ireland. A few days after the rising in Dublin, orders were issued for the defence of the Shannon followed by a substantial programme of fortification, permanent and temporary, which occupied the years 1804–6. The designs fell to Lieutenant-Colonel Benjamin Fisher, the commanding engineer for Ireland. Further threats of invasion in 1810 and 1811 produced a second phase of building activity between 1811 and 1814. The principal concentrations of defences were: Dublin Bay, Waterford, Cork harbour, Bantry Bay, the mouth of the Shannon, Galway Bay and Lough Swilly. The distinguishing feature of these coastal works is that they employed towers to one degree or another, round towers similar to the English south coast Martellos, or rectangular towers usually associated with a substantial battery. The other major strategic consideration, perhaps owing something to the 1798 experience, was the establishment of a defensive line along the Shannon, hingeing on Athlone, in order to bar the approaches to Dublin. A further aspect of Irish defence planning was an extensive system of coastal signal stations with defensible guardhouses, following the coast from south of Dublin clockwise to Malin Head, leaving the north east uncovered.[28]

In 1804, the first Martello towers were constructed in Dublin Bay, a year or so before the English south coast towers were begun. It is ironical that these first towers, built with such alacrity, were in a location where the military men were agreed there was least likelihood of a hostile landing! The Dublin towers were closely similar to Captain Ford's design, with the chief exception that they were circular, and lacked the ellipticality of the English south coast variety. In some instances, towers were provided with machicolations above the entrance. Their armament, garrison and purpose were the same. There were fifteen towers south of Dublin, and twelve to the north. Similar towers, though later in date and with design differences, appeared in County Wexford. One was at Baginbun Head, and two near Duncannon Fort. At Cork harbour, as well as the forts at the harbour entrance (Camden and Carlisle and Fort Westmorland on Spike Island), five towers were built late in the sequence. All five were still under construction between 1813 and 1815. These are considerably larger in diameter than the Dublin variety with vertical walls instead of the battered, 'flower pot' type. Here they were used to cover communications as much as landing points. One covers the bridge leading to Great Island. Further west, in Bantry Bay, four towers were built on Bere Island, while three much larger circular redoubts were thrown up on Whiddy Island. At Glengariff harbour is one of the earliest towers, built in 1804. Moving north, towers of a different sort, usually associated with batteries, become the rule.[29]

Keelogue Battery from the south east. (Paul Kerrigan)

River Shannon and Estuary defences:

1   Athlone Batteries
2   Athlone Castle
3   Shannonbridge
4   Banagher Tower
5   Fort Eliza
6   Keelogue Battery and Tower
7   Meelick Tower
8   Cromwell's Island Battery
9   Limerick Castle
10 Kilkerin Point Battery
11 Tarbert Island Battery
12 Corran Point Battery
13 Scattery Island Battery
14 Doonaha Battery
15 Kilcredaun Point Battery
16 Finavarra Point Tower
17 Aughinish Tower
18 Galway Fort
19 Rossaveal Tower
(Author)

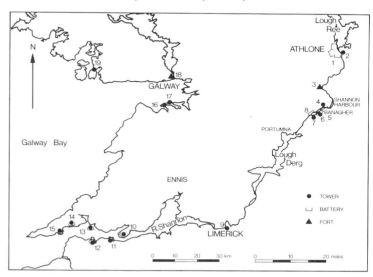

The defences of the mouth of the Shannon bear out this change of tactic. With the exception of a battery on Tarbert Island, which had a flat bastion shape and belonged to the mid-1790s, the Shannon

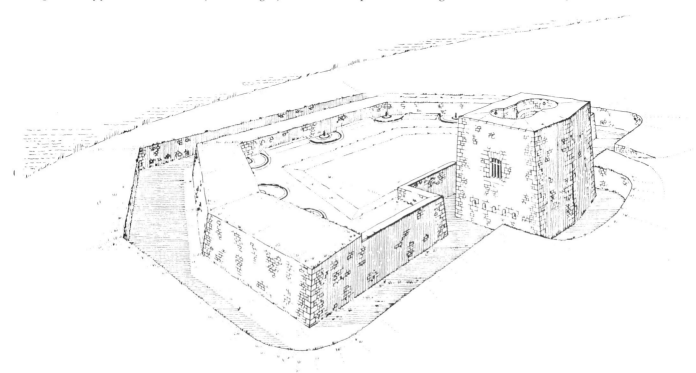

Kilcredaun Point Battery, Shannon Estuary. (Author)

Estuary defences are all of similar form. They were essentially batteries, D-shaped in plan, and generally for six guns firing over a broad parapet. They were enclosed by a dry ditch, and at the rear and built into it, was a two-storey blockhouse/tower in the centre of the landward side for the protection of the main armament in the battery. On the roof of the tower were positions for two howitzers. These batteries were well sited to cause maximum damage to an enemy fleet making its way up-river. Kilcredaun Point Battery commanded the northern side, Corran Point Battery on Carrig Island, covered the southern part of the channel between Carrig Island and Scattery Island. Doonaha Battery was on the north side, north east of Kilcredaun. This latter fort was slightly smaller than the others. Scattery Island Battery lies towards the centre of the estuary, with the early battery on Tarbert Island, further east, now demolished in the building of a power station. Killkerin Point Battery on the north side is directly opposite Tarbert Island, and with the latter commands the river at a point where it narrows considerably.

Three towers were built to cover Galway Bay. Two on the south at Finavarra Point and Aughinish, and one to the north at Rossaveal, near Cashla Bay, were also associated with batteries. The next concentration up the coast is in Lough Swilly, where the D-shaped batteries with a rectangular tower in the gorge make them similar to those in the Shannon Estuary. They were late in being built – 1811 to 1814 – and replaced temporary earthwork batteries which had

been in existence in 1798. The batteries were paired along the estuary: Dunree with Knockalla, Muckamish with Neid's Point, and Rathmullen with Down Fort on Inch Island. Further east, two towers were placed at the narrow entrance to Lough Foyle. On the west was a tower and battery at Greencastle. On the opposite side was a tower similar to the Dublin type at Magilligan Point.

Besides towers and batteries, more substantial defences were needed for Ireland's principal naval base at Cork. By the eighteenth century it had replaced Kinsale, not just for the navy but as a port for merchant vessels engaged on the North American trade. There had been earlier temporary defence works at the harbour mouth, but after 1793 these were converted into the permanent works of a somewhat old-fashioned design. Carlisle Fort, on the eastern side, is situated on a cliff, some 200 feet (61 metres) above sea level. It was in the form of a bastion with the salient to landward, flanked on each side by demi-bastions. This fort had the function of a defensible barracks. Down the cliff were detached gun emplacements better able to direct fire on incoming vessels. In 1804 a total of fifty-three pieces of ordnance were present at the fort.

Opposite Carlisle was Camden Fort in a similar cliff-top position. During the American War the site was known as Ramhead Fort. The rebuilt fort was enclosed by a rock-cut ditch with a rampart of *tenaille* trace and no bastions for local defence. In 1813, three ranges of infantry barracks were under construction. The batteries covering the harbour entrance were also detached down the hillside. In 1804 there were thirteen 24-pounders for marine defence.

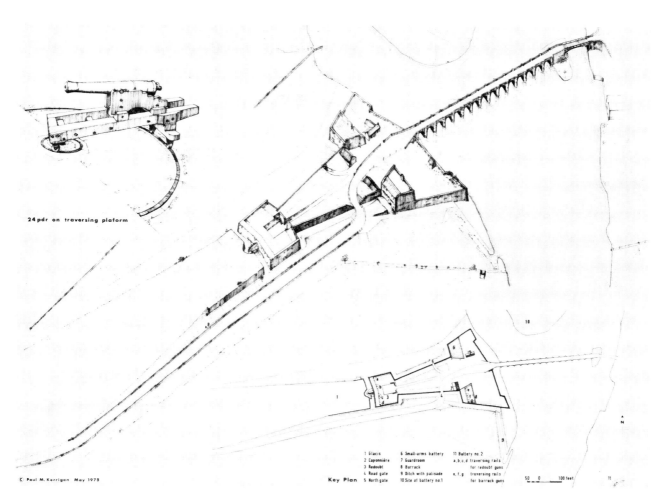

24 pdr on traversing platform

© Paul M. Kerrigan May 1975

Key Plan
1 Glacis
2 Caponnière
3 Redoubt
4 Road gate
5 North gate
6 Small-arms battery
7 Guardroom
8 Barrack
9 Ditch with palisade
10 Site of battery no.1
11 Battery no.2
a,b,c,d traversing rails for redoubt guns
e,f,g traversing rails for barrack guns

50 0 100 feet

Shannonbridge tête-de-pont. (Paul Kerrigan)

Fort Westmorland, on Spike Island, and at the apex of a triangle whose base was Carlisle and Camden, commanded the estuary directly. It also replaced an earlier earthwork position. The new fort was very large, of bastioned, hexagonal plan of fairly conventional form. The bastions have faces about 150 feet (46 metres) long and the flanks about 100 feet (30 metres). The building of the fort was extremely lengthy and costly.

The defence of the Shannon produced some works of considerable variety and importance, as well as providing the only internal line of defence of this period to leave permanent fortifications. The line of the Shannon was seen to be crucial to holding up an enemy army once it had effected a landing in the west. Starting at Portumna, there was a small cavalry barracks but no fortification. The first defence work came at Meelick, about 8 miles (13 kilometres) to the north, where a battery was thrown up on Cromwell's Island, and across the river, a Martello tower was subsequently built. This was 'cam' shaped, not very dissimilar from the English east coast towers. The gun platform was arranged for three guns on traversing carriages. On Incherky Island, a permanent battery replaced an earlier, and still surviving earthwork. Keelogue Battery had a similar arrangement to those in the Shannon Estuary: a flattened D-shaped battery for seven guns with a tower/blockhouse in the gorge with mountings for two howitzers. Banagher, 4 miles upstream, was an important river crossing. Near the end of the bridge, a medieval tower, known as Cromwell's Castle, was refurbished, converted into a magazine, and a gun mounted on top in the manner of Hurst Castle or Sandgate Castle on the English south coast. Banagher or Fanesker tower stands a short distance away. This was under construction in 1812, and is of elliptical plan for one gun. A short length of former canal parallel to the river provided something approaching a bridge-head defence. Also associated with this piece of river defence was Fort Eliza, a simple four-gun battery with the two gorge walls brought together into a salient with a guard-room at the apex.

Shannonbridge, 6 miles (9.6 kilometres) north west of Shannon harbour, the point at which the Grand Canal met the Shannon, is the nearest crossing-point of the river to Galway Bay, 45 miles (72 kilometres) to the west. French infantry could be expected to reach Shannonbridge in two days, if not delayed by an artillery train. On the same basis, Dublin was only four more days march away. In July 1803

Shannonbridge: caponier projecting from the redoubt and flanking the ditch. (Author)

Fisher was requested to design a *tête-de-pont* at Shannonbridge to forestall such a manoeuvre and work began the next year. The Shannonbridge *tête-de-pont* is unique in Ireland and Britain. The earthworks constructed in 1804 were three batteries and two redoubts. One battery survives on the east bank. The masonry works were built after 1810 and were still in progress in 1814. They replaced, for the most part, the earthwork defences. Kerrigan has described the works as follows:

> The fortifications are set out on the west bank, in an almost symmetrical layout on the axis of the bridge, which was completed in 1757. Some four hundred yards west of the river is the foot of the glacis, which slopes up to mask the west face of the advanced redoubt two hundred yards to the east. The counterscarp wall supporting the end of the glacis is separated from the scarp of the redoubt by a ditch or moat, twenty feet wide. Projecting into the ditch from the redoubt is a *caponniere*, a 'bombproof' vaulted structure provided with musket-loops flanking the ditch. Loops in two adjacent vaulted galleries in the redoubt provided for additional defence of the ditch and flank the *caponniere* north and south. Above these galleries is the gun platform for four pieces of artillery on traversing platforms, probably 24-pounders, like the guns on the western salient of the Athlone batteries. These guns had a field of fire westwards down the glacis and beyond, and could also be trained to fire to the north west and south west. The protected courtyard of the redoubt, from which there is access to the casemated galleries and the *caponniere*, is approached by a sunken road on the centre line of the lay-out. North and south of this roadway are the curtain walls linking the redoubt to the flank defences further to the east; a

small-arms battery for infantrymen armed with muskets to the north, the work to the south being a massive three-storey defensible barrack. On the flat roof of the barrack, supported by barrel-vaulted apartments below, were three guns on traversing platforms, which had a field of fire to the west, directly along the road from Ballinasloe. The front or west face of the building has two rows of musket-loops, the lower level being masked by the counterscarp wall of a small glacis. Flank fire was provided along the west face of the barrack by loopholes in the adjacent curtain wall to the north. The main road from Ballinasloe originally passed beneath an arched gateway in this curtain wall . . . The exterior of this archway with its heavy timber doors was protected by flank fire from the rear of the advanced redoubt and the front of the barrack . . . The eastern part of the *tête-de-pont* is bounded by a perimeter wall extending on the north and south as far as the river bank; at these corners are half bastions, which allowed for flank fire along the river bank north and south of the bridge, which is centrally located between them.[30]

Such a full description is justified for this remarkable military work which is the most sophisticated piece of military engineering carried out by British engineers at this period.

Athlone is about 10 miles (16 kilometres) north of Shannonbridge, and represented the key to the Shannon line. The west side of the town had earlier been ringed by a mixture of detached batteries and earthwork redoubts, some connected by entrenchments. After 1810, the earthworks of the Athlone batteries and connecting lines were revetted in masonry. A report of 1804 lists eight batteries, mostly mounting 12-pounders and eleven 6-pounders in the recently rebuilt castle. Bombproof casemates were also formed for stores and barracks. The defensive ring is not spectacular but it represented the stage that military engineering had reached with the disavowal of the continuous line.[31]

THE OTHER OFF-ISLANDS

The Channel Islands were, of course, in the front line. For this reason they were comparatively well defended already, with major fortresses and beach defences of batteries and towers. St Peter Port, Guernsey, had Fort George and its attendant batteries nearing completion. It was Jersey which lacked a modern citadel to replace seventeenth and eighteenth century Elizabeth Castle, useful as it was for protecting the approach to the harbour, but unable to provide a focus for the forces on the island and act as a defensible barracks because of tidal factors. Fieldworks on North and South Hills above St Helier had been proposed in 1787, and had been built shortly afterwards. These were replaced in

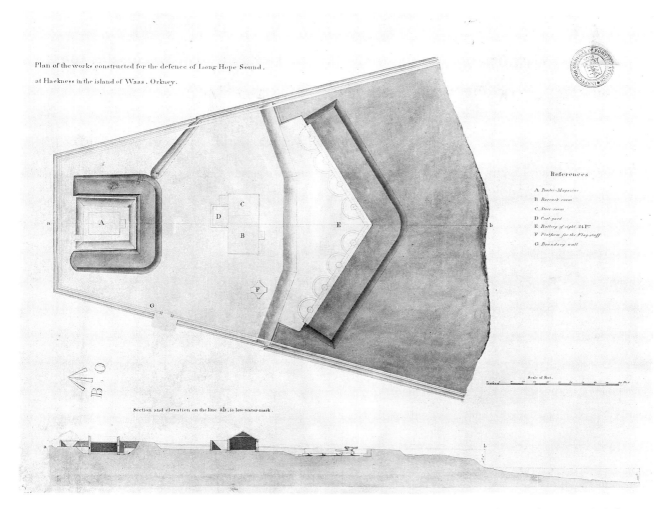

Plan of the works constructed for the defence of Long Hope Sound, at Hackness in the island of Waas, Orkney.

References
A *Powder Magazine*
B *Barrack-room*
C *Store-room*
D *Coal-yard*
E *Battery of eight 24 P.*
F *Platform for the Flag-staff*
G *Boundary wall*

Section and elevation on the line ab, to low-water-mark.

Hackness, on the south side of the Longhope Sound, Orkney: plan of the battery with barracks and magazine behind. Public Record Office, MPH 533/3. (PRO)

1806 by a large permanent work, Fort Regent, designed and supervised by Lieutenant-Colonel John Humphrey, which was to replace Elizabeth Castle as the island's military centre. The topographical conditions caused the fort to be an irregular, bastioned work, partly protected by natural cliffs. In this respect, the use of bastions was conventional, but its barrack accommodation was in casemates and casemates were used for some flanking cover. On the south side of the fort, facing the most likely direction of attack, was a counterguard and glacis over 230 yards (210 metres) long, whereby the scarp was effectively masked, and the glacis served also as a serious deterrent to a rush by infantry. The effect of this feature was somewhat similar to the long glacis at Shannonbridge, and as applied to Fort Regent meant that even if a besieger's progress was made by means of a series of saps, the approach was purposely restricted in width so that the number of men who could take advantage of this technique would be comparatively small.[32]

Elsewhere in Jersey, batteries were maintained, improved and some new towers built. In a letter of January 1811, General Don, the officer in command during the Napoleonic scares, advised that, 'a Tower was commenced by the Ordnance on l'Icho Rock last

Summer and that it is now in sufficient forwardness to admit of a guard being mounted at it.'[33] The Tour de Vinde at Noirmont was also begun at the same time. Portelet Bay tower may have been completed in 1808, and was then ready for its garrison of 1 sergeant and 12 men. Not only towers were built: the Rozel Barracks were built in 1810, and a loopholed enclosure wall survives.

Major-General Sir John Doyle, Lieutenant-Governor of Guernsey, likewise improved the coastal defensive positions. The old castle ruins at Rocquaine were pulled down, the summit of the rock levelled and a very powerful battery erected capable of containing twelve or fourteen guns, semi-circular in plan with a substantial masonry front. It was intended that the gorge should be enclosed with casemated accommodation for the garrison. The battery became known as Fort Grey, after the contractor who built it. Fort Doyle was constructed for three heavy guns and enclosed in the form of a low tower. It contained a guardroom, magazine, and shot furnace. Fort Le Marchant was

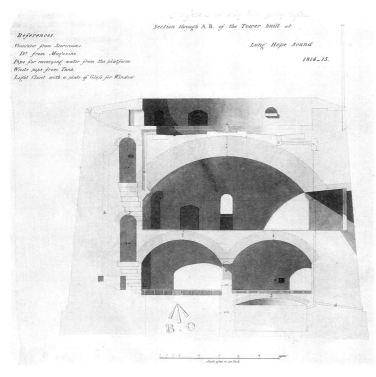

Cross section through the Hackness tower. Public Record Office, MPH 620/5. (PRO)

Internal arrangements of the barrack floor of the Hackness tower. Public Record Office, MPH 620/2. (PRO)

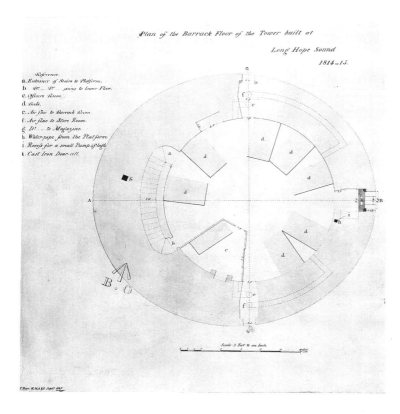

another D-shaped battery built by Doyle. Elsewhere, much attention was given to improving detail, such as the provision of breastworks and thickening parapets. By 1815, it is estimated that there were sixteen forts and barracks and fifty-eight coastal batteries in the island.

General Doyle was not at ease over the defences of Alderney, and he contemplated 'Sussex Towers' at Houmet de Longis and Houmet Herbe, east of Quesnard Point, and a place of arms at Mont Touraille, without following it up. There was a scattering of batteries in 1802, and Colonel George Cardew's map of 1842 shows that there were still ten in existence, but no major work.[34]

Towers more akin to the tall Channel Island towers appeared on St Mary's, Isles of Scilly. Major Daniel Lyman's persistence saw the erection of three 'Corsican' towers in 1803. They were 20 feet (6 metres) in height, only 18–20 feet (5.5–6 metres) in diameter, with walls 5 feet (1.5 metres) thick at the base. They contained two storeys of accommodation for 8 to 10 men, and were intended to mount a 32-pounder carronade on the top. These seem to be only the additional works on the islands put into effect during the Napoleonic Wars.[35] By contrast, a number of small batteries were created in the Isle of Man.

Conventional Martello towers of English type sprang up in Scotland, at Leith on an islet in the harbour in 1810 and two in Orkney three years later. The Leith tower has the familiar tapering design, and was for three guns. The spread of towers to Orkney had the purpose of protecting the battery at Hackness and guarding the entrance to the Longhope Sound. The two towers were not built to resist invasion but to protect the convoys of ships, assembling for the Baltic trade, from the attention of American privateers following the declaration of war by the United States in 1812. The battery at Hackness was built between 1813 and 1815, wedge-shaped, with eight guns mounted in two faces, with guardhouse and magazine symmetrically arranged to the rear. The Hackness tower was set apart from the battery, and the tower at Crookness, on the opposite side of the water, stands in isolation. Both towers were for single guns.[36] In response to similar threats, new batteries were erected at Aberdeen, and at the mouth of the Clyde at Greenock, where the small, conventional work received the grandiose title of Fort Matilda.

CHAPTER 9

The Changing Shape of Fortification

INVASION SCARES AND FALSE ALARMS

When Napoleon Bonaparte was safely in exile on St Helena, over a century of intermittant war between France and Britain was over. There were to be no circumstances after 1815 which were to bring the two into serious military conflict again. Indeed the future was one of increasing military alliances. Yet for the first half of the nineteenth century, if not longer, Britons and Frenchmen could feel no certainty that peace would last. Distrust and fear of one another, coupled with mutual feelings of superiority, were deeply engrained. The pattern of centuries of common hostility could not be lightly expunged. There were always Frenchmen who would publicly devise schemes to diminish British imperial power, and publish pamphlets, as late as the 1850s, analysing the effectiveness of British coastal defences, and speculating how Britain could be successfully invaded. Such imaginative schemes would not pass unnoticed by the British popular press, and indignation aroused. On the other hand, the often recorded confusion displayed by the British commander-in-chief during the Crimean War, Lord Raglan, over whether the French were our enemies or allies, is a fatuous example of how set in their chauvinism people could become. If this was to happen at the highest level of military command, how much more was hatred and fear of France to be fixed in folk memory.

There were three periods of popular alarm caused by imagined French aggressive intentions during the fifty years after Waterloo. On each occasion, in 1847, 1851–2 and 1859, a general feeling of national insecurity and lack of preparedness against possible invasion stimulated the building of new coastal defences. The last crisis in 1859, led to the setting up of a Royal Commission on the Defences of the United Kingdom, which was to produce the greatest wave of fortress building that has been seen in Britain before or since.

Behind the sometimes trumped up alarms and popular panics, there was a genuine case for improved defensive effectiveness, stimulated by the dramatic advances in technology, and most of all in the significance of steam power to warships. Steam completely changed the conditions governing naval tactics. It affected speed, range of operations, and manoeuvrability, by diminishing the effects of wind and tide on the operation of a warship. Naval strategy was to be profoundly altered. It did not take long for the more alarmist of observers to perceive that the English Channel was no longer the obstacle it had been to the sailing ship. Lord Palmerston expressed this point effectively when he told the House of Commons on 30 July 1845, that 'Steam navigation has rendered that which was before impassable by a military force nothing more than a river passable by a steam bridge.'[1] At the same time as steam was changing sea power, the railway systems facilitated the rapid mobilisation and concentration of troops. All of which could contribute to the element of surprise. The fact that these new advantages held good equally for the defence as the attack did not seem to carry the same weight. Then there were the revolutionary changes affecting explosive shells, such as General Paixhan's advocacy of a system for French naval gunnery based on standardisation, and the use of shell guns.[2] Following the Crimean War, there came a sudden interest in developing guns and improving the range and accuracy of artillery itself. Krupp and Schneider, Armstrong and Whitworth are just some of the best known ordnance engineers. Then there was the addition of armour plate to the sides of the traditional wooden battleship. Of these developments the public were well aware, and it was the combination of the new rifled artillery and steam-driven ironclads in the hands of the French, which lay behind the crisis of 1859.

The public was also aware of the often polemical debates on matters of defence which engrossed the military in their professional papers as well as in the newspapers. They discovered that there were widely different view on national security, and the best means of ensuring it – between the two services, as well as between individuals. It seemed that there was no appreciation among senior officers of the need for a

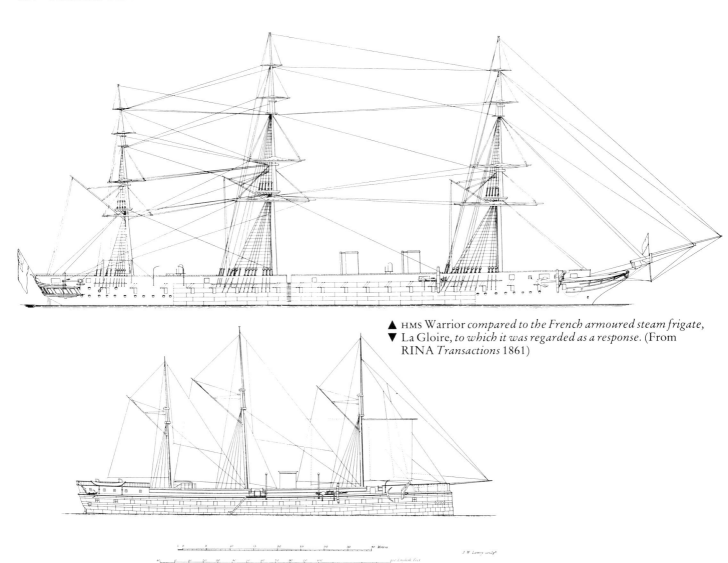

▲ HMS Warrior *compared to the French armoured steam frigate,*
▼ La Gloire, *to which it was regarded as a response.* (From RINA *Transactions* 1861)

co-ordinated strategy which involved Britain's growing imperial interests as well as the domestic. Of the two services, the preference of the soldiers for substantial fortifications at home was more forcibly expressed. British military engineers had emerged from the Napoleonic Wars with much practical experience, a wide knowledge of fortification theory at a time of radical change, and the confidence to experiment. The engineers believed that they had a contribution to make in the improvement of the nation's defences, and the time to make these improvements was the present. Of them there was none more persistent than General Sir John Fox Burgoyne, Inspector-General of Fortifications, who drew up a lengthy paper in November 1846 entitled, 'Observations on the Possible Results of a War with France under our Present System of Military Preparation'.[3] The paper repeated the long standing argument that the French might obtain temporary naval superiority in the Channel long enough to stage an invasion in great force, and given the current level of military capability and preparedness, he concluded that they would probably succeed. Inevitably, Burgoyne

stressed the need for modern fortresses and improved defences of the naval dockyards.

It was Burgoyne's paper which was the immediate source of the 'First Panic' of 1847–8. Anglo-French relations had become strained over various colonial issues. Louis Philippe's son, the Prince de Joinville, who had published a number of articles which were considered hostile to Britain, had been appointed to command the French fleet, and there had been significant increases in French naval budgets. None of these French moves was seriously menacing, but Burgoyne's paper made an immediate impact on the Cabinet. Palmerston was so impressed that he drew up a similar report of his own on 'The Defence of the Country' dated 17 December 1846. Then, on 8 January 1847, came the Duke of Wellington's reply to Burgoyne fully endorsing his pessimistic view of Britain's defences, which was 'leaked' to the *Morning Chronicle*.[4] Pressure on the government was intense, and income tax had to be almost doubled to meet limited military requirements. The 'panic' quickly fizzled out when, early in 1848, Louis Philippe and the

Prince de Joinville fled to England to escape the revolutionaries.

The second 'panic' occurred in 1851–2, caused by the *coup d'etat* and the re-election of Louis Napoleon as President of the Republic. Palmerston was again the leading figure among those alarmists who forecast the worst possible scenario. Palmerston insisted that 50,000 or 60,000 French troops could be secretly transported from Cherbourg and put ashore in a single night, and would not be put off when it was demonstrated that this could not possibly be achieved without a substantial and very visible force of shipping. There were those who suggested that the alarm about invasion was chiefly got up by soldiers who could not appreciate that steam power, in conjunction with the electric telegraph, had strengthened the defensive. The panic was nevertheless increased at the end of 1852 with the election of Louis Napoleon as Emperor. In actual fact, French military capacity was at a low level, and it was not long before the two countries were in alliance against Russia's territorial ambitions in the Balkans. However artificial the invasion scare had been, it had the effect of stimulating a programme of fortification construction in the Solent, Milford Haven and the Channel Islands.

The cause of the third 'panic' was essentially due to French involvement in naval technological progress. It arose from a combination of factors. There was undoubtedly suspicion and fear of the personal motives and ambitions of Napoleon III. French military success in Italy and subsequent territorial aggrandizement were dangerous enough, but the rapid construction of ironclads and rifled guns, and the commencement of the Suez Canal all appeared to be demonstrably anti-British. After the Crimean War, the French took the building of steam warships with iron hulls more seriously than Britain. In 1859, they briefly took the technological lead by launching the armoured steam frigate *La Gloire*. Britain replied with the *Warrior*, which was totally revolutionary, being entirely of iron with additional armour plate. Nevertheless, in 1861, France had fifteen sea-going ironclads, built or under construction, to Britain's seven. Although the revolution in naval technology, in the vastly more destructive force of rifled artillery and the greater destructive power of shells, were the underlying causes of the 'panic', there was now much greater hysteria about France and its aggressive intentions than before.

One result of this popular feeling was the growth of the Volunteer Movement, inspired by Wordsworth's rallying cry to 'Form, Rifleman Form'. It was backed at the highest level by the worries of Queen Victoria and Prince Albert. They had visited Cherbourg in 1858, and Prince Albert, having noted anti-English feelings among French senior officers, wrote that 'It makes me very unhappy to see what is done here at Cherbourg and how well protected the

works are, for the forts and the breakwater which is three times the size of the Plymouth one and is extremely well defended.' Later that year he was to write to Stockmar:

> When Cherbourg is completed England's position will be greatly altered and we must strengthen our forces if we are not to be entirely at our neighbour's mercy. By the railway an army can be brought there, and transported from that gigantic haven to our Coast in four hours.[5]

Rumours of troop concentrations at the newly fortified port of Cherbourg and elsewhere in 1859 gave rise to the belief in the imminent threat of invasion not only in the popular mind but also in the War Office. Lack of faith in existing fortifications produced the Royal Commission on the Defences of the United Kingdom.

DEVELOPMENT OF THE POLYGONAL SYSTEM OF FORTIFICATION

We have seen how British engineers absorbed the changing ideas taking place in fortification design during the latter part of the eighteenth century; how belief in the universality of the continuous bastion system gave way, in Britain, to the influence of the writings of Montalembert which encouraged the separation of offensive and defensive firepower. This concept led, during the course of the Napoleonic Wars and after, to greater use of gun casemates and caponiers, and greater reliance upon detached works, towers and redoubts, with or without connecting lines.

Montalembert demonstrated the negative side of the bastion system, and showed how increased firepower could be directed towards the field by developing the *tenaille* trace, as well as encouraging the use of substantial casemated towers and developing the means of local defence by caponiers. He was followed by another French engineer, Carnot, whose belief in the possibility of achieving invulnerability, while hopelessly exaggerated, contained elements which too had considerable influence. Many of the principles contained in Carnot's *Treatise on the Defence of Fortified Places* were extensively adopted by German and Austrian engineers.[6] He placed the highest importance on his belief in the potentially devastating effect vertical mortar fire might have when used by the defenders in the closing stages of a siege. An incessant discharge of musketry and four-ounce iron balls from mortars, chiefly mounted in the salients of each bastion and ravelin, was intended to create an impenetrable curtain of missiles, but in practice such fire lacked sufficient terminal velocity. The use of mortars placed behind ramparts in small bombproof casemates, open at each end, and large enough for a mortar and a gun team of two or three men, was widely adopted. Carnot expanded on the use of detached bastions defended by casemated structures in the gorge, and with the faces covered by counterguards and *tenailles* linked to the

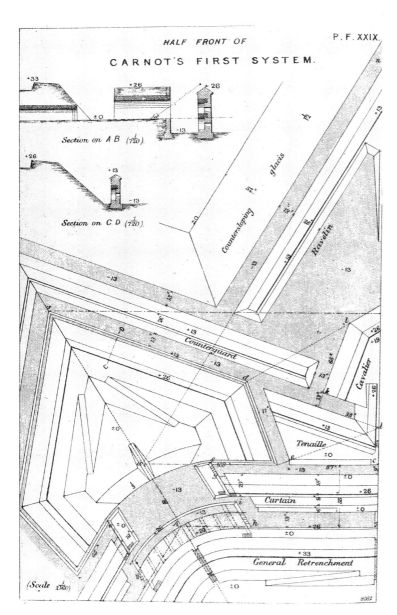

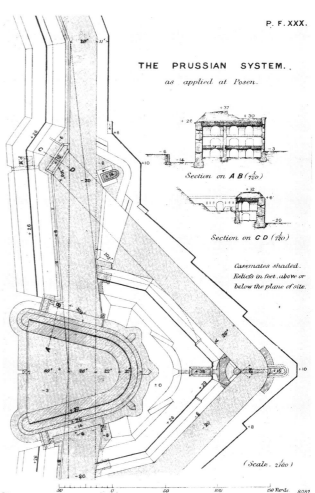

The Prussian system: section A–B illustrates a multi-storey caponier. From Textbook of Fortification *1887. (Author)*

Carnot's first system: section C–D illustrates the relationship of the Carnot Wall to the rampart. From E M Lloyd Textbook of Fortification and Military Engineering *1887. (Author)*

main work by caponiers. The rear was covered by a loopholed wall, detached and in advance of the rampart of the main work, acting as a *chemin des rondes*. This device was later known as a Carnot Wall. A further revolutionary development was the suppression of the counterscarp of the ditch, and with it the covered-way, by allowing the glacis to slope back into the ditch. This contradiction of previous practice, which had placed difficulties in the way of the attackers, allowed defenders greater opportunities for active defence through sorties. Like Montalambert, Carnot was vigorously opposed to the conventions of the bastion system, and aimed to give the defence greater security for its artillery by encouraging the construction of vast masonry casemated works containing several tiers of guns.

Another contemporary French engineer, Chasseloup, was also critical of the bastion trace, and was a firm believer in casemates. His chief contribution was to develop the use of scarp and counterscarp galleries, and to place detached caponiers in the centres of fronts and redoubts in the covered-way in order to cover ditches with reverse fire. As practical experience was to prove, too much exposure of masonry to direct gunfire had harmful effects, and there came a shift back to masking scarps, and even casemated works, by earthworks.[7]

In the new political circumstances following France's defeat in 1815, Prussian, Austrian and Dutch engineers, in striving to define and secure their new frontiers, adapted some of these theoretical ideas, and themselves evolved a novel defensive model, which became known as the 'Prussian' or 'polygonal' system. This new system was first seen in the fortified towns along the Rhine and Danube. It figured at Linz and Salzburg, protecting the western approaches to Vienna, and among the towns of the 'quadrilateral' in northern Italy, intended to stop penetration into Austria through the Tyrol. The Dutch in the Ardennes, and

Haxo casemate on the ramparts of Fort Brockhurst, Gosport.
(DOE)

elsewhere along their new southern border, produced massive casemated fortresses.

While almost all the 'Prussian' forts built after 1815 were detached works and 'polygonal' in plan, continuous lines might also be employed – as at Mainz in 1838, where a regular *tenaille* trace was used with ravelins in the re-entrant angles, but in combination with outlying detached works. Often the polygon was a version of a detached bastion with long faces at an obtuse angle, short flanks, and a straight gorge which may or may not have had a casemated, defensible barracks. An advantage of this style was the greater space for mounting more guns in the faces of the work, thus compelling the attackers to give greater lateral extent to their own siege works, and as a result, requiring larger numbers of men for effective superiority. Forts which were more truly polygonal than bastion-shaped had sides which might be 500 feet (152 metres) long, sometimes broken by short flanks in the form of caponiers, themselves covered by ravelins. Ravelins could be made salient on the glacis, preventing the body of the place being breached from the counterscarp on its salient angles. The sides of the polygon were some-

times protected by counterguards. Occasionally, a casemated redoubt was placed in the gorge of these ravelins to make them more self-defensible. On the ramparts of polygonal works there could be somewhat exposed casemated structures, usually for one and sometimes two guns, and called after their inventor, General Haxo. Additionally, a common feature of the 'Prussian' system was the two- or three-storey caponier to defend the ditch. Caponiers were sometimes separated from the curtain as at Fort Alexander outside Coblenz, or connected to the curtain as at Germersheim.

The chief and lasting contribution of the polygonal fortress, especially as developed in the 'Prussian' system, was the final impetus it gave to the development of a defensive system based upon detached works, as opposed to a continuous *enceinte*. This idea was carried to extremes by the Austrians at Linz in 1830–1. The town was surrounded by a chain of thirty-two isolated redoubts, known as 'Maximilian Towers'.[8] Each tower was sunk into the ground within a ditch, and the three floors of each tower were masked by the glacis. The eleven 24-pounders mounted on top of each tower were arranged so that their fire would graze the glacis in front. They appear to have been

Kronstadt: Fort Alexander had provision for 120 guns. (Author)

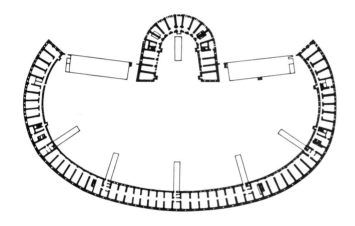

Plan of the main fort on the island of Bomarsund in the Aaland Islands. (From Quentin Hughes, Military Architecture)

influenced by the English Martello tower system, with internal and external diameters struck eccentrically, and they shared something of the characteristics of the Harwich, Dymchurch and Eastbourne redoubts. Although similar redoubts were used at Verona, they were found, on experiment, to be highly vulnerable to rockets and high-angle fire on the gun platform.[9]

Later French engineers regarded the continuous *enceinte* around the place to be protected as a retrenchment, and made the principal element of the defence consist of the works constructed outside it. This led to bastions and ravelins being covered by counterguards. The ravelins themselves were greatly enlarged with a view to detaining the besiegers longer. Eventually, French engineers recognised the advantages of detached forts, each strong enough to require a regular siege. They used such works outside Paris. Yet they did not adopt any part of Carnot's ideas, and continued to persist in the bastion system as well, even

up to 1870. The Frenchman, A Mangin, in his assessment of the polygonal fortifications constructed in Germany since 1815, was highly critical of them. While acknowledging the defects of the bastion system, he concluded that Carnot had not provided the answer, and went so far as to proclaim that 'the experience of the ages decides against caponiers'. In order to demonstrate his case he conducted a hypothetical siege of Fort Alexander, but, as his English translator noted, the fronts chosen by Mangin for his attacks 'do not fairly represent the polygonal system employed in Germany'.[10]

New developments were taking place in coastal fortification, particularly in the United States, and by the Russians in the Baltic. Casemated batteries had always shown their value against slow moving warships, but because of the gun's restricted field of fire within a casemate, the massing of guns in tiers, like the broadside of a contemporary battleship was intended to provide sufficient firepower concentrated at one point. At Kronstadt, at Bomarsund in the Åland Islands or at Fort Nicolas at Sebastopol, the Russians had constructed casemated forts of enormous length or with guns massed in as many as three tiers. The Kronstadt forts were scattered to cover the restricted deep water channel. Their plans could be square, circular or pentagonal. Here for the first time coastal batteries were associated with a system of submarine mining. At Bomarsund, the plan of the principal fort was semi-elliptical, containing sixty-two casemates on each of two floors. Behind the ellipse was a horseshoe-shaped work facing outwards, again with guns on two floors. Behind this fort, set on the waters-edge, and placed on higher ground, were three circular towers commanding the countryside between and beyond. Attacked by the Anglo-French fleet during the course of the Crimean

War, the embrasures of the fort proved vulnerable to accurate artillery which had been landed on shore, and despite their vast number of guns the defenders had great difficulty in bringing more than six to bear at a time on an attacking ship.[11]

The American multi-gun forts were also often arranged in tiers, but their plans were both simpler and more effective.[12] Joseph G Totten, who held the post of Chief Army Engineer from 1838 to 1864, carried out a policy aimed towards integrating national harbour defence systems. The most famous of all the American forts of this period was Fort Sumpter, in Charleston harbour. It had a pentagonal plan. Although under-armed and unprepared for the Confederate bombardment which started the Civil War in 1861, after capture it successfully engaged two union ironclads, sinking one and driving off the other. It also survived a determined siege from land batteries as well as a naval attack.

Coastal batteries were not just concerned with niceties of plan and arrangement of armament. Care was needed over the method of construction. In the 1850s, Totten was experimenting with iron for sea forts. Not only were the stone walls reinforced with iron but also with a device which would close the mouth of an embrasure with a form of iron shield after its gun had fired. The Russians at Kronstadt also introduced a type of iron reinforcement within the masonry. It was, therefore, in the field of coastal fortification that the first experiments with armour plate and iron turrets were to take place.[13]

THEORY AND TECHNOLOGY IN THE 1840s

British engineers were interested in the new ideas. Major-General Sir John T Jones made regular inspections twice a year of the fortresses being constructed or restored on the Rhine and in Belgium.[14] At home, experiments were conducted at Woolwich on the effectiveness or otherwise of the 'Carnot Wall'. A trial bastion had already been constructed at the Arsenal for ricochet practice, and it was found that a wall positioned between the counterguard and the scarp of the bastion could be shattered by ricochet fire from the first and second parallels of the practice siege works. The results of these experiments were communicated to their German counterparts, and the Duke of Wellington passed on his criticisms to the Prussians who were adopting Carnot's ideas whole-heartedly at Coblenz and Cologne.

The changing ideas now influencing military engineering had already appeared in Britain during the first decade of the nineteenth century under the stimulus of imminent invasion. During the thirty years following the end of the Napoleonic Wars, despite the customary limitations on finance and political will for defensive preparations, some new harbour defence

The Confederate battery at Fort Johnson bombarding Fort Sumpter in 1861, from a contemporary engraving. (Author)

Kemp Tower, St Ouen's Bay, Jersey. (Author)

works were carried out. The isolated gun-tower continued to be built, whether to protect open beaches, as in Jersey, where the South Coast form was repeated, or for flanking the enclosure wall round Pembroke Dock in Milford Haven, or commanding the mouth of the Medway from one of the shoals off the Isle of Grain. However, Fort Perch Rock, in the Mersey off New Brighton, broke new ground in its design. An early plan of 1825 shows the fort as a triangular work with curved angles, and with two round towers on either side of the gorge. This resembled some of the American harbour forts, perhaps not surprisingly in view of

Picklecombe Fort, Cornwall: medievalised barracks of the 1846 period. (Author)

Liverpool's trans-Atlantic trade. The engineer, Captain Kitson, in a revised plan of the same year, enlarged the battery from five guns to fifteen, and made it an irregular four-sided figure but still retaining the two round towers at the gorge. In other respects, the battery was unlike the American casemated 'castles' as its armament was mounted in the open with the guns firing through embrasures and *en barbette*. By contrast, at the entrance to Portsmouth harbour, the seaward battery of Fort Blockhouse which had long been 'open' was converted into a casemated battery for thirteen guns by 1825. It was referred to twenty years later, as 'one of the best specimens of military architecture we have', and except where warships can lie within 600 yards, 'can be applied generally'.[15] Similar improvements were made a few years later at Point Battery on the opposite side of the entrance to Portsmouth harbour.

At the same time as British engineers were discussing the theoretical basis of their subject, and applying change in a minor way, they were also aware of the rapid technological advances which were affecting the whole character of naval and land warfare in a quite revolutionary manner. Ships were changing, both in their design and their firepower. Shell-firing guns had been adopted by the French navy since 1837. The introduction of steam propulsion, and then the screw propeller, were technological advances which the British Admiralty ultimately accepted in 1845. At the same time, the Admiralty ordered a number of 'iron frigates'. But so slowly did the practical implications influence the naval mind that, during the siege of Sebastopol, wooden sailing ships of the line were still being used against the latest in casemated coastal batteries and, not surprisingly, to little effect. Near the end of the siege, the French covered small wooden steamers with 4½-inch (114mm) thick armour plate, which the Russian guns could not penetrate. These early steam-driven warships did not at first greatly affect coast artillery gunnery since the speed of ships of the line, even with an auxiliary engine, was still comparatively slow. Yet as early as 1847, Sir John Fox Burgoyne, Inspector-General of Fortifications, pointed out in a paper on coastal batteries the improved precision of naval gunnery that had been acquired in recent years, and drew attention to the 'force and speed of steam vessels' which had to be countered by coastal gunners.[16]

Just as steam-driven, screw propulsion, and the appearance of ironclads were revolutionary in the naval sphere, so was the improvement in range and accuracy of the rifled gun to warfare in general. The application of rifling to muzzle-loading cannon was seriously adopted by the French in 1842, and in most other European countries soon afterwards. In Britain, Sir William Armstrong experimented with breech-loading guns and produced his rifled breech-loader in 1854. This did not have immediate success, and the rifled muzzle-loader remained for some time the standard weapon in British coastal batteries. Again, Sir John Fox Burgoyne was alive to the effects rifled guns would have on existing fortifications. In 1855, he wrote:

> Towers, old castles and escarp walls in general that are exposed to view will be readily ruined from a greater distance. Although the new shot and shells are not adapted to afford the regular effects of ricochet fire, works will be subject to all the other evil consequences of enfilade, and from much greater distances, and parapets to be penetrated and ruined. The interior of works will be plunged into from heights at greater ranges than have hitherto been practicable; and where magazines, barracks or other important military establishments are exposed to such heights, and have hitherto been safe from them they will now be liable to direct cannonade or bombardment . . .'[17]

The immediate requirements were greater protection for the fortress guns, parapets needed to be thickened, and embrasures reduced in size and strengthened. The crucial factor which Burgoyne identified in his observations of the new weapon was 'the exposure of the great naval arsenals to a thoroughly effective fire from ranges that were before unattainable'.[18]

As early as 1844, the Duke of Wellington had written a Memorandum on the works of defence proposed for the naval arsenals and dockyards. In 1846, the year after his appointment as Inspector-General of Fortifications, Burgoyne drew up the paper which was to impress itself so strongly on Lord Palmerston, and thence to spark off the popular 'panic' of 1847–8. Burgoyne, while indicating Britain's hypothetical vulnerability to invasion from France, was also endeavouring to stress the urgent need for modern fortifications and dockyard defences. He was not alone among his professional colleagues. In 1845, Colonel Lewis published a 'Report on the Application of Forts, Towers and Batteries to Coast Defences and Harbours' in which he also anticipated the use of railways for mobilising the defence.[19] The debate between the traditionalist supporters of the bastion system and continuous lines, and the protagonists of the German school and detached forts, was not confined to professional military engineers. An amateur could also join in. James Fergusson, better known for his architectural writings, took issue with Colonel Lewis in 1849.[20] He proposed striking out in unconventional directions, disapproving both of the bastion system and the use of masonry towers. Fergusson believed that British engineers, unfettered by either prejudice or 'school', should burn their textbooks, and take a calm outside view of the theoretical controversies affecting military engineering at the time. His own preference was for massive earthworks containing four or five tiers of guns, and involved huge concentrations of moveable artillery. Two years later, Lieutenant-Colonel Thackerey advocated a system of detached forts encircling Portsmouth, Plymouth and London, partially anticipating the shape of things to come.[21]

There were practical results from all this theoretical speculation and feeling of insecurity. In 1844, the Mixed Committee upon Harbour Defences of the Port of Plymouth considered constructing batteries at Picklecombe Point on the Cornish side of Plymouth Sound, and at Staddon Point opposite. Two years later, it was proposed that Picklecombe should

South western of the two gun-towers flanking Pembroke Dockyard. (Author)

have a battery of nine guns, protected by two towers and a barracks. The latter, which still survives, is a remarkable architectural piece of romantic medievalism, complete with turrets and mock arrow loops. A year or so later, the defences of Milford Haven began to receive attention. As well as the two gun-towers at Pembroke Dock begun in 1848 and completed in 1851, another, more substantial tower was built at Stack

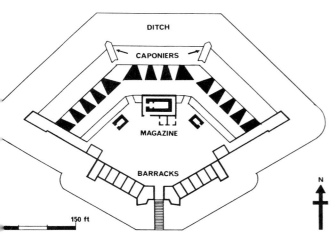

Plan of the 1850s 'polygonal' fort of Shornemead, Kent. (V T C Smith)

Fort Grosnez, Alderney. (Author)

Rock in the Haven in 1850, as the beginning of a programme of fortification which was to continue through the decade. Much more significant, because the engineers were starting to move away from both bastions and towers, was Shornemead Fort on the south bank of the Thames Estuary. This contained the hallmarks of a contemporary German polygonal fort. It was a replacement of an earlier battery, part of the forward defence line for the Thames of 1795. Not completed until 1853, because of serious problems over its foundations, the second Shornemead was a miniature 'polygonal' fort of pentagonal plan. It was the first, fully developed 'polygonal' work to be built in Britain. It consisted of an open battery for thirteen 32-pounder guns mounted on three faces. The barracks and service buildings occupied the other two. Local defence was provided by musketry caponiers which gave all-round cover in the ditch, and the corners of the barrack range in the gorge were projected into demi-bastions for defence of the entrance.[22]

JERVOIS AND DEFENSIVE MEASURES IN THE 1850s

The second 'panic' of 1851–2 had political causes which quickly dispersed. An insignificant trauma it turned out to be, but it had the effect of focussing attention on coastal defences, their inadequacies and obsolescence. It also spurred a reluctant government to put resources into a number of substantial schemes which would have been ignored or deferred in normal circumstances.

Efforts were first concentrated on three previously neglected locations: Alderney in the Channel Islands, Milford Haven, and the western approaches to the Solent and Portsmouth. With all these works the name of William Drummond Jervois became increasingly associated.

In 1844, the Admiralty commissioned a report on a proposal for providing two new defensive 'harbours of refuge' in the Channel Islands as a counterweight to the recently enlarged and fortified French naval port of Cherbourg, only 25 miles (40 kilometres) from Alderney. Work started in 1847, to designs by a James Walker, at St Catherine's Bay in Jersey, and at Braye on the north coast of Alderney. In the end, only Alderney was proceeded with, at enormous cost and with frequently changing designs. Such a great artificial harbour needed to be protected by guns, and in 1848, a Colonel Ward suggested sites for the erection of towers and a fort at Grosnez, at the head of the harbour. Nothing was done until 1850, when land was acquired by the Board of Ordnance, and a plan for Fort Grosnez was prepared. With its high level battery and steep glacis commanded by a detached cavalier giving protection from landward attack, and masking the rear of the battery, there is a close resemblance to what was later built. The engineer first in charge was Lieutenant F C Hassard, but the designer of all the other forts in Alderney was Captain Jervois, later to become Assistant Inspector-General of Fortifications, and ultimate-

Milford Haven defences:
1 *West Blockhouse Fort*
2 *Dale Point Battery*
3 *Thorn Island Fort*
4 *Chapel Bay Battery*
5 *Stack Rock Tower and Fort*
6 *South Hook Fort*
7 *Hubberstone Fort*
8 *Popton Fort*
9 *Fort Scoveston*
10 *Pembroke Dock Towers*
11 *Defensible Barracks* (Author)

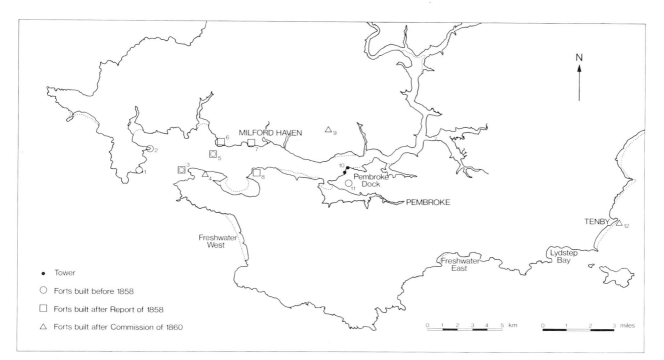

ly the Deputy Director of Works for Fortifications. In 1851, ground was purchased at Rock Tourgie, and Jervois submitted an outline plan of a fort and associated batteries. The broad defensive strategy for Alderney was prepared by Burgoyne, as Inspector-General, in 1852. He considered that Alderney's situation and potential was equal to, if not greater than, Gibraltar. Burgoyne's preference was to defend the whole island with batteries set about 500 or 600 yards (460 or 550 metres) apart. He had three main objectives: dispersal of the guns and batteries, mounting the guns at heights between 30 and 60 feet (9 and 18 metres) above sea level in order to give them an advantage over enemy warships, and to develop cross-fires rather than rely solely on direct fire. No matter how formidable the batteries, the defence of the island would depend upon an infantry garrison to deal with a landing force. The infantry was to be quartered with the gunners in self-defensible blockhouses so strong that they could only be reduced by artillery. Jervois followed up this strategy with works in progress that same year at Forts Clonque, Grosnez, Quenard Point, Rat Island and Longy Lines, while plans were afoot for Rock Tourgie, Pribette Head, Chateau à l'Etoc, Corblets and Hommet Herbe. In 1853 Jervoise prepared a plan showing the works completed with proposals for an additional four enclosed batteries.[23]

The thirteen forts and batteries designed by Jervois are a remarkable group in this transitional period of military engineering. The French writer, Vallaux, wrote of Alderney in 1913: '*L'architecture formidable et enfantine des forts construits sous Palmerston . . . vieillit les côtes presque autant que les donjons feodaux . . .*'[24] The forts do indeed have a remarkably medieval flavour, and in some of their elements have similarities with the conventions employed in the coastal forts of Henry VIII. There is, for example, much use of circular towers, semi-circular and D-shaped batteries. Fort Houmet Herbe has round bastions, including a pair which flank the entrance. Most of the batteries constructed on islands or rocky headlands are inevitably irregular in plan, and perhaps lend themselves more readily to rounded forms in order to improve their self-defensible capabilities, but their appearance is incongruous in the mid-nineteenth century. Of the two major works, Fort Albert (Touraille) and Fort Tourgie, it can be seen that Jervois still had traditional bastion forms in mind while, at the same time, using some of the new 'polygonal' ideas. At Fort Tourgie, the batteries at three levels have a large defensible, loopholed barracks or citadel in the gorge. This is flanked by projecting *bastionettes*, and the entrance is covered by a redan. Fort Albert, on the other hand, was a polygonal work with caponiers at the angles. This was one of the last of Jervois's Alderney forts, begun in 1854, and, after several changes in design, finished in 1858. For Jervois's development as an engineer, Alderney appears to have provided an opportunity and freedom for experiment, which enabled him to grasp the basic concepts of the polygonal system.

The defence of Milford Haven had never been seriously considered before except under the Tudors. The French landing at Fishguard during the Napoleonic War altered official attitudes, and the development of Pembroke Dock was influenced by security factors. A defensible barracks on the hill above the town was begun in 1841, and was the start of a gradual process of fortification which fell into two distinct stages. The first, followed up the initial defence of Pembroke Dock itself in 1849, by pushing the defences forward into the Haven, and occupying Stack Rock in 1850, and Thorn Island, where a battery was built in 1852. The outer entrance to the Haven was protected four years later, by Dale Fort and West Blockhouse Fort linking to provide a cross-fire with Thorn Island. The second, and more substantial review of the defensive needs of the Haven was prepared in 1858.

The 1852 invasion 'panic' had its most direct results in the vicinity of Portsmouth, dealing with the weaknesses apparent in its western approaches both from sea and land. The chief defence of the Needles Passage had long been Hurst Castle. Less significant batteries were sited on the Isle of Wight side, which were now replaced by substantial new works. Cliff End Fort, later known as Fort Albert, was sited on the shore opposite Hurst Castle. Fort Victoria was further east,

Fort Victoria, Isle of Wight: plan of 1897, after its modification to a submarine mining depot. (Allan Insole, from Anthony Cantwell, *Fort Victoria*)

towards Yarmouth, at Sconce Point. They were both remarkable structures. The latter was in the form of a redan, with two-storey barracks at either end of the gorge to give flanking cover across the entrance and landward approach. The main armament was housed in casemates in the two faces of the redan at the waters-edge. The fort was built of brick, the casemates had wide apertures with no form of shield, and there was an ineffective earth traverse behind the casemates. James Fergusson[25] was publicly critical of this work, and in 1860, the Royal Commission on the Defences of the United Kingdom remarked that it was 'not of the most approved construction'. The lofty, tower-like Fort Albert, which still survives, resembles a smaller version of coastal forts being erected in the United States at the time, and which were to prove extremely vulnerable to rifled artillery. Fort Albert consisted of three tiers of casemates over a basement for magazines. Although completed by 1856, it was sufficiently out of date to be ignored by the 1860 Royal Commission, and its place was taken by a less conspicuous work on the cliff above. At the same time, new batteries for shell guns as well as 32-pounders were being constructed on either side of Hurst Castle. Interestingly, the moat defence of the Tudor fort was remodelled and three brick caponiers built to flank it. One caponier remains.[26]

Much more up to date were the two forts about 6000 yards (nearly 5500 metres) in advance of Gosport: Gomer and Elson, also begun in 1852. These were unequivocally 'polygonal' fortifications of broadly bastion shape. They were land forts, and were essentially brick revetted earthworks sited at either end

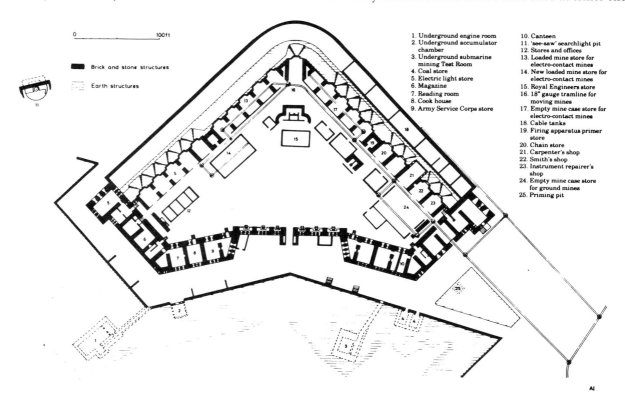

Fort Albert, Isle of Wight: looking towards Hurst Castle across the Needles Passage. (Author)

of what was to become a line of detached forts across the 'peninsula' west of Gosport. The armament was clearly separated, with local defence concentrated in the caponiers in the ditch. The forts were fully enclosed without any substantial defensive provisions in the gorge.

Of equal interest, since it shows the degree of experimentation in the 1850s, is the battery built to defend the entrance to Shoreham harbour in 1856. This was an earthwork *barbette* battery for six heavy guns firing through wide embrasures, which permitted a wide traverse, important when dealing with shipping. The novel element of its design was the employment of a 'Carnot Wall', behind which a *chemin des rondes* was reached by a flight of steps from the *terre-plein*. The ditch was also flanked by three caponiers. A 'Carnot Wall' may have been adopted because of difficulty in contriving a deep ditch in shingle. It remains the first example of a feature of fortification much derided in the writings of earlier English engineers.[27]

Towards the end of the 1850s, British en-

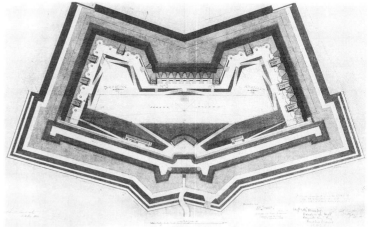

Fort Gomer, Gosport: plan at terre-plein *level showing the arrangement of the armament. Casemated barracks occupied the whole of the gorge beneath the ramparts.* Public Record Office, WO 505. (PRO)

gineers, in particular Burgoyne, obtained first-hand experience, not only of the advances in technology, but also of practical siege work and coastal defence during the Crimean War. The Russian coastal defences earned considerable interest for their weaknesses as well as

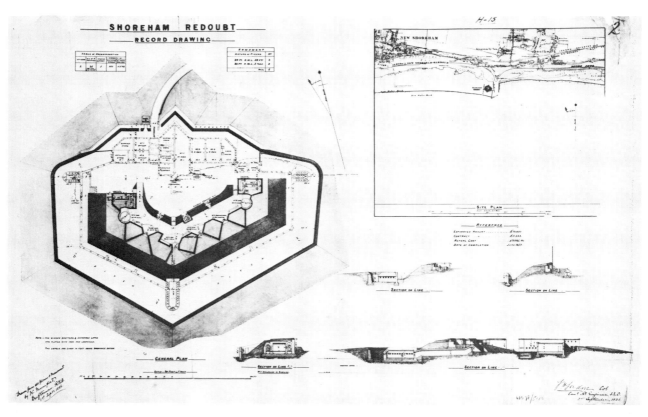

Shoreham Fort: plan and sections demonstrating the employment of the Carnot principles. Public Record Office, WO 78/5110. (PRO)

their strengths. The lessons learnt were to be assimilated in reviews of defences at Portsmouth, Plymouth and Milford Haven carried out during 1858. Compiling these reports, or in attendance on the small working parties concerned, and representing the Inspector-General of Fortifications or, indeed, producing memoranda in his own right, was William Drummond Jervois, now with the rank of Major.

At Portsmouth, Jervois noted the strength of the defences of the harbour and along the Southsea seafront. Like others before him, including Fergusson, he was particularly concerned about its vulnerability to land attack from a beach-head to the west, in the Stokes Bay area. Jervois proposed a line of detached works from a position north of Portchester Castle, through Horsea Island to link up with a reconstructed Hilsea Lines to cover an advance from the north. Behind Hilsea Lines would be a central 'polygonal' fort to act as a citadel. On the west, he wished to complete the 'Gosport Advanced Line' with three detached, 'polygonal' forts between Gomer and Elson, linking all five by a ditch and rampart. Along the coast, Forts Gomer and Monkton should be connected by a wet moat and given additional batteries. In practice, the completion of the Gosport line was approved and begun right away. The three new forts carried the development of the 'polygonal' system substantially further than their older neighbours. The northern defences were limited

to the reconstruction of Hilsea Lines. The old irregular line was replaced by a regular bastioned front of three whole and two demi-bastions which was to be the last full bastioned trace to be constructed in the United Kingdom.[28]

Plymouth's defences were limited and outdated by comparison. The only forward positions covering Plymouth Sound were the two batteries for nine guns each at Picklecombe and Staddon Points. Jervois recommended their replacement by massive three-tier batteries for sixty guns, of which two tiers would be in casemates. Casemated batteries were proposed at each end of the breakwater, and more guns on Drake's Island. As at Portsmouth, Jervois was worried by the possibility of landings some distance away, in this case at Cawsand and Whitesand Bays, and enemy advances on the dockyard from the west. His advice for a defence line in front of Anthony, with forts on either flank at Tregantle and Scraesdon, was put into effect, along with the other coastal batteries. Jervois also recognised the need for a line of detached works along the high ground north west of Plymouth, between St Budeaux and Staddon, in advance of the inner *enceinte* represented by the Devonport Lines. Burgoyne also suggested an outer line of detached forts north of Plymouth, each to be self-defensible and mutually supporting at distances varying between 600 and 800 yards (550 and 730 metres).[29]

The Committee's objectives at Milford Haven were not just to prevent the destruction of Pembroke Dockyard but to prevent an enemy using the waters of the Haven as an anchorage. The existing defences were all at the entrance to the Haven, and were too distant from each other to prevent steam-powered ships running between them. The Committee proposed two lines of defence behind West Blockhouse Fort, Dale Fort and Thorn Island. The first would include a strengthened Stack Rock and batteries at Chapel Bay, on the south, and South Hook Point on the north. The second line lay between Signal Staff Battery (Fort Hubberstone) and Popton Fort, with a floating battery between them. Behind each battery was to be a defensible barracks, capable of withstanding the fire of light guns only. It is significant that the Committee felt that even if the outer line failed, the inner line, 7000 yards (nearly 6.5 kilometres) from the dockyard would prohibit its bombardment. Sunken towers, perhaps a throwback to the Linz Towers, were proposed for landward defences. The main elements of these proposals, except the land defences, were approved by government and were in progress in 1859.[30]

Even while these fortifications were being planned, technology was overtaking them. In 1858, the first 'modern' gun had appeared. This was Armstrong's gun with the built-up breech, which had a rifled barrel and threw an elongated shell. It displaced for ever the old cast-iron cannon firing round shot. It not only revolutionised gunnery by increasing range enormous-ly, and imparting an undreamed of accuracy with its cylindrical rotating shell, it also forced the pace in every department of ship construction, armament and armour. The *Report upon the probable influence of the new Rifled cannon upon existing Fortifications and future Plans for new Works of Defence* was published on 22 February 1859.[31] Engineers were now faced by the need to keep an enemy at a distance of 9000 yards, or 5 miles (over 8 kilometres), from the point to be defended. Jervois himself had already written, a month previously, a 'Memorandum relative to the Defences of Portsmouth proposed with reference to the Long Range and Accurate Aim of Armstrong's Rifled gun'. 'When the works were designed', he wrote, 'it was universally admitted that if an enemy could be kept at a distance of 4000 yards [over 3.5 kilometres] from the place to be protected, that place would be safe from bombardment. Now, 9170 yards [over 8 kilometres] has been achieved with a 32-pounder and one might be able to direct guns with the aid of a map.'[32] A year later, Jervois set out the theoretical basis for his current thinking in a paper entitled 'Observations relating to the works in progress and proposed for the defence of the Naval Ports, Arsenal and Dockyards'.[33] It is a highly significant statement for understanding the reasoning behind the most extensive programme of fortress construction to be carried out in the United Kingdom which was to follow the 1859 Royal Commission.

Jervois started from the premise that since the

Fort Brockhurst, Gosport: plan at ground floor, casemate level, with cross sections. (Author)

FORT BROCKHURST

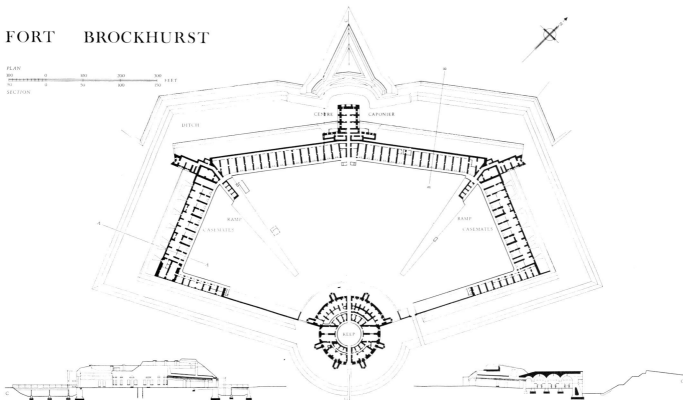

Fort Brockhurst from the air. (English Heritage)

Fort Brockhurst, main entrance through the keep. (Author)

British Empire was dependent upon the maintenance of its maritime power, its naval ports and dockyards must be protected. He argued that the fleet had more important duties than protecting its own bases. The cost of providing floating batteries was also more expensive than land fortifications. In the event of an enemy landing, the small British standing army would be limited, of necessity, to opposing an advance on London. By entrusting the garrisoning of the forts to irregular levies, stiffened by a small number of professional soldiers, instead of 'locking up' troops behind fortifications, both the fleet and the regular army were freed to carry out their principal roles.

The first of Jervois's general observations on fortifications themselves was to adopt open batteries instead of casemated works, except when sea batteries were constructed on small sites, or whenever it was necessary to build a battery in tiers. While gun casemates could provide accommodation for the garrison, the general plan adopted in open sea batteries or in those which were partly casemated was to build a fireproof (not bombproof) defensible barrack at the gorge where it could act as a keep. With land defences, Jervois favoured tactically sited, detached works capable of supporting one another rather than continuous lines. If the terrain was reasonably clear and level, detached works could be about a mile (1.6 kilometres) apart, but the intervals which could be commanded by musketry or grapeshot were limited to about 700 yards (640 kilometres).

As for the principles in the design of forts, 'it will be found in almost all cases that a fort with straight faces flanked by caponiers will adapt itself to the ground much better, and that it will be much more applicable in every other respect, than one of a bastioned trace.' He recommended the polygonal trace, making the angles of the polygon of the rampart sufficiently obtuse to allow the fire from one face to take up that of the face adjacent to it. Converging fire could thereby be arranged, as well as sweeping to front and flanks. Care should be taken in laying out the faces of the rampart to avoid enfilade fire, and by using earth traverses and Haxo casemates, which when mounted on the flanks were less susceptible to direct fire. Ditches should be flanked by bombproof caponiers, so placed that the besiegers could not silence them by batteries established on the prolongation of any particular face. Caponiers should be designed for light guns or howitzers, and not only for musketry. Counterscarp galleries were useful places from which to run out countermines but were themselves susceptible to mining.

In order to protect the escarp as much as possible from distant fire, the ditch should be narrow and deeper than it usually was. The depth should be at least 30 feet (9 metres), and be at least 45 feet (14 metres) wide. Jervois also favoured *chemin des rondes* at the top of the escarp.

One of the most important considerations in the design of these fortresses was that they should be defensible by a comparatively small number of men. With this in mind, Jervois favoured placing casemated keeps at their gorges. They were to command the interior, and, by projecting sufficiently in the rear, to flank the ditches of the gorge, and to provide artillery fire along the crest of the glacis of adjacent works. The keep was usually to be given two tiers of guns, and should be self-defensible with its own ditch flanked by musketry caponiers. The keep should not be so high that it attracted enemy fire, which was a drawback of some of the German keeps.

Examples of the practical application of Jervois's theories in works designed before 1860 can be seen at Fort Brockhurst in the Gosport Line, and at Popton Fort, Milford Haven; the former a land fort, and the latter a sea battery. Brockhurst was begun in 1858.[34] The plan took the form of a six-sided polygon with an obtuse salient, so that the long faces were less liable to enfilade fire. The flanks contained gun casemates, and additionally, Haxo casemates were placed on the ramparts. The gorge was closed by a brick wall, but in the centre was a self-contained, circular keep, complete with its own wet moat covered from eight small musketry caponiers. The keep had a command of 7 feet (2 metres) over the fort. The main work was enclosed by a wet moat, 112 feet (34 metres) wide, with

Popton Fort, Milford Haven: plan based on a WD plan of 1887. (Author)

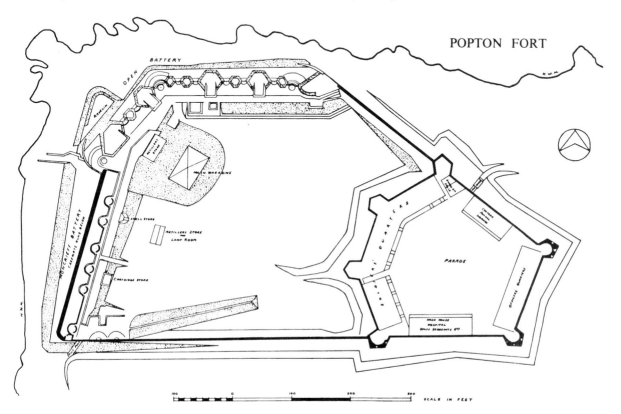

POPTON FORT

a glacis and covered-way on the counterscarp protecting the escarps of the faces from direct fire. An earthwork redan covered the centre caponier on the salient angle of the fort. This caponier was double, covering both faces with cannon fire as well as musketry. It too had to be flanked from musketry galleries on either side. Single caponiers at the north and west shoulders covered the flanks. The main armament was mounted on the ramparts behind an earthen parapet and the *terre-plein* was served by two long ramps to the north and west angles. As designed, there was provision for nineteen guns on the faces, sixteen on the flanks, of which four were in Haxo casemates. The lower tier of nine guns in each flank was contained within casemates, and were intended to cross their fire with those of the neighbouring forts. The keep was to be armed with ten guns on its *terre-plein*, and ten in the casemates flanking the gorge. Beneath the ramparts and in the keep was casemated accommodation for 11 officers and 300 NCOs and men. The main magazines were behind each single caponier, and there were expense magazines partially acting as traverses on the ramparts beside the gun positions. The supply of ammunition seems to have been cumbersome, and possibly hazardous when under fire. Access to the fort was originally through the keep. There was a rising drawbridge at the external entrance, and a horizontal sliding bridge at the inner gate giving on to the large open parade.

By contrast, Popton Fort, although begun a year later, has an anachronistic touch in the bastioned appearance of its defensible barracks. However, it demonstrated Jervois's main criterion for sea defences, the employment where possible of open batteries and, where these would be vulnerable to counter-battery from the sea, housing those guns in bombproof masonry faced casemates. The casemated guns were 45 feet (14 metres), and the parapet of the open battery 77 feet (23 metres) above high water mark. Forty-five guns, arranged in two faces, were originally conceived to be the right number to bear on the whole space between Chapel Bay and Milford Church. The batteries were later modified. In the rear, and connected with the battery by a wall and ditch, was the defensible barracks for 10 officers and 240 men. The barracks was in the form of an irregular hexagon enclosed by a ditch flanked by *bastionettes* at the angles, which were probably adopted in this instance in preference to the more usual caponiers because of the need to cover the field beyond with light guns. The defensible barracks at the other two main forts on the Haven, Hubberstone and South Hook, were substantial, two-storeyed keeps, roughly D-shaped in plan, with caponiers covering the ditch in more conventional style.[35]

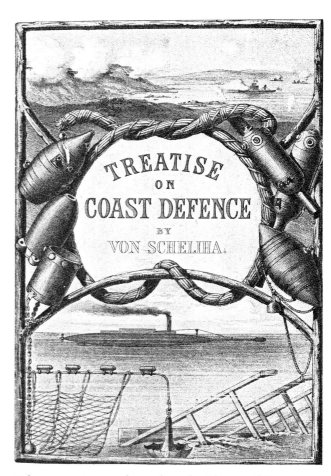

Submarine mining and torpedoes: the title page of Von Scheliha's Treatise on Coast Defence. (Author)

CHAPTER 10

The Forts of the 1859 Royal Commission

THE ROYAL COMMISSION'S PROPOSALS

The third and most serious 'panic' came in 1859, through a combination of events which suggested in the public mind that France was once more a threat, and Britain was again at risk. Military opinion at home had repeatedly and publicly described British defences as inadequate, so that for a brief while there was pressure in Parliament for something to be done. In fact, a good deal of fortress construction was already under way somewhat discreetly, as we have seen, under pressure from the military interests, and with the support of Palmerston, prime minister from 1855 to 1858, and then again from 1859 till 1865. The crisis served to bring this construction into the open, and to expand its objectives still wider. As so often happens in such circumstances, a Royal Commission was set up. This was to report on the Defences of the United Kingdom, and was instructed in August 1859, 'to examine the plans of the works now in progress at Portsmouth (including the Isle of Wight and Spithead), Plymouth, Portland, Pembroke, Dover, Chatham and the Medway', to inspect them on the ground and to consider 'the best means of rendering these dockyards and places defensible within as short a time as possible, in order to be prepared for any sudden emergency, and how they can be put in the most complete state of defence by permanent fortifications'. It had to take account of the small military forces available in the country and disposable for defences. Commissioners were additionally asked to consider what steps should be taken for defending the approaches to Woolwich. The Commission was to start its tasks at Portsmouth 'where the greatest difficulties are supposed to exist'. Subsequently in November, the dockyard of Haulbowline at Queenstown (Cork) was added to the list to give it an Irish dimension.[1]

The composition of the Commission was dominated by military men, though the naval point of view was represented. Among the most significant were Captain Astley Cooper Key, an authority on naval armament, and Lieutenant-Colonel John Henry Lefroy, one of the foremost artillerymen of his day. The most interesting choice was that of James Fergusson, representing the Treasury, and reflecting his earlier, layman's, challenge to the conventional opinions of the professional military engineers. In the key and influential position of secretary to the Commission was the Assistant Inspector-General of Fortifications, Major W F D Jervois.

The general conclusions of the Commission, whose Report appeared on 7 February 1860, were that the fleet alone was insufficient for the defence of the Kingdom.[2] The introduction of steam power, the practice of firing shells horizontally, and 'the enormous extent to which the power and accuracy of aim of artillery have been increased' were, surprisingly, held to operate to Britain's disadvantage and would enable an enemy to concentrate superior naval power and a large body of troops at any point along the coasts. 'At the same time we fully recognize the immense importance of the Channel as a first line of defence, and of the Channel Fleet to maintain it; and cannot urge too strongly on the Government of the country that every means should be taken to ensure the efficiency of that fleet.' Therefore, the protection of the naval arsenals and dockyards was of primary importance. The Report was not a scheme for preventing invasion. It was recognised that it would be difficult to prevent the landing of an invading force. Even the direct defence of the capital was not considered. 'Having carefully weighed the foregoing considerations we are led to the opinion that neither our fleet, our standing army, nor our volunteer forces, nor even the three combined can be relied on as sufficient in themselves for the security of the Kingdom against foreign invasion.' The alternative was to look to fortification as the most economical solution. Therefore, given that the fleet was the first line of defence, it was agreed that fortifications should be at the most vital points: the royal dockyards, the strategic harbours, and, indirectly, London. In practical terms this was an endorsement of the practice of the previous two or three years. The Commission indeed gave general approval to the systems of fortification adopted at Portsmouth, Pembroke, Plymouth and Portland.

The protection of the dockyards against attack from the sea had the greatest priority:

> Of late years the application of steam power to ships-of-war, the introduction of vessels plated with iron, and the invention of artillery of longer range and more accurate aim, have rendered all defences designed for the earlier state of war incapable, without very extensive additions, of defending the places for the protection of which they were designed, and require the adoption of a style of sea defences suited to the present state of the science of naval warfare.

Floating batteries were considered as a suitable adjunct to land batteries. Stationary floating batteries were not recommended under any circumstances, but iron-plated steam-driven batteries together with booms were thought to be very effective.

Where the land defences of the dockyards were concerned, the first requirement was to limit the risks of bombardment, and the second was to secure them against capture. Because of the enormously increased range of the new guns, the defences had to occupy ever more advanced positions. A bombardment range of 8000 yards (7300 kilometres) was now considered likely, and defences had to be arranged to command the ground within that limit. The Commission did not feel that its task was to consider the details of construction of the various works proposed, but rather to concentrate on the positions which ought to be occupied. However, it stressed in general terms the defensive principles which should be adopted. The forts and batteries were to be designed so as to be defensible by a small body of men against a sudden attack, and also to have 'capabilities of resistance that will enable them to withstand any attack likely to be brought against them'. Consequently these works should be provided with redoubts at the gorge. The main ramparts should be capable of providing heavy artillery and musketry fire over the approaches. Ditches, whether water-filled or not, should be flanked both by artillery and musketry. Emphasis was placed on speed of construction. The design should be so arranged that the main ramparts and ditches may be formed without being delayed by the building of revetments or bombproof barracks and permanent magazines. By these means a certain degree of protection could be provided by earthworks within three or four months from commencement. Since 'the description of duty and amount of training required for the ordinary service of garrison guns are comparatively of so simple a nature', the use of the Royal Artillery was to be limited, and more made of ordinary infantry or Volunteers.

Shortage of labour for the construction of the earthworks was not felt to be a problem. Acquisition of the land, however, was; its cost was estimated at slightly more than a quarter of that for construction, which was estimated in the region of a little over £7 millions. With about £500,000 allowed for armaments, about £1 million for floating defences, and, if the £1,460,000 already sanctioned for the works in the course of construction were taken into account, the total sum required for this massive programme was £11,850,000, to be spread over four years.

One of the most instructive aspects of the 1860 Report today is the detailed analysis of the strategic considerations at each of the places to be fortified. Of all the various elements, the siting of the defensive systems over very wide spreads of country brings home the enormous change that had overtaken warfare in the mid-nineteenth century. These considerations, and the placement of fortifications, deserve to be described fully, both to understand the broader objectives as well as the forms taken by the individual defences.

As the Commissioners' brief specified, Portsmouth Dockyard and the anchorage of Spithead took pride of place (see illustration on p13). The main objectives of the sea defences here were five in number:

> The immediate defence of the entrance to the harbour, to prevent an enemy running his fleet in and destroying the dockyard and shipping. To prevent an enemy obtaining a footing upon any part of the shore within the fortified positions to landward, between Brown Down and Fort Cumberland, and effecting the destruction of the naval establishments by a force landed for that object. The protection of the anchorage at Spithead; and that of the dockyard against bombardment by sea. The defence of the Needles Passage. [And lastly] To prevent an enemy obtaining a footing upon the Isle of Wight.

Of the first two objectives, the existing defences, or those in progress, were nearly sufficient for these purposes. The importance of Spithead had been recognised in 1852, and suggestions were made at that time for forts on the shoals of No Man's Land and Horse Sand. It was now proposed that three more sea forts, each with three tiers of casemates and more guns and mortars on the roof, backed up by batteries on the Isle of Wight, should command the eastern approaches. On the Isle of Wight, Sandown Bay was the best and only good landing place for an enemy, and therefore required defence.

The land defences of Portsmouth had been considered in 1857, and a plan begun to be put into effect. Subsequently, the effects of the rifled gun required a drastic revision of that plan. It was now necessary to occupy the whole 7-mile (over 11 kilometres) long ridge of Portsdown Hill, between 6000 and 9000 yards (5.5 and 8.25 kilometres) north of the dockyard, with four principal and three minor works. The Commissioners also thought that the flanks of the position would be secured by lines of ditch and rampart connecting the Portsdown position with Portsmouth and Langstone harbours. A further four detached works were suggested in advance of the existing Gosport Advanced Line.

Plymouth was considered the second great naval arsenal and port in the United Kingdom (see illustration on p11). The sea defences embraced three objectives: 'the defence of the entrance to the Hamoaze, the security of the Sound as an anchorage for our own ships and against its occupation by an enemy, and the adoption of means to prevent the bombardment of the dockyard at long range.' The entrance to the Hamoaze required a new substantial casemated battery on Drake's Island, together with a battery at Mount Edgecombe on the Cornish side, and additional guns elsewhere. The new powerful batteries under construction at Staddon Point (Fort Bovisand) and Picklecombe would serve to cover the Sound, together with a new fort on the Breakwater.

It was considered that a land attack on Plymouth could come either from the west or the east. The land defences had therefore to cover

the peninsula between the St Germain's [sic] River and the sea, which might be called the 'Western Defences', the country between the St Germain's River and the Tamar, which might be termed the 'Saltash Defences', the country between the Tamar and the Catwater, which may be termed the 'North Eastern Defences' and the high ground between the Catwater [sic] and the Sound which may be called the 'Staddon Heights Defences'.

The Western Defences were already in progress with a powerful fort on either flank, Tregantle and Scraesdon. The Commission recommended linking these two with a permanent ditch and rampart, and also providing protection for Whitesand and Cawsand Bays. The Saltash Defences needed three works on the high ground above Saltash, also connected by earthworks. The North Eastern Defences required an advanced line of detached works, its left resting on the Tamar, near St Budeaux, and its right at Catdown upon the Cattewater. Instead of an interior *enceinte*, which was desirable but impracticable, the outer line of works should be connected by earthworks. The Staddon Heights defences could likewise be effectively taken up by two works.

Pembroke Dock was a building yard rather than a fitting-out yard like Portsmouth and Plymouth. While its destruction would not be so disastrous, the loss of Milford Haven would be severe. It was most open to attack by a fleet running up the Haven, but the dockyard was also vulnerable to land attack. The Commission accepted the proposals which had been put forward the year before for strengthening the sea defences. It was more concerned by the lack of land defences. There were at least four places where an

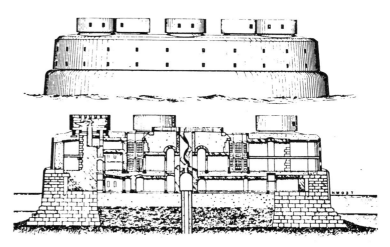

An elevation and cross section of one of the proposals for the Spithead sea forts. There were to be two tiers of guns in casemates capped by five revolving turrets. From Jervois, 'Coast defences and the application of iron to fortification', Journal of the Royal United Services Institution, XII, 1868. (Author)

enemy might land: Tenby, Lydstep Bay, Freshwater Bay (East) and Freshwater Bay (West). As a defence against the capture of the dockyard, a line of works was proposed across the peninsula from Pennaer Pill to East Llanion Pill. To protect the dockyard against bombardment, it was thought preferable to establish self-defensible batteries at the four landing places on the south coast, while, to the north, a line of six small detached works should be considered. This was a repeat of the scheme for sunken towers.

The construction of the breakwater at Portland harbour was nearing completion in 1859, providing a very large and safe anchorage on the Dorset coast. An attack here might threaten any shipping in the harbour, or its capture might facilitate a full scale invasion. Fortifications were already in progress at this time, notably the Verne Citadel.[3] The Commission proposed to complement the Verne and its batteries with a part-casemated, part-earthen battery on the headland of the Nothe, at Weymouth, which would cover the eastern side of the harbour in conjunction with a powerful casemated fort on the breakwater. Ideas for land defence were held in abeyance.

'The defence of the Thames involves interests of vast magnitude', said the Report:

it includes the security of the great powder magazine establishment at Purfleet; the important arsenal at Woolwich and the adjoining dockyard; the Government victualling stores and shipbuilding at Deptford; the large amount of valuable property extending for many miles on either bank of the river; the fleet of merchant shipping moored in the port of London: and lastly, the metropolis itself.

No practical project could be devised for protecting the entrance to the Thames by means of permanent forti-

Sheerness, Kent: bastioned trace beyond 'Blue Town', the dockyard in the centre and Garrison Point Fort. (Hunting Aerofilms)

fications, but moveable floating batteries were suggested which would be stationed at Sheerness. The existing defences were recognised as insufficient, and a new line of defence was proposed with powerful batteries between Coalhouse Point and Cliffe Creek on the opposite Kent bank. A second defence line between the long established forts at Tilbury and Gravesend was to be maintained (see illustration on p10).

The defence of the naval establishments in the Medway came under three heads: the security of Sheerness Dockyard against bombardment; to guard against the occupation of the anchorage in the entrance of the Medway, and the subsequent capture of the dockyard; and to deny the navigation of the river to an enemy, thus securing Chatham Dockyard against attack. The proposed answer was the building of a powerful multi-tiered casemated work, somewhat similar to that proposed by Major-General Sir John Jones as early as 1840 at Garrison Point. In addition, it was proposed to enclose the existing three-gun tower on Grain Spit with a casemated battery, with more batteries on the Isle of Grain. Further upstream, two small islands, Hoo and Darnet, should receive batteries. The land fronts of Sheerness required advancing further into Sheppey. Chatham could be threatened by land attack from the east from the direction of Dover, from the west of the

Medway, and from the north, between the Thames and the Medway. To counter the eastern threat, six detached works were needed in advance of Fort Pitt. The western defences had several options which could be linked with the works on the Thames. An attack between Cliffe Creek and the Isle of Grain could be met by a fort near the village of Slough, and by the flooding of the marshlands.

While it was possible to indicate lines of defence for Woolwich, this was considered prohibitively expensive and, with the extended defences of Chatham, not strictly necessary. There was, however, a recommendation that Shooter's Hill be permanently fortified.

Dover was somewhat unusual in comparison with the other fortified locations. It did not have a dockyard or arsenal which required protection. 'It is, in fact, the only place in England which partakes of the nature of a strategical fortress or intrenched camp in its primary object.' As well as its position in relation to the continent, the scheme for constructing a large harbour of refuge had progressed quite far. The completion of the works on the Western Heights and other improvements were in progress. The only new work recommended was to the north of Dover Castle, in order to prevent an enemy establishing his batteries on the high ground which overlooks the castle.

Finally, Cork harbour, 'possesses great capabilities as a naval port'. In time of war it would occupy an important naval strategic position for the defence of

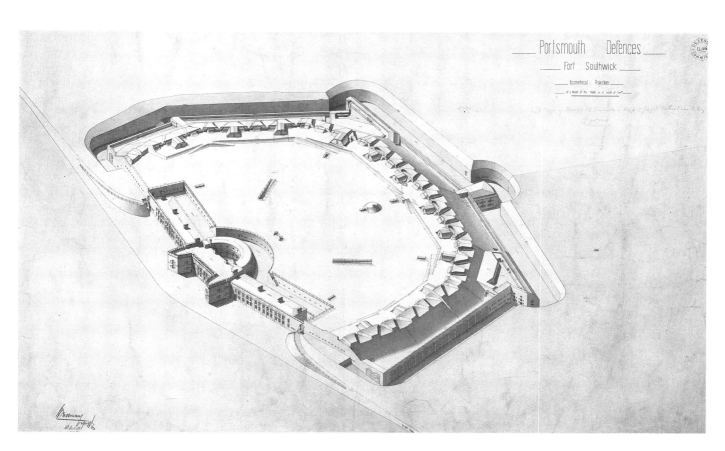

Fort Southwick, Portsdown: isometric projection. Public Record Office, WO 78/4520. (PRO)

Ireland and the western coasts of England and Wales. There were already considerable existing fortifications, and it was recommended that the land defences of Camden and Carlisle Forts should be remodelled to avoid them being taken in reverse, and the sea batteries extended. Protection against land attack could be improved by an additional four towers and further works at Youghal to the east.

The Report was not debated in Parliament until 23 July 1860. By then it had been revised by the Defence Committee, composed of military officers. Palmerston considered that a total budget of £9 millions would be sufficient, with armaments and floating defences coming out of annual revenue. Palmerston pointed out that this was very reasonable when compared with expenditure abroad; Cherbourg alone cost over £8 millions. Although it was acknowledged that the desire for improved defences was popular, there was considerable opposition to the Report in Parliament. A year had gone by since the initial crisis, and relations with France had improved. Many of those who had loudly demanded the setting up of a Royal Commission now harshly criticised its findings. Permanent fortification was declared to be 'un-English', and there was a constant demand that our defence should rest on an augmented navy and Volunteers alone. Detailed criticism, often from the older military and naval men, centered on the provision of land defences. This last point produced more hard feeling than the proposed cost, although Bright re-

minded the House of the inevitable optimism of estimates, and attacked the whole basis of the Report, declaring the Commissioners to be an 'aggregate of lunatics'.[4] The Bill received the Royal assent on 28 August 1860, but the Report's proposals were twice reduced, and in 1862, the government deferred to pressure and postponed the building of the sea forts in the Solent. The cabinet continued to be divided over the whole question of fortifications – in particular, Gladstone, who three times threatened to resign from the Chancellorship on the issue. Yet, as Palmerston wrote to the Queen, it was better to lose Mr Gladstone than to lose Portsmouth.[5]

THE FORTS OF THE 1860s

The result of the 1860 Report was a prodigality of fortress building unmatched in the British Isles, and which, in its geographical spread, went far beyond the extent of the schemes of Henry VIII and Charles II. By 1867, seventy-six forts and batteries were in the process of being built or had already been completed. The presiding influence over the designs of these fortifications lay with the now Lieutenant-Colonel Jervois, Deputy Director of Works for Fortifications. He had already set out the principles of military engineering which were to be implemented, and he achieved close oversight over the subsequent technical problems

A 13.5-inch rifled muzzle-loader in a casemate at Shoeburyness, Essex. (DOE)

which had to be met. Other engineer officers worked out the detailed designs of individual works. Captain Edmund Du Cane reconstructed the defences on the Western Heights at Dover, and designed Fort Burgoyne, adjacent to Dover Castle. He was also responsible for the North Eastern Land Defences and the Staddon position at Plymouth. Captain William Crossman was responsible for many of the forts at Portsmouth and the Isle of Wight, including the Gosport Advanced Line, and those on Portsdown Hill. He had earlier designed Forts Scraesdon and, with Du Cane, Tregantle in Cornwall, and he had also worked on the Verne Citadel. Captain Herbert Siborne covered the whole of the sea defences of the Thames and Medway, and was also responsible for the Breakwater Fort at Plymouth. Major Porter dealt with the sea defences of Milford Haven and the principal batteries defending Plymouth Sound. Captain Edwards was concerned with the Needles defences, including the extensions to Hurst Castle. Captain E H Steward was responsible for the Solent sea forts and the Breakwater Fort at Portland. Lieutenant-Colonel Fisher worked mainly on the forts in Cork harbour, but also on the Puckpool Mortar Battery, part of the Solent defences, Gilkicker Battery and Southsea Castle.[6]

The original proposals of 1860 had been considerably reduced in number following Parliamentary debate. The omissions at Portsmouth included two Spithead forts, three minor works on Portsdown Hill, and part of the Gosport advanced position. Plymouth lost the inner line of the North Eastern Defences, and a reduction in the Breakwater works. Pembroke had most of the land fortifications omitted, and, in the Medway, Grain Spit Fort was also affected. Subsequently, further works were left out: the connecting lines between the forts at Portsdown; at Plymouth, part of the North East Defences, the whole of the Saltash position and the connecting lines of the Western Defences; the Western Defences of Chatham, and a further reduction of land defences at Pembroke. Later, in order to find money for the provision of iron shields for coastal casemates, it was suggested that the Chatham Eastern Defences should be omitted, and the site for a Central Arsenal abandoned.

Changes of another kind also affected those forts which were being built, almost from their beginnings. The threat of more powerful ironclads had led to much experimentation, and it was felt, as a result, that forts should be armoured too. The Spithead forts were first planned as masonry structures but, by the time they were built, they were wholly or partly of iron.

Interior view of an iron shield with the rope mantlet lying on the floor. (DOE)

Every casemated work was reconsidered, and the insertion of iron shields was eventually regarded as essential. The lessons to be learnt from the American Civil War had a profound effect on the forts under construction during the 1860s, leading to a greater appreciation of the shot-absorbing qualities of earthwork. By 1866, the rifled muzzle-loader (RML) was accepted as the best weapon for countering ironclads, and the forts were remodelled for the 7-inch (178mm) RML of 7 tons and the 9-inch (228mm) of 12 tons. These weapons were heavier and larger than the smooth-bores and Armstrong guns which were originally conceived as the principal armament. The numbers of guns intended could no longer be fitted into the works as originally designed. Changes had to be made, often by losing one planned casemate in order to increase the space between the guns.

   Nevertheless, despite the omissions and the modifications necessary to keep the works up to date, the amount of fortification carried out was enormous. On 20 February 1867, a report prepared by Jervois on the progress made in defence construction was presented to Parliament.[7] The report covered the period up to the end of 1866, and included proposals for complet-

The construction at Shoeburyness of an iron shield within a casemate showing the first layer of horizontal plates in position. (DOE)

ing the programme. Estimates were given to show the probable cost of completing certain batteries with iron shields in the embrasures, together with proposals for the addition of turrets whenever possible. 'The improved means of protection against modern ordnance, which have been developed since these works were first planned, are necessarily very costly, and it has been an object to provide the requisite protection as economi-

An RML on a Moncrieff disappearing carriage in the loading position. (DOE)

cally as possible,' wrote Burgoyne in a letter to the Secretary of State for War.[8]

The Report of 1867 described progress in some detail. At Portsmouth, the most notable advance had been made in the construction of the now reprieved Spithead forts. Horse Sand and No Man's Land Forts were now intended to have two tiers of casemates and provision for four revolving turrets on top, each to contain two powerful guns. At Spit Bank and Rye Sand Forts there was to be a single tier of casemates for seventeen guns each, and two revolving turrets. Fort St Helens, close to the Isle of Wight, was slightly smaller. At all five work was now under way. The North Eastern Defences of Plymouth were rationalised. They extended over 5 miles (8 kilometres), with Fort Efford on the right, the centre occupied by Crown Hill Fort, and the left with Fort Agaton and Ernsettle Battery respectively, commanding the approaches to Plymouth and Devonport along the peninsula. The line of detached forts and earthen batteries here supported one another. Their ditches, where unseen from an adjacent work, were flanked by caponiers, and the escarps and counterscarps were cut into the rock. At Pembroke, work was in progress at Stack Rock, South Hook Battery, Hubberstone Battery and Popton Fort. Chapel Bay, an earthen battery for six guns, was still to be started. The only piece of land defence undertaken at Milford Haven was Fort Scoveston. Sites had been purchased for defences on the south side of the Haven but nothing was done. Only the foundations and some of the superstructure of the Portland Breakwater Fort had been completed. The new works on the Thames were in hand but no estimate had been prepared for the new batteries at Tilbury and Gravesend. On the south bank of the Medway, the Queenborough Lines were intended to be secured by a tower prepared for the reception of an iron turret for two guns. The Chatham Eastern Defences were not begun but the land had been

acquired. Nor had the line of forts between the Thames and the Medway been sanctioned. 'Unless therefore it is considered desirable to add a large sum to the estimate for land defences of Chatham, with a view of carrying out the whole plan, it appears doubtful whether the "Eastern Defences" above should be carried into effect.' When Dover Pier was completed, a small fort would be added which, in conjunction with sea batteries on either flank of the existing works would defend the harbour to seaward. In a number of instances in the Isle of Wight and in the Isle of Grain, an inland fort would act as a keep for several batteries.

The 1867 Report was followed by another, published in 1869, from the Parliamentary Committee appointed to enquire into the construction, condition and costs of the fortifications.[9] Inevitably, it was found that the costs of the works had greatly exceeded the estimates. Among the reasons was the fact that improvements in armaments had caused changes in design. This factor had led to the substitution of iron for masonry in the sea forts. Several works were now on a much larger scale than recommended by the Commissioners, and there had been a not unexpected rise in the prices of labour and materials. The committee inspected each work, and provided a detailed description. It was satisfied that the forts were well built and were of great value. It appreciated that it was fortunate that the success of the heavier rifled guns was established before the works were generally too far advanced. The space between the guns could therefore be increased, the disposition of the magazines and shell stores altered, and the need for armour and iron shields taken into account. The committee, however, was concerned by the omission of some of the Commissioners' recommendations, such as the Saltash defences at Plymouth.

One set of recommendations demonstrated the improvements falling to the common soldier at the end of the 1860s. The basic allotment of 400 cubic feet (11 cubic metres) per man in barrack rooms was increased to not less than 600 cubic feet (17 cubic metres), and twice as much was required in hospitals. The number of men that could be accommodated in barrack rooms was thus reduced by one-third. Libraries, canteens, recreation rooms and schools were also added where practicable.

One of the major concerns was the powers of resistance to powerful rifled shot and shell provided by granite walls and earthen parapets. Granite walls 14 feet 6 inches (4.5 metres) thick were concluded to be sufficient to meet an attack from ship-borne guns, but it was thought necessary to substitute concrete for earth to a certain extent in the parapets. Concrete was especially applied to the Moncrieff system of gun mounting. The introduction of the Moncrieff Disappearing Gun Carriage was a serious issue by 1869, and was most applicable to open batteries. It was proposed to substitute Moncrieff gun pits for turrets.[10]

An RML on a Moncrieff disappearing carriage in the firing position. (DOE)

Space forbids descriptions of each fort or battery, and it is sufficient to examine in detail an example of the three main types of fortification employed: a land fort, a coastal battery and a sea fort.

The choice of Fort Wallington as the representative land fort may seem strange since it has been largely demolished, but, during that unfortunate event, its constructional details were examined and recorded, so that it serves as a good comparison with the other surviving Portsdown forts which are the most impressive of the Commission's land defences.[11] Wallington also requires comparison with neighbouring Fort Brockhurst, begun three years earlier. It was the westernmost of the line of detached forts along the Portsdown ridge. It faced north west, and covered Fareham Common and the open ground before the woods in Wickham parish 2 to 3 miles (3.2 to 4.8 kilometres) away. The fort is almost 2000 yards (1828 metres) from Fort Nelson to the east, and 2840 yards (2596 metres) north of Fort Fareham, the fort which

Fort Wallington, Portsdown: aerial photograph before demolition. (DOE)

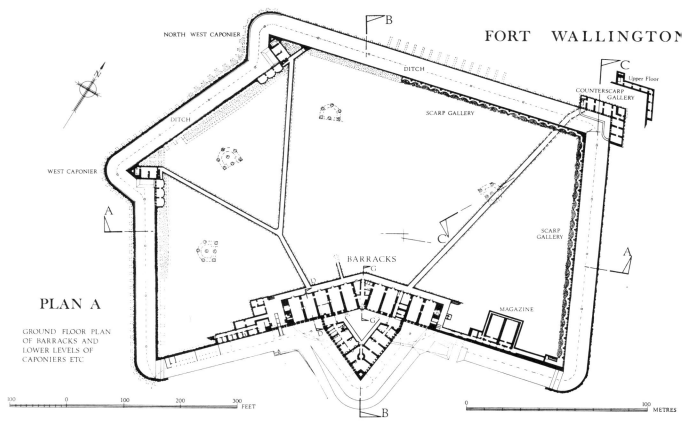

NORTH WEST CAPONIER

DITCH

FORT WALLINGTON

SCARP GALLERY

DITCH

Upper Floor

COUNTERSCARP
GALLERY

C

WEST CAPONIER

N

A

SCARP
GALLERY

A

PLAN A

BARRACKS

GROUND FLOOR PLAN
OF BARRACKS AND
LOWER LEVELS OF
CAPONIERS ETC

MAGAZINE

B

100   0   100   200   300 FEET

0   100 METRES

*Fort Wallington: ground floor plan of the barracks and the
lower levels of the caponiers and subterranean access to them
and to the counterscarp gallery.* (Author)

acted as a link between the Portsdown line and the
earlier Gosport Advanced Line. Work began in
September 1861, and was completed in December 1874.
The other Portsdown forts were constructed in two
stages, with two distinct contracts. Wallington was
built in three stages. The first involved the main lines of
the fort – the ditches, escarp galleries, caponiers, and
communication passages – and was completed by
March 1865. The second stage, the building of the
barracks, redan etc, was finished in September 1867.
The third contract involved the completion of the
ramparts. The eventual cost was £100,570 (£3,275 below the estimates – a surprising fact since there had
been failures in building the revetment walls owing to a
seam of 'blue slipper' clay).

The fort was six-sided. The east and west
sides were roughly parallel and can be regarded as the
flanks. The north and north west faces met to form an
obtuse salient angle. On the south, the gorge was closed
by two brick walls forming a re-entrant angle, in the
centre of which was a defensible barracks. From the
barracks projected a massive redan which could give
flanking fire across the gorge. The fort was built from
red, stock bricks with stone dressings. All the load-
bearing roofs, carrying the earth of the ramparts above,
were brick tunnel-vaults. Over them a cover of weak

concrete was poured and levelled, and then sealed with
a bitumen damp course. The floors separating the
upper and lower floors of the caponiers and the floors
of the barrack block were supported on iron girders.
The joinery, although simple, was of high quality
throughout.

As designed, the armament of the fort was
intended to consist of seventeen guns on the ramparts,
six mortars in casemates in the northern angle and other
guns in the gorge and flanks. In all these forts armament
strengths varied over time, and gun positions were
always being revised to meet the requirements of improved artillery. In the early 1890s, there were at
Wallington: four 64-pounder RMLs, three 8-inch
(203mm) RMLs, three 6.3-inch (160mm) RML howitzers, ten 7-inch (178mm) rifled breech-loaders (RBLs),
eight 40-pounder smooth-bore breech-loaders (SBBL),
and ten 32-pounder SBBLs. They were distributed as
follows: twenty on the ramparts, eight in the barracks,
and ten in the caponiers.[12] The number of guns on the
ramparts was later much reduced. There was accommodation for 8 officers and 172 NCOs and men, 16
hospital patients and 37 horses.

The fort was surrounded by a dry ditch. At
the gorge it was shallow and of little consequence, but
in front of the flanks and faces it was a considerable
obstacle, 33 to 40 feet (10 to 12 metres) wide. The escarp
wall was 29 feet (nearly 9 metres) high. It and the
counterscarp were revetted in brickwork of counter-

fort construction. There was no covered-way but on the escarp there was a discontinuous *chemin des rondes* below the rise of the ramparts, approached by tunnels through the earthworks. Elsewhere, the parapet of the gorge wall was pierced by musketry loopholes. The whole local defensive concept of the fort lay in the ditch, each arm of which could be scoured by cannon and musketry fire provided from two-storey caponiers in the west and north west salients, and from a counterscarp gallery in the north east. The two caponiers were almost identical. There were pairs of casemates at two levels, each containing a gunport with musketry loops on either side, except on the lower level adjacent to the curtain where the loop beside the curtain was omitted because of the batter of the escarp. Each caponier was itself flanked by one escarp gallery. The salient of each caponier was, as it were, bevelled off so that they could be flanked completely from the gallery. As an additional protection from close attack, a pit was dug in front of the caponier to prevent an enemy getting too close to the loops on the lower level. From the start, the casemates in the caponiers were equipped for barrack use. The counterscarp gallery had six casemates at the lower level, each with gunport and attendant loops to fire down the east and north ditches. Access to the gallery was by a long passage under the ditch.

For the whole of the length of the east flank, and for most of the north face, was a two-tiered escarp gallery for musketry only. It was part of the original design, but by 1867, and during the completion of the ramparts, chalk rubble was allowed to pour into the open bays of the counterforts. Access was then virtually sealed. Elsewhere the gallery was affected by failure of the escarp, and part had been filled with concrete.

The influences of Choumara, whose *Memoires sur la Fortification* was published in 1827, may have led to the fact that the parapet and *terre-plein* did not follow the line of the escarp.[13] There were in fact eight facets to the rampart outline, and the guns were arranged so that all points of the compass, except the south, could be covered by direct fire. The main weight was directed towards the north and north east where it could cross with the guns of Fort Nelson to the east. Besides a version of a 'Carnot Wall' at the junction of escarp wall and foot of the rampart, there was another feature derived from Carnot: a mortar battery for 'vertical fire'. In the northern salient there was an arc of six brick casemates for mortars firing through a gap in the earthworks below the level of the *terre-plein*. The casemates were intercommunicating and a passage to the rear gave access to the loopholed traverses flanking the *chemin-des-rondes*. A small magazine or shell room was placed behind, served by a tunnelled approach from the East Parade. The battery was well protected from counter-fire by a substantial curved bank in front and a massive traverse on the line of the salient. Further provision against more general enfilade

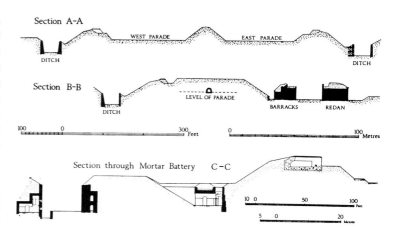

Fort Wallington: *cross-sections through the parade, the traverse, barracks and redan, and the mortar battery.* (Author)

Fort Wallington: *elevation and sections through the north west caponier.* (Author)

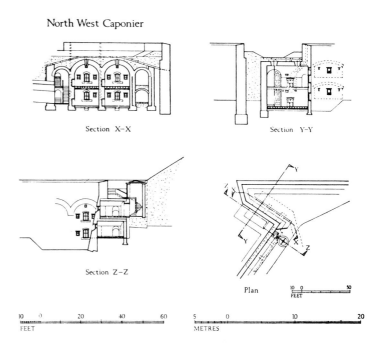

across the fort proper was the enormous earth traverse, over a 100 feet (30 metres) wide, which divided the parade. The main magazine was located in the most secure corner, the south east.

The barrack was defensible, covering the entrance and gorge. Its roof was capped with earth to render it bombproof. The top of the redan was treated in the same way, except that a *terre-plein* was created to provide room for four gun positions in between traverses. The barrack arrangements were carefully distinguished according to rank. The men were housed on the ground floor of the main range. On the first

Garrison Point Fort, Sheerness: drawing by Jervois of the application of iron to the two-tiered casemated fort. From an article in the RUSI Journal *1868.* (Author)

floor, were the rooms for the sergeants and a set of rooms for a field officer. The other officers occupied the upper floor of the redan.

Of the seventy-six forts and batteries erected, or in the course of erection in 1867, only nineteen were land forts. The remainder were sea batteries of one sort or another, or keeps serving sea batteries. Unlike land forts, the sea batteries, because of their situation, were highly variable in plan. They ranged from simple open gun platforms behind earthwork, to lines of granite-faced casemates in one or two tiers, with or without a barbette battery on the roof. Although casemates provided much superior protection to both guns and their crews, they severely restricted the field of fire of the guns. Additionally, the huge rifled muzzle-loaders took time to load and aim – nearly two minutes for each shot. There was therefore only a limited time for a casemated gun to strive to hit a moving warship. This meant that guns had to be spread along a line so that there was a better chance of the battery as a whole being successful. In contrast, the provisions for self-defence were often limited. On occasions the gorge was given a substantial brick or masonry keep, but often it was closed by a rudimentary brick wall containing, and flanked by, musketry loops.

The two-tiered casemated forts were at Garrison Point, Sheerness, to provide massive firepower at the mouth of the Medway, and at Picklecombe on the

Hurst Castle, Hampshire, from the south east. (Hunting Aerofilms)

Hurst Castle: casemated front with iron shields. (Author)

west side of Plymouth Sound. The others were single-storey, and one of the most impressive and largest of the sea batteries is Hurst Castle on the north side of the Needles Passage, the western entrance to the Solent. Hurst is an enormous single-storey battery arranged on either side of Henry VIII's castle: thirty-seven casemates on the western wing, and twenty-four to the east. The masonry wings replaced two earthwork batteries which had been thrown up between 1852 and 1858 to complement the casemated Fort Albert opposite.[14] In plan, with the hook-like terminal to the western wing of the 1860s fort, there is a resemblance to some of the Russian coastal batteries, in particular, Fort Nicolas at Sebastopol.

Essentially, the casemates were simple structures, granite-faced, brick vaulted chambers, topped with concrete, and surfaced with asphalt, in all about 5 feet (1.5 metres) thick. The outline of the flat roofs was broken by the chimneys serving the barrack accommodation to the rear of the gun positions, and by two blisters, one on each wing, which were embryonic fire control points and lookouts. Each casemated front was about 9 feet (2.7 metres) thick with segmental headed gunports recessed from the face in two 'orders'. The casemates themselves were restricted areas in which to hold a heavy gun and its team. They could quite rapidly fill with smoke and fumes. To mitigate the worst effects, most casemates were open at the rear when the gun was being fired. During peacetime, the back of the casemate was closed by a wooden frame containing windows and doors since the casemate doubled as barrack accommodation. If the gun was to be fired the glass and timber screen could be easily removed.

The estimated cost for these two new wings

Hurst Castle: fire control blister on the flat roof of the casemates. (Author)

was £108,000. The contractors, Rogers and Booth of Southsea, began work on the foundations in February 1861, and took just over a year to complete. The granite-faced superstructure was not begun until 1864 by G Tyrell of Great Yarmouth, Norfolk, and not completed until June 1870. There was accommodation for 1 field officer, 3 officers, 7 married NCOs and 120 other ranks.

The embrasures are now filled with iron shields, but these were not part of the original proposals, and were inserted in the early 1870s to counter the increased effectiveness of naval artillery. It can be seen

Plymouth Breakwater with the sea fort behind. (Author)

Spitbank Fort, Portsmouth. (Author)

that the granite surrounds have been cut back for the insertion of the shields. The armour was based on an experimental design which was made up of three 5-inch (127mm) plates of wrought iron, separated by 5-inch gaps filled with concrete. Within the armour plate was a lozenge-shaped opening for the muzzle of the gun. The guns employed were 7-inch (177mm) 7-ton, or 9-inch (228mm) 12-ton, rifled muzzle-loaders on dwarf casemate carriages and traversing platforms (see illustrations on pages 176 and 177). As a means of preventing casualties from masonry splinters under enemy fire, a rope mantlet was suspended inside the iron shield. Two mantlets were hung in each casemate and pulled close about the gun. Such mantlets were also damped with a

mixture of calcium chloride and water to lessen the flash of the gun, as well as to absorb splinters. By 1886, the armament of the East Wing of Hurst was two 12.5-inch (317mm) 38-ton RMLs, five 10-inch (245mm) 18-ton RMLs, five 9-inch (228mm) 12-ton RMLs; in the West Wing, eight 12.5-inch (317mm) 38-ton RMLs, ten 10-inch (254mm) 18-ton RMLs, and one 64-pounder. In the old castle there were two 64-pounders for covering the gorge.

Among the more dramatic of the coastal defences are the sea forts, not only in the Solent, but also at Plymouth and Portland where they are associated with the breakwaters. The idea of establishing forts on the shoals of Spithead was politically controversial. The Royal Commission recommended five casemated sea forts, and work began in 1861. The foundations were designed and laid by the civil engineer, Sir John Hawkshaw. They consisted of a ring of masonry made of large concrete blocks with the outer face in granite. The space inside was filled with clay and shingle capped by a thick bed of concrete to provide a base for the inner portion of the superstructure. The original intention was to build the works entirely of granite, but before the foundations were completed, it was decided to give them an iron superstructure. Horse Sand and No Man's Land were to be three-tier forts with guns and mortars on the roof. This was modified to produce a two-tier work with internal piers to take five projected turrets on the roof.[15]

Construction was suspended during the years from 1862 to 1864 while the whole scheme for sea forts in Spithead was questioned and debated in Parliament. However, Horse Sand and No Man's Land were eventually completed by 1880. These were the largest of the four which were built, and were armoured completely from the level of the lower gun floor to the roof of the

Plan view of the armoured face of Horsesand and No Man's Land Forts. (Author)

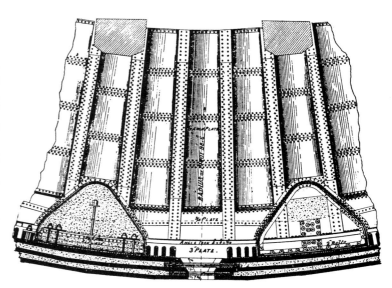

upper gun floor, 22 feet 6 inches (6.85 metres) in height. In front of the piers to support the intended turrets, the plating consisted of three wrought iron 6-inch (153mm) plates, separated by 5-inch (127mm) layers of concrete and 1 inch (25mm) of cement between the inner plate and the pier. Elsewhere, the armour was thicker on a similar 'sandwich' formula. Surrounding the gunports it was made up from the outside of 5 inches (127mm) of wrought iron, 1 inch (25mm) of teak, 2 inches (50 mm) wrought iron, 1 inch (25mm) teak, 5 inches (127mm) wrought iron, then similar plates in reverse order. The casemates themselves were constructed using iron girders tied into a circular base plate let into the masonry to form the basis of the iron structure. No part of the floor or roof structure was attached to the 3-inch (76mm) thick iron rings on which they rested, the surfaces being free to slide. The purpose of this was to prevent any movement caused by shot striking the fort from being transmitted to the gun floors and disturbing the gun mountings.

The forts were designed by Captain E H Steward but the development of the armour and shields was handled separately by Captain Inglis and Lieutenant English.[16] The most expensive to build was No Mans Land Fort, costing £462,000, without the guns. At Horse Sand, the two tiers of casemates were intended for forty-nine guns, and, in addition, the fort was supposed to act as a control station for a network of controlled submarine mines in the Spithead entrance. The intended turrets were each to be provided with two 12-inch (305mm) 35-ton RMLs, but for financial reasons these were never fitted. Rifled muzzle-loaders of 12.5-inch (317mm) and 10-inch (254mm) calibres were installed, though the casemate armament was amended several times.

The basements of the forts contained the magazine, with provision for twenty-four shell stores and lifts, opening off an outer passage, and fourteen cartridge stores and lobbies off the middle passage. In the central core, a flight of steps led down to a laundry, cookhouse and ablution room and coal store. Later, the outer ring of shell stores was blocked with concrete, and the passage filled with sand to increase protection for the magazine. The inner core was altered to take steam boilers for powering the later armament.

Accommodation for the garrison was in the two upper floors and in a central 'tower'. Even so, it was limited to the small regular garrisons, with hammock hooks provided for many more in an emergency. Horse Sand and No Mans Land had accommodation for 5 officers and 90 men, and 3 officers and 90 men respectively, with hammock hooks for 207 and 199 in addition. The smaller Spitbank was intended for a regular garrison of only 1 officer and 26 men.

THE 'BRITISH SCHOOL' OF MILITARY ENGINEERING

The recommendations of the Royal Commission of 1859 were under close scrutiny by those who were sceptical of their political necessity, by those who considered that the navy was a more than sufficient defence, and by those who were opposed to forts simply on grounds of expense. There were also some who were critical on professional grounds, and it says much for the open-mindedness of the department of the Inspector-General of Fortifications that constructive criticism was accepted and changes made. It is surprising, however, that as late as 1863, Colonel Cunliffe Owen was to revive the arguments in favour of continuous lines.[17] He pointed out that the decision of the French engineers in 1840 for a continuous *enceinte* for Paris followed an initial proposal for detached forts on the German model. He reminded his readers that even the 1859 Royal Commission had recommended that the forts in the Gosport Advanced Line, those on Portsdown, and in the Plymouth North Eastern Defences should be connected by a continuous ditch and rampart, but this was not being put into effect. The opposite point of view was that continuous lines would be too expensive to man, but Cunliffe Owen believed that the lines would save the need for Haxo casemates. In addition, 'keeps are in their way excellent things if we can afford them but they are after all mere adjuncts.' He argued strongly for open bastions. 'Caponiers have not yet stood the test of actual war.' They should be few and large. 'The opportunities for skulking which our hole-in-the-corner flanks afford always give me great uneasiness.' Finally, he claimed that a continuous line was as cheap as a line of detached works. It could be defended with fewer and less well trained men, its defence was simpler, easier to understand by officers and men, and appealed to patriotism! This conservative

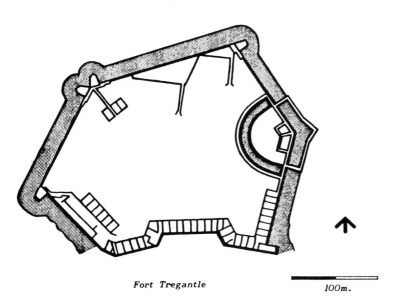

Fort Tregantle

100m.

Tregantle Fort, Cornwall, simplified plan. (Ian Hunt, 'Plymouth sound. The defence of the naval station', *Fort*, 1983)

and 'blimpish' point of view was countered by Captain J J Wilson who demonstrated the fallaciousness of the costs argument.[18] Detached works were at their most advantageous as an advanced defence on grounds of economy, in terms of cost, and in numbers of defenders. The introduction of the electric telegraph answered the communications problem. It was perfectly possible, he felt, to create fieldworks in the gaps between forts during the build-up to war. The casemated flanks in the detached works would in any case make such gaps untenable.

Constructive criticism of a prestigious kind emerged from the visit to England of General, Count Todleben, the engineer in charge of the Russian defences of Sebastopol during the Crimean War, which had proved so successful in holding up the Allied armies. Todleben had also strengthened the coastal defences at the mouth of the Dneiper and at Kronstadt, acquiring a considerable reputation. In 1864 Todleben was invited to visit the defences of Portsmouth and Plymouth, and to express his opinions on their worth.[19] His first general observation on seeing the plans was on the great extent of the works, and his doubts over how sufficient garrisons could be provided to man them. He was complimentary on the details of the works themselves. Many of the arrangements appeared novel to him, and were approved. Others were mentioned with satisfaction as precisely what 'He had himself adopted in Russia'. His position in the debate over the relative value of detached works or continuous lines was clear as a determined 'partisan of the former'. His practice was for a few very strong works on commanding sites affording a powerful fire, not only on the front and flanks, but crossing fire with

each other to the rear. Such works should have good casemates, revetted escarps and counterscarps, and thereby be impregnable to any assault. On the North East Line at Plymouth, he would have had four such works. In front of them, and supported by them in time of war, he would place a chain of earthen batteries. If these batteries were attacked, the men in them would retire behind or into the forts. In the rear, he would have more open batteries to fire on troops assembled to pass through the gaps. He was very appreciative of Tregantle Fort, approving the keep as a check on a successful assault on the main body of the work, giving time for reinforcements to arrive and drive the enemy out. He did not see it, or recommend its use, as 'a keep of last resort'. In reply to Todleben's criticism that the exposed masonry of the keep was vulnerable to battery without a glacis to cover it, Jervois dissented from this view on a number of grounds, not least because 'the proposed glacis would occupy a great part of the interior space of the fort'.[20] Nevertheless, Jervois's Portsdown forts, which were completed much later, met Todleben's point by including massive traverses in the interior. Todleben was critical of the masonry at the throats and sills of the embrasures on the *terre-plein*, an opinion shared by some British engineers. Jervois's answer was that iron shields would be provided. Todleben much approved of the *chemin des rondes* and the retired rampart which enabled repairs to be done to the exterior slopes. He was also full of praise for the siting of the North Eastern Line of forts at Plymouth in relation to the ground they had to cover. He was, however strongly against the principle of works depending for the flank defence of their ditches upon neighbouring forts. Jervois noted subsequently that this was only used exceptionally where the works were so close that 'they are more like bastions on a line of continuous fortification'. At Southsea, Todleben approved the great distance between the guns in the auxiliary batteries. He was a strong advocate of turrets for sea forts since they helped to concentrate fire. Of the two fortified places he visited he preferred Plymouth, 'for the positions looked finer and the girdle of the works more complete'. This remark was more in connection with the general appearance than with the comparative strength of the two places.

The Commission's forts were successful because they were adaptable to rapidly changing technology. 'We as a nation may consider ourselves fortunate that the defence of our principal ports had been postponed to the present time' wrote G Sydenham Clark.[21] With few exceptions, these works were constructed after rifled ordnance had unmistakably proved its powers. The development of shell-fire had tended to produce high-front protection, and the evolution of the stone or brick fort using casemates. The development of penetrative power which the rifled gun attained led naturally to the adoption of iron shields. Iron almost

Landguard Fort, Felixstowe: casemated south western front and caponier. (Author)

became a universal panacea. Captain Du Cane pointed to the drawbacks of caponiers in the forts being built in 1863; that they were vulnerable to vertical fire and a breach in the escarp could blind the casemates in the caponiers.[22] Jervois, in response to a similar point made by Todleben, insisted that in time of war caponiers would be covered by iron sheets. Du Cane was also in favour of covering the works with iron and providing iron blockhouses in the covered way or in the *chemin des rondes*. But there were disadvantages in the use of iron in the embrasures of casemates. The junction of the stone and the iron was weak, and too much of the intervening piers had to be cut away to insert the shields. The later adaptation of the forts and batteries to the Moncrieff system of disappearing gun mounting was further proof of the rapid acceptance of technical progress.

The vast range of fortifications carried out in the 1860s was not solely due to the recommendations of the 1859 Royal Commission. Lesser ports and harbours without obvious naval significance were also protected. The defences of Harwich were improved by open batteries, leaving the long established Landguard Fort to be remodelled early in the next decade.[23] A line of batteries begun in 1866, protected the Bristol Channel, from Lavernock in South Wales across to the islands of Steepholm and Flatholm, and on to Brean Down in Somerset.[24] On the south coast, works of some technical significance were constructed, such as the fort at Newhaven.

Newhaven was said to be a fort of 'enormous strength' intended for forty-two guns and accommodation for 300 men, and with many of the characteristics of a land fort. Newhaven harbour was just being developed as a commercial port and defences were thought essential. Construction on the fort began in 1864, and was completed in six years. It was described as being 'built of brick with an irregular lunette trace, the gorge and right flank being protected by a wide ditch and escarp wall, 30 feet (9 metres) high.'[25] Its unusually wide ditch of 50 feet (15 metres) was flanked by counterscarp galleries with embrasures both for cannon and musketry, and the foot of the cliffs on the south and west was covered by a substantially built single-storey brick caponier, linked to the fort above by a tunnel and stairs. The fort was designed by Lieutenant Ardagh at the period of transition from smoothbore to rifled ordnance, and completed at the moment Moncrieff's disappearing carriage and mounting were being adopted. It is not Newhaven's design, novel as it was in some respects, that demands attention today, but its form of construction in comparison with the normal run of Royal Commission forts. Begun three or

Newhaven Fort, Sussex: concrete revetted ditch on north front. (Author)

four years later than them, there is a quality of crafts-manship and detailing which mark it out. The passage behind the barrack casemates below the north rampart is wide and lofty, the communicating passages and stairs are also on a scale which makes similar features in the Commission forts appear mean. Newhaven is also the first example of the use of concrete as a revetment for ditches in a British fort.[26]

While this was a time of fundamental change for guns, there were major developments in other forms of weaponry for coastal defence. In particular, the 1860s saw the improvement and increasing use of the submarine mine: 'From a modest beginning – a "Floating obstructions Committee" assembled in 1863 – an elaborate and expensive system had been gradually developed.'[27] Minefields were planned for the Spithead defences and elsewhere. Boom-defence was considered from the outset at Milford Haven. The experiences gained from observing the American Civil War encour-aged the development of mines and torpedoes (see illustration p170). Indeed, it was said that no fort now built could keep out a large fleet unless the channel was obstructed so that the passage was kept under fire of heavy batteries.[28] This form of defence was more ap-plicable, however, to rivers but less so against attack from the open sea. The defence of estuaries such as those of the Thames and Medway, and the narrow waters like that of the Needles Passage was eventually to lead to experimentation with torpedoes and, later still, electric lights.

The Royal Commission forts, including those begun before 1859 and subsequently approved, and if some of the long deferred Chatham ring forts are also included, though excepting a few later sea forts, were the last self-defensible combination of barrack and battery to be built in Britain. Jervois, as responsible for overall design policy, wrote retrospectively in 1874 that:

> The scale upon which the fortresses were then de-signed was so large and the area covered by them so extensive as to excite much comment at the time. After fourteen years experience, however, it is now universally acknowledged that the principles of de-fence recommended by the Commission were sound. Other nations of Europe have constructed, or are now engaged in constructing, advanced land forts at much greater distances than previously from the points to be defended, of the same character and in some cases resembling the design some of the forts at Portsmouth and Plymouth.[29]

While strategic principles remained the same, details of fortification had undergone a complete change owing to the introduction of iron armour, and to a consequent enormous increase in the size and weight of guns. In 1860, armour plating in ships was in its infancy. The armour of the navy's first capital ship built of iron throughout, the *Warrior* (1860), was originally 4½ inches (114mm) thick. In 1862, construction of the Spithead forts stopped, partly because it was thought doubtful whether artillery could be produced capable of piercing the *Warrior*'s side at 1000 yards (914 metres). The subsequent increase in the weight and power of ordnance affected the construction of fortifications two-fold. It was now necessary to have additional and external protection by the application of wrought iron, and elaborate new arrangements were also necessary for the installation of the larger calibre and heavier guns. 'The experiments which have been carried out and the study which has been devoted to the subject have placed England in the foremost position as regards iron defences and the most advanced among other nations have accepted our conclusions.'[30] Such a reputation was due to the work of Colonel Inglis and Lieutenant English of the Fortification Branch. It was found as a result that batteries for the new rifled guns had to be more spacious, the use of machinery was necessary, and elaborate arrangements had to be made for the storage and conveyance of ammunition. The work of designing and executing the fortification was more difficult and complicated than in any former period.

Jervois had no false modesty about British military engineering of the 1860s.

It is satisfactory, under these circumstances, to know that our fortifications have not as yet been surpassed by those of any other countries who have had the benefit of our experiments and practice, and of their own experience in actual warfare. Our own

coast defences are in fact acknowledged by engineers of other nations to be superior to anything of the kind attempted elsewhere. Formerly English engineers sought instruction in foreign treatises and works of defence abroad; now foreign engineers resort to England to learn the latest improvements and the most modern practice in the art of fortification.[31]

A more detached view of British military engineering at the time of the 1859 Royal Commission, and of Fort Brockhurst in particular, is provided by Lendy, writer of a work of instruction on fortification. Describing the detached works then under construction he wrote,

though they bear some resemblance to the German tracing, their construction is far better and contains many of the improvements which have been proposed by the advocates of the bastion tracing. . . . If taken in their ensemble, [Gosport Advanced Line] the system may be severely criticised as not answering the purpose in view, yet taken singly these forts are constructed on decidedly superior principles.[32]

In the heated parliamentary debates of August 1860, Bright quoted the criticism of the renowned Belgian engineer, Brialmont, who objected to the Commission's plans on the grounds that they were drawn up in violation of one of the first principles of military tactics – 'never rely for security on your first line of defence'.[33] As it turned out, the general opinion on the continent was later to bear out the self-congratulations expressed by Jervois. Even Brialmont was to admit some years later that the forts and batteries of Portsmouth and Plymouth were a great advance on the work of engineers and other countries.[24]

CHAPTER 11

The Decline of Permanent Fortification and the German Threat

'BLUE WATER' VERSUS 'BOLT FROM THE BLUE'

With the virtual completion of the Royal Commission forts by the close of the 1860s, (although they were not yet fully armed), it might have been expected that there would now be a feeling of national security. The military disaster suffered by France during the Franco-Prussian War of 1870–1 clearly meant that she was no immediate danger. Yet, the manner of that defeat showed how far the techniques of warfare in Europe had changed, and the balance of political power altered. This provoked doubts and uncertainty in Britain about the soundness of her own military strength. It was now possible for the radical reform of the Army by Cardwell to succeed, and for there to be a substantial jump in the army estimates for 1871, but fear of British vulnerability to invasion was still prevalent. This is nowhere more apparent than the response to a short story written by a Royal Engineer officer, Lieutenant-Colonel Sir George Chesney, which appeared in *Black-wood's* magazine in May 1871. This was *The Battle of Dorking Gap*, whose plot focussed on an account of a successful German invasion of England. The invasion was possible because Chesney had invoked the time-old justification for land defences, the temporary absence of the fleet. He had hypothetically dispersed the bulk of the British fleet to the West Indies, the China Seas and the Pacific coast of America. The Channel fleet he had destroyed dramatically by a combination of torpedoes and mines.

Chesney's real objective was to urge the development of the Volunteer Movement and greater preparedness in home defence. Within a month the story had gone into eight printings, and was soon translated into French, German and other European languages. It was praised in the official *Naval and Military Gazette* as a timely warning. It also had the effect of drawing attention to the fact that the Home forces, though numerous, could not be considered a

A typical French torpedo-boat. (NMM)

co-ordinated army. Chesney provided further support for the widely held view that defence against invasion ultimately was the responsibility of the regular and auxiliary troops stationed at home, and the fixed defences along the coast.[1] In this climate, it was possible for the Royal Engineers to construct forts during the 1870s and 1880s on land south and west of Chatham which had already been purchased for the purpose following the 1859 Royal Commission, but where actual construction had been shelved.

The dominant approach to home defence had been that expressed and developed by military men since the Royal Commission, but an alternative point of view had been expressed in 1867, in a pamphlet written by Captain Sir John Colomb, an officer of the Royal Marine Artillery, which has been held to lay the foundations of what was to become known as the 'Blue Water School' of defence.[2] He attempted to view defence from a national stance rather than seeing it as pertaining to either the army or the navy alone. The navy, he believed, was the first and also the last line of defence; while the army's role was less to provide the country's principal obstacle to invasion but rather to provide its means of attack. The navy had a positive role in defence, blockading the enemy's ports and controlling the sea routes of empire. The army's function was to garrison India, protect the naval bases and home ports from cruiser raids, and be ready to attack the enemy's own territory. Invasion would not be risked while the navy existed, and would only occur after Britain had been comprehensibly defeated at sea, isolated and blockaded into submission.

For the rest of the century the argument fluctuated between the 'Blue Water School' and what has been called the 'Bolt from the Blue School'. The latter was impressed by the speedy mobilisation of European armies, achieved by effective use of railway systems, and the ability to transport troops quickly by steamer whatever the state of weather and tide. In 1886, the newly appointed Director of Military Intelligence, Major-General Sir Henry Brackenbury presented the Prime Minister, Lord Salisbury, with a situation report which posed the threat of a Franco-Russian alliance, and stated that Britain's coastal defences were inadequate and that London was undefended. Others, such as General Sir Edward Hamley, were publicly opposed to placing too much reliance on the fleet as the first line of defence. Hamley, too, was concerned about London. He advocated surrounding the capital with a ring of entrenched positions to be manned by Volunteers leaving the field army free to combat the invaders.[3]

This point of view had some validity since, by the mid-1880s, the navy was suffering from the policy of financial retrenchment pursued by the Liberal government under Gladstone since 1868. Britain's naval superiority over other countries was no longer unchallenged. France was building a modern fleet based on torpedo-boat warfare which potentially could be directed against British commerce with devastating effect. Although the Royal Navy was still superior to the French fleet alone, it could not confidently match the hypothetical alliance of the French and Russian naval forces. Awareness that the navy was no longer absolutely confident of preventing an invasion in certain circumstances led to a new popular invasion scare in 1888. In May that year, a National Defence Bill was introduced into Parliament to speed up the mobilisation of Volunteers and the Yeomanry in an emergency. The strengthened Army-orientated home defence faction saw the possibility for the implementation of the defence scheme for London. As a counter-blast, Admiral Philip Colomb stressed that steam power had actually made invasion more difficult, and that invasion was impossible unless the enemy gained complete command of the sea. A colossal inter-service row ensued between the rival schools of thought. The army faction was convinced that France could mobilise and embark 100,000 men within a week. An article in the *Daily Telegraph* inspired by Field Marshal von Moltke gave credence to this belief by stating that the French could land by surprise some 20,000–30,000 men between Dover and Portsmouth and advance upon London. In the face of the conflicting advice, and despite the earlier invasion panic, the Army and Naval estimates of 1889 showed that the 'Blue Water School' had won the debate. The resulting Naval Defence Act led to eight new battleships being built, armed with 13.5-inch (343mm) guns, thirty-eight cruisers of varying size, and fast torpedo-carrying gunboats besides. While the bulk of the money went to re-equipping the navy, a sop was thrown to the army faction. In 1889, Edward Stanhope, Secretary of State for War, agreed to a series of earthwork fortifications, 'mobilisation centres', to protect London from attack from the south and south east.[4]

Invasion was not the only threat that caused alarm during the 1880s. The possibility of destructive raids on commercial ports and shipping from hostile cruisers produced its own response. For example, by about 1879–80 there was considerable public demand in Scotland that the Firth of Forth should be, to some extent, defended. There was at the time no naval base in Scotland. The feeling of vulnerability elsewhere in the country among those who increasingly had much more to lose was widely held and was growing through the 1880s. It led to the appointment of a parliamentary committee to enquire into the defences of the mercantile ports in 1882, which was to be as significant for the commercial ports as the 1859 Royal Commission had been for the naval bases and anchorages. But France was still thought of as the potential enemy and for several years afterwards little was done in the way of defence north of Harwich.

Rapidly   changing   weapon   technology

affected naval developments still further when a new pattern of big guns, using cordite as a propellant, made earlier battleships obsolete. There was a risk that a few up-to-date foreign ships might destroy the whole British navy. Another naval 'scare' in 1893–4 led to the construction of the even more powerful *Royal Sovereign* class of warships to bring Britain back into the lead. Complementing these naval improvements in 1894, came the recognition of the need to defend a wider range of mercantile ports, and recommendations were made for the provision of defences against a single hostile cruiser for the Tees, Hartlepool, Sunderland, the Tay, Aberdeen and Holyhead. On the Tyne it was asserted 'that there are important private dockyards and an arsenal'. While the Clyde 'is the greatest shipbuilding port and will serve as a Naval centre to ships patrolling the northern entrance to the Irish Channel.'[5] In 1901, there were further improvements in respect of the east coast, and more especially, the Firth of Forth. The increasing spread of up-to-date fortifications up the north eastern coasts now reflected the growing unease at Germany's rapidly expanding naval strength.

With the turn of the twentieth century, home defence came to occupy a major place in military thinking. It was marked by a rationalisation of the armament in the forts and batteries. The breechloading gun was now the standard issue: 9.2-inch and 6-inch calibres, together with 4.7-inch and 12-pounder quick-firers supported by the occasional machine gun. At last there was much greater co-ordination than ever before, and collaboration between the War Office and the Admiralty, culminating in the creation of the Committee of Imperial Defence. Britain was also seeking alliances, first with Japan in 1902, and then with France in 1904. Increasing technological innovations in weaponry, particularly in the development of torpedoboats and submarines, as well as the range and firepower of naval guns, meant that defensive measures could not remain static. The prospect of danger arising from German naval expansion, and thence to the threat of invasion from this direction, found its way into popular literature with such novels as *The Riddle of the Sands* by Erskine Childers.

Out of this atmosphere in Edwardian Britain came three inquiries into the likelihood of invasion, and the remedies. These were held in 1903, 1907, and, just before the First World War, in 1914. The first produced a report on the possibility of serious invasion which generated an optimistic belief that an invasion could not be launched successfully with a force of less than 70,000 men, which would require 200 boats and at least twenty hours to disembark. Such an event was thought highly unlikely. The report envisaged the Royal Navy having the principal defensive role, and resulted in the Forth being considered a Dockyard Port and Principal Naval Base by a joint Naval and Military Committee. This led to the construction of the dockyard of Rosyth,

and improved defences in the Firth of Forth. Although land defensive measures elsewhere were thought to be now largely irrelevant, a handbook was issued in 1903 providing officers with instructions on the use of the London Defence Positions.[6]

The second invasion inquiry began late in 1907, when a German offensive still seemed likely. At first it confirmed the 'Blue Water' conclusions of the earlier committee of 1903, and the Committee, under the chairmanship of General Ruck in 1908, examined all War Department land, especially near the land forts, to see if any of it could be sold. Land defences were now thought to be redundant. But two years later, the War Office approached the Admiralty to propose the formation of a Home Ports Defence Committee. It said that 'the naval situation has changed considerably of late years, and the defences at several of the home ports, particularly on the east coast, require consideration.'[7] The actions of this committee confirmed the shift in the geographical emphasis of defence from the south coast to the east, although a defended station for destroyers and torpedo-boats was intended for the Isles of Scilly and where the supporting land batteries were in the process of completion and arming in 1901.[8] As well as Rosyth on the Forth, as the new chief naval base, Cromarty and Scapa Flow were to be naval anchorages. At this stage, the navy was to be responsible for the defence of the former, and Scapa Flow was to have no fixed defences at all. The Admiralty and the War Office began to diverge again in their respective approaches to coastal defences. Agreement was finally achieved in 1913, when the military were allotted responsibility for the Forth, Tyne, Sheerness and Dover, and the Admiralty took on the defence of Cromarty, Aberdeen, the Tay, the Tees, Hartlepool, the Humber and Harwich. As far as constructions were concerned, this was left to the Home Ports Defence Committee. The land disposal policy of the Ruck Committee was reversed in 1911 by Lieutenant-General Franklyn's Committee on the Land Defences of Portsmouth, Plymouth and Chatham. Whereas in 1907 the type of attack to be guarded against was mere raids, now an invasion by at least 70,000 men was considered possible.[9]

On the eve of the War, the growing tension between Britain and Germany coincided with the results of naval manoeuvres in 1912 and 1913. On both occasions the 'enemy' fleet evaded detection long enough to throw on shore on the east coast forces of between 12,000 and 48,000 men. April 1914 saw a report entitled 'Attack on the British Isles from Overseas'. It recognised that protection of all east coast ports was impracticable and too costly. The report instead recommended increases in the defences of the Humber, the Tyne and Harwich.[10] The construction of the Humber forts was in progress when war began. The navy had left the protection of Scapa Flow to the last minute.

FROM ARTILLERY FORT TO INFANTRY REDOUBT

The accelerating rate of development in military technology in the last years of the nineteenth century was inevitably transmitted to defence works. The Commission forts had been built at a time when the improvements in big guns could be accommodated without too much structural change, and even in the 1870s, could be adapted to take the new Moncrieff disappearing carriages. Jervois, still Deputy Director of Works (Fortifications), went to France to observe the effects of the Prussian siege work on the Paris fortresses and other forts such as Belfort. What he saw did not, however, lead him to rethink the basis of current British fortress design but rather it reinforced his views on the value of the Moncrieff carriage in gun pits on the front faces alongside shielded emplacements, as an alternative to the open *barbette* positions, and leaving open embrasures only on the least vulnerable flanks. His ideas were expressed in his 'plan Exemplifying the Principles on which it is proposed that forts to resist land attack should be armed'.[11] Fort Southwick in the Portsdown line was used as a model. There is little evidence, however, that these proposals were carried through to any extent during the 1870s which were quiet years for British fortress building.

More significant for its influence upon the direction which future British fortification design was to follow was the manner of the Turkish defence of Plevna, Bulgaria, in 1877–8, against vastly superior Russian forces. This action demonstrated the effectiveness of theoretically deficient field fortifications when manned by troops armed with magazine rifles. The Russians had immense superiority in artillery during the siege, but the use of temporary trenches enabled great flexibility for the defenders.[12] There were those, such as George Sydenham Clarke, his namesake, Sir Andrew Clarke (who had become Inspector-General of Fortifications and Director of Works in 1882), and Captain J F Lewis, who, in 1881, saw the effectiveness of infantry redoubts and mobile artillery as an alternative to evermore substantial fixed defences. 'Forts can no longer be thought of as constituting a fortress.' The infantryman's capability for rapid fire from a magazine rifle together with the evolving machine gun could, in Lewis's view, lead to a situation where 'the whole circumference of the fortress will in a sense be a line of rifles.'[13] In Sydenham Clarke's polemical book, *Fortification*, the magazine rifle, capable of averaging at least fifteen aimed rounds a minute, acquired particular significance in changing the nature of defence. He was to add that 'from the point of view of the defence, the development of rifled howitzers is second in importance only to the introduction of the magazine rifle' for applying high angle fire to the advantage of the defence. Throughout the military scene there was indeed a

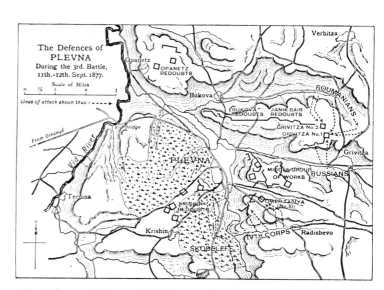

The Defences of Plevna, 1877. (Author)

growing use of the Maxim gun and other machine guns and quick-firer artillery. These weapons no longer required to be secreted and shielded within a complex and massively built fortress. They were weapons of mobility, and could be used in rapidly dug trenches or earthwork redoubts. Such observations gradually acquired practical application, first in the slowly evolving Chatham ring forts of the late 1870s and 1880s, and then in the London defence positions of the 1890s.

Sir Andrew Clarke, in a memorandum of 1886, summed up the changes he had pursued as Inspector-General. The differences from the Commission forts of the 1860s were principally three. First, that instead of grouping heavy guns for coast defence in comparatively small and confined batteries, they should be placed at wide intervals and at different levels. Second, was greater reliance on earthworks in preference to masonry and iron. Lastly, he summarised the new line of thought as follows:

> For the future we must rely as much upon concealment as upon resistance, and the use of earth alone admits of a combination of these qualities. The power of small arms, which has grown concurrently with the improvements in ordnance, and the introduction of machine and quick-firing guns, have also had an important influence on the design of works of defence. Flanking fire is of less importance than formerly, deep ditches and costly caponiers can in most cases be dispensed with, and much complication and expense are thereby avoided. Fortified posts will not in future be marked by batteries conspicuously frowning, or granite casemated forts with tiers of guns, rivalling rows of targets in regularity and clearness of definition. On the contrary, defences if skilfully designed will be indistinguishable from the ground on which they stand, and while they retain all the advantages of the defence, will offer no mark to the enemy's fire.[14]

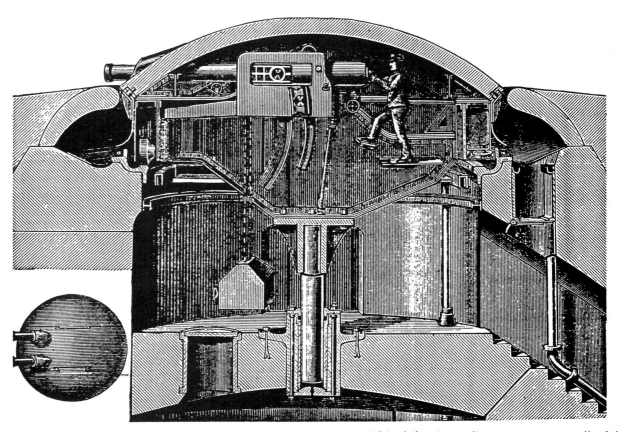

The armoured turret designed by Mougin and adopted for the defences round Bucharest. (Author)

Plan of one of the forts surrounding Liege designed by Brialmont in 1888. (From Quentin Hughes, *Military Architecture*, 1974)

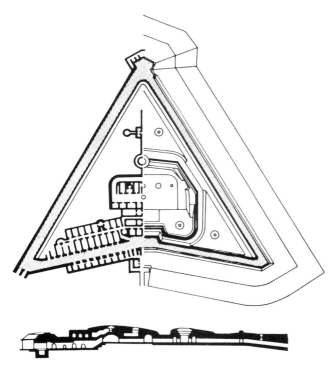

This defensive policy was not generally followed in the rest of Europe. As artillery became even more effective, fortification grew a harder carapace with massed concrete, and guns protected in armoured, revolving turrets. Of all the great ring fortresses, Antwerp was the strongest of its time. The Belgian engineer, Henri Brialmont, used detached polygonal forts with large pointed caponiers which were virtual forts in their own right, covered by a massive redan with large defensible barracks to the rear. Between 1878 and 1898, Brialmont's ring forts were extended by five new works, built some 10 to 14 kilometres farther out. In a more modern vein, Mougin invented a type of fort consisting of underground concrete structures from which rose three iron-domed cupolas each mounting two 150mm (5.9-inch) guns with four disappearing machine gun cupolas for close defence. General von Sauer, of the Bavarian artillery, regarded detached forts of the sort developed in Germany, and belatedly adopted in France, as useless. Instead, he proposed to employ a line or lines of the two-gun cupolas in something of the same manner as the earlier Linz towers. The Prussian engineer Lieutenant-Colonel Schumann held that, 'armour-plated Fortification is really advantageous only when it is applied without stint', and he actually built an armoured front into the Sereth Line in Roumania between 1889 and 1892.[15]

The progress which was being achieved by the makers of heavy artillery lay in two directions, but both equally destructive for fixed fortifications. The

Inchkeith, Firth of Forth: the defensible gorge of the West Fort dated 1880, which was designed for a single 10-inch gun. The concrete emplacement was later altered for a 6-inch BL gun. (HBM)

first was in the development of more accurate high angle fire at longer ranges. A range of 3000 yards (2.75 kilometres) was possible in the early 1880s. This made caponiers at the forward angles of a fort more suscepti- ble to direct fire, and the bombproof gun emplacements which had been sufficient in the 1860s were safe no longer in 1883, 'owing to the accuracy and destructive- ness of the new siege artillery'.[16] The other factor lay in the improvements in the destructive qualities of explo- sives filling the shells. The introduction of breech- loading guns firing shrapnel and high explosive shells made exposed guns or bodies of troops extremely vulnerable. The French had adopted Melinite as a high explosive of considerable destructive force. The Ger- mans used guncotton, and the British developed an explosive called Lyddite. As we have seen, British and Continental engineers in their respective land forts responded to this enormous increase in destructive firepower in radically different ways.

While the lessons of the siege of Plevna were strongly to affect British land forts, the bombardment of the forts at Alexandria by the British Mediterranean fleet in 1882 was also influential for the future of coastal forts and batteries. The old fashioned defences at Alex- andria had undergone an enormously heavy bombard- ment at close range, yet when Captain G Sydenham

Clarke and a gunner officer closely inspected the effects after the city had been taken, they found surprisingly little damage had been done to the forts or their guns. This was because the guns had been effectively pro- tected by earthworks. Parapets of earth or sand with exterior slopes were found to divert the incoming shells over the works themselves. This event was to have profound influence when the 'Colonial Defence Com- mittee', of which Sydenham Clarke was a member, was set up in 1885 to plan defences for the coaling stations at Aden, Trincomalee, Columbo, Hong Kong, Singa- pore, Sierra Leone, St Helena, Simon's Bay, Mauritius, Jamaica, and St Lucia. It also produced a similar design factor for coastal defences in Britain, especially at the commercial ports, notably on the Clyde and the Tyne in the late 1880s. The Firth of Forth received its first modern defences, taking some of these lessons into account, in 1881, with the fortification of the island of Inchkeith.[17] Only at Dover in 1882 was there a pair of steam-powered, 80-ton 16-inch (406mm) guns mounted in an armoured turret – the only turret to be built in the British Isles.[18] The new coastal batteries avoided casemates and armour. The guns in these *bar- bette* batteries were now protected by a long earthen slope in front of the guns, running out into an unrevet- ted ditch with sloping sides, producing a 'Glacis Para- pet'. Shells from hostile warships striking the 'Parapet' would ricochet upwards as had been observed at Alex- andria. Local protection was given by an unclimable iron fence in the bottom of the ditch.[19]

The mid-1880s saw the introduction of a new generation of breech-loaders: 6-inch (150mm), 9.2-inch (233mm) and 10-inch (254mm). By now the gun emplacements were constructed in concrete.[20] Another innovation appearing in 1885 was the hydropneumatic mounting, which was an improvement on the Moncrieff disappearing gun of the late 1860s and 1870s, using the force of the recoil to compress air which was then used to raise the gun to the firing position. Most of these new mountings were employed in the colonial stations, but some guns on this type of hydropneumatic mounting were added to the Thames defences at East Tilbury Battery and Slough Fort. Other elements in the newly armed coastal defences were controlled minefields, the guided Brennan torpedo, electric searchlights in association with quick-firing (QF) guns, initially 6- and 12-pounders, for use against fast torpedo-boats and gunboats. Brennan torpedo positions are still detectable at places such as Cliffe Fort in the Thames Estuary and a submarine mining establishment can be seen at Landguard Fort.[21] The employment of searchlights can probably be best appreciated at the Needles Battery, Isle of Wight. Between 1889 and 1892 the Needles Passage was the base for trials where searchlights illuminated British torpedo-boats for gunnery practice. Five cave-like positions for lights and

The Dover turret: one of its two steam-powered 80-ton 16-inch guns shown arriving. (DOE)

An RML on a traversing carriage in a new concrete barbette emplacement on the western wing battery of Southsea Castle, Portsmouth. (IWM)

▼ *Plan and section of the Old Needles Battery, Isle of Wight, showing gun emplacements and the searchlight positions with access to them.* (P Sprack)

▲ *Cliffe Fort, Kent: Brennan torpedo position.* (V T C Smith)

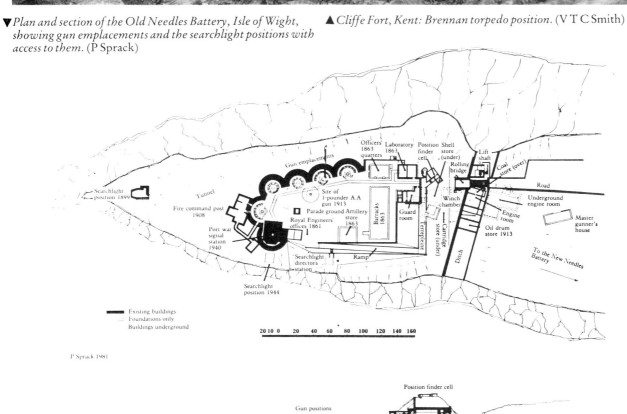

QFs were excavated at the foot of the cliff, and a fixed beam shone across the channel. A new armoured 'fighting' light emplacement was built in 1898–9 at the furthermost tip of the promontory, connected to the parade by a tunnel. From here an observer could also watch the Needles Passage, and, by means of electric cables, could detonate a selected mine under any enemy ship entering the minefield. Augmenting QFs, and searchlights were boom-defence systems; at first designed to hamper the movement of surface ships, and later to combat submarines. All the major estuaries were provided for in this way. At the entrance to Southampton Water a boom, initially of hulks secured stem to stern, was stretched across the channel from Calshot Castle to the site of Bungalow Battery opposite. These were linked to 'dolphins' – wood and iron towers each armed with two 12-pounder QFs and a machine gun. The boom was the responsibility of the navy which provided four or five elderly gunboats adapted as boom-defence vessels.[22]

By the early years of the twentieth century, Sydenham Clarke, a powerful advocate for the 'Blue Water School' was expressing the belief that coast batteries now needed no land defences. It was a view that was short-lived as far as home defences were concerned, and was disproved by the practical example of the Port Arthur defences under siege in 1905, but it was to have dire implications for the defence of Singapore in 1942.[23]

THE CHATHAM FORTS: A PERIOD OF TRANSITION

A ring of detached forts to the south and east of Chatham had been proposed in the Royal Commission Report of 1860, but had been omitted subsequently on grounds of cost. However, the land for some of the projected forts had already been bought and remained in War Department hands, although there were still no funds in the defence budget for construction. An ingenious solution was found by the engineers during the 1870s. The Director of Convict Prisons was Major-General Sir E F Du Cane, who had previously designed the Commission forts at Dover and the land forts at Plymouth. He saw to it that a new prison was built at Borstal, south east of Chatham, in 1875, and it was the adjacent prison labour which was first to build Fort Borstal alongside, and then another fort at Bridgewoods. The eventual construction of the crescent of forts, south and east of Chatham, was to take more than twenty years. During that time the form and function of fixed land defences were to evolve rapidly, and it is possible to see the radical ideas of Sydenham Clarke, Lewis and others taking shape, perhaps experimentally, in one limited area.[24]

The first of the Chatham forts – Borstal, Bridgewoods, Horsted and Luton to the south of the town – exhibited a superficially similar plan to the

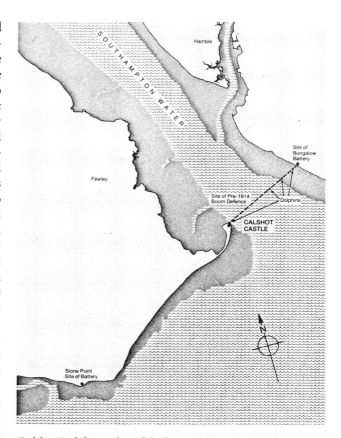

Calshot Dolphins: plan of the boom defence. (English Heritage)

Royal Commission land forts of the Jervois model. They were polygonal, but here caponiers were omitted from the front faces because of their increasing vulnerability to high angle fire. Counterscarp galleries were used instead to control the ditches. Fort Borstal was given a caponier but this was low in height, and relegated to the less exposed role of gorge defence. All accommodation for garrison or stores was mounded over with chalk rubble and earth excavated from the ditch. Indeed, as low grassed humps, these forts were much more inconspicuous than previously, with little, if any, visible masonry or concrete structure even in the gorge. Their shapes blended into the natural contours. Concrete was used extensively for the internal structures as well as for the counterscarp galleries and the ditch revetments. The forts were designed to fire to the front and to the flanks for the defence of the ground between. Borstal controlled a large area of the Medway valley; Horsted and Luton overlooked a shallow valley running south west; and Horsted and Bridgewoods commanded the high ground between these two valleys.

Fort Horsted was the largest of the Chatham forts. It was also unusual in being divided into two halves by a massive earthwork traverse containing a tunnel access from the entrance in the gorge to a position behind the front casemates, as well as protect-

▲ *Fort Borstal, Kent: gorge wall constructed in concrete.* (Author)

▼ *Fort Horstead, Kent: cut-away plan of the largest of the Chatham forts. The inset shows relation between serving rooms and expense magazines.* (V T C Smith)

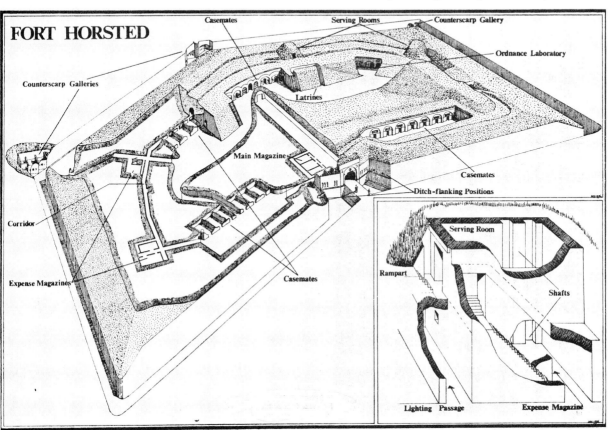

FORT HORSTED

Counterscarp Galleries

Corridor

Expense Magazines

Casemates

Serving Rooms

Counterscarp Gallery

Ordnance Laboratory

Latrines

Main Magazine

Casemates

Ditch-flanking Positions

Casemates

Serving Room

Rampart

Shafts

Lighting Passage

Expense Magazine

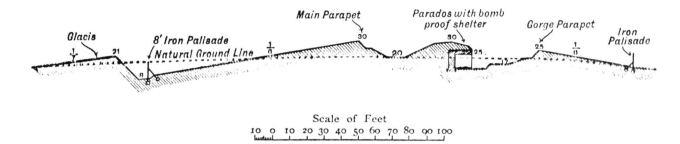

The Twydall Profile. From H F Thuillier, The Principles of Land Defence, *1902.* (Author)

ing the main magazine. There was a rear line of casemates on either side of the tunnel. The ditches could be swept by rifle and cannon fire from counterscarp galleries approached by tunnels from within the fort. It had been observed that there are blind exits in the galleries, probably intended to be used for countermining in the event of siege. The only exposed structure was the entrance at the rear which was protected by a drawbridge, and flanked in demi-bastion form from rifle slits and ditch-flanking positions. The other three forts in this first phase varied in size, and were designed to fit the ground rather than follow a prescribed plan. Ditches tended to be much narrower than the Royal Commission forts. There were no hints of a keep in the gorge, and indeed at Bridgewoods and Luton, there were no defensive provisions for protecting the gorge ditch.

The four southern forts were far from complete by 1880, with only Borstal and Bridgewoods well advanced. Work was suspended for much of the 1880s, and a good deal of the work already done was allowed to fall into disrepair. The completion of the forts was urged by Colonel J C Ardagh in a memorandum of 1888[25], and with work restarted, Horsted was complete by 1889. However, work had also begun on the eastern part of the Chatham ring in 1886, and it is here that a fundamentally different concept was developed and also completed in 1889. On the left flank towards the sea, the defences were not artillery forts but infantry redoubts armed with rifles and machine guns. Grange was built first, and with Woodland, they were known collectively as Fort Twydall.[26] Artillery firepower was separately provided in a sunken battery between the two redoubts. They were designed by Major G R Walker under the direction of Sir Andrew Clarke, Inspector-General of Fortifications. These redoubts were very low-lying, essentially earthwork, but with open-backed concrete casemate shelters for the 200-strong garrison to take cover in during bombardment. The significant element was the profile. The principal element was a firing step in an earthen parapet which sloped gently down to a ditch in which was an unclimbable vertical iron fence set at the base of an unrevetted counterscarp following an angle of 45°, and

with a sloping glacis beyond. Behind the infantry firing step was the bank containing the concrete shelters. The so-called Twydall Profile put into practice the thinking of engineers like Sydenham Clarke and Lewis. It dispersed the infantry into earthworks which were difficult to identify, and therefore to hit. It detached the artillery, and placed it into concealed and increasingly mobile positions. Such works made the deep ditches and elaborate ditch defences of regular fortresses unnecessary. Best of all for the politician, they were cheap. One of these redoubts cost only £6000, being built by contract labour in only thirty-one working days, as opposed to £45,000 and more, for the conventional fort. A War Office paper referring to these infantry redoubts noted prophetically: 'it will be ere long universally recognized that it is only on these principles that the defence of London is practicable.'[27] It is a very great loss to archaeology that these redoubts, which have been considered as a prototype for future land fortifications, no longer exist.

One more fort remained to be built to fill the gap between the Twydall redoubts and the southern forts. Fort Darland was started in 1893 and finished in 1899. In some ways this was a compromise between the two styles. It was a large work similar in plan to Fort Horsted. It reverted to the deep revetted enclosing ditch but without counterscarp galleries for its close defence. Surprisingly, it had a caponier in the gorge which carried the roadway into the entrance of the fort. Casemates were provided under the front and rear ramparts. Novel components were eleven semi-circular machine gun emplacements set into the front rampart. An unclimbable fence was provided but on the glacis not in the ditch. Finally, it was intended to provide emplacements for 6-pounder QF guns. Though Darland represents a compromise between a return to a conventional fort with some of the intentions of an infantry redoubt, it set a precedent for providing a store for moveable field guns with a wing rampart, separate and to the right of the fort, where the guns could be deployed when the threat materialised.

The Chatham forts, in their evolving form, demonstrate a move towards a decentralised and more fluid type of defence. The new doctrine was striving for a situation where the artillery defence was to be based on moveable armaments. Guns might be present in the strategically placed forts at the beginning of a siege but would be removed to external tactical positions once the enemy's breaching batteries were established. The mobile guns would be dispersed to concealed positions, using indirect fire techniques wherever possible. Forts were increasingly seen as infantry works rather than artillery positions with greater use of quick-firing guns deployed against hostile troops attempting to move through the intervals between the fixed defences. In addition, the advanced ground would be barred by barbed-wire and unclimable fences. The emphasis was now towards dispersement of the defence in order to make best use of the country, and spread the enemy's fire rather than to concentrate it. Only the decentralised groupings of mutually supporting forts and batteries, with barracks and infantry trenches, all surrounded by barbed-wire entanglements exemplified by the German *feste*, offered another European attempt to break away from the traditional fortress at the end of the nineteenth century.[28]

THE DEFENCE OF LONDON

Unlike most European capitals, London had no defensive system of its own, apart from those forts and batteries controlling access by river, sited between the first substantial narrowing of the Thames Estuary at Lower Hope Point, and the Gravesend–Tilbury crossing. Even the protection of Woolwich Arsenal and the establishment of a fortified post on Shooters Hill, both proposed by the 1859 Commission, had been abandoned. Burgoyne, as Inspector-General of Fortifications in 1860, had declared that the idea of defending London was 'futile' and that 'no city scarcely could be less favourable for defensive positions than London'. There were other engineers, however, who believed that London could and should be defended, including Jervois, who had written papers on the subject, and Colonel Shafto Adair who produced detailed plans in 1861 and 1863.[29] The political sticking point was the prohibitive expense of permanent works on the continental, or indeed Portsmouth, model.

The new doctrine being developed at Chatham in the late 1880s was for defences based on simple earthworks, principally intended for infantry, and on moveable armaments. This could be achieved at remarkably low cost, and now made the protection of the capital a practical proposition. A paper published by Major Elsdale in 1886 suggested that an effective defensive scheme could be devised on the basis of rapidly thrown-up fieldworks at the time of war along a pre-determined line, backed up by previously established magazines at five-mile intervals around the agreed defensive perimeter, so that ammunition and stores were already available in the event of an invasion.[30] General Sir E Hamley, MP for Birkenhead, also pressed for the use of Volunteer units to man any defensive positions of this nature. The author of the

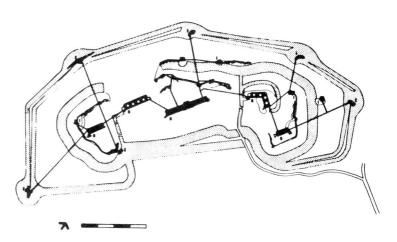

German feste. (From Quentin Hughes, *Military Architecture*, 1974)

scheme which ultimately obtained approval in 1888, and which embodied both contingency planning and a core of permanent works, was Colonel J C Ardagh, Assistant Adjutant-General. His ideas were approved by Parliament the next year, and a small committee of three was appointed in 1890 to work out the details. Their work was completed by 1892.[31]

The scheme, known as the London Defence Positions, was for a defence line 70 miles long, running along the escarpment of the North Downs, from Guildford in the west to the Darenth Valley, concentrating on the strategic gaps in the Downs through which road and rail communications passed to London; then to the Thames at Dartford. The line then resumed at Vange, on the north bank of the Thames, and continued along the low hills to North Weald near Epping (see illustration on p131). The Ardagh proposals were for thirty permanent works of a simple kind, ditched and banked enclosures containing store buildings for guns and munitions. They were mobilisation points. In real war conditions, these permanent works would be improved and supplemented by additional redoubts, batteries for moveable artillery and trenches. As the scheme developed, it was thought necessary for a field army of 200,000, regulars and volunteer divisions, to be maintained between London and the coast. Continuing supplies of war material would come via the radial system of railway lines springing from central London. The handbook, prepared in 1903, for the instruction of the officers expected to carry out the scheme, nominated ten railway stations as advanced depots to provide fresh supplies once those kept at the permanent works had been exhausted. Woolwich, Bishopsgate and Nine Elms railway stations were to be the base depots. The artillery intended for the scheme were thirty batteries of 4.7-inch (120mm) BL field guns, seventy batteries of 15-pounder BLs, as well as obsolete 40-pounder, 20-pounder and 16-pounder RMLs: a total of over 400 guns. It was hoped that seven days' warning of invasion

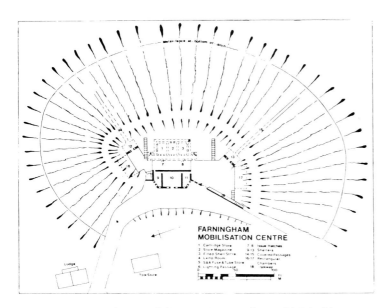

Farningham Mobilisation Centre, plan. (V T C Smith)

would be possible in order to co-ordinate the force, civil as well as military, necessary to construct and man the field defences.

In the event only thirteen sites were chosen, and the land purchased. They were: Pewley Hill, Henley Grove, Denbies, Box Hill, Betchworth, Reigate, West Merstham, Fosterdown, Woldingham, Betsoms Hill, Halstead, Farningham and North Weald. Tilbury Fort and Brentwood were existing ordnance stores which were brought into the system. The 'forts' had a dual purpose. They were to be mobilisation storehouses for the volunteers, holding entrenching tools and ammunition, and they were also useable as redoubts in an emergency. Most of them consisted of a magazine inside an earthwork enclosure, with a rampart of Twydall profile together with an unclimbable fence. Some, which were sited to have command over extensive tracts of country, were intended to deploy artillery, and others were just infantry positions of two basic types. There were those whose rampart, casemates and magazines were arranged round a central parade, and those whose casemates and magazines were in a single block surrounded by rampart and ditch. In some instances, as at Fort Farningham, there was a loopholed wall at the gorge. The first of the works to be built was the North Weald Redoubt, completed in 1891. It was oval in plan, and, on the rampart, had positions for seven or eight field guns firing *en barbette*, with casemates below. As at Fort Darland in the Chatham line, its entrance was over a caponier covering the gorge. This was the only caponier provided in the London positions. The largest of the works was Fort Halstead, which came closest to becoming a traditional fort. The ditch scarps were revetted in concrete, and it had a substantial rampart of regular form with parapet, banquette and *terre-plein* divided by traverses. The

main magazine lay under a central traverse, and there were expense magazines on the ramparts, but even here it was anticipated that the armament would be moveable, and there were no fixed gun positions. The smaller, simpler works had a roughly semi-circular plan with magazines under the rampart. A common feature at most was a caretaker's cottage and tool store outside the defensive perimeter.

Defensive thinking was however changing rapidly in the early years of the twentieth century, and for a time the views of the 'Blue Water School' were supreme. Within three years of the *Handbook for the London Defence Positions (Provisional)* being published by the War Office, they were abolished. The Committee of Imperial Defence meeting on 9 March 1906 minuted that 'in view of the conclusion that a serious invasion of the United Kingdom is impossible, so long as our naval supremacy is maintained, the London defences should be abolished.' The forts, with the exception of Fort Halstead, were sold after 1907.

THE COMMERCIAL PORTS AND THE DEFENSIVE SHIFT TO THE NORTH AND EAST

The recognition of the commercial ports as places worth defending occupied the last twenty years of the nineteenth century. Two areas in particular received much attention: the Firth of Forth and the Tyne. About 1878–80, there was already considerable public demand in Scotland that the Firth of Forth should be protected. The developing ties between France and Russia had introduced a northern and Russian element to the concern. There was not at the time any naval base north of the Medway, and there was much concern that the defenceless state of Edinburgh and the east coast of Scotland generally might incite a landing in the event of war. Three forts, for four 10-inch (254mm) rifled muzzle-loaders, were built on the island of Inchkeith in the Forth in 1879, and another two 10-inch RML battery built at Kinghorn on the Fife side of the Forth. Those on Inchkeith were designed by Colonel John Yarbery Moggridge, and are much in the style adopted by the 1859 Royal Commission – masonry with vaulted casemated barracks, enclosed by narrow ditches flanked by musketry caponiers. The forts were not, however, armed until 1881.[32]

In 1882, the Morley Committee was appointed by Parliament to enquire into the defences of the mercantile ports, but as France was still regarded as the potential enemy, little was done north of Harwich.[33] The Committee did, however, recommend a number of improvements for the Forth, together with proposals for the Clyde, the Tay and for Aberdeen. New breech-loading guns were recommended for Inchkeith but the main improvement of the Forth defences during the 1880s lay in a submarine mining system. More significant developments were not

Firth of Forth, nineteenth and twentieth century defences:

1	*Leith Battery*	7	*Carlingnose Battery*	13	*Kinghorn Battery*
2	*Crammond Island Battery*	8	*Downing Point Battery*	14	*Pettycur Battery*
3	*Hound Point Battery*	9	*Braefoot Battery*	15	*Inchkeith batteries*
4	*Dalmeny Battery*	10	*Charles Hill Battery*	16	*Kincraig Battery*
5	*Inchgarvie Battery*	11	*Inchholm batteries*	17	*Fidra Battery*
6	*Coastguard Battery*	12	*Inchmickery Battery*		(Author)

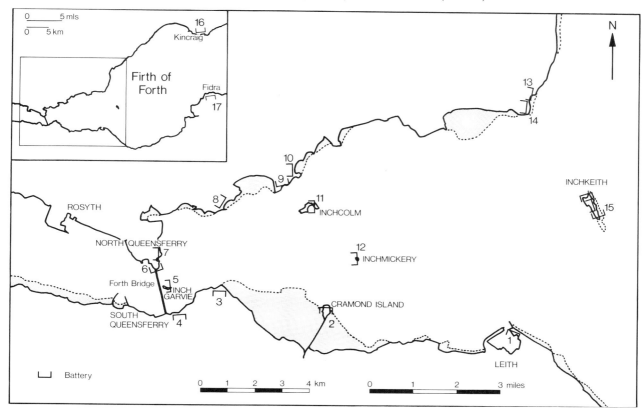

A 12-pounder quick-firer. (V T C Smith)

achieved until the next decade. By 1894, the need to protect the mercantile ports took on greater urgency, and the Firth of Forth received a great deal of attention. It was thought that any attack in force was improbable, but a raid by several cruisers could not be ruled out. Moreover, the increasing importance of the docks, and the value of the Forth Bridge, which had been completed in 1890, had made the question of defence more significant. Batteries were proposed near Leith but not carried out. Fixed defences in place of moveable armament were provided, however, on both shores at Queensferry and on Inchgarvie, the island close to the main central pier of the Forth railway bridge. What was of great importance was the establishment of inner and outer defence lines for the first time, even before the creation of the naval base at Rosyth. By 1901 a heavy battery for two 6-inch (152mm) guns was built on the cliffs at Carlingnose near North Queensferry, and another for two 12-pounders at Coastguard Battery. On the south side, Dalmeny Battery had emplacements for two 4.7-inch (120mm) guns, while on Inchgarvie there were two 12-pounder quick-firing guns.

In 1903, the Joint Naval and Military Committee decided that the Forth should now be classified

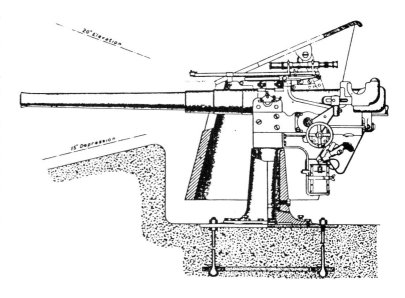

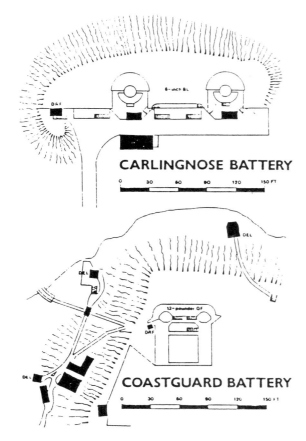

CARLINGNOSE BATTERY

COASTGUARD BATTERY

Carlingnose and Coastguard Batteries (Firth of Forth), for two 6-inch guns and two 12-pounder QFs respectively. (V T C Smith)

as a Dockyard Port and Principal Naval Base, with the creation of the Rosyth dockyard. Wider strategic considerations in the next two years led to the definition of the 'fortress' to include not only the Firth and its shores but as far out as a line drawn from Elie on the eastern Fife coast to North Berwick opposite. The probable forms of attack were specified. The Precautionary Period might involve minor raids by a few daring men for the purpose of damaging locks, lights, bridges and batteries on vulnerable points on the coast. The War Period might take two forms: an attack by cruisers and torpedo-boats to damage the docks and shipping; or an attack on Edinburgh, or the batteries on the Forth by a landing party of about 2000 men, supported by cruisers. As for the forts themselves, their armament was brought up to date. By 1898 Inchkeith, in the outer line, had one 9.2-inch (233mm) breech-loader, two 10-inch (254mm) rifled muzzle-loaders, two 6-inch BLs (152mm) and two 4.7-inch (120mm) QFs. At Kinghorn in 1904, there was a similar range of armament.[34]

The Firth of Forth was not alone in receiving protection during the last two decades of the century. Aberdeen, the mouth of the Tay, and the Clyde, all had their share of new batteries. The English east coast defences were also brought up to date, from Harwich

to the Humber, the Tees and the Tyne. Harwich (or more particularly, Landguard Fort) and Tynemouth are the best surviving examples of this period to be seen today. Tynemouth has had a long and consistent history of defensive provision. The principal defensive position was Tynemouth Castle itself, which had been amongst the first English fortresses to be given an early Italian style bastion. In 1841, it was described as 'an old irregular work consisting of the ruins of a monastery and a castle with some modern works attached, situated on a projecting point of high land on the north of the entrance to the river Tyne.'[35] It was supported by Spanish Battery lower down the cliff since the mid-sixteenth century, and, until the end of the Napoleonic wars, by a battery at South Shields on the opposite side of the river. Towards the end of the nineteenth century, the Tyne defences expanded to include those around Sunderland and the mouth of the Wear, and also north of Tynemouth to Seaton Sluice.

In 1881, Spanish Battery was described as an earthen work 300 yards (274 metres) to the right of Tynemouth Castle but on a lower level. Although obsolete with just three smooth-bore guns, it occupied an excellent position which could bear directly on the harbour mouth. Despite this advantage, the Morley Committee did not propose the expense of remodelling it 'at the present time'. Although the Inspector-General of Fortifications, in 1884, recommended mounting there one heavy and two medium guns which had been previously allocated to Tynemouth Castle, nothing was done until 1893. Then it was said that 'The battery is approaching completion and the approved armament of one 6-inch [152mm] BL and two 6-pounder QF guns has been provided.'[36] It was later to receive another 6-inch (152mm) BL and this was its complement throughout the First World War.

By 1881, Tynemouth's commanding position had been so recognised that it was described as 'an extensive work armed with twenty guns of which six are modern rifled guns'. Lord Morley's Committee, the next year, recommended that four 10.4-inch (264mm) BLs should be mounted to command the entrance to the harbour and the open water in front, and that the medium rifled guns already there should be retained. By 1905, the armament consisted of one 9.2-inch (233mm) Mark X BL, two 6-inch (152mm) Mark VII BLs and two 12-pounder QFs.

From 1900 to the outbreak of the First World War, two major considerations, technological and political, dominated the theory and practice of the nation's defences. The first was the final development in the mounting of coast defence guns, and a rationalisation of their types and calibres. The second was the realisation that Germany was now the major threat to Britain's naval supremacy, and that this created fresh vulnerability to invasion.

The return of Sydenham Clarke from Malta

Tynemouth Castle: QF positions. (DOE)

to be Superintendent of the Carriage Department of the Royal Arsenal, Woolwich, saw the replacement of the hydropneumatic disappearing gun mounting for something much simpler. The exception to this policy was in the low-lying forts of the Thames Estuary, particularly at East Tilbury, just outside Coalhouse Fort. Lord Sydenham, as he became, returned carriage design to first principles. The purpose of a gun carriage was to allow the gunners to shoot as rapidly, and as accurately as possible. Previously, heavy guns were attached to a carriage which recoiled up an inclined slide. The gun was then reloaded and allowed to move back to a firing position; at best a slow and cumbersome operation. Now, totally new mountings were designed which employed axial recoil with hydropneumatic control. Recoil distances were kept short, and the gun crew could cluster round the gun, protected from light weapons and splinters by a shield, ready to maintain a rapid rate of fire. With central pivots, and hydraulic power providing ammunition supply for the heavier guns, the manoeuvrability and rate of fire was increased enormously. So fundamentally sound were these advances that, with only minor modifications, these mountings remained in service until the end of coast artillery in 1956.

Mountings of this design were produced for the 9.2-inch (233mm), 6-inch (152mm) and 4.7-inch (120mm) guns which became the standard weapons of coast defence by the turn of the twentieth century. New emplacements were designed, requiring deep concrete pits in which the mounting was protected while the shielded gun fired over the concrete parapet. There were other types of armament. In 1884, the Inspector-General of Fortifications suggested that it might be possible to use the existing, but by now obsolescent, rifled muzzle-loaders in a high angle role. This was thought to be of value for attacking hostile stationary ships intending to bombard shore installations while out of range of flat trajectory fortress guns. Trials were carried out at Warden Point Battery on the Isle of Wight, and some of these guns were installed elsewhere. Lighter guns, with great manoeuvrability and a rapid rate of fire, were increasingly necessary to deal with a naval development which had appeared in the early 1880s – the fast torpedo-boat. The 4.7-inch (120mm) quick-firer was supplemented by a number of Hotchkiss and Nordenfeldt 3-pounder and 6-pounder guns which could fire at a rate of 30 and 25 rounds a minute respectively. In the 1890s, machine guns also became standard equipment.

The coming of the twentieth century saw even more serious concern for home defence. In the years following the Boer War, the bureaucratic machinery for creating defence policy and plans achieved previously unheard of levels of co-ordination. The development of the General Staff and the Naval

Tilbury Fort, QF positions. (Author)

War Staff was amplified by the reconstitution of the Imperial Defence Committee in 1903. Sydenham Clarke became its secretary. This was as well. At the same time as the Russo-Japanese War had important lessons for attack and defence, Britain began to show a decline in her former self-confidence, departing from her long adopted diplomatic principle of 'Splendid Isolation', with the realisation of growing German power and ambition. To all this political and popular anxiety, technological advances played their customary part. 'The increase in the number of torpedo craft, the range and accuracy of naval guns and increasing development of submarines made the whole question of coast defences ripe for revision.'[37]

The Owen Committee on the Armaments of the Home Ports, meeting in 1905, recommended three categories of defended port. Class A included the major naval bases of Portsmouth, Plymouth, the Medway and Pembroke Dock, which might be attacked by battleships and should have 9.2-inch (233mm) guns. Class B were those ports considered to be liable to attack from armoured cruisers and included Cork, Berehaven, Lough Swilly, Portland, Dover and the Forth. These were to have 6-inch (152mm) guns. The remainder – the Thames, Harwich, the Humber, the Tees, Hartlepool, the Tyne, Sunderland, the Tay and Aberdeen – were thought to be vulnerable only to light unarmoured

vessels which could be dealt with by 4.7-inch (120mm) guns, though 6-inch (152mm) would be needed against blockships. All the naval and commercial ports were to have 4.7-inch (120mm) QFs against torpedo-boats. Guns covering the inner waters of harbours were removed and none was allowed for land defence.[38] This last decision was surprising in the light of the example of the siege of Port Arthur. There, the Japanese fleet was driven off by the Russian coastal batteries which had then to be attacked from the land by 50,000 men, and only fell after a siege of five months. In the light of subsequent events it is interesting to note that the only attack on a C Class port was that on Hartlepool in 1914. In this case the assailant included battlecruisers and a heavy cruiser which retired with some damage from the accurate fire from inadequate defences.

Changes of emphasis resulted from the German threat. The establishment at Harwich had increased in value. Formerly it was simply classified as a defended commercial port but it came to be regarded as a War Anchorage, with corresponding additions to its armament. There was also a proposal for an anchorage for battleships to the east of the Forth Bridge. This led to a new battery at Braefoot on the mainland opposite Inchcolm, sited so that its fire enfiladed the main channel between Kinghorn and Inchkeith. By 1915, two 9.2-inch (233mm) guns were mounted there, and at the same time, the inner line was strongly defended against torpedo-boats.

Opinion, as we have seen, had begun to turn back towards the risk of invasion, and the possibility that the navy might not be the total answer. The First Lord of the Admiralty, Winston Churchill, was fearful lest the torpedo threaten the survival of the Grand Fleet. This, and the evidence of weakness shown by the naval manoeuvres of 1912 and 1913, led Lieutenant-General Franklyn's committee to argue once more that fixed defences did have a role. There was then a revival for the land defences of Portsmouth, where the Portsdown line was to be prepared for infantry defence, together with emplacements for heavy field and machine guns. The Portsdown line was also to be extended from Farlington Redoubt to Langstone harbour in the east, and from Fareham to Fontley in the west. At Plymouth, Crownhill Fort was still regarded as the key position on the northern line, and at Chatham the Borstal–Darland–Twydall line was regarded as the final position for the defence of the Dockyard. Yet another committee under Brigadier-General Wilson in 1912, considered the 'Defence of Coast Fortresses and Coast Batteries against Land Attack'. All works were regarded at risk from surprise attack. The committee recommended that they should therefore be protected by ditches, walls, palisades or barbed wire entanglements, covered by flanking fire and lights. Batteries should be protected from rifle fire from the rear and blockhouses built at places which might be used by attackers.[39]

Although little of the Wilson Committee's report was acted upon before the outbreak of war in 1914, one locality did receive special attention in a surprisingly old-fashioned way. This was the strengthening of the Humber defences, which arose partly from the opening of Immingham Docks, and the existence of a large Admiralty oil storage depot nearby. It was decided in 1913 to build two batteries for 6-inch (152mm) guns with defence lights on the north and south shores of the estuary below Immingham Docks. The alluvial nature of the soil, and the resulting difficulty in raising the guns to sufficient elevation, were said to be serious obstacles to rapid construction. Also, as a result of visits by the Home Ports Defence Committee, it was decided that two more batteries should be built, one at each end of the Spurn peninsula. The estuary, which at its mouth is four miles wide, should be guarded by an island fort constructed on Bull Sand about a mile from Spurn Point, with another similar work on Haile Sand near the Lincolnshire coast. These sea forts were harking back to those in the Solent, though they were to be of different construction. They could also only be built with great difficulty because both shoals were covered at high tide, and Bull Sand had 11 feet (3.3 metres) of water even at the lowest tide. Because of these difficulties, nothing was done until after the commencement of war, and then changed circumstances led to a revision of the defensive strategy.[40]

A 9.2-inch gun on its mounting. (IWM)

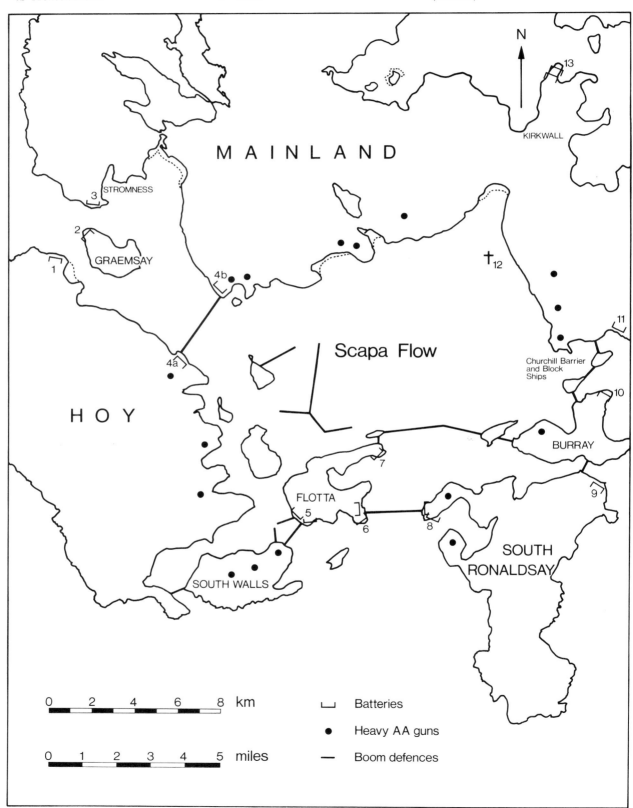

Scapa Flow defences:
1 Skerry
2 Graemsay
3 Ness
4a Scad Head
4b Houton Head

5 Innan Neb and Gate
6 Stanger Head and Buchanan
7 Roan Head
8 Hoxa Head and Balfour
9 Cara

10 Burray
11 Holm
12 Royal Oak
13 Car Ness and Wellington
(Author)

N

KIRKWALL

MAINLAND

STROMNESS

GRAEMSAY

Scapa Flow

HOY

Churchill Barrier
and Block
Ships

BURRAY

FLOTTA

SOUTH
RONALDSAY

SOUTH WALLS

0   2   4   6   8 km

0   1   2   3   4   5 miles

⊔ Batteries

● Heavy AA guns

— Boom defences

CHAPTER 12

Coastal Defences in Two World Wars

1914–1918

The Edwardian defence strategists were partially vindicated by events on the English north east coast on 16 December 1914: firstly, on account of their acknowledgement of the vulnerability to cruiser attack of certain coastal towns and harbours (in this instance Whitby, Scarborough and Hartlepool); and secondly, by the resistance put up by the batteries at Hartlepool. What had not been sufficiently appreciated by the Chiefs of Staff was that the torpedo and the mine were to be more significant naval weapons during the First World War then surface battle fleets. The naval strategists had in fact planned for the wrong sort of war. The German High Seas Fleet, for most of the time, remained in harbour, and, at the first (false) alarm of the presence of a U-boat, Sir John Jellicoe led his Grand Fleet out of the then undefended Scapa Flow and into the western Atlantic, not to return until well into 1915. Coastal raids were not in fact to play much of a part in naval activities.

British coastal defences as a whole, however, were in a high state of readiness at the outbreak of war, thanks to the close attention to home defence, and the appreciation of the potential German naval threat during the previous ten years. There were exceptions, such as Scapa Flow, where the navy only belatedly recognised the need to protect the base of the Grand Fleet. Although a force of Royal Garrison Artillery had been specially raised to man the Scapa Flow defences, not a coast defence gun had been mounted by August 1914. At first, 12- and 3-pounder QFs were taken off warships in order to get some guns ashore, and it was only gradually that 4-inch (102mm), 6-inch (152mm) and 12-pounder guns were in position covering all approaches and entrances to the Great Harbour. In 1915, plans were made to construct permanent barriers across the eastern entrances but, because of the urgency of the situation, boom-defences, blockships and underwater anti-submarine defences of steel trestles were put in place.[1] Elsewhere in the country, many additional batteries were already in hand, filling gaps in an other-

wise well ordered system of fortress control, and with an eleventh-hour revival of concern for the threat of enemy landing parties, field fortifications protected every fortress.

The action off Hartlepool in 1914 was, however, the only occasion when the home coastal defences actually fought off German warships. German battlecruisers had earlier opened fire on Great Yarmouth and Gorleston. The next raid was to consist of four battlecruisers (*Seydlitz, Moltke, Von Der Tann and Derfflinger*), one heavy cruiser (*Blücher*) with supporting light cruisers and destroyers. The *Von Der Tann* and *Derfflinger* turned aside to bombard the defenceless towns of Scarborough and Whitby. The *Seydlitz, Moltke* and *Blücher* made for Hartlepool, which was defended by Heugh Battery with two 6-inch (152mm) guns, and Lighthouse Battery with just one. The first shell from the *Seydlitz* fell between the two batteries cutting all the fire-commander's telephones. In spite of many shells falling close to the batteries there were only four fatal casualties among the gunners, though 112 civilians were killed in the town, and much damage done to its buildings and docks. The coast defence guns, despite the initial damage, hotly returned the enemy fire, and when the guns of Heugh Battery were able to turn on the *Blücher* several hits were obtained including one on the forebridge which put two guns of the secondary armament out of action. It was held to be a creditable performance by a severely under-gunned coast artillery unit, and the principal members of the batteries were decorated.

Despite this readiness among British coast defences, some places needed substantial additional works, principally on the east coast. The most important included a heavy battery at Felixstowe to increase protection for the approaches to Harwich, and the defences of the Humber which had barely been started. Additional works were needed for the Tyne, and a new scheme for the Forth. There were similar works elsewhere, at Plymouth, and in the Bristol Channel, batteries to flank the Solent boom-defence, others to protect the entrances to Belfast and to the Clyde at Gourock,

Fletcher Battery, Sheppey: constructed in 1917 and armed with two 9.2-inch guns. (IWM)

Bull Sand fort in the Humber Estuary. (IWM)

and alterations to the siting of guns at Sheppey and Dover.

The major work at Felixstowe was Brackenbury Battery, to the north of the town. Work began in

April 1915 to accommodate two 9.2-inch (233mm) guns transferred from Berehaven, in south west Ireland, and barrack accommodation was provided for 2 officers and 71 other ranks, and also for an infantry force of 3 officers and 160 other ranks alongside.[2] Moving up the coast, the most extensive works were in the Humber where many new positions had been anticipated. A war anchorage of considerable importance was established on the north side of the river opposite Grimsby. To protect it, two heavy guns were needed at each end of the Spurn peninsula, at Spurn and Kilnsea, with more guns and lights at Bull Sand and at Haile Sand Forts. The construction of these two sea forts was a remarkable engineering feat. Built on ingeniously constructed foundations, the forts were circular, four-storeyed masonry structures, protected by 12 inches (305mm) of armour. They were armed with four 6-inch (152mm) guns.[3]

Another remarkable engineering enterprise was the installation of the Tyne turrets. In October 1916 the Admiralty offered the two turrets, each containing two 12-inch (305mm) guns from the old *Majestic* class battleship HMS *Illustrious*, for mounting on shore. Sites at Hartley, near Seaton Sluice, north of the Tyne, and at Marsden near Lizard Point, south of the river, were selected for Roberts and Kitchener Batteries respectively. With the exception of the Dover Turret guns, these were the heaviest fixed guns available in coastal defence at the time.[4]

Shortly after the outbreak of war, temporary works were carried out to improve the inner line of the Forth defences, so as to give better protection to the anchorage west of the Bridge (see illustration on p203). In the spring of 1916, however, there was a change of policy. It was decided to have an anchorage east of the Bridge protected by a further line of guns and lights. The effect of these proposals was the construction of new batteries at Leith to the south, and at Pettycur to the north; by additional batteries – two 6-inch (152mm) – and lights at Inchkeith; batteries for two (later four) 6-inch (152mm), four 4.7-inch (120mm) guns and four 4-inch (102mm) QFs on Inchcolm; batteries for four 4-inch (102mm) QFs on Inchmickery; and minor modifications on the inner defence line, where, at Downing Point, two 4.7-inch (120mm) guns were mounted. The line of defence covering the new anchorage thus took full advantage of the scatter of islands across the estuary north of Edinburgh. The works were finished, with the exception of a few details, by the autumn of 1917. The guns were mounted in concrete emplacements, with or without shelters, with magazines below. Close protection consisted of barbed wire, trenches and concrete pillboxes. The battery garrisons were housed in hutted camps, often some distance away. The batteries were therefore not self-sufficient, nor were they planned in isolation. Their fire interlocked with each other under a common fire con-

Inchcolm, Firth of Forth: pillbox. (Author)

trol. The Firth of Forth, as far east as the Elie/North Berwick line, was considered a 'fortress', with the groups of guns and individual batteries only elements of the whole.[5]

The First World War owed its painful reputation to the success of defence over attack. The effectiveness of trenches and fieldworks in depth when defended by machine guns and magazine rifles, and the horrendous loss of life incurred by futile attempts to meet these fortifications head-on, were the abiding themes of this war. The expensively constructed lines and rings of permanent fortresses which divided France and Belgium from Germany, and which had been built or rearmed during the generation before 1914, played a less significant part than might have been expected. The Belgian forts designed by Brialmont, which had been castigated by Sydenham Clarke – rightly as it turned out – succumbed rapidly to the penetrative power of the German 42cm (16.6-inch) howitzer. The French

Maidstone–Swale line: a front-line fire trench on Detling Hill. (IWM)

Maidstone–Swale line: Thrognal Redoubt. (IWM)

forts around Verdun, however, were more stoutly constructed. Even when partially disarmed, they proved capable of effective resistance, and were a critical factor in holding back the German advance during the battle of the Marne. Elsewhere, some permanent fortifications proved their worth. The Austrian works at Przemysl held out against the Russians for five months, and were eventually starved into surrender. In the Far East, the German fortress of Tsingtao on the Chinese coast took the Japanese a month to reduce.

In Britain, the strategy that had evolved from the Chatham defences into the London Defence Positions still held good. Given the existence of advanced mobilisation centres, the digging of field defences was to await hostilities or the imminence of invasion. To the rear was a mobile force intended to deal with the invader if he succeeded in advancing inland. The German advance on the Belgian coast in 1914 did indeed stimulate fears of invasion. It was thought possible that an effective invasion could be mounted with a force of 70,000 men carried in barges, and escorted by secondary units of the German navy, while the main British and German fleets fought a major battle elsewhere. It was not until after the battle of Jutland, in the early summer of 1916, that invasion could be seen to be highly unlikely. Nevertheless, preparations had been made in the south east, in Kent and Essex, since the Cabinet were convinced that London would be the principal target.[6]

Between the capital and the coast were a series of 'stop lines' of fieldworks. The earlier line of London Defence Positions was brought back into use, equipped with some 6-inch (152mm) and 9.2-inch (233mm) howitzers. The Chatham line also returned to favour. Further out still, there was a line of entrenchments and pillboxes between Maidstone and the river Swale. It has

Garrison Point, Sheerness: the West Boom machine-gun emplacement on the berm of Garrison Point Fort. (IWM)

Warden Point, Sheppey: concrete machine-gun emplacement of the First World War. (IWM)

been established that as late as 1917, during the Ludendorff Offensive, General French was organising further internal defence lines in Kent, with 6-inch (152mm) howitzers and 60-pounder guns for artillery support.[7]

There was little in the way of land defences to the north and east of London. From October 1914, there came into being three trench systems, the outermost running north of Chelmsford by Maldon and Danbury Hill, and the innermost by Ongar and Epping. Other parts of the east coast were entrenched, and that winter some 300,000 troops were deployed there. Concrete pillboxes were added later, some facing inland to defend the naval ports from landward attack. These first pillboxes were mainly circular in plan (hence the nickname pillbox) and built of concrete blocks.[8] A few in this early form still survive in East Anglia. Pillboxes in the Thames and Medway area were of the more familiar hexagonal type, later in use in the 1940s. Although the British army had used a form of pillbox in association with lines of barbed wire as a means of restricting the mounted Boer commandos during the South African War, it was the Germans who developed the use of reinforced concrete construction, and established the pillboxes's effectiveness against infantry attack.[9] Larger versions of the pillbox could house

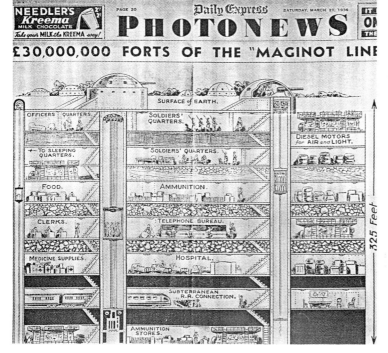

NEEDLER'S Kreema MILK CHOCOLATE *Take your MILK the KREEMA way!*

PAGE 20

Daily Express SATURDAY, MARCH 21, 1936

PHOTONEWS

£30,000,000 FORTS OF THE "MAGINOT LINE

SURFACE of EARTH.

OFFICERS' QUARTERS.

SOLDIERS' QUARTERS.

DIESEL MOTORS for AIR and LIGHT.

TO SLEEPING QUARTERS.

SOLDIERS' QUARTERS.

FOOD.

AMMUNITION.

CLERKS.

TELEPHONE BUREAU.

MEDICINE SUPPLIES.

HOSPITAL.

SUBTERRANEAN R.R. CONNECTION.

AMMUNITION STORES.

325 Feet

Diagrammatic section through a Maginot Line fort as it was popularly imagined in 1936. (From the Daily Express, 21 March 1936)

artillery, but essentially it was an infantry fire-support position, and when well made, could resist direct hits from 6-inch (152mm) and 8-inch (203mm) shells. This was the main novel contribution of the First World War to the story of defensive structures.

MAGINOT LINE MENTALITY

After the 'War to end all Wars' none of the belligerents gave up their national defences; on the continent of Europe they improved them. Since German generals protested that their defeat stemmed from collapse at home, and that their army had not been defeated in the field, it was not surprising that the French General Staff soon returned to its defence studies. France was, in fact, now politically weaker than 'defeated' Germany. Her traditional ally, Russia, was separated from Germany since the war by newly independent Poland, and with its civil war following on the 1917 Revolution, the Soviet Union was no longer an immediate threat to Germany's eastern borders. France was faced by a country with a population nearly twice as great as her own, increasingly resentful of the policy of 'Germany must pay', and enjoyed only temporary occupation of the Rhineland which was to act as a replacement for the buffer that Alsace and Lorraine formerly provided.

The French army was divided into two schools of thought. The traditional belief was in the offensive, to which Napoleon's directive that 'It is an axiom of war that the side which stays within its fortifications is beaten' was prayed in aid. Others believed that France could not stand another war of launching its armies against an entrenched enemy, and that since trenches had been so successful in the last war

it followed that permanent defences would give France the greater security it craved. Yet permanent defences had had limited value during the Great War, although the French were entitled to feel that those around Verdun had been particularly successful. While temporary fieldworks had been supreme until near the war's end, some of the more far-sighted military observers appreciated the potential of the tank to break through trench systems. The French, after the divergent arguments among their military chiefs of staff during the 1920s, staked their security on permanent defences. It was a policy which depended upon the continuing military alliance with Belgium, and the existence of a strong line of fortifications based upon the route of the river Meuse and along the Albert Canal to Antwerp. And therein lay its weakness. The French objective was not to defend the whole length of its frontiers itself. Its new line was essentially limited to serve as a shield for Alsace and Lorraine, and to protect the vital iron and steel industry of the Saar. The basic design was outlined by General Belhague, Inspector-General of Fortifications in 1927. It was, however, the politician, André Maginot, who had pressed for a system of fixed defences, and helped to obtain the resources from government for their construction, whose name was associated with what came to be the most complex system of permanent fortification ever built.[10]

Stemming from the French decision to invest in massive works of concrete and steel, the 1930s saw prodigious new systems of permanent border defence in Europe. As well as the Maginot Line, there was, in Belgium, the fortress of Eben Emael, and eventually in Germany too, where the West Wall was mistakenly called the Siegfried Line by the British. The French had absorbed the lessons of Verdun. The Maginot Line was a system of strongly protected underground forts which were set so deep, and encased in such heavy concrete, that they were capable of resisting the heaviest bombardment. Only the small armoured cupolas of the retractable gun turrets showed above ground. Beneath, were several levels of living accommodation, each with their own lighting and ventilation systems, kitchens, hospitals, storerooms and magazines. Troops could be moved about by small underground electric trains. Apart from the technological advances necessary to house an underground garrison, and deploy its firepower by remote control, the Maginot Line and the West Wall demonstrated an appreciation of the tank as a new factor in twentieth century warfare. The advanced posts, covering all the likely approaches to the main fortresses of the Maginot line, were associated with anti-tank barriers of concrete pyramids or forests of vertically-set railway lines, all covered by machine guns and anti-tank guns. Each fort supported another, and could bring down the heaviest fire on a neighbour without risk of structural damage in order to deal with parachute troops or other assault parties who might penetrate to the cupolas. The Belgian fort of Eben Emael fell in 1940 because it was not capable of receiving support from neighbouring forts. The Germans were able to land parachutists and glider troops on to the fort itself, and place charges in the barrels of the guns in the cupolas with remarkable ease.[11]

Defensive strategy in Britain differed little from that adopted at the beginning of the century, except that during the 1920s there was a return to the thought that France might again be a potential future aggressor. There was thus continuing military opposition to any revival of the plans for a Channel Tunnel. More seriously, there was an appreciation that the 'bolt from the blue' might now come from the air as well as from the sea, and that the needs of defence should be viewed more widely. In defence papers of 1925, it was still thought that the need for fixed defences was limited, and that the actual defence positions could be left until the immediacy of war. Any peacetime works might consist of anti-tank obstacles, and the establishment of defended localities consisting of mutually supporting concrete pillboxes. In practice, nothing was done inland but coastal defence remained in being. The old high angle, rifled muzzle-loaders on disappearing mountings, however, were ultimately made obsolete, and the sites sold, but the land forts around Portsmouth, Plymouth and Chatham were retained, although not armed. They remained as barracks and stores. Following trials at Portsmouth and Malta in which coastal guns had achieved disturbingly poor results when firing at moving targets at 18,000 yards (16.5 kilometres), a report on coast defence requirements in 1929 produced a modernisation programme for the 9.2-inch (233mm) guns, and a recommendation for coast defence guns to adopt salvo firing. This became necessary because of the increased speed of modern warships, and their ability to mount guns of greater range, and to maintain sophisticated fire control systems. While the defences on the Channel Islands were abolished, most batteries elsewhere were retained with improvements made to their equipment and observation facilities. Protection against air attack required reinforced concrete shelters. The batteries were manned by the Territorial Army.

An improvement in armament against fast motor torpedo-boats was the replacement of the 12-pounder QF guns by twin 6-pounders with a higher rate of fire. However, the War Office admitted that the role of coast artillery in future was not so much that of sinking hostile ships approaching our defended ports 'as of inflicting on them sufficient damage as to place them at a disadvantage in subsequent naval action, or to

compel their immediate return to a base for repairs.'[12] Its future role would be more of deterrence. Nevertheless, following an enquiry into the relative merits of the gun and the aeroplane in modern warfare, it was concluded that the gun was still the main deterrent against naval attack.

During the 1930s, it was increasingly recognised that there might be another war with Germany, and the menace of Japan to British colonial and trading interests was foreshadowed by the Japanese invasion of Manchuria in 1931. By 1934, the Committee for Imperial Defence made recommendations on the basis of the possibility of a war with Germany by 1939. Early in 1937 there was a major inquiry into the possibilities of invasion. As in previous considerations of such an event, a scenario involving the absence of the navy had to be visualised. In this case, the diversion of warships to the Far East had some validity. Even so, a minimum invasion force of 17,000 men would have been detected early on from aerial or sea reconnaisance, and failing that, the landing would be made more vulnerable from air attack on the invasion beaches. Invasion was therefore thought improbable but sea-borne raiding was more likely. During the last two years of peacetime rearmament, priority was given instead to the creation of an effective air defence for Britain, with fighter planes the main objective.

1939–1945

By the time of the Munich crisis in 1938, an awareness of the inevitability of war meant that the coast defences of the United Kingdom were once again fully manned. New works were under way, with additional 6-inch (152mm) batteries at Scapa Flow, Invergordon and Spurn Head, and experiments in early warning systems had been put in hand. For example, concrete acoustic mirrors were built in 1927 on the eastern side of Dungeness in the hope that they would detect aircraft at a range of at least 25 miles (40 kilometres).[13] Yet, once war had been declared, there seemed little danger of sea-borne attack, other than by submarines. When the fleet returned to Scapa Flow on the outbreak of war, they found the anchorage only slightly better protected than in 1914. An early German success, in October 1939, was the sinking of the *Royal Oak* while at anchor at Scapa. The fleet was withdrawn until the defences had been improved, and the Churchill barriers fully blocked the eastern entrances. The batteries themselves were improved, particularly by the introduction of the twin 6-pounder.

Any early feelings of security elsewhere in the country evaporated once the seriousness of the German offensive against France and the Low Countries in May 1940 was recognised. After only nineteen days of fighting, the Chiefs of Staff believed that a full-scale attack on Britain was imminent. On 10 May, the Home Defence Executive was set up under General Sir

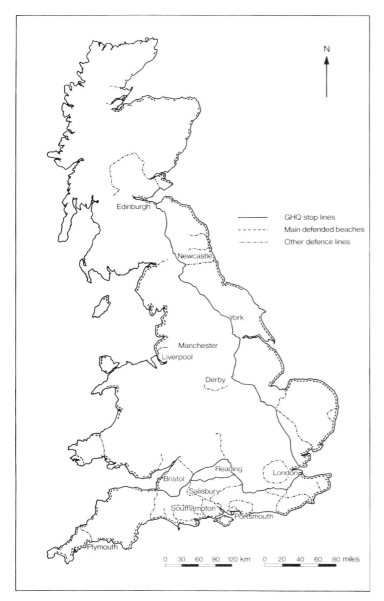

Map showing the principal lengths of coastline protected by 'Emergency Batteries', the main 'GHQ' defence line and local 'stop lines'. (Author)

Edmund Ironside, Commander-in-Chief Home Forces, to deal with everything related to possible invasion. Three days after the collapse of France, General Ironside was summoned on 25 June to outline his strategy for dealing with such an eventuality.[14]

Ironside's strategy had three main elements. The first line of defence was an 'extended crust' along probable invasion beaches, and a ring of gun batteries right around the coast. The 'Emergency Coast Batteries' which were to protect the minor ports, and cover every possible landing place, were armed from a naval store of guns and mountings from the ships which had been scrapped after the First World War. Most of the weapons were 6-inch (152mm), 5.5-inch (140mm), 4.7-inch (120mm) and 4-inch (102mm) guns. Ammunition

was also supplied by the navy but in very small quantities. Work was also in hand on anti-tank obstacles on the beaches supported by wire and pillboxes. The troops were to hold these positions as best they could, and gain time for mobile forces to arrive and counter-attack the landing force. The second defence line was a series of road blocks, manned by the Home Guard, to obstruct German armoured columns with some local 'stop lines' of pillboxes. The third element was the main, 'GHQ', defence line which followed the course of rivers and canals and employed them as ready made anti-tank obstacles. Intended to cover London and the industrial Midlands, this was essentially a line of pillboxes both for small arms and anti-tank guns, and was also manned by the Home Guard. Behind the GHQ line was the mobile reserve. In the main, the siting of pillboxes was allowed to follow a linear fashion, and was not used in groups, creating defended localities as had been recommended in the pre-war manual.[15] This may have been due either to the speed of construction, and lack of experience of local commanders, but also to the point of view which regarded the lines of pillboxes not so much for resisting a major assault, as preventing fast moving and lightly armed German troops from ranging across the country ahead of the main force.

Although these plans were approved by the prime minister, Winston Churchill, 'gravest concern' was expressed by the Vice-Chiefs of Staff. To them 'it appeared that the main resistance might only be offered after the enemy had overrun nearly half the country, and obtained possession of aerodromes and other vital facilities.'[16] They believed that it was crucial to oppose any invasion while it was still in the vulnerable state of disembarkation. Nevertheless Ironside's plan went forward. Churchill, in the meantime was developing his idea for the formation of well-armed, highly mobile units which he characteristically called 'Leopard Groups' but which eventually became known as Commandos. On 26 June, however, General Alan Brooke, who had just seen action in France, was appointed General Officer Commanding-in-Chief of Southern Command. After little more than three weeks, on 19 July, he had replaced Ironside as C-in-C Home Forces. There was an immediate change in defence planning. Brooke disapproved of the earlier system of extensive inland defences, while developing the notion of highly mobile forces which could concentrate rapidly on the point of danger. He condemned the concept of linear defence. Many of the road blocks were removed because they also hindered the mobility of the defending forces. Work on building pillboxes in the secondary GHQ line was stopped but continued elsewhere. Something in the region of 8000 pillboxes had been built at this stage, of which about a quarter were 'shellproof'. Some 17,000 more were proposed or under construction. In addition, many miles of concrete anti-tank obstacles were erected, mostly behind

TWO WORLD WARS 217

Camouflaged coastal strongpoint in Northern Command.
(IWM)

beaches, nearly 100 miles of anti-tank ditches were dug, mainly around London, and anti-glider trenches criss-crossed large expanses of open land. Airfields were ringed with fixed defences. Special designs were sometimes adopted for this specialised use. The F C Construction Company produced a circular pillbox with a concrete cantilevered roof which gave complete all-round fire. Another was the Pickett-Hamilton Counterbalance Fort which was flush with the ground so as not to obstruct the movement of aircraft; with a crew of five, it could be raised on the standard garage car-lift principle to allow 360° cover at ground level.[17] Elsewhere, steel cupolas were used. On the coast, long range guns were needed, particularly in the Dover Straits. Before the end of June, the Germans were busy mounting 11- to 16-inch (280mm to 406mm) guns from

Anti-tank defences on the east coast. (IWM)

▲ *The Pickett–Hamilton Counterbalance Fort re-erected outside the D-Day Museum, Southsea.* (Author)

Cape Gris Nez to Calais in the Batterie 'Lindermann', Batterie 'Todt' and Batterie 'Grosser Kurfurst'. The best, but only, answer to that degree of firepower were two 14-inch (356mm) naval guns, manned by the Royal Marines, and known locally at Dover, as 'Winnie' and 'Pooh'. By September 1940, it was decided to construct three new batteries in the Dover area for counter-battery fire. These were Fan Bay Battery for three 6-inch (152mm) guns with an extreme range of 25,000 yards (22.9 kilometres), South Foreland Battery for four 9.2-inch (233mm) guns with a range of 31,000 yards (28.3 kilometres) and Wanstone Battery for two 15-inch (381mm) guns whose extreme range was 42,000 yards (38.4 kilometres). These were not ready, however, until 1941, and in the case of Wanstone, not until the middle of 1942.

As in the time of Napoleon Bonaparte, from 1803 to 1805, the danger of invasion in the late summer of 1940 was very real. By the end of June, German forces were in occupation of the western coast of Europe from the North Cape to the Spanish border. In addition, the Germans could move their airfields up to the Channel. The eastern and southern coasts of Eng-

▼ *'Pooh', one of two 14-inch counter-bombardment guns at St Margaret's Bay, Dover.* (IWM)

Tentsmuir, Fife: Polish soldiers constructing the anti-tank defences. (IWM)

land were now under constant threat of attack from the air, as well as from light motor torpedo-boats operating along the Channel. British expectations of the likely landing place for the main invasion was the east coast, between Southwold and East Kent, with the immediate objective of seizing London. The German plan of invasion, code-named 'Operation Sealion', was for the landing to take place between Ramsgate and the Isle of Wight, employing nine infantry divisions and two airborne divisions, supported by 250 amphibious tanks and 72 rocket launchers. The first wave was to be followed by a second of four armoured, two motorised and two infantry divisions. The invasion was intended during the week of 19–27 September, when moon and tides would be most favourable.[18] Essential for success, however, was German mastery of the air, and it was here that the Battle of Britain was fought and won by the Royal Air Force. The invasion was postponed on 12 October until the following summer of 1941. By then Hitler's attentions were concentrated on Russia. Although the British Defence Chiefs maintained their guard, the threat of invasion had passed.

From November 1940, no more shellproof pillboxes were built on the beaches as there were thought to be sufficient. Instead, there were better planned groupings of fixed defences into anti-tank 'islands'. By the time of the German invasion of Russia in June 1941, all work on the stop-lines was abandoned but what had been constructed was maintained and co-ordinated. Soon, however, the conspicuous pillbox lost favour because it could be demonstrated that it was vulnerable to high velocity guns. By September 1941 all pillbox construction stopped, and in February the next year they were forbidden altogether by the Commander-in-Chief. While existing pillboxes could remain, future defences were to be fieldworks.

The pillbox is still the most recognisable and most widespread survival of Britain's last-war defences. The astonishing thing is that they are mainly an archaeological survival since their written record is extremely patchy. This may be due to the fact that some defences were erected on the initiative of local commanders without reference to a co-ordinated strategy, and the urgency of the moment did not allow for the niceties of bureaucratic records. For example, the only detailed list of the GHQ Line defences which appears to survive in the Public Record Office is that for Southern Command. The understanding of the defence lines, and the elements that they contained, depends principally upon archaeological observation and the recollections of participants.[19]

Pevensey Castle, Sussex: strongpoints incorporated into the ruins of the Roman Saxon Shore fort and the later Norman castle. (Author)

The pillbox was not new. It had become part of the trench system of the First World War, and was later seen as an obstacle to a more mobile warfare incorporating tanks. The design of British pillboxes was the responsibility of FW 3, a branch of the directorate of Fortifications and Works at the War Office. This branch issued a series of drawings to the army commands which in turn passed them on to the various building contractors employed. The Commander Royal Engineers at the various commands modified the specifications to suit local circumstances. Some of the designs were based on those used in France in 1939–40, while others were of the hexagonal type of the first war. For the most part, the pillboxes were intended for the use of rifles, machine guns and anti-tank rifles. The largest ones were for anti-tank guns, the 2-pounder being the most common, though some heavier weapons were occasionally accommodated. Walls, 3½ feet (89mm) thick, were considered to be shellproof in 1940. More considered research was applied to their powers of resistance to shell-fire during 1941, and in some instances walls were thickened. More than a dozen different designs were issued varying from the hexagonal Bren gun emplacement, a rectangular emplacement for land and air defence, square and round forms, anti-tank 2-pounder emplacements, and a sea-wall pattern for use in the Thames and Medway. As well as more specialised types for airfield defence already mentioned, there were one- and two-man tur-

rets, known as the Tett Turret, formed from a standard 4-foot diameter concrete pipe sunk into the ground, and a revolving turret projecting only some 13 inches. Frequently, pillboxes were part of long stretches of anti-tank defences. A remarkable survival of this linear defence is to be seen along the Fife coast at Tentsmuir, between St Andrew's and the Tay, opposite Dundee.

The construction of these fortifications was carried out at great speed, and caused a crisis for the national stocks of cement. Steel reinforcement was often in short supply, so that in some instances bedsprings were used. In June 1940, some contractors were working a seven-day week averaging twelve hours a day. In many places all able-bodied men and boys were drawn into the work of building beach defences, often under fire from German planes. While many pillboxes are only too conspicuous today alongside railway lines and canals, much was done to camouflage them, and ingenious lengths were taken to incorporate pillboxes into the rural scene. Camouflage and continuity of defence is illustrated at Pevensey Castle where strong-points were incorporated into the ruins of the Roman Saxon Shore fort and the later Norman castle.

Preparations to thwart a sea-borne invasion were only some of the defensive works which were necessary. Anti-aircraft positions were constructed in large numbers throughout the war, but few have survived into recent times. The heavy anti-aircraft guns were generally of 3.7-inch (94mm) and 4.5-inch (114mm) calibres. Most of these had prepared positions for four or more guns with the gun pits protected by low concrete octagonal blast walls. Some of the old land

A 3.7-inch AA Fixed Defence in Richmond Park, London.
(IWM)

forts ringing the naval bases mounted anti-aircraft batteries, which in some cases, as at Chatham, were the only
armament they ever received. The most remarkable and
most visible of the anti-aircraft defences were the flak-
towers in the Thames and Mersey estuaries which were
conceived in 1941 by the civil engineer G A Maunsell
and built in 1942–3. There were two types of sea fort,
one designed for the navy, the other for the army. The
former consisted of two concrete cylindrical towers
containing storage and living accommodation which
were towed out and sunk into position. The towers
carried a superstructure armed with two 3.7-inch
(94mm) anti-aircraft guns, and two Bofors 40mm light
anti-aircraft guns. A number of these were sited in the
Thames estuary but they were not suitable for the
Mersey because of the shifting sea bed. The alternative
design was the 'Army Fort' manned by gunners of
Anti-Aircraft Command. They were used in the
Mersey and in the Thames where they were closer
inshore than the 'Navy Forts'. These forts consisted of
seven tubular steel towers connected above the water
by lattice steel bridges. Each tower carried a two-storey
steel superstructure for accommodation of all sorts,
with gun positions on the roof. One tower was for
control, one for searchlights, one for Bofors guns, and
four for 3.7-inch (94mm) guns. The military objectives
of these sea forts were to break up enemy aircraft
formations approaching London or Liverpool, to prevent the laying of mines in the estuaries, and preventing

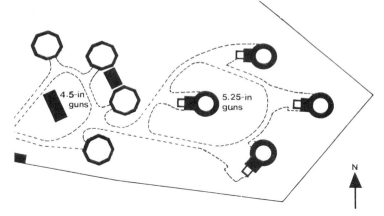

Bowaters Farm AA site, East Tilbury, Essex. (V T C Smith)

enemy E-boats carrying out raids on shipping and
coastal targets. Elsewhere, the other notable defensive
structures were the radar towers, and the accompanying but unobtrusive surface installations of the underground control centres, which had such a part in the
successful outcome of the air war, and also had no small
part in the deployment of naval guns.

As the threat of invasion became more remote, the new long-range batteries, commanding the
Dover Straits with the aid of radar, concentrated instead on destroying German shipping attempting to
slip past while hugging the French coast, and in
counter-bombardment. Elsewhere, the danger of E-
boat attack on harbours remained. However, by the
beginning of 1943, it was determined that coast artillery

'Army' AA sea fort in the Thames Estuary. (IWM)

strengths could be reduced, and by July certain batteries were consigned to care and maintenance, and others to be manned by the Home Guard. The general policy was to retain only the counter-bombardment batteries capable of closing the Straits of Dover. Close defence batteries were to be reduced to two guns per port, anti-motor torpedo-boat guns were to be retained and manned by regulars, but beach defence batteries were either to be manned by the Home Guard or relegated to care and maintenance. In October the number of active batteries was further reduced.

While mainland Britain escaped invasion, and its fortifications for that emergency were not put to the test, part of the United Kingdom was occupied by the German army. It would be wrong therefore to conclude this review of fortifications without some mention of those considerable defences built by the Germans in the Channel Islands as part of the Atlantic Wall against Allied invasion of the continent. Although Hitler had ridiculed the failure of the French Maginot Line, his insistence on a static, concrete, defensive wall

along the coasts of western Europe was as much for psychological reasons as for physical protection. He was much influenced by the Allied raid on Dieppe in August 1942, and it served to convince him of the value of permanent fortifications. Having accepted such an idea, the German military recognised that the permanent defences must be capable of resisting initial air and naval bombardment, and involved the development of a network of self-sufficient strongpoints capable of absorbing enemy attacks and mounting local counter-attacks. The main concentrations of defences followed a central directive dated 28 May 1942. This referred to setting up four types of coastal defence. The first, and the smallest of these types, was the Resistance Nest, for defence against local attacks by infantry and armour. The position was intended to be self-contained, arranged around at least one anti-tank gun, with machine gun and mortar emplacements interconnected by communications and rifle trenches, and surrounded by barbed wire and minefields. The second type was the Strongpoint, comprising either a group of smaller positions to form an infantry strongpoint with a core of heavier weapons, or a battery position for artillery. The battery was either mounted under concrete casemates or in open emplacements with separate bunkers housing command posts. Strongpoints were also surrounded by a system of fieldworks. The Strongpoint Group was a combination of strongpoints grouped for unity of command in the vicinity of a major port. The largest defence complex was the Defence Sector at places of strategic importance.[20]

There were two readily distinguishable types of German coastal battery. Some were capable of engaging sea targets and were under navy control, while the army batteries covered the beaches and the hinterland. The navy sited those batteries under its control in forward positions to obtain the greatest range out to sea, and engage sea targets with direct visual fire. Those army batteries which were not positioned on the beach, were sited some distance inland to bombard the beaches at long range by employing forward observation positions.

There were therefore gun sites ranging from multi-storey casemates such as the 'Lindemann' and 'Todt' batteries, or with a naval turreted gun in the open, surmounting a single-storey bunker. The most visible and architectural structures were the coastal observation posts in the Channel Islands, with their tiers of cantilevered canopies for visual observation, use of radar and range finding. A further type was the command post, combining the activities of observation and command with fire control. This could vary from an underground bunker with a low profile, and dual or single armoured observation turret, to the multi-storey platform. The last type was the bunker associated with all the major artillery and infantry strongpoints, provided for housing the garrison and intended to withstand the heaviest naval and aerial bombardment. These had many forms.

The Channel Islands were among the most effectively fortified locations on the Atlantic Wall. This was both for strategic reasons, and because of Hitler's obsession with the capture of British soil. The islands of Jersey, Guernsey and Alderney were each treated as separate defence sectors. Guernsey was ringed with eleven strongpoints and fifty-three resistance nests. Of the fifteen coastal artillery batteries, the largest battery was 'Mirus' at Le Frie Baton to the west of the island, mounting four 30.5cm (12-inch) naval turreted guns with an effective range of 32 kilometres (20 miles). There was a total of thirty-one anti-aircraft batteries, six of which were 8.8cm installations with six guns in each. For much of the shoreline, the main strongpoints were placed on the low headlands to enfilade the beaches. The defences of Jersey were similar, though the long beaches of St Ouen's Bay and St Aubin's Bay presented considerable problems. Along the length of the former, were a number of strongpoints providing interlocking fire and connected by a continuous concrete anti-tank wall. The Jersey defences contained

German observation tower at Corbiere Point, Jersey now in peaceful use. (Author)

thirteen strongpoints and fifty-two resistance nests with seventeen batteries of guns, not counting thirty-four anti-aircraft batteries. Elizabeth Castle, Mont Orgueil and St Aubin's castles, as well as a number of eighteenth century towers, were strengthened with new works. Alderney, despite its small size had thirteen strongpoints and twelve resistance nests, and the mid-nineteenth century forts were almost all strengthened. The Channel Islands, for all their enormous firepower, were never tested. They were by-passed with the liberation of France, and surrendered after the ceasefire in Germany on 5 May 1945.

St Ouen's Bay, Jersey: anti-tank wall and strongpoint.
(Author)

Epilogue

The emergency batteries were dismantled in 1945, and the permanent batteries were put into care and maintenance. Yet, within two months after the end of the war in Europe, the Chiefs of Staff began to plan for post-war coastal defence on the basis of past experience. Then came the explosion of atomic bombs at Hiroshima and Nagasaki. Even so, the organisation of home defence barely comprehended the new weapon. But as the political attitude towards the Soviet Union changed from alliance to hostility, there were those who revived the view of an earlier Chief of the Imperial General Staff, Sir George Milne (1926–33), that Britain's natural strategic frontier lay on the Rhine.

The government in 1946 decided to continue with conscription with the expectation of avoiding a return to large scale unemployment but also with the declared aim of deterring future aggression and defending British interests abroad against attack. The international political scene worsened, and the blockade of Berlin in 1948 led to the North Atlantic Treaty Organisation, to which Britain was a signatory. The issue of home defence was still under discussion, and the Home Fleet exercises that year were designed to test the organisation for defence of the British coastline. Changing technology also had a bearing on the nature of British defences, particularly the development of the guided missile. The outbreak of the Korean War in 1950 produced a considerable increase in defence expenditure, and the next few years saw a reactivisation of home defence in case a remote and limited war became more general. Mobile columns were organised and trained, and the Home Guard and similar services built up. The more significant coastal batteries retained their guns.

Increasingly, the development of nuclear weapons continued side by side with traditional expedients. Then the test explosions of thermo-nuclear devices by the United States in the early 1950s completed the revolution in weaponry. NATO strategy was publicly based on the use of nuclear weapons in a major war, and with it was associated the British nuclear deterrent. Conventional coastal defence was now irredeemably obsolete. By 1956, a complete review of Britain's defence policy had been carried out, and coastal defence was finally abolished that year. Since that time, the forts and batteries of many periods have been abandoned, sold for new development, or levelled – except for those which have been statutorily protected as historic monuments, and from these some are deliberately preserved for the future, displayed and explained by a variety of public and private bodies.

NOTES

Chapter 1

1 A J Pollard, *John Talbot and the War in France 1427–1453* (London 1983), pp137–9.

2 D F Renn, 'The *enceinte* wall of Quarr Abbey', *Fort* 8 (1980), pp5–6.

3 D F Renn, 'The Southampton Arcade', *Medieval Archaeology* 8 (1964), pp226–8.

4 J R Kenyon, 'Early artillery fortifications in England and Wales: a preliminary survey and reappraisal', *Archaeological Journal* 138 (1981), pp205–40; and J R Kenyon, 'Early gunports: a gazetteer', *Fort* 4 (1977), pp4–6.

5 *Cal Patent Rolls*, 1385–9, p123.

6 D Knoop *et al*, 'Some building activities of John, Lord Cobham', *Trans Quattuor Coronati Lodge* 45,1 (1932), pp48–53.

7 A D Saunders, 'The Cow Tower, Norwich: an East Anglian Bastille?', *Medieval Archaeology* 29 (1985), pp109–119.

8 F Taylor and J S Roskell (eds), *Gesta Henrici Quinti* (Oxford 1975).

9 Pollard (1983), pp59–60.

10 John Gillingham, *The Wars of the Roses* (London 1981), p153.

11 C J Tabraham and G L Good, 'The artillery fortifications at Threave Castle, Galloway', in D H Caldwell (ed), *Scottish Weapons and Fortifications 1100–1800* (Edinburgh 1981), pp55–72.

12 A Emery, 'The development of Raglan Castle and keeps in late medieval England', *Archaeological Journal* 132 (1975), pp150–86.

13 A H Thompson (ed), 'The building accounts of Kirby Muxloe Castle, with introduction and notes', *Transaction of the Leicestershire Architectural and Archaeological Society* 11 (1913–20), pp193–345.

14 L T Smith, *The Itinerary of John Leland*, vol 2 (London 1908), p40.

15 Stewart Cruden, *The Scottish Castle* (Edinburgh 1960), p219.

16 B H St J O'Neil, 'Dartmouth Castle and other defences of Dartmouth Haven', *Archaeologia* 85 (1936), pp129–57.

17 R N Worth, *Calendar of the Plymouth municipal records* (Plymouth 1893), p97.

18 *Fifth Report of the Royal Commission on Historical Manuscripts* (London 1876), p492.

19 John de Waurin, *Chronicles*, 1447–71 (*Rolls Series*) (London 1891), pp385–8.

20 Worth (1893), pp89–90.

21 Iain MacIvor, 'Artillery and major places of strength in the Lothians and the East Border, 1513–1542', in D H Caldwell (ed), *Scottish Weapons and Fortifications 1100–1800* (Edinburgh 1981), pp119–122.

22 J R Hale, 'The early development of the bastion: an Italian chronology c1450–c1534', in J R Hale (ed), *Europe in the late Middle Ages* (London 1965), p484.

23 MacIvor (1981), pp107–19.

24 *Ibid*, pp124–6.

25 *Ibid*, p105.

26 J R Kenyon, 'Wark Castle and its artillery defences in the reign of Henry VIII,' *Post-Medieval Archaeology* 13 (1979), pp50–60.

27 H M Colvin (ed), *The History of the King's Works*, IV,1485–1660 (Part II), (London 1982), p417, and Kenyon (1981), p221.

28 Gillingham (1981), p27.

Chapter 2

1 Sir H Ellis (ed), *Hall's Chronicle* (1809), p829.

2 H M Colvin (ed), *The History of the King's Works*, IV, 1485–1660 (Part II), (London 1982), p369.

3 *L & P, For & Dom*, 1539 xiv (1), 770.

4 *Ibid*, xiv (1), 223–4.

5 *Ibid*, xiv (1), 223.

6 Colvin (1982), pp415–447.

7 *L & P, For & Dom*, 1539 xiv(1), 670.

8 G Owen, 'The Description of Milford Haven', *Cymmrodorion Record Series*, i (2), pp543–4, 547.

9 BL Cotton MS, Augustus I.i.35–6, 38–9.

10 *SP Henry VIII* v, p155 (*L & P* xv (1), 625).

11 J R Hale, 'The Defence of the Realm, 1485–1558', in Colvin (1982), p377.

12 Colvin (1982), pp415–447, and H Susan Ames, 'A note on the results of recent excavations at Camber Castle, Sussex', *Post-Medieval Archaeology* 11 (1975), p233.

13 Facsimile edition, Gregg International Publishers (1972) with introduction by Martin Biddle.

14 BL Harleian MS 353, 90, 'Charges of the Kings Warres . . .'.

15 WL Rutton, 'Sandgate Castle, AD 1539–40', *Archaeologia Cantiana* 20 (1893), pp228ff.

16 BL Cotton MS App XXVIII f19.

17 *L & P, For & Dom* xiv(2) 785.

18 *Cal SP Dom, Elizabeth I 1601–3* Add 329.

19 J R Hale, 'The Early Development of the Bastion: an Italian Chronology, c1450–c1534', in J R Hale (ed), *Europe in the Late Middle Ages* (London 1965), pp466–94; Quentin Hughes, *Military Architecture* (London 1974); J R Hale, *Renaissance Fortification: Art or Engineering?* (Norwich 1977).

20 Francesco di Giorgio, *Trattati di Architettura, Ingegneria e Arte Militare*, C Maltese (ed) (Milan 1967); Simon Pepper and Quentin Hughes, 'Fortification in late fifteenth century Italy: The Treatise of Francesco di Giorgio Martini', in H McK Blake, T W Potter, D B Whitehouse (eds), *Papers in Italian Archaeology* I, part ii, BAR Supplementary Series 41(II), (Oxford 1978).

21 Hale (1965), p473.

22 *The Ten Books on Architecture*, translated by M H Morgan (New York nd), p23.

23 Hale (1982), p387.

24 *Historical MSS Commission, Salisbury MSS* (1883), i, p49.

25 Staffs Co Record Office D1778/III/01, f8v.

26 Lynn White Jnr, 'Jacopo Aconcio as an Engineer', *American Historical Review* 72, 1966–7, p425.

Chapter 3

1 J R Hale (1977); Horst de la Croix, *Military Considerations in City Planning: Fortifications* (1972).

2 J R Hale (1977) and, for a contrary view, John Bury 'Are renaissance fortifications beautiful?', *Fort* 8 (1980), pp7–20.

3 S E Rigold, *Yarmouth Castle, Isle of Wight*, Ministry of Works (English Heritage) Official Guide, (1959).

4 A D Saunders, 'The Building of Upnor Castle, 1559–1601', in M R Apted, R Gilard-Beer & A D Saunders (eds), *Ancient Monuments and Their Interpretation* (1977), pp263–84.

5 *Cal SP Dom Eliz*, 1601–3, p162, 58 (14 March 1602).

6 A D Saunders, 'Harry's Walls, St Mary's, Scilly: a new interpreta-

tion', *Cornish Archaeology* 1 (1962), pp85–91.

7 T J Miles and A D Saunders, 'King Charles's Castle, Tresco, Scilly', *Post-Medieval Archaeology* 4 (1970), pp1–30.

8 N V Quinnell, 'A sixteenth century outwork to King Charles's Castle, Tresco', *Cornish Archaeology* 17 (1978), pp142–3.

9 Marcus Merriman and John Summerson, 'The Scottish Border' in H M Colvin (ed), *The History of the King's Works*, IV, 1485–1660 (Part II) (London 1982), pp607–726.

10 *Ibid*, p719, *Correspondence politique de Odet de Selve*, p366.

11 *Ibid*, p725.

12 *Ibid* pp613–664; Iain MacIvor, 'The Elizabethan fortifications of Berwick-upon-Tweed', *Antiquaries Journal* xlv(1965) and *Fortifications of Berwick-upon-Tweed* (1967), HMSO.

13 H M Colvin (ed), *The History of the King's Works*, IV, 1485–1660 (Part II), (London 1982), pp488–527.

14 Frank McLynn, *Invasion From the Armada to Hitler 1588–1945* (1987), p24.

15 C J Young (forthcoming).

16 Paul Ive, *The Practice of Fortification* (1589, reprinted by Gregg International Publishers with introduction by Martin Biddle 1972).

17 *Ibid*, pp12–13.

18 H M Colvin (1982), p533.

19 *Ibid*, pp522–3; BL Lansdowne MS 116, ff65–6.

20 James Sheriffe's 'Table of English Ordnance', 1592; Oliver F G Hogg, *English Artillery 1326–1716* (London 1963), p26; M Lewis, *Armada Guns* (London 1962).

21 Paul M Kerrigan, 'Seventeenth century fortifications, forts and garrisons in Ireland: a preliminary list', *The Irish Sword* XIV, No 54 (1980), p3; M D O'Sullivan, 'The Fortifications of Galway', *Journal of the Galway Archaeological and Historical Society* xvi (1934–5), pp1–47.

22 Maurice Craig, *The Architecture of Ireland: From the earliest times to 1880* (London 1982), and 'Portumna Castle', *gatherum* 7 (Dublin 1976).

23 H M Colvin (1982), pp471–2; Charles Trollope, *The Defences of Harwich*, reprinted from *Fort* 11 (1983), pp5–30.

Chapter 4

1 Joshua Sprigge, *Anglia Rediviva, Englands' Recovery* (London 1647), p130.

2 Lupton, *Warlike Treatise of the Pike* (1642), p131.

3 Christopher Duffy, *Siege Warfare: the Fortress in the Early Modern World* (London 1979), p145.

4 Robert Ward, *Animadversions of War* (1639), Bk I, p72.

5 Simon Stevin, *La Castramentation* (Leyden 1618), and *Nouvelle Maniere de Fortification par escluses* (Leyden 1618); Samuel Marolois, *Fortification ou architecture militaire tant offensive que defensive* (The Hague 1615); Adam Freitag, *Architectura Militaris Nova et Aucta oder Neue Vermehrte Fortification* (Leyden 1630).

6 Duffy (1979), p91.

7 Mrs Lucy Hutchinson, *Memoirs of the Life of Colonel Hutchinson* (London 1904), p215.

8 Joshua Sprigge (1647), p84.

9 Lieutenant-Colonel W G Ross, *Military Engineering during the Great Civil War, 1642–9* (1887, reprinted London 1984), pp29–30.

10 *Ibid* pp22–7.

11 Sprigge (1647), p14.

12 C H Firth, *Cromwell's Army* (1902, reprinted London 1962), pp 165–6.

13 MS at Rockingham Castle.

14 Sprigge (1647), p167.

15 A Kemp, 'The fortifications of Oxford during the Civil War', *Oxoniensia* 42 (1977), pp237–46; F J Varley, *The Siege of Oxford* (Oxford 1952).

16 Ross (1887), Appendix A.

17 Royal Commission on Historical Monuments (England), *Newark on Trent: The Civil War Siegeworks* (London 1964).

18 Ross (1887), pp58–62, 66–9; Patrick McGrath, *Bristol and the Civil War* (Bristol 1981).

19 Sprigge (1647), pp94–118.

20 Hutchinson (1904), p282.

21 Sprigge (1647), p130.

22 Royal Commission on Historical Monuments (England) (1964).

23 B H St J O'Neil, *Castles and Cannon* (Oxford 1960), pp108–10.

24 *Ibid* p 106–7.

25 *Ibid* p110.

26 PRO, SP Dom, Ch I, ccclxviii, 110 (30 September 1637).

27 *Mercurius Politicus* (8 May–15 May 1651).

28 Colonel Courtenay Vyvyan, 'Defence of the Helford River, 1643–46', *Journal of the Royal Institution of Cornwall* XVIII, pt 1 (1910).

Chapter 5

1 E S de Beer (ed) *The Diary of John Evelyn* (Oxford 1955), III, p486.

2 Henry B Wheatley (ed) *The Diary of Samuel Pepys* (London 1895), VI, p404–5.

3 Menno van Coehorn, *Nieuwe vestingbouw op een natte of lage horisont* (Leeuwarden 1685), translated by T Savery as *The New Method of Fortification* (London 1705).

4 Lt-Col W G Ross, *Military Engineering during the Great Civil War 1642–9* (1887), p30; *Dictionary of National Biography*; H M Colvin, *A Biographical Dictionary of English Architects 1660–1840* (London 1954), p240.

5 Samuel Pepys, *Naval Minutes*, J R Tanner (ed), Navy Records Society (London 1926), p28.

6 *Ibid*, p205.

7 Howard Tomlinson, 'The Ordnance Office and the King's forts, 1660–1714', *Architectural History* 16 (1973) p13; Staffs RO, D 1778, 1.i 1077.

8 *Ibid* p19; Staffs RO, D 1778, I.i 591 & 1077.

9 G H Williams, *The Western Defences of Portsmouth Harbour 1400–1800* (Portsmouth 1979), p17; MS House of Lords, III(NS), 1965, pp305–6.

10 SP Dom Chas II, cxxxvii, 22 (17 November 1665); F W Woodward, *Citadel* (Exeter, 1987), p24.

11 PRO E 3512/3608.

12 PRO WO 30/57.

13 Staffs RO, D 1778, V 4.

14 A D Saunders, 'Tilbury Fort and the development of artillery fortification in the Thames Estuary', *Antiquaries Journal* xl (1960), pp152–174.

15 Patricia M Wilkinson, 'Excavations at Tilbury Fort, Essex', *Post-Medieval Archaeology* 17 (1983), pp111–162.

16 Howard Tomlinson (1973), and *Guns and Government* (London 1979).

17 Whitworth Porter, *History of the Corps of Royal Engineers* I (London 1889), pp49–50.

18 *Ibid*, p50.

19 Howard Tomlinson (1979), p43.

20 G H Williams (1979), p17; PRO SP 29/401(65).

21 A D Saunders (1960).

22 John Evelyn, *Diary*, III, 609, (21 March 1672).

23 Howard Tomlinson (1973), p13; Sir Jonas Moore, *Modern Fortification or Elements of Military Architecture* (1673), p73.

24 John Childs, *The Army of Charles II* (London 1976), p230.

25 C H Firth, *Cromwell's Army* (1962 ed), p176n.

26 Howard Tomlinson (1973), p11; PRO SP 32/11, ff318–9.

Chapter 6

1 Quoted by D M Waterman in 'Some Irish Seventeenth Century Houses and their Architectural Ancestry', in E M Jope (ed), *Studies in Building History* (London 1961), p251.

2 Paul M Kerrigan, 'Seventeenth century fortifications, forts and garrisons in Ireland: a preliminary list', *The Irish Sword* XIV (1980), pp3–24.

3 A A Tait, 'The Protectorate Citadels of Scotland', *Architectural History* VIII (1965), p9.

4 *Ibid*.

5 *Cal SP Ireland 1666–69* (April 1666).

6 Paul M Kerrigan, 'Charles Fort, Kinsale', *The Irish Sword* XIII (1978–9), pp323–338.

7 *Ibid*, p330, National Library of Ireland MS 3137, Report on the principal fortifications and harbours in Ireland by Thomas Phillips.

8 Stewart Cruden, *The Scottish Castle* (Edinburgh 1960), p236, Report of the Committee anent this peace off the Highlands, 1699.

9 *Ibid*, pp234–8; G Stell 'Highland Garrisons, 1717–23: Bernera Barracks', *Post-Medieval Archaeology* 7 (1983), p185.

10 *Ibid*, pl 46, plan in National Library of Scotland.

11 *Ibid*, p237, W J Allardyce, *Historical Papers relating to the Jacobite Period 1699–1750* (Aberdeen 1895–6).

12 *Ibid*, p237, King's Warrant Book.

13 Iain MacIvor, *Fort George*, HMSO Guidebook (Edinburgh 1970), p11.

14 *Ibid*; Iain MacIvor, 'Fort George, Inverness-shire I & II', *Country Life* (12 & 19 August 1976).

15 Louis de Cormontaigne, *L'Architecture militaire, ou l'Art de fortifier* (The Hague 1741).

Chapter 7

1 Howard Tomlinson, 'The Ordnance Office and the King's forts, 1660–1714', *Architectural History* 16 (1973), p8, PRO WO 46/5, p101.

2 *Ibid*, p8, PRO WO 47/18, p57.

3 G H Williams, *The Western Defences of Portsmouth Harbour, 1400–1800* (Portsmouth 1979), p18, PRO WO 55/1548/10.

4 Talbot Edwards's report and estimates, 14 August 1708; PRO WO 55/1548/10.

5 J H Leslie, *The History of Landguard Fort in Suffolk* (London 1898); Charles Trollope, 'The defences of Harwich', *Fort* 11 (1983), pp5–30; D A Wood, *Landguard Fort: Felixstowe* (Felixstowe 1983).

6 Christian Lilly's report on the south west district, BL King's MS 45, reports, 1714–17.

7 Whitworth Porter, *History of the Corps of Royal Engineers* (London 1889), 1, pp141–2.

8 BL King's MS 45.

9 PRO SP 41/38.

10 *Ibid*.

11 Rex Whitworth, *Field Marshal Lord Ligonier* (Oxford 1958).

12 J R E Hamilton-Baillie, 'The Fixed Fortifications of the Sixteenth to Nineteenth Centuries Illustrated by the Defences of Chatham', *The Royal Engineers Journal* LXXXVIII, 1 (1974), pp2–14; Keith Gulvin, *Fort Amherst: a brief history and guide* (Maidstone, no date).

13 Woolwich, G3N 177, 73–74.

14 V T C Smith, 'The Artillery Defences at Gravesend', *Archaeologia Cantiana* LXXXIX (1974), pp141–168.

15 Keith Gulvin *(Fort Amherst)*.

16 G H Williams (1979), p44.

17 *Ibid*, pp44–60.

18 M M Oppenheim, *The Maritime History of Devon* (Exeter 1968), p94.

19 J G Coad and P N Lewis, 'The later fortifications of Dover', *Post-Medieval Archaeology* 16 (1982), pp141–200.

20 H R S Pocock, 'Jersey's Martello Towers', *Bulletin of the Société Jersaise* 20, pt 3 (1971), pp289–298.

21 *Ibid*, p290.

22 Information from Howard Tomlinson.

23 William Cobbett, *Parliamentary History of England from the Earliest Period to the Year 1806*, XXV, pp1096&1157.

24 *Ibid*.

Chapter 8

1 E H Stuart Jones, *The Last Invasion of Britain* (Cardiff 1950).

2 J Holland Rose and A M Broadley, *Dumouriez and the Defence of England against Napoleon* (London 1909).

3 Richard Glover, *Britain at Bay: Defence against Bonaparte, 1803–14* (London 1973); Report of the Duke of York to the Secretary of State (25 August 1803), PRO WO 30/76, pp106–203.

4 Sir David Dundas's report (February 1798), PRO WO 30/68, pp1–72.

5 Christopher Duffy, *The Fortress in the Age of Vauban and Frederick the Great 1660–1879: Siege Warfare II* (London 1985), p161.

6 *Ibid*, p154.

7 Sir George Sydenham Clarke, *Fortification: its Past Achievements, Recent Development, and Future Progress* (London 1907), pp6–7.

8 V T C Smith, 'The Artillery Defences at Gravesend', *Archaeologia Cantiana* LXXXIX (1974), pp158–161, and *Defending London's River* (Rochester 1985); A D Saunders, 'Tilbury Fort and the Development of Artillery Fortification in the Thames Estuary', *Antiquaries Journal* XL (1960), pp152–174.

9 J G Coad, 'Hurst Castle: the evolution of a Tudor fortress 1790–1945', *Post-Medieval Archaeology* 19 (1985), pp63–104.

10 Edward C Harris, 'Archaeological Investigations at Sandgate Castle, Kent, 1976–9', *Post-Medieval Archaeology* 14 (1980), pp53–88.

11 J G Coad and P N Lewis, 'The later fortifications of Dover', *Post-Medieval Archaeology* 16 (1982), pp141–200.

12 *Ibid*, pp153–4, PRO WO 30/68.

13 *Ibid*, p160, PRO WO 55/778, Twiss to Dundas, 17 July 1803.

14 *Ibid*, pp163–5.

15 PRO WO 30/64, pp67–76.

16 PRO WO 30/68, pp97–107.

17 S G P Ward, 'Defence Works in Britain, 1803–1805', *Journal of the Society for Army Historical Research* 27 (1949), pp18ff.

18 *Ibid*, PRO WO 55/778; B K Pegden, 'The purchase of bricks for Martello Towers in the year 1804', *Fort* 8 (1980), pp55–60.

19 *Ibid*; Commander Hilary P Mead, 'The Martello Towers of England', *The Mariner's Mirror* [Journal of the Society for Nautical Research] 34 (1948), pp205–17, 294–303; Sheila Sutcliffe, *Martello Towers* (Newton Abbot 1972).

20 Kenneth Walker, 'Martello Towers and the Defence of North East Essex in the Napoleonic Wars', *Essex Review* 47 (1938), pp171–185.

21 P A L Vine, *The Royal Military Canal* (London 1972); Richard Glover (1973), pp119–122.

22 Richard Glover (1973), pp111–114; PRO WO 30/56, pp147–150, WO 30/76 p308, WO 1/628 pp643–4.

23 V T C Smith, 'The Later Nineteenth Century Land Defences of Chatham', *Post-Medieval Archaeology* 10 (1976), pp104–117.

24 Paul M Kerrigan, 'The Defences of Ireland 1793–1815, 4 – The Dublin Area and Wicklow Mountains', *An Cosantoir: The Irish Defence Journal* (August 1974), pp285–290.

25 Paul M Kerrigan, 'Defences of Ireland, Part 15, Naval and Military Aspects (1793 to 1815) and General', *An Cosantoir: The Irish Defence Journal* (May 1983), pp142–9; Correspondence of Napoleon, 29 September 1804.

26 Lieutenant-General Sir Henry Sheehy Keating [then (1795) Lieutenant Keating], *On the Defence of Ireland* (Dublin 1860).

27 Memorandum by Sir Alexander Hope (13 November 1801), Murray Papers, 6 ff1–60, PRO WO 25/3247.

28 Paul M Kerrigan, 'The Defences of Ireland 1793–1815, 3 – The Signal Towers', *An Cosantoir: The Irish Defence Journal* (July 1974), pp225–227.

29 Paul M Kerrigan, 'The Defences of Ireland 1793–1815, 2 – The Martello Towers', '5 – Shannon Estuary', '6 – The Shannon – Portumna to Shannon Harbour', '10 – Cork Harbour and Kinsale', *An Cosantoir: The Irish Defence Journal* (May 1974), pp148–9, (September 1974), pp310–314, (February 1975), pp59–63, (May 1978), pp145–150; Victor J Enoch, *The Martello Towers of Ireland* (Dublin no date).

30 Paul M Kerrigan, 'The Shannonbridge Fortifications', *The Irish Sword* XI (1973–4), pp234–245. 'The Defences of the Shannon: Portumna to Athlone, 1793–1815', in Harman Murtagh (ed), *Irish Midland Studies: Essays in commemoration of N W English* (1980), pp168–192.

31 Paul M Kerrigan, 'The Batteries, Athlone', *Journal of the Old Athlone Society* 1, No 4 (1974–5), pp264–270.

32 William Davies, *Fort Regent* (St Helier 1971).

33 H R S Pocock, 'Jersey's Martello Towers', *Bulletin of the Société Jersaise* 20, part 3 (1971), pp289–298.

34 M S Partridge, 'The Defence of the Channel Islands, 1814–1870', *Journal of Army Historical Research* LXIV, No 257 (1986), pp34–42; John Winkworth, 'Alderney's run-down batteries', *Alderney Society and Museum Quarterly Bulletin* (March 1971).

35 G Forrester Matthews, *The Isles of Scilly* (London 1960), p98; PRO WO 1/626, 12 October 1803.

36 R P Fereday, *The Longhope Battery and Towers* (Stromness 1971).

Chapter 9

1 Richard Cobden, 'The Three Panics', *Political Writings*, vol 2 (London 1868), p23; Hansard LXXXII col 1223.

2 Ian V Hogg, *A History of Artillery* (Feltham 1974), p72.

3 G Wrottesley (ed), *The Military Opinions of General Sir John Fox Burgoyne* (London 1859), pp1–23.

4 G Wrottesley, *Life and Correspondence of Field Marshal Sir John Burgoyne* (London 1873), I, pp435–451.

5 Theodore Martin, *The Life of His Highness the Prince Consort* (5th ed, London 1879), 4, pp117, 122, 267, 19 July 1858.

6 'Memoir on the Fortifications in Western Germany, compiled from various sources', *Professional Papers of the Corps of Royal Engineers*, II (1844), pp51.

7 Francois, Marquis de Chasseloup-Lambat, *Extraite de memories sur queleues parties de l'Artillerie et des Fortifications* (Paris 1805).

8 J Corréard Jeune (ed), *La Defense*, (Paris 1837).

9 Quentin Hughes, *Military Architecture* (London 1974), pp168–170.

10 'Memoir on the Polygonal Fortification constructed in Germany since 1815 by A Mangin', translated by Captain J Williams, *Professional Papers of the Corps of Royal Engineers*, NS III (1853), p167.

11 Quentin Hughes (1974), p183.

12 Emanuel Raymond Lewis, *Seacoast Fortifications of the United States: An Introductory History* (Washington DC 1970); Willard B Robinson, *American Forts: Architectural Form and Function* (Fort Worth 1977).

13 Quentin Hughes (1974), p178.

14 General Sir Howard Douglas, *Observations on Modern Systems of Fortification including that proposed by M Carnot . . .* (London 1859).

15 Colonel Lewis, 'Report on the Application of Forts, Towers, and Batteries to Coast Defences and Harbours', *Professional Papers of the Corps of Royal Engineers*, VII (1845), pp185ff.

16 Major-General Sir John Burgoyne, 'Coast Batteries', *Corps of Royal Engineers, Papers and Memoirs on Military Subjects*, I (1849–50), p1ff.

17 Sir John Fox Burgoyne, Inspector-General of Fortifications, 'Memorandum on the probable effect of the Rifled Cannon on the Attack and Defence of Fortifications' (1855), PRO WO 33/7, p112.

18 *Ibid.*

19 Colonel Lewis (1845).

20 James Fergusson, *An Essay on a Proposed New System of Fortifications with hints for its application to our National Defences* (London 1849).

21 Lieutenant-General Thackeray, 'Remarks on Fortification with reference to the Defence of the United Kingdom', *Professional Papers of the Corps of Royal Engineers*, NS I (1851), p96ff.

22 A D Saunders, 'Tilbury Fort and the Development of Artillery Fortification in the Thames Estuary', *Antiquaries Journal* XL (1960), p167; V T C Smith, *Defending London's River: The Story of the Thames Forts 1540–1945* (Rochester 1985), pp21–2.

23 Plan for projected breakwaters in Braye Bay and Port Longy referred to in Mr Walker's Report (8 October 1849) PRO WO 55/815, MPHH 679; Colonel Ward's plan for Grosnez PRO MPHH 679; Burgoyne's proposals (20 May 1852) PRO WO 55/816; T G Davenport & C W Partridge, 'The Victorian fortification of Alderney', *Fort* 8 (1980), pp21–46 and Supplement on Alderney in *Fort* 8.

24 C Vallaux, 'L'Archipel de la Manche' (1913), quoted by C E B Brett, *Buildings of the Island of Alderney* (Belfast 1976).

25 James Fergusson, *Portsmouth Protected: A sequel to the Peril of Portsmouth with notes on Sebastopol and other sieges during the present war* (London 1856).

26 J G Coad, 'Hurst Castle: the evolution of a Tudor fortress 1790–1945', *Post-Medieval Archaeology* 19 (1985), pp76–84.

27 F G Aldsworth, 'A Description of the Mid-Nineteenth Century Forts at Littlehampton and Shoreham, West Sussex', *Sussex Archaeological Collections* 119 (1981), pp181–194.

28 Major W D Jervois, Report to Accompany the Project for the Defences of Portsmouth (5 December 1857), Appendix to the Report of the Royal Commission on the Defences of the United Kingdom (1860); Garry Mitchell, *Hilsea Lines and Portsbridge*, Solent Papers No 4 (West Wickham 1988).

29 Major W D Jervois, Assistant Inspector-General of Fortifications (26 February 1858), Memorandum on the Defences proposed for the protection of the Naval Arsenal at Devonport and Plymouth, Appendix to the Royal Commission on the Defences of the United Kingdom Report (1860).

30 Report of the Committee on the Sea Defences of Milford Haven and Pembroke Dockyard (16 December 1858), Appendix to the Royal Commission on the Defences of the United Kingdom Report (1860).

31 Appendix to Report of the Royal Commission on the Defences of the United Kingdom (1860).

32 PRO WO 33/7, p115.

33 Major Jervois, 'Observations relating to the works in progress and proposed for the defence of the Naval Ports, Arsenals and Dockyards', *Professional Papers of the Corps of Royal Engineers* NS IX (1860), pp129ff.

34 A D Saunders, 'Hampshire Coastal Defence since the Introduction of Artillery', *Archaeological Journal* CXXIII (1967), pp150–1.

35 A D Saunders, 'Harbour Fortresses of a Century Ago', *Country Life* (4 May 1961), pp1040–2, and 'Popton Fort', *Archaeological Journal* CXIX (1962), pp345–7.

Chapter 10

1 A D Saunders, ' "Palmerston's Follies" – A Centenary', *Journal of the Royal Artillery* LXXXVII, No 3 (1960), pp138–144; Hansard (29 July 1859) 3.S. vol 155 p676.

2 The Report of the Commissioners appointed to consider the Defences of the United Kingdom, together with the Minutes of Evidence, Appendices and correspondence relating to the site of an internal arsenal (22 August 1859).

3 The defence works around Portland Bay were designed in 1857 as a result of the French initiative in fortifying Cherbourg on a grand scale. The ditch of the Verne citadel was started as early as 1848, since stone was needed for the construction of the breakwater for the new Portland harbour. E A Andrews & M L Pinsent, 'The coastal defences of Portland and Weymouth', *Fort* 9, Supplement (1981), pp4–43.

4 Hansard (2 August 1860), 3.S.vol 160, p486.

5 Philip Guedalla, *Gladstone and Palmerston* (London 1928), p58.

6 Whitworth Porter, *History of the Corps of Royal Engineers* (London 1889), II, pp221–2. A general description of the principles, designs and construction of the Royal Commission forts can be found in Lieutenant-Colonel Philips, *Elementary Course on Field and Permanent Fortification and of the Attack of Fortresses* (London 1879).

7 Lieutenant-Colonel Jervois RE, CB, Deputy Director of Fortifications, Report with Reference to the Progress made in the construction of the Fortifications for the Defence of the Dockyards and Naval Arsenals etc of the United Kingdom, War Office (19 February 1867); Quentin Hughes, 'Letters from the Defence Committee in 1861', *Fort* 8 (1980), pp71–102.

8 G Wrottesley, *Life and Correspondence of Field Marshal Sir John Burgoyne*, 2 vols (London 1873).

9 Report of the Committee appointed to enquire into the construction, condition and cost of the fortifications erected, under 30th and 31st Victoria and previous statutes (1869).

10 Ian V Hogg, *Coast Defences of England and Wales 1856–1956* (Newton Abbot 1974), pp61–3.

11 A D Saunders, 'Hampshire Coastal Defence since the Introduction of Artillery with a description of Fort Wallington', *Archaeological Journal* CXXIII (1967), pp136–171. See also Gary Mitchell & Peter Cobb, *Fort Nelson and the Portsdown Forts*, Solent Papers No 3 (West Wickham 1987).

12 CRE statements on Armaments in the Portsea sub-district, Isle of Wight sub-district and Gosport sub-district (c1891–3).

13 Theodore Choumara, *Memoires sur la Fortification* (1827). Choumara's principles were strongly recommended by A F Lendy.

14 J G Coad, 'Hurst Castle: the evolution of a Tudor fortress 1790–1945', *Post-Medieval Archaeology* 19 (1985), pp63–104; Jude James, *Hurst Castle: An Illustrated History* (Wimborne 1986).

15 Ian V Hogg (1974), pp127–135; Garry Mitchell with Anthony Cantwell, Peter Cobb & Peter Sprack, *Spitbank and the Spithead Forts* (West Wickham 1986).

16 Whitworth Porter (1889), p223.

17 Colonel Cunliffe Owen, 'Fortification versus Forts or Remarks on the Relative Advantages of Continuous and Detached Lines of Works', *Professional Papers of the Corps of Royal Engineers* NS XII (1863), p165.

18 Captain J J Wilson, 'On Detached Works versus Continuous Lines', *Professional Papers of the Corps of Royal Engineers* NS XII (1863), p185.

19 Todleben's observations, PRO WO 55/1548; Quentin Hughes, 'Russian Views on the English Defences in 1864', *Fort* 7 (1979), pp69–79.

20 *Ibid*. Jervois was in Canada at the time of Todleben's visit and subsequently added technical comments in the margin of the report on the visit.

21 G Sydenham Clarke, *Fortification* (London 1907), p75.

22 Captain E F Ducane, 'Fortification in Iron', *Professional Papers of the Corps of Royal Engineers* NS XII (1863), p11; W D Jervois, 'Coast Defences and the application of iron to fortification', *Journal of the Royal United Services Institution* XII (1868)

23 Charles Trollope, 'The defences of Harwich', *Fort* 11 (1983), pp5–30.

24 J H Barrett, *A History of Maritime Forts in the Bristol Channel 1866–1900* (privately published, no date); Margaret Pinsent, 'The defences of the Bristol Channel in the last two centuries', *Fort* 11(1983), pp63–76.

25 R J Goulden and A Kemp, *New-haven and Seaford Coastal Fortifications* (1974), quoting Mark Lower's *History of Sussex*.

26 Andrew Porter, 'Concrete in nineteenth century fortifications constructed by the Royal Engineers', *Fort* 9 (1981), p31.

27 G Sydenham Clarke (1907), p263.

28 Von Scheliha, *A Treatise on Coast Defence* (London 1868).

29 W D Jervois, Report of Progress in the Construction of the Fortifications for the Defence of the Dockyards, Naval Arsenals etc in the United Kingdom (February 1874), PRO WO 33/26.

30 *Ibid*; James Phinney Baxter 3rd, *The Introduction of the Ironclad Warship* (Harvard 1968).

31 W D Jervois (1874).

32 A F Lendy, *Treatise on Fortifications or Lectures delivered to Officers reading for the Staff* (London 1862).

33 Hansard (2 August 1860), 3.S vol 160, p480.

34 Henri Alexis Brialmont, *Progrès de la défense des Etats et de la Fortification permanente depuis Vauban* (Brussels 1898).

Chapter 11

1 I F Clarke, 'The Battle of Dorking 1871–1914', *Victorian Studies* VIII, No 4 (1965), pp309–71.

2 J C R Columb, *The Protection of our Commerce and Distribution of our Naval Forces Considered* (London 1867).

3 Sir E B Hamley, *The Operations of War Explained and Illustrated* (Edinburgh 1889).

4 J K Dunlop, *The Development of the British Army 1899–1914* (London 1938), pp12–14.

5 Report of the Committee appointed to enquire into the Defence of Mercantile Ports (1882).

6 *Handbook for the London Defence Positions* (War Office 1903).

7 R H Brade to Sir Charles Ottley (14 June 1909), PRO Cab 3/2/3/45A.

8 'A Naval Base in the Scilly Isles', *The Navy and Army Illustrated* (12 October 1901), p90.

9 PRO Cab 3/2/1/44A.

10 Attack on the British Isles from Overseas: Report of Standing Committee (15 April 1914), PRO Cab 3/2/5/62A.

11 V T C Smith, 'Chatham and London: the changing face of English land fortification, 1870–1918', *Post-Medieval Archaeology* 19 (1985), pp105–149; RE Corps Library, Plan 420/SE/1/0001.

12 Rupert Furneaux, *The Siege of Plevna* (London 1958).

13 Captain J F Lewis, 'Permanent Fortification', *Professional Papers of the Corps of Royal Engineers* VII (1882), p12.

14 Whitworth Porter, *History of the Corps of Royal Engineers* (London 1889), II, pp224–5.

15 G Sydenham Clarke, *Fortification* (London 1907), pp81–101; Quentin Hughes, *Military Architecture* (London 1974); Ian V Hogg, *Fortress: A History of Military Defence* (London 1975).

16 Major E M Lloyd, 'On the Forts of Today', *Journal of the Royal United Services Institution* XXVI (1883), pp164–79.

17 A D Saunders, 'The Defences of the Firth of Forth', in *Studies in Scottish Antiquity* (Edinburgh 1984), pp469–480; V T C Smith, 'Defending the Forth: 1880–1910', *Fort* 13 (1985), pp89–102.

18 J G Coad and P N Lewis, 'The later fortifications of Dover', *Post-Medieval Archaeology* 16 (1982), pp192–6; David Burridge, *The Dover Turret, Admiralty Pier Fort* (Rochester 1987).

19 G Sydenham Clarke (1907), pp241 & 243.

20 Ian V Hogg, *A History of Artillery* (Feltham 1974).

21 V T C Smith, *Defending London's River: The Story of the Thames Forts 1540–1945* (Rochester 1985), pp31–33.

22 J G Coad, *Calshot Castle*, English Heritage Handbook (1986).

23 W David McIntyre, *The Rise and Fall of the Singapore Naval Base* (London 1979).

24 V T C Smith (1985), and 'The Later Nineteenth Century Land Defences of Chatham', *Post-Medieval Archaeology* 10 (1976), pp104–117.

25 PRO WO 33/46/A65.

26 V T C Smith (1985); Keith Gulvin and Quentin Hughes, 'Twydall profile', *Fort* 5 (1978), pp39–43.

27 PRO WO 33/46.

28 Quentin Hughes (1974), pp226–30.

29 V T C Smith, 'The London Mobilisation Centres', *The London Archaeologist* (Spring 1975), and (1985 *op cit*); Colonel Shafto Adair, 'The Defence of London', *Journal of the Royal United Services Institution* IV (1861), pp291–310, and 'The Lines of London', *ibid* VI (1863), pp521–538.

30 Major H Elsdale, 'The Defence of London and of England', *Journal of the Royal United Services Institution* XXX (1886), pp601–670.

31 V T C Smith (1985), p128; L B Timmis, notes on the History of the Old Fort (Halstead) and the London Defence Positions (1957), generously given to the writer.

32 A D Saunders (1984); V T C Smith (1985).

33 Report of the Committee appointed to enquire into the Defence of Mercantile Ports (1882).

34 G K Scott Moncrieff, A Summary of the Policy and Work of Coast Fortification in Great Britain during the past 60 years (March 1918), PRO WO 32/5528.

35 PRO WO 55/718.

36 PRO Cab 13/1.

37 G K Scott Moncrieff (1918).

38 *Ibid.*

39 Major J C Matheson, 'RE Siege and Fortress Units with reference to fortress warfare', *Professional Papers of the Corps of Royal Engineers* 4th series (Chatham 1912).

40 G K Scott Moncrieff (1918).

Chapter 12

1 J R E Hamilton-Baillie, 'The coast defences of Orkney in two world wars', *Fort* 9 (1981), pp21–30; W S Hewison, *This Great Harbour Scapa Flow* (Stromness 1985).

2 Charles Trollope, 'The defences of Harwich', *Fort* 11 (1983), p24; G K Scott Moncrieff, A Summary of the Policy and Work of Coast Fortification in Great Britain during the past 60 years (March 1918), PRO WO 32/5528.

3 G K Scott Moncrieff (1918).

4 *Ibid*; R Hogg, 'The Tyne turrets: coastal defence in the First World War', *Fort* 12 (1984), pp97–104.

5 A D Saunders, 'The Defences of the Firth of Forth', in *Studies in Scottish Antiquity* (Edinburgh 1984), pp469–480; Norman H Clark, 'Twentieth century coastal defence of the Firth of Forth', *Fort* 14 (1986), pp49–54.

6   Lord Hankey, *The Supreme Command 1914–1918* (London 1960), I, p218.

7   V T C Smith, 'Chatham and London: the changing face of English land fortification, 1870–1918', *Post-Medieval Archaeology* 19 (1985), pp143–5.

8   Keith Mallory and Arvid Ottar, *Architecture of Aggression: a history of military architecture in North West Europe 1900–1945* (London 1973), p65.

9   Henry Wills, *Pillboxes: A Study of UK Defences 1940* (London 1985), p2.

10 Anthony Kemp, *The Maginot Line: myth and reality* (London 1981).

11 Quentin Hughes, *Military Architecture* (London 1974), p235.

12 Special Committee on Coast Defence Requirements: Interim Report Part III (10 October 1929), p3, PRO WO 33/1201/3.

13 Andrew Graham, 'It was all done with mirrors: A 1920s experiment in sound detection', *Country Life* (4 December 1986), p1820.

14 W S Churchill, *The Second World War* (London 1948–54), II, p155.

15 *War Office Manual of Coast Defence (Provisional)* (1930).

16 Chiefs of Staff (40) 195 (meeting of 26 June 1940), PRO Cab 79/5.

17 Henry Wills (1985), p20–21.

18 Frank McLynn, *Invasion From the Armada to Hitler 1588–1945* (London 1987).

19 Henry Wills (1985).

20 Colin Partridge, *Hitler's Atlantic Wall* (Guernsey, 1976).

GAZETTEER

There are many fortifications across Britain and Ireland which are opened and displayed to the public by national institutions, local authorities or private individuals and preservation trusts. Included with these in this gazetteer are those fortifications which are available for inspection by appointment; together with others where there is no restriction on entry, and whose interior is accessible. Not listed are those which are in private grounds.

The fortifications listed below are, or have recently been, open to the public, but it is impossible to guarantee that they will be available at the time of visit. Inevitably there will be omissions from this list since, with increasing interest in the subject, more and more former defensive works are becoming cared for and displayed.

Opening hours or admission fees are not given since these are usually subject to frequent revision.

Channel Islands

In the three main islands there are many small forts, batteries, towers and other defensive works around the coastline which can easily be appreciated and, in some instances have descriptive labelling.

Alderney

Fort Clonque
Coastal fort for ten guns of the mid-1850s designed by Jervois on the west side of island.
Landmark Trust (by appointment).

Guernsey

Castle Cornet
Medieval castle reconstructed in the sixteenth century as an irregular bastioned artillery fort. Built on an isolated rock and defended the town and harbour of St Peter Port. Much of the medieval core was destroyed in 1672 when lightning ignited the powder magazine; after repair it remained an active fortification into the nineteenth century.
States of Guernsey.

Fort Grey, Rocquaine
Circular battery enclosing a round gun-tower, constructed in 1803.
States of Guernsey, now houses maritime museum.

Pezerie Battery
Small coastal battery on west side of island, of unusual plan, reformed in 1804 for three 18-pounders. Magazine intact and platforms complete.

Jersey

Elizabeth Castle
Built on an island south of St Helier. Original core is the 'Upper Ward', a small irregular, bastioned fort designed by Paul Ive 1594–1601. Enlarged in seventeenth century to present extent and remodelled by John Henry Bastide 1731–34. Considerable adaptation during German occupation of 1940–45. Bastioned lines, barracks, magazines etc.
Jersey Heritage Trust.

Kempt Tower, St Ouen's Bay
Gun-tower, similar in appearance to the English south coast Martello towers, behind a three-gun barbette battery. Built in 1834 as part of a series of towers and batteries commanding the long open beach. The Bay was re-fortified by the Germans 1940–45.
Jersey Heritage Trust.

Mont Orgueil Castle
Medieval castle above Gorey harbour. Adapted in fifteenth century for artillery but substantially remodelled 1537–50, with the addition of the Somerset Tower and the Great Rampire flanked by an *orillon* bastion. Castle superseded by Elizabeth Castle in seventeenth century.
Jersey Heritage Trust.

Fort Regent
Irregular bastioned fort on the hill above St Helier and built 1806–14 to the design of John Humphry. Superseded Elizabeth Castle as the principal military establishment on the island. Elaborate outworks on eastern side of hill together with a long sloping glacis. Interior now occupied by a leisure centre.

St Aubin's Fort
A tower was built on islet in St Aubin's Bay in 1542. Extended in seventeenth century and remodelled by John Bastide 1742, and again 1838–40. German casemates added 1940–45.
Water sports centre.

Victoria Tower
Built 1837 on heights above Anne Port Bay and as an advanced work for Mont Orgueil Castle. Circular gun-tower.
Jersey Heritage Trust.

England

Avon

Brandon Hill Fort, Bristol
Much eroded earthworks with bastioned trace, part of the Civil War defences of Bristol. Extends from the vicinity of the Cabot Tower to the Water Fort.

Berkshire

Donnington Castle
The gatehouse of the late fourteenth century castle survives and also the earthworks of the Civil War irregular bastioned outer defences added by the Royalist, Colonel Boys. Donnington was of very great strategic importance commanding the London to Bath road, and the road from Oxford to Portsmouth and the south coast.
English Heritage.

Buckinghamshire

Quarrendon
South east of Church Farm are remains of Civil War earthworks consisting of lines of entrenchments and four gun platforms.

Cambridgeshire

The Bulwark, Earith
Square earthwork fort with angle bastions at each corner and with a covered-way and glacis beyond the ditch. A Parliamentarian work between the Old and New Rivers guarding the approaches to Ely. Well preserved.

Horsey Hill Fort
A pentagonal earthwork with a bastion at each angle. Near Stanground, close to a bridge over the old River Nene carrying the main road to Peterborough. Well preserved.

Cornwall

Dennis Fort
On Dennis Head, St Anthony in Meneague, covering the entrance to the Helford river and Gillan harbour. Square earthwork with bastions, with outworks protecting the landward approach and a subsidiary battery towards the sea. Built in the Royalist interest c1643 by the Vyvyans.

Mount Edgecumbe or Barnpool Blockhouse
Small square stone blockhouse of two storeys of c1540 opposite Devil's Point controlling the entrance to the Hamoaze. Cornwall County Council, in grounds of Mount Edgecumbe Park.

Pendennis Castle
Initial fortification of the late 1530s or 1540 on the headland on the west side of Falmouth Haven was the small blockhouse of Little Dennis at the waters-edge. Modified in 1540 when Henry VIII's Pendennis Castle begun. The latter consisted originally of a central circular gun-tower. The governor's lodging added to north side and later an outer polygonal curtain and gatehouse. Fortifications were greatly extended in an irregular bastioned trace by Paul Ive in 1597. Defences maintained and armed with 6-inch BLs in two world wars.
English Heritage.

Polruan Blockhouse
Two-storey, square masonry tower of the fifteenth century, protecting the Polruan end of a chain boom across Fowey harbour. Keyhole gunports on the upper floor. Ruins of the Fowey blockhouse opposite.
Polruan Town Trust.

St Catherine's Castle, Fowey
Small two-storey blockhouse on the headland at the entrance to Fowey Haven, built c1520 by Thomas Treffry and the townspeople.
English Heritage.

St Mawes Castle
As at Pendennis opposite, there are the remains of a small blockhouse at the waters-edge which preceded the main castle of the early 1540s. This is architecturally the most decorative of all Henry VIII's castles. In plan an 'ace of clubs' with a round tower rising above three round bastions. Batteries of the 1780s. Four 12-pounder QFs intended for the 1905 battery. Battery and searchlights maintained during the Second World War.
English Heritage.

Cumbria

Carlisle Castle
Major medieval Border castle adapted for artillery by Stephan von Haschenperg in 1541. Principal survival of this period is the Half-Moon Battery, a casemated ditch defence for the inner ward. Castle remained armed throughout the seventeenth to nineteenth centuries.
English Heritage.

Devon

Bayards Cove, Dartmouth
Small battery protected by a high wall and built 1509–10 to cover the entrance to the inner harbour.
English Heritage.

Berry Head Batteries, Torbay
Three extensive detached batteries erected in 1779 and armed with a total of twenty 20-pounders protected by an earthwork cutting off the headland.
Torbay District Council.

Berry Pomeroy Castle, near Totnes
The late fifteenth century gatehouse, curtain and the Margaret Tower at the south east angle of the medieval *enceinte* were built with artillery in mind. The gatehouse has small vertical slits for hand-guns and the roof was strengthened for heavy artillery. St Margaret's Tower has elaborate multi-purpose loops.
English Heritage.

Crownhill Fort, Plymouth
The centre and key of Plymouth's North Eastern defences built in the 1860s as a result of the 1859 Royal Commission. A little altered example of a land fort of the period with monumental architecture and impressive earthworks.
Landmark Trust (by appointment).

Dartmouth Castle
Innovative blockhouse begun by the townsfolk in 1481 to guard the entrance to Dartmouth Haven. Contains large, square gunports for heavy guns at ground level. Medieval castle later extended in eighteenth and mid-nineteenth centuries. Later casemated battery adapted for use in the Second World War.
English Heritage.

Firestone Bay Blockhouse, Plymouth
Seven-sided blockhouse, one of a number built along the waters-edge of the Hoe. Two-storey with rectangular gunports.
Plymouth Corporation.

Kingswear Castle
Opposite Dartmouth Castle and built a little later in 1491. Similar in its main characteristics to Dartmouth with nine rectangular gunports.
Landmark Trust (by appointment).

Mount Batten Tower
Circular gun-tower built in the 1650s and commanding the Cattewater and the Pool of the town of Plymouth. Battery mounted on roof with ten embrasures in the parapet.
English Heritage (by appointment).

Plymouth Citadel
Large, irregular bastioned fort on the site of, and incorporating portions of the late sixteenth century Plymouth Fort on the Hoe and commanding the town and the entrance to the Cattewater. Designed by Sir Bernard de Gomme and begun in 1665, construction continuing into the 1680s. A fine example of a little altered (apart from the outworks) seventeenth century bastioned fortification. Handsome Baroque main gate.
English Heritage (in military occupation).

Salcombe Castle
Blockhouse constructed c1540, perhaps as a result of local initiative at the mouth of Salcombe harbour. A half-round tower towards the land is the principal surviving fragment. Foundations of a larger D-shaped bastion also visible.

Dorset

Brownsea Castle
Built 1545–47. Originally a square, single-storey building with an hexagonal gun platform on one side to protect Poole harbour. Later converted into a residence.
National Trust (by appointment).

Maumbury Rings, Dorchester
Neolithic henge monument, later Roman amphitheatre, converted into a Civil War strongpoint. Internal terracing and gun platform in the south west corner still visible.

Nothe Fort, Weymouth
On the Weymouth side of Portland Bay. Designed in 1857 but not begun until 1860, a D-shaped, casemated, granite fort for ten heavy guns behind iron shields. Armed with two 6-inch BLs in both world wars.
Weymouth Civic Society.

Portland Castle
Henrician fort built in 1540. Plan forms a sector of a circle with a single-storey gun room for five guns with an upper

tier of guns, backed by a segmental two-storey barrack building. Controlled Portland Bay in association with Sandsfoot Castle. Later bastioned enclosure to rear and six-gun battery to south.
English Heritage.

Rufus or Bow and Arrow Castle, Portland
East side of Isle of Portland. Blockhouse, possibly of fifteenth century. Walls contain five circular gunports, remains of machicolated parapet.

Sandsfoot Castle
Henrician castle in existence by 1541. Octagonal gun room almost entirely lost through coastal erosion. Tall rectangular residential block to rear the main survivor. Rectangular bastioned earthwork enclosure on landward side.
Weymouth District Council.

Sherborne Old Castle
Fortified palace of the bishops of Salisbury, principally of the twelfth century but in 1592 passed to Sir Walter Raleigh. Fortified during Civil War. Large earthwork bastion flanking entrance front and other outer defences.
English Heritage.

East Sussex

Bodiam Castle
Built 1386 by Sir Edward Dalynrygge both as a defensible house and as an officially approved coastal fortification following French raids along the south coast. In its northern gatehouse there is a series of keyhole gunports for small hand-guns one each side of the gateway.
National Trust.

Camber Castle
West of Rye. The large and elaborate Henrician castle of the 1540s has an early sixteenth century gun-tower as its core. It originally protected a harbour (camber) now completely silted up. Castle in ruins but little altered since the sixteenth century; recently excavated and consolidated.
English Heritage.

Eastbourne Redoubt
One of the two south coast redoubts associated with the Martello system. Constructed 1805–10. Circular work for eleven guns firing through embrasures over a glacis, barrack accommodation in casemates below.
Eastbourne District Council.

Wish Tower, Eastbourne
Martello Tower No 73 on the extremity of cliffs which extend from Eastbourne

to Beachy Head. Now a museum of the Martello system. Eastbourne District Council.

Newhaven Fort
Constructed 1864–70 on the cliffs to protect the newly developing port. Irregular lunette trace with wide, deep ditch on two sides, unusually for this date revetted in concrete. Defences at harbour level largely destroyed but brick caponier still projects from foot of cliffs. Partly restored with some guns on the open battery.

Pevensey Castle
Roman fort partly occupied by a medieval castle. On the cliff edge west of the castle is an eroded earthwork thought to be an Armada battery for two sakers, one of which is mounted in the castle on a reproduction Elizabethan field carriage. Second World War strongpoints and pillboxes built into the medieval and Roman ruins.
English Heritage.

Seaford, Martello Tower No 74
Westernmost of the south coast line of towers.

Essex

Coalhouse Fort, East Tilbury
Large casemated fort, part of the advanced line of Thames defences built in 1860s and now the best preserved of the three. Incorporates the plan of an earlier battery on the site. Later 6-inch and 12-pounder guns and then searchlights mounted on the roof. Restoration in progress.
Thurrock District Council.

Tilbury
At West Tilbury at the Essex end of the ferry to Gravesend. Nothing of the Henrician or Elizabethan defences survives but the fort is the best example in the country of a late seventeenth century bastioned fort of the Dutch School, designed by Sir Bernard de Gomme. Double moat, ravelin and little altered outworks. Riverside bastions and curtain modified in the late 1860s to take improved armament.
English Heritage.

Greater London

Tower of London
The castle of the Norman Conquest constructed in the angle formed by the eastern wall of the Roman city and the river and enlarged and developed through the Middle Ages was also adapted for artillery defence in the late seventeenth century. The large rounded

gun-towers of Legge's Mount and Brass Mount were constructed in 1682 at the west and east angles of the northern outer wall after the Restoration for internal security reasons.
The Tower was the home of the Board of Ordnance until its dissolution in the 1850s.
Department of the Environment.

Hampshire

Basing House
A Royalist stronghold throughout the Civil War and fortified palace of the Marquis of Winchester. The massive circular earthwork enclosing the 'citadel' was further strengthened by an earthwork *enceinte*. The large angled bastions, of which three survive, appear to have been added a little later. Basing was finally stormed by Cromwell in October 1645.
Hampshire County Council.

Fort Brockhurst
One of the five mutually supporting detached forts comprising the Gosport Advanced Line, conceived in the late 1850s as protection for Portsmouth from any landward threat from the west. Fort constructed between 1858 and 1862. Large polygonal fort enclosed by a wide wet moat, with the hexagonal parade enclosed by casemates under the ramparts which carried the main armament. Close defence from three caponiers and a self-defensible circular keep in the gorge, complete with its own moat and caponiers.
English Heritage.

Calshot Castle
One of the first of Henry VIII's 1539 programme of coastal defence, constructed on the spit at the entrance to Southampton Water, part of the Solent defences with East and West Cowes and Hurst Castle. It has a circular keep rising from an octagonal wall within a sixteen-sided curtain wall and lower battery, surrounded by a wet ditch. Adapted in the nineteenth century.
English Heritage.

Fort Cumberland
At the south east corner of Portsea Island and designed to control the entrance into Langstone harbour. An earlier fort was built on the site in 1746 but was replaced between 1794 and 1820 on a much larger and more regular bastioned scale. The present fort was the last major bastioned fortress to be constructed in England and is unusual in combining a bastioned trace with great use of casemated guns.
English Heritage.

Gosport Lines

The rebuilding of the seventeenth century fortifications enclosing the town of Gosport began in 1748 and continued during the rest of the eighteenth century. Much of the bastioned *enceinte* has since been demolished but traces remain at its southern end and to the north east at Priddy's Hard and at Weevil.

Hilsea Lines, Portsmouth

Bastioned lines across the north of Portsea Island defending access from landward. Remodelled in the mid-nineteenth century with substantial earthworks and moat.
City of Portsmouth.

Hurst Castle

On the pebble spit opposite the Isle of Wight and part of the defences of the Needles Passage. Best approached by boat from Keyhaven. Begun as part of Henry VIII's 1539 scheme of coastal defence with a twelve-sided keep rising above a similarly multangular curtain wall from which project three prominent rounded bastions. Additional batteries were built outside it in the eighteenth century, to be replaced in the 1860s by long single-storey, granite-faced, casemated wing batteries for 61 heavy guns on either side of the Tudor fort. There are also remains of First and Second World War batteries and fire control positions.
English Heritage.

Fort Nelson

One of the line of detached forts on Portsdown Hill protecting the naval and military installations of Portsmouth from attack from landward. Commenced 1861 and completed in 1870. Six-sided polygonal fort with ditches protected by demi-caponiers on the east and west and a central caponier on the northern salient. Above each caponier was a mortar battery. The brick walled gorge is flanked by a defensible barrack in bastioned form.
Hampshire County Council.

Portchester Castle

At the head of Portsmouth harbour the Norman and later castle occupies the northern angle of the late Roman 'Saxon Shore' Fort and has evidence of adaptation for artillery in the late fourteenth century. Hand-gun loops in the parapet south west of the keep and a keyhole gunport in Assheton's Tower are confirmation of the issue of three guns from the Tower to Robert Assheton, Keeper of the castle in 1379.
English Heritage.

Portsmouth

Round Tower
Originally one of two towers on either side of the harbour entrance guarding the ends of a chain boom and built early in the fifteenth century. Known as Ridley's Tower in 1536 it had by then three gunports at ground level and an upper gun platform. Much altered and refaced since, and its height raised in the nineteenth century. At the western end of Eighteen-Gun Battery and forming part of Point Battery.
City of Portsmouth.

Point Battery
Guns were mounted along the Camber shore in 1540 but the Battery became a permanent feature in de Gomme's reconstruction of Portsmouth's defences in the 1670s with eighteen casemates somewhat shallower than they are today, with that part adjacent to the Round Tower set at an angle in order to flank the beach. In 1847 an enclosed barrack was created to the rear (now demolished) and the casemates were deepened to accommodate 68-pounder carronades and a second tier of four casemates for 32-pounders added to the top of the flanking battery.
City of Portsmouth.

Square Tower
Built in 1494 as a gun-tower, it was also intended as a residence, perhaps for the master gunner. In the late sixteenth or early seventeenth centuries it became a magazine before being adapted by the Victualling Board as a meat store. With the reorganisation of the seaward defences in 1848–50 the top was reinforced to take three 8-inch guns.
City of Portsmouth.

Ten-Gun Battery and Saluting Platform
East of the Square Tower. The Saluting Platform was constructed in the late fifteenth century or early sixteenth century. Rebuilt in 1568 but continued to suffer sea damage. The Ten-Gun Battery was part of de Gomme's improvements to the seaward defences in the late seventeenth century. In the 1860s the level of the battery was raised to the height of the Saluting Platform.
City of Portsmouth.

King's Bastion and Long Curtain
Last surviving stretch of the town defences as remodelled by Sir Bernard de Gomme in 1670s. Further works were done here in the 1730s when the bastion known in the sixteenth century as the Greene Bulwark, later as Wimbledon's Bastion, was renamed after George II.
City of Portsmouth.

King James's Gate
The facade of King James's Gate was removed to its present position at the entrance to the United Services Officers' Club recreation ground in c1860. It had been built in 1687 as part of the de Gomme's reconstruction of the town defences. This monumental gateway gave access from the Point through the defences between the Camber and the sea.
English Heritage.

Landport Gate
On the north side of St George's Road and the men's entrance to the United Services Recreation Ground. This was once the main land entrance through the town's fortifications. The original Land Port was further to the east astride the London Road but moved to its present position when the defences were improved in c1585. The present gatehouse was built in 1760.

Southampton Town Walls

During the latter half of the fourteenth century, portions of the town walls were constructed or improved for the deployment of guns, and in the early fifteenth century additional defensive works were designed, principally for employing artillery at key positions.

Arcade
A battlemented wall-walk carried on a series of arches built outside the blocking walls which cross the backs of twelfth century houses. In the blocking walls are long keyhole gunports inserted in the late 1370s or early 1380s and therefore among the earliest gunports in the country.
Southampton Corporation.

Catchcold Tower
Built in the early fifteenth century towards the northern end of the western defences. The tower has deep projection in order to flank the curtain wall. A stone vaulted chamber at wall-walk level contains keyhole gunports and the vault suggests an intention to mount heavy guns on the platform above.
Southampton Corporation.

God's House Tower
Built in the early fifteenth century outside the God's House Gate and previously known as the Mill Tower. Projects across the line of the town ditch and was a considerable strongpoint as well as the house of the town gunner and magazine. The first floor of both the link building and the tower are pierced by keyhole gunports, likewise the second floor of the tower. The parapet of the tower has single embrasures

on three sides for heavy guns.
Southampton Corporation Museum.

Southsea Castle

Built in 1544 as part of Henry VIII's scheme of coastal defence. Unusual in having a square tower with rectangular batteries to east and west linked by two angled salients. Remodelled by de Gomme in the 1670s. The outer curtain wall was completely rebuilt in 1814 and a counterscarp gallery constructed to command the dry ditch and reached through a caponier from the seaward salient. Large earthwork wing batteries constructed on either side of the castle in the 1860s, now very mutilated and transformed into municipal gardens.
City of Portsmouth Museum.

Spitbank Fort

The northernmost of the Spithead sea forts, south west of Southsea Castle, built in the 1860s. One of the smaller of the sea forts, it is circular and only armoured on the side facing the open sea. Single tier of casemates over basement magazines and further gun emplacements in the parapet.
Special programme of visits in summer.

Fort Widley

One of the detached forts built in the 1860s on Portsdown Hill to protect the naval and military installations of Portsmouth from landward attack. Polygonal plan of six sides with the wide and deep ditch flanked by two demi- and one central caponiers. The main armament, including mortar batteries, mounted on the ramparts. Defensible barrack in the gorge flanked by two demi-bastions.
City of Portsmouth.

Winchester West Gate

The altered western face contains two keyhole gunports probably belonging to the early 1390s.
Winchester City Council.

Hereford and Worcester

Fort Royal, Worcester

Quadrangular earthwork with angle bastions commanding the London road south east of the city.

Humberside

Paull Fort

An advanced work of the Hull defences on the north bank of the Humber. Constructed in 1856 and remodelled in 1899 for three 6-inch guns, quick-firers and machine guns.

Isle of Wight

Carisbrooke Castle

The medieval castle was for many years the principal stronghold on the island and was first adapted for guns when the gatehouse was heightened in 1380. Between 1585 and 1588 two mural towers on the curtain wall were converted to angle bastions. In 1596–7 in response to a continuing Spanish threat, Frederigo Genebelli completely enclosed the castle by a 'Italian' *orillon*, bastioned *enceinte*.
English Heritage.

Freshwater Redoubt

Small fort built in 1855–6 to prevent a landing in Freshwater Bay. Two batteries enclosed by a ditch and rampart flanked by a large caponier. Barracks now a private house.

Golden Hill Fort

Defensible barracks built between 1863 and 1872 to serve the batteries of the Needles Defences. Hexagonal in plan with three caponiers flanking the ditch and six guns on the bombproof roof.

Needles Batteries

Needles Point Battery for six 7-inch Armstrong RBLs built 1861–3 to protect the westerly entrance to the Solent. 1889–92 subject to searchlight experiments to counter fast torpedo-boats, and in 1913 was the location for the testing of the first British anti-aircraft gun. New Needles Battery for three 9.2-inch guns built higher up the cliff 1893–5.
National Trust.

Fort Victoria

West of Yarmouth and built following a French invasion scare in 1852–6. Single-tier casemated battery arranged in a salient angle with defensible barrack to the rear. Later used as a submarine mining depot. Barracks demolished in 1969.
Isle of Wight County Council.

Yarmouth Castle

Last of the coastal defence forts built by Henry VIII. Built to protect the harbour and Yarmouth Roads, and the first surviving example of an italianate *orillon* bastion which flanks two sides. The other two sides of the square battery are washed by the sea.
English Heritage.

Isles of Scilly

Cromwell's Castle, Tresco

Tall, circular gun-tower built c1650 to protect the anchorage of New Grimsby between Tresco and Bryher. In mid-eighteenth century a gun platform was added near the waters-edge.
English Heritage.

Garrison Walls, St Mary's

Irregular and incomplete bastioned trace around the headland west of Hugh Town, begun in the late sixteenth century with further construction in the mid-eighteenth century. Inside this military area is Star Castle (*qv*), the master gunner's house, the 'black hole' (prison), a Napoleonic gun-tower and early twentieth century batteries.
English Heritage.

Harry's Walls, St Mary's

Unfinished *orillon* bastioned fort built in 1551 to command St Mary's harbour. The first fully accomplished italianate fort to be planned in England.
English Heritage.

King Charles's Castle, Tresco

Built 1551–4 as part of the fortification of the islands. Hexagonal gun room with domestic accommodation behind in the style of Henrician coastal forts ten years earlier. Later enclosed within earthworks of bastioned form.
English Heritage.

Old Blockhouse, Tresco

Small blockhouse and gun platform built in the 1550s to protect the anchorage of Old Grimsby on the east side of the island.
English Heritage.

Pellew's Redoubt, Toll's Island, St Mary's

Small earthwork battery of Civil War date consisting in plan of two demi-bastions back to back.

Star Castle, St Mary's

Built in 1593 by the engineer Robert Adams for Francis Godolphin as the focal point for the defence of the islands. Central building in the form of an eight-pointed star surrounded by a similarly planned curtain wall. Gun embrasures in the re-entrant angles.
Hotel.

Kent

Fort Amherst, Chatham

The southern end of the Brompton Lines begun in 1756 to protect Chatham Dockyard and its associated military installations. In the 1770s, additional

works and retrenchments were added to either end. Amherst Redoubt, Cornwallis Battery, Belvedere Battery and the casemated barracks at Prince William's Battery occupied the southern end which was completed in its present form in 1820. In course of restoration.
Fort Amherst and Lines Trust.

Canterbury West Gate and City Walls
Begun in 1380, and the twin-towered gatehouse still stands to full height. The towers contain three tiers of keyhole gunports and the gatehouse is the earliest example of an English fortification purpose-built for guns. Subsequently the city wall was provided with mural towers also with keyhole gunports.
Canterbury District Council.

Deal Castle
The largest and most powerful of all Henry VIII's 1539–40 scheme of coastal defence, and the central fort of the three which 'keep the Downs', an important anchorage. Central circular keep has six small rounded bastions attached and is surrounded by a curtain wall with six larger rounded bastions enclosed by a dry moat. Converted in the eighteenth century for residential use.
English Heritage.

Dover Castle
One of the great fortresses of Europe with its nucleus in the twelfth and thirteenth century castle within the earthworks of the Iron Age. Considerably altered in the mid-1750s and more so during the Napoleonic Wars when it was adapted to an artillery fortification of great strength. The medieval towers were cut down, the Spur remodelled, earthen bastions built outside the northern ditch and the ditches themselves made defensible with musketry galleries and caponiers. The batteries protecting the harbour were maintained during the nineteenth century and the castle was the headquarters for the Dover and Channel defences during both world wars.
English Heritage.

Western Heights, Dover.
The hill which dominates the west side of Dover was first fortified on any scale in 1779 when fieldworks were constructed to protect the port and town. Substantially strengthened in 1803–15, they were again improved in the 1860s. Irregular, with Drop Redoubt to the north east, North Centre Bastion and Citadel and Western Outwork linked by continuous lines. The Grand Shaft, with triple stair, linked the now demolished barracks with the town below.
Drop Redoubt (English Heritage), Grand Shaft (Dover Council).

Dymchurch, Martello Tower No 24
Tower No 24, one of 74 towers built along the south coast between 1805 and 1812 to resist the threatened French invasion. Small exhibition inside.
English Heritage.

Gravesend Blockhouse
The excavated half of the D-shaped front of an artillery blockhouse of 1539. The only visible fragment of Henry VIII's five blockhouses guarding the Thames Estuary and the river crossing between Gravesend and West Tilbury. In front of the Clarendon Royal Hotel.

New Tavern Fort, Gravesend
Battery built in 1778 to the east of Milton Chantry to cross fire with an enhanced Tilbury Fort opposite. Of irregular bastioned trace. Remodelled in 1868–9 for improved armament.
Gravesend Corporation.

Royal Military Canal
Defence work associated with the south coast Martello tower system carried out in 1804 by the Royal Engineers under the direction of Sir John Rennie. It was a wet ditch and rampart with batteries some 30 miles long from Shorncliffe in Kent to the Rother at Rye in Sussex, cutting off and isolating Romney Marsh. Later extended from Rye to Pett Level south west of Winchelsea.
Parts accessible to the public.

Sheerness
The site of a Henrician blockhouse, the point was fortified once a dockyard was established in the seventeenth century. Parts of the seventeenth century seaward lines designed by Gomme remain and the eighteenth century bastioned front to Blue Town but the massive two-tiered casemated Garrison Point Fort of the 1860s is not readily accessible.

Upnor Castle
Built 1559–63 to protect Queen Elizabeth's warships while moored in the Medway; designed by Sir Richard Lee. Large angle bastion projects into the river with a towered front built on and above the river bank behind. In action during the Dutch raid on the Medway in 1667 but later converted into a powder magazine.
English Heritage.

Walmer Castle
Associated with Deal Castle as one of the three fortresses 'which keep the Downs'. Built in 1539–40 with a central circular tower and an outer ring of four large rounded bastions with wide dry ditch. In eighteenth century converted into the residence of the Lords Warden

of the Cinque Ports which it remains. Close associations with Wellington and the visits of Queen Victoria.
English Heritage.

Leicestershire

Kirby Muxloe Castle
Brick-built, fortified manor house designed for the use of guns. Regular, square-towered plan with gunports at ground level. Begun in 1480 by William, Lord Hastings but never completed.
English Heritage.

Merseyside

Fort Perchrock
Built at the entrance to the Mersey at New Brighton between 1826 and 1829. Accessible by land at low-water. Lozenge-shaped and constructed for fourteen 32-pounders on the ramparts, two 32-pounders on the two towers and with two 18-pounders in casemates in the towers.

Norfolk

Great Yarmouth Town Walls
Well preserved medieval town walls with mural towers. Strengthened with an internal rampart in 1544 and improved in 1569 and during the Armada crisis with earth mounts and ravelins.

King's Lynn
First fortified in the thirteenth century with rampart and ditch. The South Gate built in 1437–40 has circular gunports. The surviving bastioned earthworks were added during the Civil War.

Norwich, Cow Tower and City Walls
Much of the medieval city wall and towers survive. The existence of guns and gunners occurs as early as 1365 and a few gunports remain. The Cow Tower is a detached gun-tower at a bend of the river Wensum and built in 1398-9.
Cow Tower, English Heritage.

Northumberland

Berwick-upon-Tweed Town Walls
One of the outstanding fortified towns of Europe. Parts of the medieval castle and town walls survive. Small gun-towers were added to the northern defences and a massive circular tower (Lord's Mount) added to the north west angle. The principal work is the complete Elizabethan *enceinte* of bastioned ramparts in 'Italian' fashion designed by Sir Richard Lee. Within the town is Ravensdowne Barracks, the first purpose-built barracks in England begun in 1717.

Lindisfarne Castle

Gun platforms and batteries first constructed in 1542 and maintained fitfully until the end of the nineteenth century. Partly incorporated into the 'castle' built by Lutyens after 1902.
National Trust.

Norham Castle

One of the Border strongholds commanding a ford across the Tweed. This medieval castle was adapted for artillery after 1513 with gunports in the outer ward and with angle-fronted towers on the inner and outer baileys.
English Heritage.

Nottinghamshire

Queen's Sconce, Newark

Best preserved element of the once extensive Civil War defences and siege works around Newark. Large, square earthwork, bastioned fort south west of town. Well defined angle bastions and surrounded by a large ditch.
Newark Corporation.

North Yorkshire

Scarborough Castle

Medieval castle subsequently armed with artillery. By 1841 four carronades mounted on mural towers. Remains of the South Street Battery on south side of castle intended for eleven 18-pounders. Castle damaged by Germans in 1914.
English Heritage.

Somerset

Brean Down Battery

Sited at the western end of Brean Down and the southern end of a chain of batteries across the Severn estuary. Begun 1865, completed 1870 for seven 7-inch RMLs. Defended to the rear by high wall and concreted ditch flanked by caponiers. Masonry defensible barracks.
National Trust.

Suffolk

Aldeburgh Martello Tower

Northernmost of the East Coast Martello towers, 1808–12, and the most unusual of the British towers. Quatrefoil in plan for four guns with an additional platform on the sea-side now missing through coastal erosion.
Landmark Trust (by appointment).

Landguard Fort

At the entrance to the Orwell estuary and fortified since the 1540s. Present fort is principally the pentagonal bastioned fort of the 1740s which serves as the core of successive associated batteries. Fort substantially remodelled in 1870 with granite-faced casemates and adjacent batteries improved or added in the two world wars.
English Heritage.

Tyne and Wear

Tynemouth Castle

Medieval castle enclosed by primitive Italianate bastioned earthworks c1546 including the site of Spanish Battery. Batteries maintained at the castle although main strength lay in Clifford's Fort below. Nineteenth century battery on cliff edge remodelled for 9.2- and 6-inch guns in 1880s–1890s.
English Heritage.

Warwickshire

Warwick Castle

Unfinished gun-towers (Bear and Clarence) on outer curtain wall, begun by Richard III c1484. Contain circular gunports.

West Sussex

Littlehampton Forts

Commanding the entrance to the river Arun. On the east side, the rampart of 1759 battery behind the lighthouse. On the west side is the bastioned shape fort of 1859 with a loopholed Carnot wall below the ramparts.

Shoreham Redoubt

Built at entrance to Shoreham harbour in 1857. Polygonal plan, for six guns mounted on ramparts, barracks to rear now demolished. Carnot wall in ditch with caponiers and loopholes.

Ireland

Antrim

Carrickfergus Castle

Medieval castle on the north shore of Belfast Lough. The castle was converted to artillery defence in the 1560s and the gatehouse also altered for guns. Infantry barracks were inserted in 1715 and gun-towers created on the gatehouse with the grand battery commanding the north eastern flank. In the later nineteenth century the east battery had the function of controlling shipping on Belfast Lough.
Department of the Environment for Northern Ireland (DOENI).

Carrickfergus Town Walls

Town was enclosed with stone walls from 1610 onwards having had earthwork defences since c1570, and at least half of this circuit is still visible including the north east corner angle bastion.
DOENI.

Dalway's Bawn

North east of Carrickfergus. An unusually well preserved example of an early seventeenth century planter's fortified enclosure with three surviving flanking towers, built c1609.
DOENI.

Grey Point Fort

On the south shore of Belfast Lough opposite the contemporary Kilroot Battery on the north. Battery for two 6-inch breech-loading guns and first manned in 1907 by the Antrim Royal Garrison Artillery. Gunhouses added in 1940 as protection against air attack and three searchlight emplacements were built on the foreshore in 1936 and 1940.
DOENI.

Armagh

Charlemont

One of the principal Ulster forts throughout the seventeenth century, first built by Mountjoy in 1602. The house within the square bastioned fort was burnt in 1920 and the ruins subsequently demolished but the gatehouse and earthworks remain.

Cavan

Belturbet

Fort constructed by the townspeople in 1666. Part of the earthwork bastions and ramparts still survive, surrounding the Church of Ireland church and graveyard.

Clare

Aughinish Island Martello Tower
One of three towers guarding Galway Bay, cam-shaped in plan and therefore different from those in Dublin Bay. Constructed in 1811 or slightly later.

Doonaha Battery
North side of the Shannon Estuary, north east of Kilcredaun Point. Similar to other Shannon batteries with half-demolished oblong tower in the centre of the gorge of an enclosed D-shaped battery for four 24-pounder guns.

Finavarra Point Martello Tower
Cam-shaped three-gun tower of c1811, similar to that at Aughinish Island. There is a large guardhouse at the side.

Kilcredaun Point Battery
Commanded northern side of the mouth of the Shannon. D-shaped battery for six 24-pounder guns. Oblong blockhouse or bombproof barracks in centre of gorge, dated 1814. Positions for two howitzers on top of blockhouse.

Kilkerin Point Battery
Opposite Tarbert Island and the best preserved of the Shannon batteries. Of similar plan and size as Kilcredaun Point Battery.

Cork

Ardagh Martello Tower
On Bere Island in Bantry Bay, one mile west of Lawrence's Cove. Drum-shaped with near vertical sides, built in 1804. One of four towers built on Bere Island, two of which survive.

Belvelly Tower
Drum-shaped commanding the bridge on to Great Island, and like the other four Cork harbour towers, has vertical sides. Under construction 1813–5.

Charles Fort
The best preserved example of a seventeenth century artillery fort in Ireland. Begun in 1678 under the supervision of William Robinson and Captain James Archer on the site of Ringcurran Castle. An irregular bastioned hexagon with well preserved outworks. Sited to command the approaches to Kinsale harbour but overlooked from high ground from where it was overpowered by Marlborough in 1690. The mainly ruined barrack buildings in the interior belong principally to the eighteenth century.
Nat Mon.

Cloonaghlin Martello Tower
On Bere Island in Bantry Bay, one mile south west of Lawrence's Cove. Drum-shaped with near vertical walls. Built in 1804.

Cove Fort, Cork Harbour
Three levels of gun emplacements overlooking the harbour, part of the wall for musketry defence survives on the landward side. Constructed by 1743.

Dunboy Fort
During the Cromwellian period a star fort constructed around the castle near Berehaven, traces of the earthworks survive.

Elizabeth Fort, Cork
To the south of the old city. First constructed in 1601–2, rebuilt 1603 and reconstructed in 1625–6. A key point in the siege of Cork in 1690. Outer walls and bastions survive.

Garinish Island Tower
Defending Glengariff harbour and among the earliest of the Irish Martello towers, started in 1804. Vertical exterior face. Battery associated with the tower.

James Fort
Built on the site of the earlier Castle Park occupied by the Spanish during the siege of Kinsale, 1601. Castle Park Fort, later known as James Fort is a pentagonal earthwork bastioned work constructed 1602–4 to the design of Paul Ive. The central building – a square enclosure with demi-bastions and two towers – is a few years later, completed by Bodley by 1611. A water-level masonry blockhouse to the north west appears to be sixteenth century in date but could belong to the 1640s.
Nat Mon.

Ringaskiddy Martello Tower
On high ground on the western side of Cork harbour, still under construction 1813–5. Drum-shaped with vertical exterior face. Unlike other towers it is surrounded by a ditch.

Donegal

Greencastle Martello Tower
With Magillan Tower commanded the entrance to Lough Foyle. Built for two 5½-inch howitzers on the roof in 1812, elliptical in plan and forming the landward salient of a fort or battery mounting five 24-pounders.
Part of an hotel.

Lough Swilly
Seven batteries in existence in 1798; six were converted into permanent works

in the early 1800s and circular, cam-shaped and rectangular towers added. Distributed on either side of the Lough but restricted public access, except for Dunree Fort which is now open to the public.

Down

Carlingford Lough Blockhouse
On a small island in the Lough. Plan and surviving features suggest a blockhouse of mid-sixteenth century date, but it may be associated with Lord Mountjoy's activities c1601.

Hillsborough Fort
Square, bastioned stone revetted earthwork fort built by Colonel Arthur Hill in the 1650s to command important routes. A rectangular gatehouse in the centre of the north side was remodelled in 1758 in a gothick style.
DOENI.

Dublin

Dublin Bay Martello Towers
Built in 1804 along the Bay, twelve towers to the north ending with Balbriggan, fourteen to the south. 'Joyce's Tower', Sandycove, is open to the public as a museum to James Joyce; others are in private hands.

Magazine Fort, Dublin
In Phoenix Park. A fort with four demi-bastions, constructed 1736–8. A ravelin on the east front added in the early nineteenth century.

Fermanagh

Enniskillen Castle and Barracks
Nucleus of the castle is a late medieval tower-house of the Maguires remodelled in the seventeenth century into a workable Plantation fort. This reworking included the 'Watergate'. Barrack buildings erected after 1796 and others c1825 and after 1835.
DOENI.

Enniskillen Forts
The east fort on Fort Hill was constructed in 1689 as an outwork to the defences. A square earthwork bastioned fort, later modified in the 1790s, now in a public park. A massive redoubt of c1796 commands the west side of the town from a hilltop.

Monea Castle
The largest and best preserved of the 'plantation' castles of the early seventeenth century. Built by 1618 for Malcolm Hamilton. A tower-house of Scottish type at one corner of a square bawm

whose high wall was covered from two flankers.
DOENI.

Tully Castle
On Tully Point on the western shore of Lower Lough Erne. 'Plantation' castle of the Humes and built in 1613, burnt in 1641. Rectangular tower-house, showing Scottish influence, along one side of a square bawn having square flankers at each angle.
DOENI.

Galway

Meelick Martello Tower
Cam-shaped like the English east coast towers for three guns on its roof platform supported by a stone central pier. Built in 1811–2 at the time of the construction of Banagher tower a short distance upstream.

Rossaveal Martello Tower
Cashla Bay, on the north side of Galway Bay. Oval or elliptical in plan and for one gun. Built c1811.

Leitrim

Manorhamilton
Square masonry fort with corner bastions on high ground east of the town. Larger than the typical Cromwellian period forts and possibly early eighteenth century. The Church of Ireland church stands in the centre of the enclosure which now forms the churchyard.

Limerick

Limerick Castle
The medieval castle had one of its four towers replaced by a bastion in 1611 and all were lowered to carry artillery. It was used as a barracks in the eighteenth century.
Nat Mon.

Londonderry

Culmore Fort
Linear earthwork flanked by a single central bastion, cutting off peninsula where Lough Foyle narrows. Dates from 1600 and constructed under the supervision of the Dutch engineer Jose Everaert by an English force which landed at Lough Foyle.

Londonderry Town Walls
Built 1614–8 for the Irish Society to the design of Captain Edward Doddington, the stone-faced ramparts and bastions are the outstanding seventeenth century town defences in Ireland. Five of the eight bastions survive and two shallow

gun platforms. Survived the siege of 105 days by the forces of James II in 1689. Eleven of the cannon given to the city by the London companies surviving.
DOENI.

Magilligan Tower, Lough Foyle
Martello tower built in 1812 on the east side and defending the entrance of Lough Foyle and opposite another at Greencastle. Circular with five-corbelled machicolation over first floor entrance. Designed for two 24-pounders operating from the same central pivot.
DOENI.

Offaly

Banagher Martello Tower
Elliptical or oval in plan for one 24-pounder similar to the English south coast towers commanding the bridge and opposite Cromwell's tower. Being on the west bank of the Shannon is, strictly, in County Galway.

Fort Eliza
Banagher. Small five-sided battery for four guns south east of the bridge. Ruined gatehouse in rear salient, magazine in centre of enclosure.

Keelogue Battery
Similar to the Shannon Estuary batteries. D-shaped battery for seven guns, with rectangular bombproof barracks at the rear with two gun emplacements on the roof. Defended a ford over the Shannon.

Roscommon

Shannonbridge
A unique example in Ireland or Britain of a *tête-de-pont* defending the western approaches to the bridge and begun in 1804 as part of the Shannon Defence Line in response to the French invasion of 1798 and later invasion plans. The masonry works were constructed after 1810 and replaced the earthwork de-

fences. A complex of redoubts, defensible barracks and batteries fronted by a massive earth glacis.
Nat Mon.

Sligo

Green Fort
Small, square, bastioned earthwork fort of Cromwellian date outside Sligo town. The fort formed an important salient of the defences of Sligo during the campaigns of 1688–91.

Westmeath

Athlone Castle
Strategic importance of Athlone as a principal crossing of the Shannon. Medieval castle repaired in 1798 initially for musketry defence but also the walls and towers were adapted for eleven artillery positions during the Napoleonic Wars. Only remains of one of the seven batteries built west of the town in 1803–4 survive.
Nat Mon.

Waterford

Duncannon Fort
Defends Waterford harbour. Medieval castle adapted for artillery 1587–90 but commanded on the landward side. Sea battery built for twenty-five guns during the eighteenth century, and there were further alterations c1805–15 and later in the nineteenth century. In 1814 the high ground was occupied by two Martello towers of elliptical form which both survive.

Wicklow

Black Castle Battery, Wicklow
To the south west of the castle ruins is the site of a late nineteenth century battery for four guns. Two emplacements for 6-inch BLs of c1900 survive. The battery was used by the Wicklow Militia artillery.

Isle of Man

Castle Rushen
Medieval castle mainly of fourteenth century construction. In 1536–42 renovated and modernised by Edward, Earl of Derby into an artillery fortification. Curtain masked by the addition of a glacis to the counterscarp. On the glacis were three round gun-towers one of which remains.

Derby Fort
On St Michael's Island, commanding Derby Haven. Circular fort of 1536–42 attributed to the Earl of Derby. The thick walls 10–12 feet high have seven large embrasures for guns at ground level.

Peel Castle
Medieval castle improved and converted to artillery in 1536–62. The

round gun-tower on Horse Rock with three gunports protecting the harbour was linked by a gallery to the castle.

Half-Moon Battery west of the cathedral constructed in 1595–6. New battery added in nineteenth century.

Scotland

Borders

Eyemouth Forts
Among the earliest angle bastion fortifications in Scotland or England. The first fort devised by Thomas Petit for the invading English army in 1547. Single massive earthwork bastion within the re-entrant angle of a rampart and ditch across the promontory. The second, beyond the earlier work, was built by French engineers after the English withdrawal in 1557. The earth rampart was flanked by a bastion at either end.

Hermitage Castle
The original manor-house of the Dacres was built between 1385 and 1365, with two blocks flanking a small open court. It was later converted into a tower-house and by about 1400 projecting square towers were added. There is also a redan-shaped earthwork on the western side, and the remains of an earthwork bastion front on the north. Both are probably of the third quarter of the sixteenth century.
Historic Buildings and Monuments, Scottish Development Department (HB&M, SDD).

Roxburgh Castle
The scene of the mortal wounding of James II by an exploding cannon at the siege of 1460. Medieval castle refortified for artillery in 1548, though not in Italianate style, as part of the English campaign.

Central

Blackness Castle
North east of Linlithgow on the Forth Estuary. Strong, oblong tower of the fifteenth century built for artillery defence by the Crown, modified in 1537 by a casemated reinforcement to the south front.
HB&M, SDD.

Stirling Castle
Medieval royal castle on the great basalt rock above the battlefield site of Bannockburn and the strategic centre of Scotland. As a fortress and royal palace its buildings were frequently destroyed and rebuilt. The sixteenth and seventeenth century irregular bastioned *enceinte* was begun to a design by Theo-

dore Dury but remodelled to its present form by Talbot Edwards early in the eighteenth century
HB&M, SDD.

Dumfries and Galloway

Threave Castle
The mighty tower of the 'Black Douglasses' stands on an islet in the River Dee. The tower was enclosed by an early form of artillery defence with loopholed walls flanked by round towers with two tiers of gunports probably in 1454.
HB&M, SDD.

Fife

Inchcolm
Island in the Firth of Forth. Batteries for four 4.7-inch guns and four 4-inch QFs completed in 1917; two 6-inch added shortly after as part of the inner defences of the Forth. Much damaged but elements still visible, and the only parts of the First World War defences which are readily accessible.
HB&M, SDD.

Ravenscraig Castle
On a narrow promontory between Dysart and Kircaldy, begun in 1460 by James II as a fortress wholly designed for artillery and in this respect the first example in Scotland. The wide-mouthed gunports on top of the frontal cross wall were probably added later in the fifteenth century.
HB&M, SDD.

St Andrew's Castle
The archiepiscopal castle of the primate of Scotland. The medieval castle strengthened by Cardinal Beaton with the massively thick walls of a circular blockhouse of which a fragment survives, pierced by large, horizontal gunports. The mine and counter-mine belong to the siege of 1546–7.
HB&M, SDD.

St Andrew's West Port
One of the few surviving examples of a city gate in Scotland. Built in 1589. Central archway flanked by two semi-octagonal towers equipped with gunports.
HB&M, SDD.

Grampian

Corgarff Castle
By Cock Bridge at the foot of the Lecht road it commands the passes of the Dee, the Avon and the Don and was of considerable strategic importance. Sixteenth century tower-house, converted into a garrison post and enclosed within a loopholed wall of *tenaille* trace in 1748.
HB&M, SDD

Spynie Palace
The episcopal tower-house of the bishops of Moray was built between 1461 and 1482. Substantially fortified with numerous inserted gunports in the sixteenth century by Bishop Patrick Hepburn.
HB&M, SDD.

Tentsmuir
Long length of Second World War anti-tank obstacles and pillboxes north east of Leuchars.

Highland

Fort George
One of the finest mid-eighteenth century fortresses in Europe. The bastioned fort and its outworks on a promontory at the mouth of the Moray Firth have survived almost unaltered since they were built. Begun in 1748 following the Jacobit defeat at nearby Culloden to the design of William Skinner. Still garrisoned in part.
HB&M, SDD.

Ruthven Barracks
One of the series of fortified barracks built to control the Highlands. Not built until 1719 after the first Jacobite rising. Square, walled enclosure with two opposed barrack blocks within. Exterior flanked by two opposed bastion-like towers.
HB&M, SDD.

Lothian

Dunbar Battery
Well preserved battery near the harbour of the early 1780s and a survival of the war with America.

Dunbar Castle
Medieval castle, slighted in 1488, was reconstructed for James IV in 1496–1501. Later, the 'great outer blockhouse' was built on an island linked by a traverse wall to the castle in 1512–23 and equipped with advanced forms of gunports. Perhaps built by French.

Edinburgh Castle

The most famous of all Scottish castles, on its great basalt rock. The enclosing walls with their distinctive sentinel boxes at the angles mostly belong to the seventeenth and eighteenth centuries when the castle was refortified as a result of the Jacobite risings. The Half-Moon Battery was built by the Regent Morton and encloses the remains of the great tower built by David II and destroyed by English guns in the siege of 1573. Still partly garrisoned.
HB&M, SDD.

Leith Citadel

Leith was the last of the Cromwellian forts to be erected and was begun in 1656. A fragment of curtain wall survives.

Tantallon Castle

On the cliff opposite the Bass Rock in the Firth of Forth. The great frontal curtain wall flanked by round towers and with an imposing central gatehouse dates from the fourteenth century but was later adapted for guns. Outside the castle are extensive earthworks, some of which represent the defences thrown up against the artillery of James V in 1528, others probably belong to the period 1538–9 and were a major obstacle during the Cromwellian siege.
HB&M, SDD.

Strathclyde

Ayr Citadel

Part of a bastion with corbelled angle turret of the Cromwellian citadel designed by Hans Ewald Tessin in 1654 survives near the harbour.

Craignethan Castle

Private stronghold of the Hamiltons, built c1530. Neck of its promontory site cut by a deep, straight and narrow ditch with high vertical masonry scarp to shield the inner tower from fire from higher ground and with a masonry counterscarp. The ditch defended by a caponier, a vaulted and loopholed gallery across the ditch and the earliest example of this form of defence in Britain.
HB&M, SDD.

Dumbarton Castle

Medieval castle on a volcanic plug of basalt. Refortified during early eighteenth century. The main defence was a curtain wall which had occasional platforms and turrets according to the terrain. Armament maintained there as part of the Clyde defences until the 1850s.
HB&M, SDD.

Tayside

Broughty Castle

On the Tay estuary. A fifteenth century tower-house converted into a coastal defence battery in 1860–1. Open batteries for two 68-pounders and five 10-inch guns in 1882.
HB&M, SDD.

Orkney

Hackness Martello Tower and Battery

With the tower of Crookness opposite at the entrance to the Longhope Sound, Hoy, the tower and battery was built in 1814–5 in order to protect Baltic convoys of merchant ships from American privateers. Tower similar to the English south coast variety for one 24-pounder on the roof. Battery for eight 24-pounders on traversing carriages. In good state of preservation.
The tower is HB&M, SDD; the battery is in private hands.

Hoxa Head Battery

A well preserved battery on South Ronaldsay belonging to the defences of Scapa Flow of both world wars. Emplacements for two 6-inch guns.

Shetland

Fort Charlotte

A fort was begun in 1665 to protect the Sound of Bressay against the Dutch. In 1673 it was burnt with the town of Lerwick but it was repaired in 1781. A pentagonal work with bastions at the angles, it is now closely surrounded by the houses and streets of the town.
HB&M, SDD.

Wales

Dyfed

Carmarthen Civil War Earthworks

One remaining angle bastion, accessible behind the Police HQ.

Dale Point Battery

Open battery for nine guns constructed as part of a defensive scheme for Milford Haven in the 1850s. Now in use as a Field Studies Centre.

Pembroke Defensible Barracks

A square bastioned work with barracks around a central parade erected c1845 on a hill immediately behind the dockyard to provide a substantial barrack and some protection against an attack by land. Loopholed parapets in the bastions and barracks.

Pembroke Dock Towers

Two towers at north east and south west angles of the dockyard wall inaccessible at high tide. Built in c1845. The NE tower could mount three guns, the SW only one.

West Blockhouse Battery

The smallest of the Milford Haven defences, completed in 1857; L-shaped in plan for six 68-pounders with an inner two-storey keep with facetted angles and separated from the cliff by a ditch. Supplanted by an open battery in 1902 on cliff behind.
Landmark Trust (by appointment).

Gwent

Raglan Castle

Majority of the castle probably built 1461–69 by William Herbert, Earl of Pembroke for political reasons during the Wars of the Roses. Designed both as a fortress and residence. The Great Tower standing in its own moat in advance of the main entrance was originally only linked by a drawbridge to the rest of the castle. Great Tower and other towers and entrance front liberally provided with gunports of various sizes. Outside are remains of Civil War earthwork defences.
Cadw.

SELECT BIBLIOGRAPHY

Allmand, Christopher, *The Hundred Years War: England and France at war c1300–c1450*, Cambridge 1988.

Barnett, Correlli, *Britain and her Army 1509–1970*, London 1970.

Baxter, James Phinney, *The Introduction of the Ironclad Warship*, Cambridge, Mass, 1968.

Best, Geoffrey, *War and Society in Revolutionary Europe, 1770–1870*, Leicester 1982.

Blackmore, H L, *The Armouries of the Tower of London: I Ordnance*, London 1976.

Blondel, Maréchal, *Nouvelle Manière de Fortifier Les Places*, Paris 1683.

Bond, Brian, *War and Society in Europe, 1870–1970*, Leicester 1985.

Brialmont, Henri Alexis, *La Defénse Des États et La Fortification A La Fin Du XIXe Siècle*, reprinted Osnabruck 1967.

Bruijn, C A de & Reinders, H R, *Nederlandse Vestingen*, Bussum 1967.

Caldwell, David H, *Scottish Weapons and Fortifications 1100–1800*, Edinburgh 1981.

Callender, Sir Geoffrey & Hinsley, F H, *The Naval Side of British History 1485–1945*, London 1954.

Carnot, Lazare-Nicolas Marguerite, *De la défense des places fortes . . . Memoire sur la fortification primitive . . .*, Paris 1810.

Cataneo, Giralmo, *Opera nuova di fortificare, offendere et defendere . . .*, Breschia 1564.

Cataneo, Pietro, *I quattro primi libri di archittura di P Cataneo*, Venice 1554.

Churchill, Winston, *The Second World War*, London 1948.

Clarke, George Sydenham, *Fortification: its past achievements, recent development, and future progress* 2nd ed, London 1907.

Coad, Jonathan, *Historic Architecture of the Royal Navy: An Introduction*, London 1983.

Cockle, Maurice J D, *A Bibliography of Military Books up to 1642*, London 1957.

Coehorn, Menno Van, *The New Method of Fortification, translated from the Original Dutch . . . by Tho Savery*, London 1705.

Cormontaigne, Louis de, *L'Ar-*

chitecture militaire, ou l'Art de fortifieer*, The Hague 1741.

Corneweyle, Robert, *The Maner of Fortification Of Cities, Townes, Castelles And Other Places*, 1559, reprinted 1972.

Cruden, Stewart, *The Scottish Castle*, Edinburgh 1960.

Cruickshank, C G, *Elizabeth's Army*, Oxford 1966

——, *The English Occupation of Tournai 1513–1519*, Oxford 1971.

Davies, William, *Fort Regent*, Jersey 1971.

Dietz, Peter, *Garrison: Ten British Military Towns*, London 1986.

Douglas, General Sir Howard, *A Treatise on Naval Gunnery 1855*, reprinted London 1982.

Duffy, Christopher, *Fire and Stone: The Science of Fortress Warfare 1660–1860*, Newton Abbot 1975.

——, *Siege Warfare: the Fortress in the Early Modern World 1494–1660*, London 1979.

——, *The Fortress in the Age of Vauban and Frederick the Great 1660–1789 (Siege Warfare Vol II)*, London 1985.

Dürer, Albrecht, *Etliche underricht zu befestigung der stett, schloss und flecken*, Nuremberg 1527.

Eis, Egon, *The Forts of Folly – the history of an illusion*, London 1959.

Errard de Bar-Le-Duc, Jean, *La fortification reduicte en art et demonstrée . . .*, Frankfurt-on-Main 1604.

Fergusson, James, *An Essay on a Proposed New System of Fortification; with hints for its application to our national defences*, London 1849.

Firth, C H, *Cromwell's Army*, London 1962.

Fraser, Antonia, *Cromwell Our Chief Of Men*, London 1973.

Freitag, Adam, *L'Architecture Militaire ou La Fortification Nouvelle . . .*, Paris 1668.

Furneaux, Rupert, *The Siege of Plevna*, London 1958.

Gaunt, Peter, *The Cromwellian Gazetteer: An Illustrated Guide to Britain in the Civil War and Commonwealth*, Gloucester 1987.

Gille, Bertrand, *The Renaissance Engineers*, London 1966.

Gillingham, John, *The Wars Of The Roses: Peace and Conflict in Fifteenth Century England*, London 1983.

Gooch, John, *The Plans of War: The General Staff and British Military Strategy c1900–1916*, London 1974.

Hale, John R, 'The Early Development of the Bastion – An Italian Chronology, c1450–c1534', in *Europe in the late Middle Ages*, ed J R Hale, London 1965.

——, *Renaissance Fortification: Art or Engineering?*, London 1977.

——, *War and Society in Renaissance Europe 1450–1620*, Leicester 1985.

Hogg, Ian V, *Coast Defences of England and Wales 1856–1956*, Newton Abbot 1974.

——, *A History of Artillery*, London 1974.

Hogg, Oliver F G, *English Artillery 1326–1716*, London 1963.

Hughes, Quentin, *Military Architecture*, London 1974.

Ive, Paul, *The Practice of Fortification*, 1594, reprinted London 1972.

Jobé, Joseph (ed), *Guns: an illustrated history of artillery*, London 1971.

Jones, E H Stuart, *The Last Invasion of Britain*, Cardiff 1950.

Kemp, Anthony, *The Maginot Line: Myth and Reality*, London 1981.

Kennedy, Paul M, *The Rise and Fall of British Naval Mastery*, London 1986.

Le Blond, M, *The Military Engineer, or a treatise on the attack and defence of all kinds of fortified places*, London 1754.

Lendy, Auguste Frederic, *Elements of Fortification, field and permanent*, London 1857.

——, *Treatise on Fortification: or Lectures delivered to Officers reading for the Staff*, London 1862.

Lewis, Emanuel Raymond, *Seacoast Fortifications of the United States*, Washington DC 1970.

Lewis, Michael, *The History of the British Navy*, Harmondsworth 1962.

Liddell Hart, B H, *The Defence of Britain*, London 1939.

Lloyd, E M (ed), *Textbook of Fortification and Military Engineering*, London 1884.

——, *Vauban, Montelembert, Carnot: Engineer Studies*, London 1887.

Lloyd, E W & Hadcock, A G, *Artillery: Its Progress and Present Position*, Portsmouth 1893.

Longford, Elizabeth, *Wellington: The Years of the Sword*, London 1969.

Mallory, Keith and Ottar, Arvid, *Architecture of Aggression: a history of military architecture in North West Europe 1900–1945*, London 1973.

Marchi, Francesco de, *Della archittura militare . . . libri tre*, Brescia 1599.

Marolois, Samuel, *The Art of Fortification*, Amsterdam 1638.

Martin, Colin & Parker, Geoffrey, *The Spanish Armada*, London 1988.

Maurice, Le Baron P-E, *De La Défense Nationale en Angleterre*, Paris 1851.

Maurice-Jones, Colonel K W, *The History of Coast Artillery in the British Army*, London 1959.

May, Lieutenant-Colonel Edward S, *Principles and Problems of Imperial Defence*, London 1903.

McLynn, Frank, *Invasion: From The Armada To Hitler, 1588–1945*, London 1987.

Montalembert, Marc René, *La Fortification Perpendiculaire; ou, essai sur plusieurs manières de fortifier*, Paris 1776–84.

Montgomery of Alamein, Field Marshal Viscount, *A History of Warfare*, London 1968.

Muller, John *A Treatise containing the Elementary Part of Fortification, Regular and Irregular . . .*, London 1756.

O'Neil, B H St J, *Castles and Cannon: A Study of Early Artillery Fortifications in England*, Oxford 1960.

Partridge, Colin, *Hitler's Atlantic Wall*, Guernsey 1976.

Pasley, Charles William, *A Course of Elementary Fortification*, London & Chatham 1822.

Porter, Whitworth, *History of the Corps of Royal Engineers*, London 1889.

Ritter, Raymond, *Chateaux Donjons et Places Fortes: l'architecture militaire française*, Paris 1953.

Roland, Alex, *Underwater Warfare in the Age of Sail*, Bloomington, Indiana 1978.

Rose, J Holland & Broadley, A M, *Dumouriez and the Defence of England Against Napoleon*, London 1909.

Ross, Lieutenant-Colonel W G, *Military Engineering during the Great Civil War 1642–9*, 1887, reprinted London 1984.

Saxe, Field Marshal Count, *Reveries or Memoirs upon the Art of War . . . translated from the French*, London 1757.

Scheliha, Von, *A Treatise on Coast Defence*, London 1868.

Schukking, W H, *De Oude Vestingwerken van Nederland*, Amsterdam 1941.

Shelby, L R, *John Rogers, Tudor Military Engineer*, Oxford 1967.

Speckle, Daniel, *Architectura von Vestungen*, Strasbourg 1589.

Spiers, Edward M, *The Army and Society 1815–1914*, London 1980.

Sprigge, Joshua, *Anglia Rediviva; England's Recovery: being the History of the Motions, Actions, and Successes of the Army under the Immediate Conduct of his Excellency Sr Thomas Fairfax, Kt Captain-General of all the Parliament's Forces in England*, London 1647.

Stevin, Simon, *Nouvelle Manière de Fortification Par Escluses*, Leyden 1618.

Strachan, Hew, *European Armies and the Conduct of War*, London 1983.

Straith, Hector, *A Treatise on Fortification, deduced from established principles, with observations on the increased effects of artillery*, Croydon 1833.

Sutcliffe, Sheila, *Martello Towers*, Newton Abbot 1972.

Tait, A A, 'The Protectorate Citadels of Scotland', *Architectural History* 8, p9.

Tomlinson, H C, *Guns and Government: The Ordnance Office under the later Stuarts*, London 1979.

Vauban, Sebastien LePreste de, *A Manual of Siegecraft and Fortification*, 1737, translated by George A Rothrock, Michigan 1968.

——, *The New Method of Fortification as practised by Monsieur de Vauban, Engineer-General of France*, by A S, 6th ed, London 1762.

Venn, Captain Thomas, *Military & Maritime Discipline*, in three books (Book II: *An exact method of Military Architecture, the art of Fortifying Towns; with the ways of Defending and Offending the same*), London 1672.

Whitworth, Rex, *Field Marshal Lord Ligonier: A Story of the British Army 1702–1770*, Oxford 1958.

Viollet-le-Duc, E, *An Essay on the Military Architecture of the Middle Ages*, 1860 translated by M Macdermott, Oxford & London 1860.

——, *Annals of a Fortress*, translated by Benjamin Bucknall, London 1874; reprinted with a new Introduction by Simon Pepper and Quentin Hughes, 1983.

Webb, Henry J, *Elizabethan Military Science: The Books and the Practice*, Madison 1965.

Wills, Henry, *Pillboxes: A Study of UK Defences 1940*, 1985.

Yule, Henry, *Fortification for Officers of the Army and Students of Military History*, Edinburgh and London 1851.

Zastrow, A de, *Histoire de la Fortification Permanente*, Paris 1856.

GLOSSARY

Advanced works
Additional works beyond the glacis but still commanded from the main defences.

Approaches
Siege works: trenches dug towards a fortress in order to approach under cover from fire.

Bailey
Medieval fortified enclosure often associated with a motte.

Banquette
An infantry firing step.

Barbette
Breastwork of a battery sufficiently low so that guns may fire over it without the need for embrasures.

Barbican
Outwork for the protection of a gateway or approaches to a bridge.

Bastion
Projection from the general outline of a fortress from which the garrison can defend by flanking fire the ground before the ramparts. From the mid-sixteenth century generally a four-sided projection.

Bastionettes
Small bastions which give local flanking cover but are not the principal defensive element.

Batardeau
Dam retaining water in a ditch. Often given an angled top to prevent access along it.

Batter
Inward slope of the face of a wall or revetment.

Battery
Any place where guns or mortars are mounted.

Berm
Level space between the edge of a ditch or moat and the foot of the rampart.

Blockhouse
Small detached fort at a strategic point, later often a wooden structure.

Bonnet
Small triangular work in front of the salient angle of a ravelin.

Bulwark
Early term for a bastion or blockhouse.

Capital
Theoretical centre-line through the salient angle and dividing the work into two equal parts.

Caponier
Covered communication across a dry ditch leading to outworks, usually loopholed. Also a powerful casemated work projecting into or across a ditch to provide flanking fire.

Carnot wall
Detached wall at the foot of the rampart and separated from it by a *chemin des rondes*

Casemate
Bombproof vaulted chamber within the ramparts providing an emplacement for a gun and/or a barrack room.

Cavalier
Raised battery usually built on a bastion to provide an additional tier of fire.

Chemin des rondes
Passage or sentry path at top of the scarp wall with a parapet for cover.

Circumvallation
Entrenchments surrounding a place being besieged for investment or defence.

Citadel
Self-contained fortress usually within a town's fortifications intended as a place of last resort.

Command
Elevation of one work above another or above the surrounding country.

Contravallation
Continuous line of redoubts and breastworks constructed by besiegers to protect themselves against sorties from the garrison.

Cordon
Continuous rounded projection at the junction of the sloping scarp revetment with the vertical parapet.

Counterforts
Buttresses built behind scarp walls, and often arched over, to provide additional strength within a rampart.

Counterguard
Work of two faces forming a salient angle, usually placed in front of a bastion to cover the opposite flanks from being seen from the covered-way.

Counterscarp
Exterior slope or revetment of a ditch.

Counterscarp gallery
Loopholed passage behind the counterscarp wall to defend the ditch.

Covered-way
Continuous communication on the outer edge of the ditch protected by an earthwork parapet from enemy fire.

Crémaillère
Indented or saw-toothed trace to allow greater flanking cover, usually applied to fieldworks.

Crenel
Gaps in a parapet between merlons enabling the fire of archers or gunners, hence *crenellations* or battlements.

Crochets
Passages round the head of traverses to allow continuous access on the covered-way.

Crownwork
Projecting outwork consisting at the head of a central bastion supported by demi-bastions on either side.

Cunette
Narrow trench cut into the bottom of a ditch.

Cupola
Armoured dome to protect guns, searchlights or observation equipment above an underground position.

Curtain
Length of rampart between two bastions on the main line of a defensive work.

Demi-lune
Detached work in front of a curtain, resembling a bastion in shape with a crescent-shaped gorge.

Echaugette
Sentry box projecting from the angle of a bastion at parapet level.

Embrasure
Opening in a parapet or wall through which a gun can be fired.

Enceinte
Also known as 'the body of the place'. The main defensive enclosure of a fortress excluding the outworks.

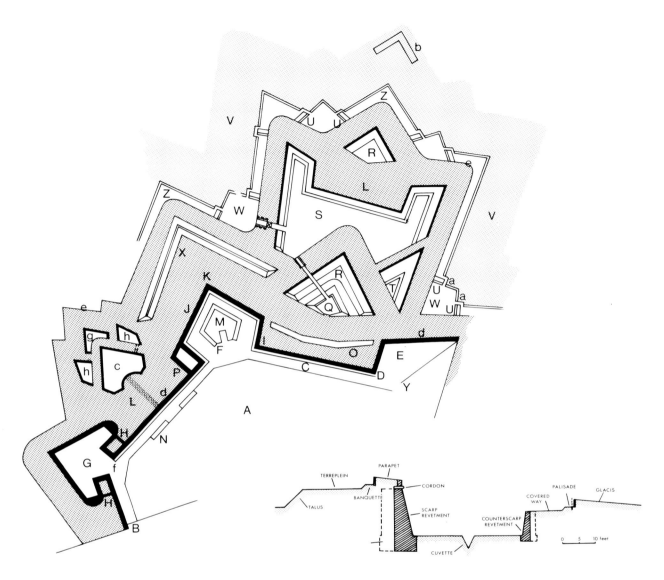

Parts of the Bastion System:

A	*Parade*	**X**	*Counterguard*
B	*Rampart*	**Y**	*Line of capital*
C	*Terre-plein*	**Z**	*Covered-way*
D	*Banquette*	**a**	*Crochet*
E	*Demi-bastion*	**b**	*Fleche*
F	*Bastion*	**c**	*Demi-lune*
G	*Orillon*	**d**	*Escarp*
H	*Flanker*	**e**	*Counterscarp*
I	*Flank*	**f**	*Gorge*
J	*Face*	**g**	*Bonnet*
K	*Salient*	**h**	*Lunettes*
L	*Ditch*		(Author)
M	*Cavalier*		
N	*Ramps*		
O	*Tenaille*		
P	*Fausse-braye*		
Q	*Redoubt*		
R	*Ravelin*		
S	*Hornwork*		
T	*Tenaillon*		
U	*Traverses*		
V	*Glacis*		
W	*Places of Arms*		

Enfilade
Fire coming from a flank which sweeps the length of a fortification.

Entrenched camp
Protected area for the assembly or re-grouping of an army.

Escalade
The climbing of walls by means of ladders.

Escarp
Outer slope or revetment of a rampart. Also scarp.

Esplanade
Open space between a citadel and the buildings of a town.

Expense magazine
Small magazine close to a battery in which a small supply of ammunition is kept for immediate use.

Parts of the Polygonal System:

A *Traverse*
B *Terre-plein*
C *Ramp*
D *Parade*
E *Redan*

F *Ditch*
G *Mortar Battery*
H *Caponier*
I *Counterscarp Gallery*
J *Scarp Battery*

K *Expense Magazine*
L *Chemin des rondes*
M *Counterforts.*
(Author)

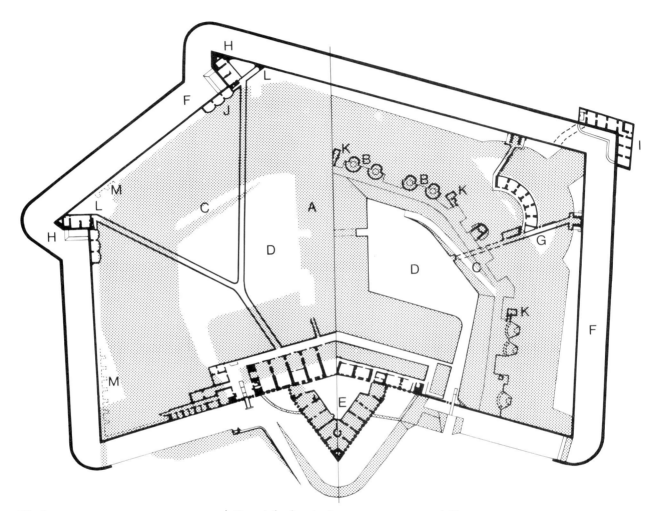

Flanker
Battery mounted in the flank of a bastion from which flanking fire is directed across a curtain.

Flèche
Small arrow-shaped outwork placed at the foot of a glacis.

Fort
Position or building designed primarily for defence

Fortress
Major fortified place, often a town, capable of containing a large force.

Front (of fortification)
Distance between the salients of two adjacent bastions.

Face (of a bastion)
Outer sides of a work which meet at a salient angle projecting towards the field.

Fausse-braye
Outer rampart separated from and lower than the main rampart.

Feste
Group of defences which include long range and close-support artillery and infantry works.

Flank
Side of a work, usually a bastion, between the face and the curtain. The principal defensive element of a bastioned fortification.

Fougasse
Small mine charged with explosive and rocks.

Fraises
Stakes or palisades set horizontally on the outward slope of a rampart to counter an infantry rush.

Gabion
Cylindrical wicker basket filled with earth and used to protect batteries etc and to supplement parapets.

Glacis
Parapet of the covered-way extended in a long slope towards the field.

Gorge
Rear, whether open or closed, of any work. Usually the neck of a bastion or a detached work.

Guérite
'See *echaugette*.

Haxo casemate
Vaulted casemate for a gun built on the *terre-plein* of a rampart, invented by General Haxo.

Hornwork
Detached work beyond the main ditch. The front is made into two demi-bastions on either side of a curtain.

Keep
Principal and strongest tower of a castle and the final point of defence.

Line of defence
Theoretical line drawn from the junction of a flank and a curtain to the salient of an adjacent bastion.

Lunette
Large advanced work, consisting of two faces and two flanks and an open gorge.

Machicolation
Projecting gallery corbelled out from a wall-top with openings for vertical defence of the foot of a wall.

Mantlet
Moveable timber protective screen for a gun or head of a sap.

Merlon
Solid part between two crenels of a battlemented parapet.

Motte
Generally artificial steep-sided mound on or in which is set the principal tower of a castle.

Mount
Artificial mound of earth on which guns can be mounted.

Orillon
Projection of the face of a bastion beyond the line of a retired flank, serving to protect a flanker.

Palisade
Obstacle of close-set pointed wooden stakes.

Parade
Ground on which regular musters and exercises are held.

Parallel
Wide trench dug by besiegers parallel to the works intended to be attacked.

Parapet
Wall or earthen breastwork for the protection of troops on the forward edge of a rampart.

Place of arms
Assembly point at the re-entering or salient angles of the covered-way to enable the formation of troops for a sortie or for the defence of the outworks.

Platform
Hard surface of timber, stone etc on which guns in battery can be placed.

Postern (or sallyport)
A small entrance and tunnel leading out of the fortifications.

Ramp
Inclined track on the rear slope of a rampart to allow the movement of troops and guns on to the *terre-plein*.

Rampart
Mass of excavated earth on which the troops and guns of the garrison are raised and forming the main defence of the fortress.

Ravelin
Triangular, detached work with or without flanks in the ditch in front of a curtain and between two bastions.

Redan
Outwork consisting of two faces forming a salient angle.

Redoubt
Small enclosed work without bastions, sometimes in the form of a redan, either used as an outwork or placed inside a bastion or ravelin.

Reduit
Small citadel of last resort, sometimes used to protect parts of a town independent of its citadel.

Re-entrant
Angle facing inwards from the field as opposed to salient.

Retired flank
Recessed platform or casemate within a bastion flank.

Retrenchment
Interior works behind the *enceinte* to provide defence in depth and to make good a breach.

Revetment
Retaining wall of a rampart or for the sides of ditches.

Ricochet fire
Method of firing by which the projectile is made to glance or bounce along the length of a work.

Salient
An angle projecting outwards toward the field.

Sallyport
See *Postern*.

Sap
Narrow siege trench often in zigzag form and employing gabions.

Scarp
Outer slope or revetment of a rampart or inner side of a ditch. Also *escarp*.

Shoulder (of a bastion)
Angle at the meeting of the face and the flank.

Spur
Arrow-shaped projection from the face of a curtain wall.

Storm poles
As *fraises*

Tenaille
Low-lying work in the ditch between bastions for the protection of the curtain.

Tenaille trace
Succession of redans at right angles to each other to form a zigzag front.

Tenaillon
Small irregular-shaped work to one side of a ravelin.

Terre-plein
Level surface on top of a rampart and below the parapet where guns are mounted.

Tête-de-pont
Fortification on the vulnerable side of a bridge.

Trace
Plan of a fortified place and its angles of fire.

Traverse
Earthwork thrown up to bar enfilade fire along any line of a work which is liable to it.

Wings
Long sides of exposed fortifications such as hornworks and crownworks.

Work
General term for any work of defence.

INDEX

References to captions in *Italics*. Gazetteer entries, which are alphabetical, are not included.